KHRUSHCHEV ON KHRUSHCHEV

KHRUSHCHEV

O N

KHRUSHCHEV

An Inside Account of the Man and His Era

by His Son
SERGEI KHRUSHCHEV

Edited and translated by
WILLIAM TAUBMAN

LITTLE, BROWN AND COMPANY

Boston   Toronto   London

Copyright © 1990 by Sergei Khrushchev
Translation copyright © 1990 by William Taubman

FIRST EDITION

Library of Congress Cataloging-in-Publication Data
Khrushchev, Sergei.
    Khrushchev on Khrushchev: an inside account of the man and his era
/ by his son, Sergei Khrushchev; edited and translated by William
Taubman.
        p.   cm.
    ISBN 0-316-49194-2
    1. Khrushchev, Nikita Sergeevich, 1894–1971.   2. Heads of state —
Soviet Union — Biography.   3. Soviet Union — Politics and
government — 1917–   I. Taubman, William.   II. Title.
DK275.K5K487   1990
947.085'2'092 — dc20
[B]
                                                      90-5618
                                                        CIP

10 9 8 7 6 5 4 3 2

Designed by Barbara Werden

MV-PA

Published simultaneously in Canada
by Little, Brown & Company (Canada) Limited

Printed in the United States of America

11-30-92

*I dedicate this book to the fond memory
of my parents.*

CONTENTS

EDITOR-TRANSLATOR'S FOREWORD

Of all the Soviet leaders since the Bolshevik Revolution of 1917, we probably know the most about Nikita Sergeyevich Khrushchev. Nevertheless, his son Sergei's book comes as a revelation, even to one who, like me, has written a book about Stalin and has been working on a comprehensive biography of Khrushchev for five years.

Khrushchev's time in power, approximately a decade, depending on when one dates the moment he defeated all comers to become Joseph Stalin's successor, was much less than either Stalin's quarter century or even Leonid Brezhnev's eighteen years. But Khrushchev was an irrepressible, loquacious talker in contrast to the notoriously taciturn Stalin and the bureaucratically programmed Brezhnev. And unlike his predecessor and successor he left us his memoirs to remember him by. From the moment in October 1964 when he was ousted from office until more than two decades later when *glasnost* and *perestroika* arrived in Moscow, Khrushchev's name was officially unmentionable in the USSR. But in recent years, a small flood of reminiscences and other accounts has begun to appear in his homeland.

Still and all, Sergei Khrushchev's account is unique. Sergei was Khrushchev's only surviving son, the person he took on frequent trips around the Soviet Union and abroad, as well as on walks at the end of the day when trying to relax and unwind, the one he confided in, insofar as he confided in anyone besides his wife, Nina Petrovna Khrushcheva.

We have known for a long time the main outlines of Nikita Khrushchev's career — his improbable rise to power in the Ukraine and Moscow, his dramatic de-Stalinization campaign, his nonstop changes in Soviet policy, as well as the changes he was unwilling or unable to make, and then his sudden, unexpected removal in 1964, followed by the reversal of many of his reforms. What we have not known, what Khrushchev either deliberately left out of his memoirs or was not able to include before he died in 1971, was the personal drama behind the scenes, especially during his last years in power and afterward.

How could a man who managed to survive and succeed Stalin be ousted overnight? How did his reforms unravel? When and why did he lose his touch? Could it be he never noticed the plot taking shape against him? What motivated the conspirators, and how did they pull it off? And how did a man who had been all-powerful react when his power was suddenly torn from him? These are but a few of the questions on which this book sheds new light.

Sergei Khrushchev observed close up the erosion of his father's authority. He learned of the plot against him early on and tried to warn Khrushchev. Later he worked with his father on the memoirs, editing more than two thousand pages of transcript, concealing them from the KGB, helping to transmit them abroad. Even though we know the outcome from the start, his narrative reads like a suspenseful detective story — not just the anti-Khrushchev conspiracy, and the cat-and-mouse game with the KGB over the memoirs, but the struggle to arrange a proper funeral followed by another battle to erect a memorial headstone, both in the face of open and hidden resistance from the authorities. And intertwined with all this is his son's moving account of Khrushchev's dark depression after 1964, and of his slow, painful climb back to something resembling his former self.

This book offers an intimate portrait of Khrushchev as man and leader, and an unprecedented inside account of life at the pinnacle of the Soviet elite. The view we get of Khrushchev's personal life (or rather of his lack of same) is fresh and revealing. We see him at work and on vacation (which usually meant work at a different location). We find him to be a suprisingly puritanical, gruff, yet loving father, and a husband barred by the Politburo code from discussing with his wife the life-and-death matters that hung in the balance every day in the Kremlin.

Sergei Khrushchev's portraits of his father's colleagues, particularly those who betrayed and dethroned him, are devastating: Leonid Ilyich

Brezhnev, as vain and indecisive as he was ruthlessly ambitious; Aleksandr Shelepin, the Young Turk who helped to overthrow Khrushchev and assumed he would eventually replace him, but was neatly outmaneuvered by Brezhnev; Nikolai Ignatov, consumed with envy and hatred of Khrushchev and hence willing to do Brezhnev's dirty work, only to be unceremoniously dumped when the deed was done.

Besides these and other top-level plotters, assorted lesser leaders and functionaries come to life in Sergei Khrushchev's pages. They resist and undermine his father in office, and then persecute and torment him after 1964. Yet they themselves are depicted as cogs in the mammoth party-state machine to which all must sooner or later accommodate.

This new image of Khrushchev as a victim of the system he led is one of the most striking features of this book; he is seen as a victim not only in retirement, when he and his son were hounded into becoming dissidents in all but name, but even when he was still in power. The author shows how power corrupted Khrushchev, how it surrounded him with flatterers who led him astray even when they didn't mean to, as well as provocateurs who deliberately put him in harm's way.

Throughout his book, Sergei Khrushchev connects his father's story with other eras in Soviet history, including the present. Stalin's legacy weighs heavily on his successor. The corruption of the Brezhnev era takes shape before our eyes. But the most striking link is with the Gorbachev period. Khrushchev was, of course, Mikhail Gorbachev's great predecessor as a reformer, and Nikita Sergeyevich's fate is a sobering cautionary tale for today. So close is the connection, so important the lessons, that when excerpts from the second chapter of this book, concerning the plot against Khrushchev, appeared in late 1988 in the popular Soviet magazine *Ogonyok,* many Soviets leapt to the conclusion that their publication was an urgent signal that Gorbachev was in trouble, a desperate warning to him to avoid the fate that befell Khrushchev.

Sergei Khrushchev makes no secret of his own commitment to *perestroika* and *glasnost.* Nor does he pretend to an objectivity about his father that he doesn't possess; he readily admits to a son's partiality in evaluating Khrushchev's reforms. The author also points out that he is neither a professional writer nor a politician, but rather a technocrat and engineer. Yet, as the reader is about to discover, he tells his story with directness and power.

As editor-translator, I worked with two somewhat different Russian-language versions of this book — an earlier version and one later edited for publication in the USSR. The author allowed me to choose between them, and I did so; when there were differences between the versions, I selected what I deemed most important and most likely to interest Western readers.

I should also add that in the course of reading through the Russian manuscript I came up with a long series of questions that I put to the author in writing, most of which he answered in the same way. Some of the material he provided could readily be incorporated into the text without disturbing the flow of the narrative; it has been so inserted. Other answers I included as author's footnotes along with notes he had previously provided. Editor's notes, also to be found at the foot of the page, often briefly repeat a question I put to the author and then quote his answer directly.

Finally, a few words of explanation about the official positions and titles of certain characters who move through this book. The author mentions many such titles, and readers who are not card-carrying Sovietologists are likely to need some guidance.

Nikita Khrushchev himself headed both the Communist party and the Soviet government. His formal party title was first secretary of the Central Committee of the Communist Party of the Soviet Union (CPSU). The Central Committee is a fairly large body (about 250 to 300 members in Khrushchev's time) that theoretically runs the party between even larger national party congresses, which are supposed to take place every five years. In fact, however, the Central Committee itself is usually run by its Politburo (consisting of ten to fifteen full members and a handful of nonvoting, or candidate, members), which to make matters more confusing was called the Presidium while Khrushchev was in power. The term Central Committee is also used in the Soviet Union and in this book to refer not just to the committee itself but to the party apparatus that is directed by several Central Committee secretaries, most but not all of whom are members of the Presidium/Politburo. The Presidium was supposed to exercise collective leadership, but, as his son somewhat reluctantly admits, it was dominated by Khrushchev as first secretary. (This is the same position known as general secretary in Stalin's time and again under Brezhnev and his successors.)

Khrushchev's formal title as head of government was chairman of the Council of Ministers, in effect prime minister or premier. Still another position mentioned in the book is head of state, or president; the official Soviet title is chairman of the Presidium of the USSR Supreme Soviet. In formal terms, the Supreme Soviet is the USSR's parliament, but until Gorbachev gave it real weight, it was a rubber stamp for the top party and government leadership. The chairmanship of its Presidium (not to be confused with the Presidium of the Central Committee) was largely a ceremonial position in Khrushchev's time — which makes all the more interesting Sergei Khrushchev's assertion that Leonid Brezhnev craved this post almost more than he did the first secretaryship of the Communist party.

In chapter two, especially, we encounter a series of local officials as they are recruited for the plot against Khrushchev. Several are republic or province party secretaries, the most important political figures in these realms; their formal title is first secretary of the republic central committee, or of the province party committee. Less influential, but still quite important, are the chief governmental officials in these areas — their formal position is chairman of the republic council of ministers, or of the province soviet executive committee.

So ends the Sovietological lesson. Let the book begin.

I WOULD like to acknowledge several people's assistance in preparing the manuscript for publication. Most of all, I am grateful to Vyacheslav Luchkov, who provided invaluable help with the whole translation. My rendering of chapter two is based in large part on Kate Cook's translation of the excerpts from the chapter that appeared in *Ogonyok* magazine. Lurline Dowell contributed her usual fast and reliable word processing. Peggy Leith Anderson proved to be a copy editor extraordinaire. And Roger Donald of Little, Brown offered sage advice and counsel throughout. Not to mention the author, who responded patiently to my endless comments and questions.

I would also like to thank Amherst College for providing me with the time and space needed to complete this project.

KHRUSHCHEV ON KHRUSHCHEV

INTRODUCTION

THIS is a book about the last seven years in the life of my father, Nikita Sergeyevich Khrushchev, first secretary of the Central Committee of the Communist Party of the Soviet Union and chairman of the Council of Ministers of our state. It is largely about the period after Father retired from all his posts in October 1964, when relatively little is known about his activities. But I begin with the early sixties, and I include flashbacks from earlier times, too, so as to connect Father's last seven years with his activities in previous years.

This book does not consist of diaries; rather, it is based on observations that I dictated into a tape recorder in the wake of events that seemed important. In the beginning, I intended the notes based on those tapes for my children and grandchildren — and, with luck, for historians living in what we used to call "the radiant future." In those days the possibility of publishing a book about a disgraced leader was unimaginable. All my efforts were directed at preserving my notes. God forbid that anybody might learn about them! If so, they would disappear without a trace. So they sat for more than fifteen years in a small brown suitcase tucked between a bedside table and a radiator.

Times have changed. History is beginning to resemble real history and not a set of juggled facts. Now, at last, the truth about Father can be told.

At first I was reluctant to emerge from the underground and make public this account. By profession I am very distant from the writing of history or literature. Many years of working in a rocket design bureau and in a scientific research institute taught me to fill my out box with crafty responses to complicated incoming requests. And this is a rather peculiar genre, hardly a suitable model for this book.

With the recent political thaw, history hunters of all sorts have begun to swarm around my father's name; all kinds of myths and fables have begun to appear. Some events are so distorted in recent publications that they are unrecognizable; others have been replaced with total inventions. Take, for example, the mythical attempt on my father's life on the cruiser *Red Ukraine,* or Father's "order" (reported by an "eyewitness") that he be flown to Kiev instead of Moscow when he was summoned back from vacation at his Black Sea dacha in October 1964.[1]

Another example involves the curious rehashing of Winston Churchill's warning that a precipice can't be crossed in two leaps. It's hard to think of a Khrushchev-era development to which that maxim hasn't been applied. In fact, Churchill made the remark in the spring of 1956, during Father's visit to Great Britain.[2] I was among those who accompanied the delegation.

Father was seated next to Sir Winston at a dinner given by Prime Minister Anthony Eden at 10 Downing Street. Churchill had retired from affairs of state by that time, but he had not lost interest in politics and he was curious to meet the leaders of our country.

That spring the world was excited by rumors about Khrushchev's "secret speech" at the Twentieth Congress of the Communist party. Everyone wanted to know more about the man who had dared to lift his hand against Stalin, the dreaded *vozhd* (leader). Talk at the table quickly turned to the revelations about Stalin. Father wouldn't confirm that he had in fact given the speech, but he was willing to talk about Stalin and those crimes that had been revealed. At the same time, he stressed that we had not forgotten Stalin's achievements.

1. In an early version of his book *Khrushchev: A Political Biography* (New York: Doubleday, 1983), Roy A. Medvedev reported that the *Red Ukraine* blew up at Sevastopol in the 1950s, shortly after Khrushchev had disembarked. This is not true; the cruiser was turned over for scrap. The battleship *Novorossiisk* did in fact explode, but at another time, when Khrushchev was in Kiev. After I pointed out the error, Medvedev removed it from later editions of his book. As for the October 1964 "order," cited by Fyodor Burlatsky in *Literaturnaya gazeta,* it is an invention.

2. *Editor's note:* The visit to Britain was jointly undertaken by Khrushchev, who was then first secretary of the Central Committee, and Soviet premier Nikolai Bulganin.

Father remarked in conclusion that the process of change was very complicated and painful, and therefore had to be carried out gradually, in several stages. It was this remark that provoked Churchill's famous answer. Sir Winston shook his head skeptically and said more or less the following:

"Mr. Khrushchev, I think it is just because the problem is so painful that you must resolve it once and for all. Any delay could result in the most serious consequences. It is like crossing a precipice. One may leap over it, if one has sufficient strength, but never in two jumps."

Father liked the remark and often repeated it, for example when discussing warnings from "the right," proposals to halt or slow down the pace of de-Stalinization, which far from everyone in the party apparatus accepted and acknowledged.

Many years have passed and much has been forgotten. Today Churchill's pronouncement is applied by Khrushchev's critics to all sorts of his reforms. Some people even employ Sir Winston's maxim to sum up the whole period of the Khrushchev thaw. Many such inaccuracies have appeared recently.

Human memory is inclined to play tricks. Mine is no exception. When I started writing this book I was sure I remembered everything. But when I began reading my notes from 1964–1975, I found many things that were new to me. Some events I had completely forgotten; others were totally transformed in my mind. It took considerable effort for me to reconstruct the past — not prettied up to please memory's promptings, but as it really was.

In the narrative that resulted from these labors, I have tried to be as impartial as possible, to present events as I saw them at the time. I have deliberately tried to avoid overanalyzing the past or overgeneralizing about it.

Today it may seem hard to believe, but in the last years before October 1964, I had no premonition of what was to come. On the contrary, it seemed to me that, as we are fond of saying, everything was proceeding along the path mapped out by the party. I'm not being ironic when I use this standard phrase; I'm confessing that my own thinking was quite orthodox, and that I didn't notice things which should have been obvious.

Of course, not everything was working smoothly; there were deficiencies here and there, but they seemed minor and would pass. In the last analysis, everything would turn out fine. When doubts did arise, they concerned particular concrete issues — inflated statistics contained in the party program, or quarrels with the intelligentsia, or problems in the field of genetics. I used to ask Father about cases like these. Sometimes I got answers, some satisfactory, some not.

One thing was beyond all doubt and criticism: I was convinced that the top leaders, and the whole apparatus of the party, were unconditionally giving their all to the common cause. Paradoxical as it may seem, Father himself believed in, and brought us up to believe in, these people's commitment to unblemished self-sacrifice. I had no doubt at the time that everyone from the top to the bottom lived only for the common cause, and was ready to sacrifice himself for the radiant future.

I don't want to make myself out to be naive. I had encountered petty-minded bureaucrats, official idleness, parochialism, and provincialism at work. But to me these were negative traits of particular people, not what we nowadays call the administrative-command system.

Such illusions began to be dispelled in my conversations with Aleksei Vladimirovich Snegov, an old Communist who worked in the twenties with my father and with Anastas Mikoyan, and who then spent eighteen years in the camps (out of twenty-five that had been doled out to him in 1937).

My acquaintance with Snegov begins my story.

THE THRESHOLD

I FIRST met Aleksei Snegov in the early 1960s, several years after his return from a labor camp. In the meantime, he had retired, or rather had been retired, from official employment for reasons I will shortly explain. He lived with his wife, Galina, and his little daughter on Kropotkin Street in Moscow. He had married and obtained an apartment after getting out of prison.

I was twenty-seven years old at the time. Snegov seemed to me an old man. All the more, then, was I struck by his liveliness and energy, by his capacity to flare up and rush into battle for a just cause without looking back. His apartment was crammed with books, manuscripts, magazines, and papers of all sorts. They lay on bookshelves, on the table, on chairs, and in piles on the floor.

At the time, Snegov was working on controversial historical issues. He was engaged in what is now referred to as the elimination of "blank spots" in the history of our country and the Soviet Communist party. The Twenty-second Party Congress had already taken place, in October 1961: they had removed Stalin's body from the mausoleum, but they hadn't dared to move it very far and had buried it right by the Kremlin wall. This kind of ambivalence, this effort to have things both ways, was typical of the time.

People were afraid to speak their minds, to think things through, to come to logical conclusions. Yes, Stalin was a murderer — but still he was a Marxist. He devastated the Red Army on the eve of the world war — but his contribution to victory over the enemy was immense. He undermined agriculture — but the collectivization of agriculture was a triumph. The list went on.

Today this sounds absurd, but that was then and not now. People were only beginning to unlearn the habit of inserting a reference to "the Great Leader and Teacher" into every sentence. They still had difficulty uttering the phrase "cult of personality."

Only a few years before, no one had heard this term. Father first pronounced it about the time the Pospelov Commission was formed to carry out a preliminary analysis of events that transpired in the 1930s.[1] Naturally, the functionaries cast around for a suitable phrase in the primary sources of Marxism-Leninism, and, of course, proper citations were found.

I remember one Sunday at the dacha. The regular Sunday briefcase full of documents arrived. In the presence of family members, Father took out a thin blue-gray folder with a selection of quotations from the classics. He asked me to read aloud Marx's thoughts on the dangers, the inadmissability, of a cult of a leader's personality.

I began with the heading: "Karl Marx on the culture of personality." Everybody laughed at the mistake the typist had made. But if you think about it, it wasn't very funny. In those years, you couldn't get your tongue to pronounce such things, or your typewriter to type them. Many a year was needed to comprehend what had happened.

What struck me about Snegov when I first met him was his argument that the issue was not Stalin's mistakes or delusions, but that everything was the fruit of his criminal policy. The monstrous results had not appeared all of a sudden in the thirties. Their roots, Snegov said, went back to the October Revolution and the civil war. Snegov raised his hand not only against the dogmas of the *Short Course*,[2] but against the whole canonical history since 1917.

---

1. Pyotr Nikolayevich Pospelov, a former journalist and historian, was a senior party ideologue and Central Committee secretary in 1955, when Khrushchev nominated him to head a Central Committee commission evaluating the repressions carried out in the 1930s, especially against high-ranking party officials and delegates to the Seventeenth Party Congress, held in 1934. Khrushchev used the memorandum prepared by the commission as the basis for his secret speech at the Twentieth Congress, in 1956.

2. The *Short Course* was a falsified history of the party that Stalin ordered prepared in the thirties. The book's full name is *History of the VKP(b)* [*All-Union Communist Party (Bolsheviks)*], *Short Course*. For a long time, it was required reading for all

Snegov wrote several historical articles. One concerned Stalin's position on the issue of whether Lenin should have appeared in court in the summer of 1917. In July 1917, the Provisional Government gave the order to arrest Lenin, Grigory Zinoviev, and other Bolshevik leaders. The party then debated whether Lenin should appear and unmask the government's policies in open court, or go into hiding lest he be killed while under arrest. The latter point of view won out and later became canonical. Stalin had favored Lenin's appearing in court, but his actual position was expunged from the *Short Course,* which depicted him as opposed to Lenin's appearance. Snegov exposed the lie.

Another article analyzed the tragic willfulness of Stalin and Kliment Voroshilov [a political rather than professional soldier who later rose to be Stalin's defense commissar and, from 1953 to 1960, head of state — ed.] that led to the defeat of our army in Poland in the 1920 war. During the war Stalin was with the troops near Lvov. Lenin ordered him to transfer the First Cavalry Army to the front commanded by Mikhail N. Tukhachevsky, whose troops were attacking Warsaw. Stalin refused to carry out the order; he chose to storm Lvov instead, in service of his own ambitions. As a result, Polish troops under Józef Pilsudski were able to break through Tukhachevsky's front, and Soviet Russia suffered a defeat. The official history blamed Tukhachevsky, but Snegov posed the issue of Stalin's role. Nowadays, most historians share Snegov's view.

Today these articles would be hard to distinguish from many similar pieces. Then they had the effect of an exploding bomb. I read them and thought that once others had and had learned the truth, the world would turn on its axis, and everything would be changed. But wherever Snegov sent his manuscripts, the reaction was uniformly negative.

Stalinists did everything possible to prevent Snegov's studies from seeing the light of day. Scholars and academicians, led by chief party ideologue and head of the Central Committee Propaganda Department Mikhail Andreyevich Suslov, closed ranks against Snegov. It was their "history" that Snegov had taken apart brick by brick, accusing them not only of being unscrupulous scholars but of flat-out falsification.[3]

Soviet citizens, and any deviation from its teachings was considered the gravest of ideological crimes.

3. *Editor's note:* Why didn't the response Snegov got provoke the kind of premonition of disaster that Sergei Khrushchev insists he did not have? I asked him, and

Snegov believed implicitly in the integrity of Khrushchev and Mikoyan (who was deputy premier at the time), and counted on their support in his struggle. But it was difficult for him to get in touch with them through official channels. He didn't trust Khrushchev's assistants; he considered Vladimir Semyonovich Lebedev, in charge of ideological matters in Khrushchev's apparatus, a hidden Stalinist and Suslov's man.[4]

I met Snegov through Anastas Mikoyan's son, Sergo, who was a professional historian. Sergo had been acquainted with Snegov for some time, and had given his articles to Mikoyan himself. But that hadn't produced any result. Whether the senior Mikoyan tried to help and failed, or never really tried, I don't know. All I know is the result, or rather the lack of same.

One day Sergo suggested, "Let's pay a visit to an acquaintance of mine. He's a historian, a man who's led a hard life. He has some unique material concerning Stalin that he wants to show you."

I was quick on the uptake in those days, and I agreed immediately.

A rather short, dried-out man, very animated and with stern, piercing eyes, opened the door. He was no longer young, but there were only slight touches of gray in his thick black hair. One hand was missing a finger, a memento from "there," he later explained.

Our host invited us into his study. His wife brought tea for which he cleared a small space by removing some papers from the cluttered table. For a while we scrutinized each other.

Snegov didn't stand on ceremony. He dumped a mountain of information on us about Stalin, latter-day Stalinists, and their methods. He kept pounding on one point: Stalinism was not broken. The Twentieth Congress was just a beginning; a long, hard struggle lay ahead; defeats as well as victories awaited us. The enemy was powerful, experienced, and treacherous.

---

he replied as follows: "Attitudes toward Stalin varied sharply in those days, and besides, the issue concerned history rather than the present. Father himself wavered back and forth in his assessment of Stalin. Snegov's failure to get his pieces published was nothing new. Dogmatists were doing quite well at the time, so this incident didn't put one on one's guard."

4. As will be recounted in chapter two, it turned out Lebedev was not a hidden Stalinist, but such was Snegov's firm belief. It was based in part on the fact that Lebedev hadn't forwarded Snegov's letters directly to Khrushchev, but had sent them instead, in accordance with established practice, to the Propaganda Department of the Central Committee.

I agreed with some things Snegov said. Others I had more trouble believing. I simply couldn't accept his argument about Stalinists ensconced in the Central Committee, opposing the line adopted by the congress. My own thinking hadn't gone that far yet. My mind rejected this information like an organism rejecting an alien protein.

Snegov also told us about himself, about all his reversals of fortune. The one thing he didn't talk about was prisons and labor camps. Maybe he didn't want to revive bitter memories. Or perhaps he considered the subject closed and preferred to concentrate on the current struggle.

Aleksei Snegov, Alyosha in those days, joined the revolution as a young man. Fate tossed him from place to place. It was in those years that he first met Mikoyan, and later, finding himself in the Ukraine, Khrushchev. No one had heard of Khrushchev back then. For a while, in fact, Snegov was my father's boss. Later, life separated them. Father's career moved rapidly upward, while Snegov's advanced more slowly.

By 1937 Snegov was a party secretary in one of the provinces. He was arrested as "an enemy of the people," but though he passed through all the infernal circles of the interrogation machine, he refused to implicate anyone. Sentenced to twenty-five years, he disappeared from the lives of Khrushchev and Mikoyan.

During the war, the Nazi occupiers burned Snegov's mother alive because her son was an active Communist. Meanwhile, he was serving time in a Soviet camp as a "foreign spy." Still, the end of the war left Snegov's situation unchanged, and then came 1953.

Stalin died in March. Lavrenty Beria, the notorious head of the secret police, made his bid for power. Snegov knew him well. They had worked together in the Caucasus during the first years after the revolution. Their paths had crossed later, too. But they never liked each other; Snegov knew too much about Beria, including certain things Beria preferred to forget. Snegov knew that Beria had worked for the Mussavatists, a nationalist group in Azerbaijan that opposed the Bolsheviks during the civil war. He remembered Beria's bloody rise in Georgia, and he hadn't forgotten the book in which Beria, "the historian," had turned upside down the revolutionary past of Transcaucasia. Snegov was probably arrested in 1937 because he knew too much. By the bloodbath logic of the time he should have perished, but by some miracle he survived. It's hard to say where the extermination machine broke down.

Beria himself was arrested in July 1953. With his trial in the offing, his accusers sought out witnesses. But hardly any remained alive. Apart from the defendant himself, virtually no one could testify about his past. It was at this point that someone remembered Snegov. They found him in a camp and delivered him to Moscow in a hurry. The victim and his oppressor met again. The former people's commissar, who once loved to carry out personal interrogations in his Lubyanka office, was now a pitiful sight as he begged for mercy.

When the trial was over, and Beria condemned to death, an interesting fate awaited the witness for the prosecution. Snegov's onetime close friend Roman Andreyevich Rudenko had just been appointed USSR procurator general. The two men met, Snegov having been brought to the procurator's office under armed guard. They exchanged pleasantries. As long as he could, Rudenko kept up the small talk. Finally, averting his eyes from Snegov's, he asked, "What can I do for you, Alyosha?"

Snegov raised his head in astonishment. The pause dragged on.

"You have to understand . . ." Rudenko broke the silence. "The law is the same for everyone. You've been sentenced, and the sentence has not been repealed. Even I can't change it. You'll have to return to prison. It pains me to say so, but I'm the procurator and I have to obey the letter of the law. All I can allow myself to do is to take your papers, if you've written anything, and safeguard them until your release. Even that is a violation of the rules."

Snegov was stunned. Everyone knew he was innocent. The hangman had just been shot. And now this ending! Snegov handed over his notes and diaries, and Rudenko locked them in his safe. There they lay for two more years while Snegov continued serving his term. On the way back to the camp, he was nearly killed by criminals in a transit prison. After that, time seemed to stand still. News from outside was rare, just when he desperately wanted to know what was happening. Why weren't he and his fellow prisoners freed? Could it be that everything was just as it had been?

Finally, 1956 arrived. The Twentieth Party Congress was to take place in February. Father decided to invite as guests old Communists who had survived Stalin's purges. When an assistant showed him the guest list, he suddenly remembered: "Where's Snegov? Why did they forget him? He must be invited."

No one dared inform him that Snegov was still serving out the term handed him in 1937. Instead, they rushed off to find Snegov. He was brought to Moscow straight from prison, hungry and unshaven. There he exchanged his prison outfit for a suit and was given a guest pass to the Kremlin. This time, of course, there was no talk about the unfinished prison term.[5]

Some say that the plan initially called for Snegov, Olga Shatunovskaya, and other victims of Stalinism actually to address the congress, but for some reason that never happened.

Once the congress was over, Father didn't let Snegov out of his sight. He placed great hope in people like Snegov and Shatunovskaya. He counted on their help in breaking the old punitive apparatus. He needed like-minded people he could trust, people who would be his eyes and ears.

After being freed from the camp, Shatunovskaya was assigned to work on rehabilitations at the Party Control Commission, the high-level agency that investigates violations of party rules and ethics. Snegov became a commissar at the Ministry of Internal Affairs, which controlled the corrective labor camps of the Gulag. We owe them, and others like them, a debt; they were partly responsible for the rehabilitation of victims and for the first steps in restructuring the punitive organs.

Shatunovskaya and Snegov achieved a great deal, but they also aroused the hatred of the reactionary part of the apparatus. Snegov was outnumbered and in the end defeated. A phony excuse was found for eliminating his job, and he found himself awarded "a well-deserved rest on account of his age and the condition of his health."[6]

NOW we were sitting in Snegov's study having tea. Ever more animated, he overflowed with stories, arguments, and proofs. His position could be summarized as follows:

5. *Editor's note:* Roy Medvedev reports that Khrushchev ordered Snegov released many months before the Twentieth Party Congress. I therefore asked Sergei Khrushchev to reconfirm his account, and in due course he replied as follows: "As a matter of fact, Snegov *was* released on Father's initiative significantly earlier than he told me when we first met in 1962. The two men met at the Kremlin, and after that Snegov played an active part in the difficult and nerve-racking early work of preparing political rehabilitations. He could scarcely have forgotten the date of his own liberation; the version he recounted to me must have seemed more dramatic to him. In any event, I didn't want to alter his account to correct the inaccuracy." Snegov died in September 1989 at the age of ninety-two.

6. *Editor's note:* I asked Sergei Khrushchev why his father didn't take Snegov's defeat as a sign his own cause was in trouble. He replied, "Snegov's departure didn't constitute a personal setback for Father since Aleksei Vladimirovich was on a much lower level. Of course, this marked a retreat from the line laid down at the Twentieth Congress, but such ebbs and flows occurred continuously at that time."

Khrushchev, though head of both the party and the government, was practically isolated, supported only by a very thin layer of younger people in the apparat. The overwhelming majority of apparatchiks had recovered from the shock of the Twentieth Congress. They understood that they were now home free — that they would neither be arrested nor fired from their jobs. Instead, they awaited conditions that would allow them to take revenge.

According to Snegov, the main enemy was Mikhail Suslov, the chief party ideologist, and his agitprop machine. It was they, he said, who impeded de-Stalinization, drowned attempts to criticize Stalinist methods in a sea of interagency coordination, and tried to cover up actual committed crimes. Drawing on their rich past experience, these "gardeners" carefully weeded out any timid little shoots of the new and progressive. Attempts to look at the past objectively were ruthlessly cut short. Snegov was unhappy with both Khrushchev and Mikoyan. He accused them of unforgivable tolerance and passivity.

"Nikita Sergeyevich is focusing on the wrong thing," Snegov said. "Why is he poking his nose into details of industry and agriculture? One man can't do it all anyway. We don't need to plant corn; we need to struggle against the main enemy — Stalinism and its disciples. They've lodged themselves in the very heart of the system, in the Central Committee and the government.

"Either Khrushchev will break the old apparat, or they will break him. He's got to put a real Communist, an honest man of principle, in the Central Committee, instruct him to put the place in order, and give him extraordinary powers to get the job done.

"If victory can be achieved within the Central Committee itself, progress will go faster, and there will be no turning back to the past.

"But there's practically no one around Khrushchev who could tear the apparat apart and stitch it together again. Most of them sound as if they support him, while actually hindering progressive innovations.

"The only one I trust is Mikoyan. He's the one Khrushchev should assign to purge the Central Committee apparat."

Snegov's words, more or less as I've quoted them, convinced us. He asked me to give Father a letter requesting an audience on a very important matter. I hesitated. I had received similar petitions before. When I gave them to Father, he invariably read me a lecture about interfering in what wasn't my business: "Appeals like this should be directed to the office of the Central Committee. They'll know what needs to be done."

No one likes to be reprimanded. But in this case, I agreed to deliver Snegov's letter; Snegov was not a special pleader, he was worried about our common cause.

From that day on, Aleksei Vladimirovich and I became friends. Each time we met, Snegov would recount ever more detailed facts about the growing opposition to Khrushchev personally and to his policies.

A short time later, Snegov's letter was ready. I picked a propitious moment and gave it to Father, briefly recounting what I knew. He was not exactly delighted to hear from his old comrade. Muttering something about Snegov's extremism, he put the letter in his pocket without opening it.

Evidently, the "services" don't earn their daily bread for nothing. The KGB (Committee for State Security), the Central Committee apparat, and other agencies quickly arranged for information compromising to Snegov to arrive on Khrushchev's desk. Nonetheless, Father received him in short order. But when I asked his impressions of the meeting with Snegov, Father brushed my question aside: "He's an honest man, and he's concerned about the cause. But he exaggerates a lot, and there's a great deal he doesn't understand. There's a grain of truth in what he says, but his conclusions are inflated, simply untrue, and his fears have no basis."

Father wasn't about to continue the conversation. We never returned to the subject.

I drove over to see Snegov. He was both desperate and furious.

"He didn't understand a thing. He simply didn't take me seriously. I told him what was happening in the Central Committee, about intrigues going on behind his back. I pleaded with him to be cautious and vigilant, and warned him about the imminent danger of a Stalinist restoration. But he just laughed and said that my imagination was running away with me, and that I was seeing enemies under every bed.

"He said the people working for the Central Committee are sincerely and selflessly devoted to the party. Like all of us, he said, they have their weaknesses, but each is completely dedicated. So it would be a mistake to suspect them of intrigues, or of pursuing their self-interest, let alone of attachment to Stalinist practices condemned by the Twentieth Congress.[7]

" 'We mustn't devote ourselves to settling scores. That would pro-

7. *Editor's note:* Earlier the author says that Khrushchev relied on people like Snegov to help clean Stalinists out of the secret police. Yet here Khrushchev seems to trust the Central Committee apparatus more than he did Snegov. Was Khrushchev's

voke a new wave of violence and hate.' That's how he reacted to my call for conducting an investigation and punishing the butchers.

"I tried to convince him to leave everyday economic matters to others — let *them* answer for corn and beets and rolled steel — to devote himself to key questions of party policy. But he laughed that off; he said nothing is more important than providing people with food, clothes, and shoes. He sees his main task precisely as resolving these workaday problems. He refused to transfer Mikoyan over to the Central Committee. He said everything over there is in place, and everyone is doing his job.

"He's just blind, he doesn't see a thing, and soon it will be too late," Snegov exclaimed.[8]

The conversation had been painful. Before seeing Khrushchev, Snegov had met with Mikoyan and had not achieved anything with him either.

Sitting in his apartment, I found myself infected by Snegov's mood. I wanted to do something, take action, issue warnings. I was terrified both for my country and — I won't hide it — for myself. There were plotters everywhere.

Yet, outside the apartment things felt completely different. Life still took its familiar course; it still was beautiful, as it should be when you're young. All around me were nice friendly people, smiling good honest smiles, nothing corresponding to the gloomy prophecy that had issued from the apartment crammed with books. I chose the easy way out: I appeared less and less frequently at Snegov's place. Since meeting Father, he had lost quite a bit of interest in me. There was little I could do now to help him in his struggle.

*   *   *

attitude contradictory? Sergei Khrushchev replied: "Of course, Snegov was not the only person assigned to clean up the police. And Snegov had done his job: people overtly associated with Beria had been purged. But it's true that Khrushchev did trust the apparatus. So there's no contradiction; or rather, the contradiction was in the mind of Khrushchev himself."

8. *Editor's note:* Looking back, should one conclude that Snegov was right all along? "Not necessarily," Sergei Khrushchev replied. "In retrospect, it's clear that Father's de-Stalinization had more adherents than Snegov thought. After all, even though Brezhnev wanted to put Stalin back on a pedestal, he was unable to do so. Even Suslov turned out to be opposed to that. On the other hand, Snegov's idea of having Mikoyan clean out the Central Committee was probably already unrealizable at the time he suggested it."

GRADUALLY my unease died away. Life continued, and 1964 arrived, a jubilee year for Father. He turned seventy and he had been in his high party post for about ten years. A New Year's reception had been arranged in the vast hall on the top floor of the recently completed Palace of Congresses. In recent years, Father had established the tradition of greeting the New Year not at home with his family, but in the floodlit hall of the Palace of Congresses. Here gathered not only members of the Presidium, but officials of the Council of Ministers, ministers themselves, high-ranking military officers, paragons of production, writers, directors, actors, poets, playwrights, artists, airplane and missile designers, and diplomats.

In one corner, on a raised platform, stood a brilliantly decorated New Year's tree. The reception went off splendidly, with a great number of toasts and dances. It was not until long after midnight that the guests headed home to greet the New Year again according to Berlin, London, or New York time as suited their temperaments.

Some people liked Khrushchev's innovation: in this whirlwind of merrymaking one met new acquaintances, struck up interesting conversations, made useful contacts. Others winced: for them New Year's was a family affair, to be celebrated at home. But everyone went.

Father felt himself to be the cordial host. Among the guests this year was Nikolai Aleksandrovich Bulganin. Father and Bulganin had worked together in Moscow for many years, beginning in the 1930s. After Stalin's death, Bulganin became first deputy chairman of the Council of Ministers and then chairman, but in 1957 he had supported Vyacheslav Molotov, Georgy Malenkov, Lazar Kaganovich, and others in a group opposed to Khrushchev. After the 1957 Central Committee plenum backed Father against the "antiparty group," Bulganin managed to stay afloat for a while, but his ouster as prime minister was preordained when Molotov, Malenkov, and company were dispersed to distant cities. They were away from Moscow for a long time, returning only in retirement. When Bulganin came back, he lived alone, and few if any of his old friends dared have anything to do with him.

Father had a yen to see him, whereupon the fallen ex-premier received an invitation to the New Year's reception.

I'm sure Father wasn't moved by a wish simply to see a defeated opponent. On the threshold of his eighth decade, he kept coming back to his early years; he felt drawn to old friends. For many years they had been close: Khrushchev the Moscow party secretary, Bulganin the chairman of the city soviet and thus the mayor of Moscow. They had lived in the same apartment house on Granovsky Street, on the fifth floor, right next to each other. Even during the silent years, when mutual suspicion reigned everywhere, they had visited each other's apartments. Unseen by outsiders, they had skipped across the hall to drink a glass of tea or knock back a Georgian cognac.

On that memorable New Year's Eve, Father greeted Nikolai Aleksandrovich warmly, they embraced as in the old days — and parted, for the last time.

The evening ended; the lights on the tree went out, and the music died away. Everyday concerns inundated Father again. Moreover, things were not exactly going brilliantly. He had to find a way out, the single little string which, if pulled, would start up the whole economic mechanism. But the strings broke or became tangled, and the right one was never found.

Father understood — I often heard him say it at that time — that the old economic management system, with its emphasis on the "naked" enthusiasm of the workers and its promise to "catch up to and overtake America," had run its course and had nothing left to offer. He searched feverishly for a way to get the economic machinery to function in response to something other than shouts from above. But he didn't find one. At times he thought he had, but it only seemed that way. One thing he was sure of: nothing could be done as long as the worker himself had no material incentive to work.

Not only did each new step run up against the opposition of his ideologist colleagues in the Central Committee, and of academic economists;[9] he had also to overcome opposition within himself. The market, competition, profit — all had been condemned in the twenties, all supposedly led directly to the restoration of capitalism. How was he to get past this barrier?

But there could be no standing in place either. A way had to be found to "provide food, clothing, and shoes for the people."

New and unusual ideas had a hard time breaking through. Father supported Yevsei Liberman, the Kharkov economist who favored strengthening economic rather than administrative methods of manage-

9. *Editor's note:* Was Sergei Khrushchev aware of this opposition at the time, and if so, how could he be so confident of his father's political position? His answer: "I'm not talking here about opposition to Khrushchev, but rather to any discussion of a possible retreat from the command system of economic administration. Nor do I have in mind any particular individuals. The system itself was resistant. It still is today, as Gorbachev's example shows."

ment, and Ivan Khudenko, the Kazakhstan state farm chairman who put his *sovkhoz* (state farm) on the contract system and thus turned it into a model of success. But Khudenko was removed as director in 1964, and in 1973 he was tried in Alma-Ata for appropriating government property. One of those responsible for his arrest was Kazakhstan party leader Dinmukhamed Kunaev, a member of the Politburo and a close friend of Leonid Brezhnev's. Khudenko died in prison.

The contours of a basic economic reform took shape in Khrushchev's mind about this time; fundamental decisions leading in this direction were actually taken. This time, unlike so many others, Father didn't hurry; instead, he pondered the principles underlying the reforms over and over again. For this was his last hope, and there would be no chance to correct any mistakes that might crop up. However, fate decreed otherwise. It was only in the post-Khrushchev period, in 1965, that the reform was proclaimed.

Father paid heed to other countries' experience. His conversations with Tito had made a big impression on him. Father looked carefully at the Yugoslav experience but couldn't bring himself to try to copy it. With one voice, the ideologists reiterated that Yugoslav socialism was unclean and gave off a strong capitalist smell. The Yugoslav path, they told him, was a retreat from Marxist-Leninist ideals.

At the time I am talking about, our country was under the total sway of what we today refer to as the administrative-command system. It was within the limits of that system that Father kept trying to find a way to lift the economy out of the pattern of failures that followed one after another. The very logic of that system demanded bureaucratic interference in the production process at all levels and in all areas, as well as detailed supervision not just of every factory and collective farm, but of every shop, brigade, and worker's bench, of every individual worker.

What the command approach meant, in essence, was that party leaders at every level had to analyze the most trivial details. The more specialists there were in the apparat, the worse was the state of affairs they looked after. In the end, the apparat swelled like a cell about to undergo mitosis. It remained only to give a last push.

It was in an effort to get this system to function better that the decision was taken in the fall of 1962 to divide the party's province and district committees into separate industrial and agricultural organizations. The considerations that Father laid out were simple. The economy had become extraordinarily complex, and the province party secretaries and their apparatuses could not simultaneously be experts on industry and agriculture. That dictated the establishment of two parallel apparats. As Krylov [a Russian fable writer of Pushkin's time, many of whose lines have become proverbial — ed.] said: Let's change seats and everything will be dandy. The notion that the party leadership should not interfere at all in economic matters had yet to ripen. At the time, it was simply inconceivable.

I was present when the idea for dividing the party was first mentioned. Apparently, Father had been thinking about it for a long time. In the summer of 1962 he was vacationing at a new dacha not far from Livadia, a resort in the Crimea near Yalta. Inside the house, which was made of white sandstone, it was always cool. But Father spent almost all his time under a linen awning on the beach. It was there that he read his mail and met with a steady stream of visitors: bureaucrats from Moscow, guests at neighboring sanatoria, foreigners, and our own scientists, engineers, and writers. Government telephones were set up right there under the awning. Father often spent the night there as well, in a wooden hut built close to the water, just above the beach.

On the day I'm recalling, Presidium members Brezhnev, Nikolai Podgorny, and Dmitry Polyansky, I think, were visiting. They were staying at a dacha nearby, and they drove over like neighbors who, as Father would say, "saw a light in the window." Settling themselves in wicker chairs right by the water, they began an unhurried conversation about affairs of state. After a while, they went swimming. Father, by the way, was a poor swimmer and made use of an inflated red rubber ring which reminded one of a bicycle inner tube. The conversation about dividing the party organizations began in the water, and Father pursued his idea when he came back on the beach. Finally, he fell silent. At this point, everyone supported his idea enthusiastically and all in one voice: "What a wonderful idea! It must be done immediately!" I remembered those words later. Podgorny was especially enthusiastic.

"We'll have to think about it a bit more. We'll present the issue at the next plenum," Father summed up the conversation.

For some reason the idea didn't sit well with me. But in accordance with the long-established rule, I didn't dare interfere when my elders were conversing. As usual, I told myself that I didn't understand. They must know what they are doing. If I don't agree, I must be wrong.

Soon the plenum approved the party reorganization, and the reform was implemented. However, the hopes for it were not destined to be fulfilled; the economy didn't improve, and the resulting duplication of leaders at each level deepened the muddle. In addition, the reorganization increased the size of the apparat.

The division of the party provoked deep dissatisfaction among party and economic leaders at all levels.[10] This was the last major reorganization carried out by Father. A correct resolution to our economic dilemma had yet to be found.

With things still going poorly, Khrushchev grasped at straws, trying to resolve this or that concrete problem by hanging around factories, touring the countryside, trying everywhere to find the time to see everything for himself. But there was no time left.

Nonetheless, he was able to implement many measures during these years: increased housing construction, development of the virgin lands to increase the harvest, and development of a large-scale chemical industry.

The situation in foreign policy underwent serious change as well. The Twentieth Congress thesis that war between countries with different social systems was not inevitable had proclaimed the start of a new era in international relations, one in which it proved possible to move from an endless arms race toward arms control and disarmament. Decisions concerning the Soviet-American military balance also contributed to the easing of tensions.

For many years, our government had lived with a nightmare: American bombers could easily attack the Soviet Union with nuclear weapons while avoiding any retaliation. Now, however, missiles rendered the two sides equal. This was a great victory for the notion that global nuclear war was out of the question. And that in turn opened up the possibility of arms reductions. The Soviet army was cut almost in half over a brief span of time. Father put on the agenda an even larger

---

10. *Editor's note:* Khrushchev's reasons for dividing the party have been the subject of considerable debate among Western observers and Soviets, too. The reform, adopted in November 1962, was so likely to produce opposition — especially from province party leaders who had formerly lorded it over regions as large as medium-sized countries and were now reduced to being experts on industry or agriculture — that some have wondered whether Khrushchev's critics foisted it on him as a way to discredit his cause. Yet others contend that the reform was Khrushchev's way of replacing his old political base among province party leaders with a new one among enterprising managers and agronomists. Asked about this speculation, Sergei Khrushchev replied: "My feeling is that Khrushchev's only motive was to encourage specialization among party leaders on industry and agriculture. On the other hand, it's hard to speak for him, to imagine what thoughts were going through his head."

reduction, with the aim of freeing human and other resources for economic development. The term of active service in the military was cut. Young people returned home, supplying additional working hands and minds for the economy. However, these steps incurred the displeasure of the top brass; it seemed to the military that they were losing their position and their privileges, and they were far from reconciled to the change. But Father was adamant. He knew their ways well and had no intention of dancing to a primitive militarist tune.[11] Father's view of the future allowed for only minimal deterrent forces, and he was in a hurry to put his plan into practice. The age of missiles was at its peak, but he had already broached the possibility of transferring several missile production plants to peaceful purposes.[12]

The new approach allowed us to begin negotiations with the United States on reducing nuclear weapons. These were only first steps, but someone had to take them. The signing in 1963 of an agreement to ban nuclear tests in the atmosphere, under water, and in space was a real success.

The testing of a super-powerful hydrogen bomb over Novaya Zemlya provided a last push toward this agreement. Its baneful reverberations were felt in many European countries, especially northern ones. It was now clear that the joking was over, that the time had come to think about saving the earth.[13]

Important improvements also occurred in domestic affairs. The process of unmasking the cult of personality, begun at the Twentieth

11. *Editor's note:* Apart from anything else, the military had reason to regret the way the cuts were carried out — that is, precipitously and with insufficient provision made for employing and housing officers who were demobilized. Sergei Khrushchev agrees that this was a problem and could be again today when the Soviet armed forces are again being reduced. But he insists that "the top brass was concerned most of all about preserving its role in the state."

12. *Editor's note:* Some historians of the arms race contend that Khrushchev did *not* really opt for "minimal deterrence." Soviet ICBMs may have been minimal in number in the early sixties, but that was because such rockets were in a relatively early stage of development, with full deployment possible only several years later. I therefore asked Sergei Khrushchev whether he thought his father would have produced and deployed far fewer missiles than Brezhnev eventually did, even in the face of a substantial U.S. buildup of strategic missiles during the Kennedy and Johnson administrations. "Without doubt," he replied. "There would have been fewer Soviet missiles."

13. *Editor's note:* Western historians, and some Soviet ones, contend that Khrushchev authorized the mammoth explosion, which occurred in October 1961, during the Berlin crisis, to intimidate the West, rather than to promote a test ban. "One can argue the issue," Sergei Khrushchev commented. "I have expressed my point of view."

Congress, inevitably developed into the democratization of our entire system, our whole social order. Things went slowly and painfully, but at least they went.

The problem of political power greatly disturbed Father. He worried about who would succeed him and how, and about how to create guarantees against concentration and abuse of power. How to elect deputies was another key issue. Instead of the existing one-candidate system, Father proposed nominating several candidates. That way people would be able to express their preferences, and the deputies would really depend on those who elected them. For the moment, this was just an idea, but it might well have been adopted during consideration of a new constitution, which was scheduled for late 1964.

As an example of the existing system's imperfection, Father cited the remarkable case of Wanda Lvovna Wassilewska's candidacy for the Supreme Soviet. He had a high opinion of her creativity as a writer and of her social contributions, and she often visited us at home. The warm relationship dated back to the war. Wanda Lvovna was the daughter of a major political figure in bourgeois Poland. In 1939 she arrived in liberated Lvov and cast her lot forever with our country. Together with her husband, the well-known Ukrainian playwright Aleksandr Korneichuk, she toured the war zone several times between 1941 and 1945. They saw Khrushchev at Stalingrad and during the Battle of Kursk.

But as a deputy, she didn't do a thing. Moreover, she was so obvious about it that the Ukrainian authorities, fearing possible unpleasantness, changed her district in each new electoral campaign — just far enough so that people in the new district didn't know about her behavior.

"Is that any way to behave?" Father exclaimed indignantly. "What kind of deputies are these? They palm someone off on you and you're supposed to elect them!"

However, he was not fated to reform the benighted system. Not enough time remained.

New regulations governing the soviets were discussed in the course of work on the new constitution. The idea was to give them the power and authority necessary to oversee political life under their jurisdiction. One of the variations under consideration called for the soviets to be in session all year round, as parliaments in Western countries are.

The succession problem was absolutely crucial. It tormented Father: how to arrange a natural and painless transfer of power. He thought of restricting leaders' time in office to a limited number of terms. The Twenty-second Congress adopted that approach in 1961 for party functionaries [with exceptions for top leaders, including Khrushchev — ed.]. All that remained was to extend it to government officials and to enshrine it in the new constitution. But immediately a myriad of problems cropped up: What to do with the functionary after two terms? Move him into a job next door? Send him into retirement? Where and how to apply his experience and knowledge?

On this matter, Father consulted the American model. Although he had yet to rid himself of the "image of the enemy," after two visits to the United States, he paid careful heed to its experience and even measured our own against it. To be sure, he never spoke publicly about borrowing positive features and applying them to our own state structures. Even in his own inner circle, he broached the subject rarely and cautiously. It was still premature. The fruit had yet to ripen.

The apparat had accepted other of Father's innovations with dissatisfied grumbling, whether it approved of them or not. But this one struck it where it lived. From the very top of the system to the district level, leaders went into a panic. The result was not just a group of dissatisfied people but a serious opposition thirsting to take action.

Reforms depriving apparatchiks of many privileges granted to them by Stalin added fuel to the fire. The first step in this direction, taken after the Twentieth Congress, had been to abolish the so-called packets, regular supplementary payments to certain categories of functionaries which were not subject to taxation. But Father's secret speech about Stalin froze them with fear; apparently that's why the cut went through relatively painlessly. They were too frightened, their memories of nighttime arrests too fresh, to resolve on a confrontation.

But the shock passed quickly, and the apparat soon learned it was no longer subject to executions, arrests, or exile. More and more the bureaucracy began to consider itself the decisive force, the master of the situation. After that, reform initiatives were hopelessly stalled. It took a special commission of the Central Committee to work out and implement proposals for liquidating stores open only to the elite, and for reducing the number of cars available for high-level functionaries. The commission was headed in the beginning by Aleksei Illarionovich Kirichenko, at that time second secretary of the Central Committee. The commission met, discussed, recommended, turned down, clarified — but didn't resolve a thing.

Father got anxious; he was in a hurry. They assured him that the matter was nearing completion. They showed him papers of some sort.

When he calmed down for a while, everything returned to its former state.

Soon Kirichenko wasn't around anymore. Several more chairmen were replaced in turn. Finally, after October 1964, the commission ceased to exist altogether. All Father had been able to achieve was a small reduction in the fleet of cars available for personal use. And they never forgave him for that.

Of course, establishing social justice by liquidating such privileges was primarily a moral and ethical matter. Redistribution was not the way to resolve economic problems. The only way to satisfy consumer demand was to produce a sufficient quantity of high-quality goods. But we're used to dispossessing kulaks and belt-tightening all around. We've mastered the art of taking but have completely forgotten how to give.

The measures taken greatly embittered those threatened with the loss of privileges. Not only were they alienated; their wives were too. All of this, in turn, played no small role in the fall of Khrushchev.[14]

Father's efforts to cut back the state apparatus also failed. Naturally, these measures didn't increase his popularity among the bureaucrats. Functionaries who lost their jobs in ministries overflowed into regional economic councils, state committees, and other new entities which sprang up, as if from underground.

Nowadays Father's not-so-simple relations with artists and writers are the subject of much discussion. Obviously, this demands real examination. As for me, I'll permit myself just a few remarks.

The results of the Twentieth Congress brought society, literature, and culture to life. New names appeared; so did bold works of art. People began to say aloud what they had been afraid even to think the day before. Those in authority were sent reeling. Then suddenly it became clear that the powers that be weren't about to accept the change. They hadn't expected the new developments. How had such domesticated, obedient intellectuals gotten out of control? How could they refuse to obey the usual bellow from above? Many officials were frightened, and their fright led them to take retaliatory action.

Father never engaged with these matters in earnest, for he didn't

14. *Editor's note:* I asked Sergei Khrushchev why his father didn't see the potential for open opposition in all this covert resistance? His answer: "You are confusing opposition to a particular decision with opposition to Khrushchev's whole course of action. There was support for some decisions but not for others. This was to be expected. Blind obedience was out of the question. It's only the West that expects that from the Soviet system. Opposition to Khrushchev's overall course sprang up only toward the very end."

consider himself an expert as he did in agriculture, industry, and construction. The field of ideology belonged to Central Committee secretaries Mikhail Suslov, Leonid Ilyichev, and Boris Ponomaryov. However, at critical moments, the warring camps maneuvered to get his support. Writers sent him works that had been rejected up and down the bureaucracy. At the slightest loosening of the reins, the "ideologists" sounded the alarm: "The Hungarian counterrevolution started in the Petofi Circle [a discussion club of Communist intellectuals — ed.]. It ended with hangings and shoot-outs. If we loosen the reins, the same thing will happen here."

There was a grain of truth in these words. The spread of political freedoms unreinforced by economic progress can easily lead to unpredictable results. Father understood this very well, and so, after hesitating, could not bring himself to take the steps he had intended.

Father's last years in power were darkened by sharp confrontations with writers, poets, artists, and musicians. What was so harmful was that he was clashing with people who, in essence, stood on the same side of the barricade as he did.

One must add, however, that these confrontations were carefully and deliberately provoked. Father was worked over at length and finally convinced that the "contagion" of bourgeois ideology had seized the minds of our creative intellectuals, especially the younger ones. They had to be saved. Otherwise they would destroy themselves and bring immeasurable harm to our country and to the cause of communism. Didn't everyone know that bourgeois ideology insinuated itself into every crevice, and that all it would take to bring on disaster was a small lapse of vigilance?

Carefully choosing their moment, the provocateurs set up a series of situations in which Khrushchev was sure to quarrel with people who just yesterday had been his most passionate supporters. From now on, he and they would find themselves in opposing camps.[15]

On top of all these troubles, there were also complications within the socialist commonwealth. No sooner had the storms died down in

15. *Editor's note:* This account of Khrushchev's clashes with writers, artists, and others, while supplemented by more information in later chapters, seems partial. When pressed for more concrete details about the provocations, the author replied that he simply lacked "confirmed facts." Even if Khrushchev didn't consider himself an expert on art in the beginning, didn't he do so later on? "The fact that Father appeared so often before the intelligentsia," his son replied, "does not mean that he himself developed

Europe, with the situation stabilizing in Poland and Hungary, than a new hotbed of tension arose in the form of our disagreements with China. I leave it to the historians to analyze the causes and consequences of the rift, which eventually led to armed clashes. I'll say only that Father took the entire responsibility for the conflict on his own shoulders during those difficult days. It seemed to some, and others consciously wanted to portray it that way, that the conflict was neither ideological nor political, but rather the result of ill will between the two countries' leaders, and particularly on the part of Khrushchev. It would take years before people finally realized how wrong this view was.

FATHER carried a heavy burden of problems just when, nearing his seventieth birthday, his strength began to wane. He would come home exhausted. After walking his two circuits around his Moscow residence on Lenin Hills, he would have supper and then pull several multicolored folders filled with papers out of his briefcase. The evening's work had begun. He would settle himself right there in the dining room, at the corner of the dinner table, or he would head up to his second-floor bedroom. Although there was an office in the house, he never used it.

As a rule, his work stretched until midnight. By nine the next morning, he was always at his desk in the Kremlin.

His eyes ached from the endless reading, and more and more frequently he asked one of his assistants, or one of his children, to read to him aloud. Several years before, the Presidium had adopted a decision limiting his working day, and providing him with two extra weeks of vacation. But the decision remained on paper; in fact, his job took up not only his entire working day, but all his free time as well. He did use the extra vacation time; he was glad to go to Cape Pitsunda (a Black Sea resort in the Caucasus), to the Crimea, or to the Byelovezhsky Forest, in Byelorussia, just to break up his routine. But what he did there was to gather his thoughts, and to think through fundamental problems, after which he would put his conclusions and recommendations in the form of notes to the Central Committee. Father often used his

the thoughts he expressed on these occasions. He was prompted by others whom I list in the text. This pattern continued to the very eve of his retirement. Furthermore, Khrushchev felt no antipathy toward intellectuals. On the contrary, he respected and even honored them, and had many friends among them — writers, poets, and engineers."

free time on vacation for meetings or just conversations with scientists and engineers. I remember Pitsunda gatherings attended by a great many people at which various avenues for developing aviation, rocketry, and the chemical industry were discussed.

Father took full account of the fact that his strength was ebbing. His approaching seventieth birthday was a clear signpost. More and more often, and ever more insistently, he pondered who should succeed him. Just as frequently, he contemplated retirement.

Within the family, he talked often about his wish to retire, sometimes jokingly, sometimes in all seriousness. And he kept returning to this theme in conversations with his colleagues in the Presidium.

"We're oldsters, we've done our bit. It's time to yield the road to others. We've got to give youth a chance to do some work." As I recall, this was the sort of thing he would say. Each time he would grin, and the people around him would laugh. They thought he was joking. But in April 1964, he publicly talked about retirement for the first time, at a meeting with young people, and his speech was published in all the newspapers.

Were serious intentions hidden behind these words? I believe my father actually did intend to retire. He often referred to the approaching Twenty-third Party Congress as his last hurrah.

At home his words provoked no resistance, but his comrades at work raised a storm of protest: "What are you talking about Nikita Sergeyevich? You look terrific! You're a lot stronger than most younger men." That's how they responded — aloud.

It's hard for me to say whether he would have acted on his decision. After all, he kept coming up with new projects and plans. He would have wanted to see them implemented; only then would it have been time to go. But whether his thoughts of retirement were serious or not, he never stopped thinking about his successor. The succession problem preoccupied him throughout his last years. One candidate was replaced by another, and then by a third. But a final resolution, a worthy man who must be younger and more energetic, was nowhere to be found.

At one point he settled on Frol Romanovich Kozlov. Despite conflicts, and even some sharp skirmishes, Father came to trust him more and more.[16] However, misfortune soon followed. Kozlov suffered a ma-

---

16. *Editor's note:* Western Kremlinologists, including Carl Linden, Michel Tatu, William Hyland, and Robert Slusser, have speculated that Kozlov became Khrushchev's main conservative rival, perhaps even leading an open opposition that outvoted Khru-

jor stroke. After he recovered enough to return home from the hospital, Father paid him a visit. It was Sunday, and as usual, he took me with him. Kozlov had often been a visitor in our home, and our two families knew each other well. Kozlov's dacha was just past Uspenskoe, not far from ours, which was located near the Gorki-2 state farm, about thirty kilometers west of Moscow. We drove through the standard green gates and stopped at the entrance. Frol Romanovich's wife, along with some other people, met us and we walked through the house. The bed on which Kozlov was lying occupied the center of the room so that the nurses had convenient access to their patient. A small table with medicines, syringes, and a sterilizing device stood by the wall.

Kozlov reclined on a mound of cushions and pillows, his pale face shining with a sallow glow. When we entered he recognized Father and tried to get up and speak, but his words were disconnected. The impression he made was depressing in the extreme.

Father stood next to him for a few moments, trying to cheer him up by joking in his typical manner. "Here you are taking it easy, pretending to be ill. It's time to get well and get back to work."

Kozlov mumbled something unintelligible in response.

After saying good-bye, we walked into the next room, where the doctors were waiting. They explained that while Frol Romanovich was not in imminent danger, a cure would take many months.

"Will he be able to work?" Father asked.

The medical verdict was unanimous: Of course not. He would remain an invalid. Moreover, any excitement might lead to a new seizure and to death. There could be no more counting on Kozlov.

Father remembered the doctors' warning that nervous stress could prove ruinous for the patient. Therefore, when the question of Kozlov's status came up at the next Presidium meeting, he suggested that Frol Romanovich remain a member despite his illness. No one objected. But after October 1964 they reopened the issue and sent Kozlov into retirement. The doctors proved correct. He couldn't stand the shock and soon passed away.

Kozlov's illness not only posed the question of a future successor

---

shchev. Sergei Khrushchev's comment: "Everyone is entitled to his opinion. I don't want to argue with Sovietologists. Without doubt, Kozlov expressed the views of the party's right wing, but we don't know how he would have acted in power. All I know is that Khrushchev saw him as his successor, and that there were no open clashes between them."

more sharply than ever; it also raised the issue of who would now become the second secretary. But there was no solution to be found, and meanwhile time was passing. To make matters worse, Father had no one he could consult with.[17] He kept it to himself. Evidently, it was his excruciating doubts, his deep need to talk it out, that allowed me to become a witness to my father's meditations.

Father was an energetic man easily carried away with enthusiasm, and like all people of this type, he enjoyed discussing his favorite ideas with almost anyone who would listen. Various technologies for prefabricating apartment house walls filled our ears. We learned a great deal about the advantages and disadvantages of various kinds of concrete. We could imagine how much more profitable it was to smelt steel in a converter than in an open-hearth furnace. And we analyzed the peculiarities of raising not just corn, but Chinese millet, wheat, vegetables, grapes, and fruits. We were inspired by the way plastics were replacing steel, followed the successes of our hydrofoil ships, and much, much more.

Since I was privy to defense matters, Father also discussed questions relating to planes, rockets, and tanks with me. But at no time in our presence did he ever touch on high-level personnel questions. The subject of relations within the leadership was absolutely taboo. Even in June 1957, when disagreements overflowed into stormy Presidium meetings and then into a Central Committee plenum, even then we had to deduce what was happening from indirect hints. All our information came to us in roundabout fashion. Asking Father directly was simply out of the question. The answer was predictable, and so was its form: "Don't butt in where you don't belong. Don't interfere."[18]

That's why I was flabbergasted when in answer to my question about Kozlov, Father suddenly started talking about the doubts that were tormenting him. It happened at the dacha in the late autumn of 1963. We had gone out for our evening walk. We were strolling by the

17. *Editor's note:* Did Khrushchev have no confidants in general, or just on this supersensitive subject? Would he not have discussed this with Mikoyan? Sergei Khrushchev's reply: "My observation is limited to this issue. As far as it was concerned, any Presidium member would have been self-interested. As to possible conversations with Mikoyan, I have no information."

18. *Editor's note:* Here and elsewhere in the book, Khrushchev is depicted as crudely telling his by now adult children to keep out of his affairs. How did his son feel about being treated as if he were still a child? "Father treated me very well, better, in fact, than his other children. But he loved us all. His 'crude' answers were a kind of game, a signal that we were not to press him on whatever our question was."

light of a lantern along the road that led from the gate to the house, when Father suddenly started talking about the situation in the Presidium.

"It's a pity Frol Romanovich won't be returning to work," he began. Usually he referred to his colleagues by their last name, but not this time. "I was really counting on him. He was already in place, he was the kind of person who could decide things on his own, he knew the economy. I don't see a replacement for him, but it's already time for me to think about retiring. My strength isn't what it used to be, and it's time to make way for the young. I'll carry the torch till the Twenty-third Congress and then hand in my resignation.

"I've gotten old, and the rest of the Presidium are old enough to retire as grandfathers. I was forty-five when I joined the Politburo. That's the right age for matters of state; you have the strength, and there's lots of time ahead of you. At age sixty you no longer think about the future. It's time to baby-sit for your grandchildren.

"I'm breaking my neck trying to figure out whom to propose for Kozlov's place. He has to know the economy, and defense, and ideology, but most of all how to analyze people. I'd like to find someone a bit younger. I used to have Shelepin in mind. He seemed a good candidate; he's young, he passed muster at the Komsomol [Young Communist League], and he's worked for a while at the Central Committee. True, he doesn't know his way around the economy. And he's been in the bureaucracy all the time.[19]

"I figured he'd learn a little more, accumulate a bit more real-life, on-the-job experience. That's why I suggested he go up to Leningrad to serve as province first secretary there. It's a huge organization, industry is up-to-date, and they have a great revolutionary tradition. After training like that he could hold any job in the Central Committee.

"So what does he do? He unexpectedly turns it down. He takes offense. He sees the move from a cushy bureaucratic job in the Central Committee to the first secretaryship of Leningrad province as a comedown. It's too bad: I guess I overestimated him. Maybe it's for the best. One can't afford to make mistakes in matters like this. I wasn't about to insist. I wouldn't want to offend him.

19. *Editor's note:* Aleksandr Nikolayevich Shelepin, born in 1918, was already a Central Committee secretary. He had headed the Komsomol from 1952 to 1958 and the KGB from 1958 to 1961. His successor at the KGB was his protégé, Vladimir Semichastny, whom we will meet playing a key role in the anti-Khrushchev conspiracy in chapter two.

"If he'd spent a few years in Leningrad," Father returned to the same sore subject, "he'd have become an old hand at it, and then he could have been nominated to take Kozlov's place. But now he's still a bureaucrat. He doesn't know real life. No, Shelepin won't do, and that's too bad. He's the youngest man in the Presidium."

Father stopped talking. I was silent too. My opinion hadn't been solicited; it was just that he needed to talk to someone. We reached the gate and turned back. Following his own train of thought, Father continued: "Podgorny was a possibility. He's a sensible man, he knows how to analyze economic questions, and he works well with people. He proved himself in the Ukraine. He's got a lot of experience, but he's narrow. Since coming over to the Central Committee he hasn't managed food industry matters very well at all. He isn't suited for this position."

Again a pause.

"That leaves Brezhnev," Father continued with a sigh. "He isn't suited either. The job needs someone with a different sort of character.

"It's true he's got a lot of experience, and he knows the economy and people, too. But he can't hold to his own course; he gives way too easily to the influence of others and to his own moods. Anyone with a strong will can readily dominate him. Before the war, when we appointed him Dnepropetrovsk province secretary, the boys nicknamed him 'the ballerina.' When they told me about it, I asked why.

" 'Anyone who wants to can turn him around,' they answered.

"This position demands firmness, someone who can't be easily swayed. Kozlov was like that. No. Brezhnev won't do."

Again Father fell silent. Nor did he resume the conversation. We wandered along the path from the house to the gate and back, each thinking his own thoughts.

I was depressed by this unexpected candor. How hard it must have been for Father, how alone he was, if he had to confide in me on a topic like this. It had never happened before. It would have seemed inconceivable.

Father never returned to the subject of high-level personnel, not that evening, not ever. Naturally, I never told anyone about the conversation. Father didn't warn me; I didn't need any warning.

You can imagine my amazement when I learned that Brezhnev was slated to become second secretary of the Central Committee. That meant that a more suitable candidate just couldn't be found. I was not about to ask Father about it.

On a personal level, Leonid Ilyich Brezhnev impressed me. He always wore a benevolent smile. He always had a story to tell. He was ever ready to listen and to help. It was his passion for playing dominoes that jarred a bit; it didn't fit my notion of a statesman.

Brezhnev himself didn't seem overjoyed by the flattering suggestion. He resisted it but would eventually have to accede. The new post would bring with it great power, but power that was hardly noticeable. It involved intensive work inside the overgrown party organism. One had to draft decisions, interact with the province committees, keep track of the army, answer for failures. There wasn't enough time in a day. Leonid Ilyich's character and inclinations equipped him better to perform the representational functions of the position he currently held, that of chairman of the USSR Supreme Soviet Presidium. Everything about that job pleased him — the receptions for presidents, kings, and queens, the honor guards, the state breakfasts, lunches, and dinners, the evenings at the theater. He was always in the public eye. Nor was it any less pleasant to present medals and other awards: all around him were smiling faces, people shaking hands and embracing. Those who received awards were full of sincere appreciation and love. And then there were state visits: more honor guards, receptions, press conferences, smiles, handshakes, toasts. He liked to be the center of attention, to see his face in the papers and magazines and on the newsreels.

Now all this would have to end. Ahead of him was exhausting work, a heavy load of responsibility, and the need to make all sorts of decisions with vast and at times unpredictable consequences. Brezhnev didn't like any of this; he was displeased with his appointment, but he didn't dare express his dissatisfaction. Instead, he expressed his thanks for the trust shown in him and promised to justify it.[20]

20. *Editor's note:* As described both here and elsewhere in this chapter, Brezhnev's behavior and motivation seem puzzling. Given his apparent craving for power and perquisites, one would expect him to have welcomed his new status as heir apparent. Is Sergei Khrushchev saying, then, that Brezhnev wanted to be *both* second secretary of the Central Committee and chairman of the Supreme Soviet Presidium? Does he mean to imply that Brezhnev's fondness for the glamorous easy life was so overpowering that he might have refrained from leading the effort to oust Khrushchev if only he had been allowed to stay on as head of state? Sergei Khrushchev's reply: "The main thing about Brezhnev was his ambivalence. He couldn't decide *what* he wanted. As long as Khrushchev was the leader, he preferred being president, but it would be easier to oust Khrushchev from the position of second secretary. The contradiction ate away at him until the very last moment."

The next scheduled Central Committee plenum opened on February 9, 1964. This would be the last one called by Khrushchev. Like many previous plenums, it was to be devoted to the problem of agriculture. Father was still doggedly seeking a way out of the morass, still groping his way toward abundance.

It's not fair to say that Father didn't seek new methods for managing the economy that would allow producers to exercise greater initiative and thus raise the productivity of their labor. Such issues were discussed at conferences and in the press, and various experiments were conducted. Unfortunately, however, he focused his main attention on the search for concrete innovations — in metallurgy, machine-building, chemicals, and agronomy — that would resolve all unresolved questions as if by the wave of a magician's wand.

The minister of agriculture, Ivan Platonovich Volovchenko, gave the main report at the plenum. Until quite recently he had been a state farm director; his rise had been breathtaking. He had held forth effectively at a recent conference, recounting the great results achieved on his farm and making some businesslike proposals.

Father had fallen for him. Father saw the bureaucratization of leadership, and leaders' isolation from real life, as one of the reasons for our lack of agricultural success. He imagined that a man "from the land" could radically change the situation. That's why Volovchenko became minister. However, no miracle occurred. So here he was delivering a report with the magnificent title "On the Intensification of Agricultural Production Based on the Broad Application of Fertilizer, the Development of Irrigation, All-round Mechanization, and the Introduction of the Achievements of Science and Advanced Practice Designed to Produce the Fastest Possible Increase in the Production of Agricultural Output." Obviously, nothing had been omitted.

A multitude of people from all across the country were invited to the plenum: party functionaries, bureaucrats from the ministries, agricultural specialists, scientists. In essence, it wasn't a plenum but a massive conclave. Father had recently introduced these expanded plenums at which one or another set of economic issues would be examined in detail. Far from everyone liked these sessions. The apparatchiks felt they reduced the prestige of the plenum and eroded its significance. But no one dared to voice such seditious sentiments.

Father's attempts to examine things himself, and to figure out the essence of problems, clearly defined his style. At times these methods produced positive results, for example, in missile production. But often the effect was the opposite, as in the case of Lysenko.

Trofim D. Lysenko was an agronomist who appeared on the scene of Soviet biology in the thirties. Supported at first by academician Nikolai I. Vavilov, then the dean of Soviet biology, Lysenko achieved certain practical successes in breeding agricultural crops. Very quickly, however, he began to play the demagogue — irresponsibly promising that his techniques would produce a huge increase in yields, accusing geneticists of "bourgeois idealism," and flat-out denouncing his scientific opponents to the secret police. All this garnered him the support of Stalin, with whose help he seized control of agricultural science.

Before long, Vavilov and many other scholars were arrested. Lysenko achieved full victory in 1948 when, again with Stalin's support, he managed to declare genetics a "false science" and to outlaw it in our country. What probably attracted Stalin's attention to Lysenko was his promise to carry out an agricultural revolution, to double and triple yields, in a short period of time.[21]

Alas, the story of Lysenko was hardly the best page in my father's biography. I want to recount only what I saw with my own eyes.

In the late forties and early fifties, all I knew about Lysenko and genetics was what they taught us in school, and what you could read in popular books: Trofim Denisovich had smashed the "pseudoscientific idealists" who instead of resolving our key agricultural problems were chasing after fruit flies of some sort. Now we were marching along the correct "Michurinist path."[22] I also remember the vernalization of potatoes that was supposed drastically to increase their yield.

Of course, not all of this was quite this primitive, but it seemed that way to someone like me who wasn't very interested in these matters at the time. Imagine my amazement, then, in April 1956, when I noticed two short items in huge type in the upper right corner of *Pravda*'s second page.

The first reported that Comrade Lobanov, deputy chairman of the Council of Ministers, had been relieved of his position by the USSR

21. For more on Lysenko, see Zhores A. Medvedev, *The Rise and Fall of T. D. Lysenko* (New York: Columbia University Press, 1969).

22. Ivan V. Michurin was a Russian plant breeder and developer of many varieties of fruit trees and other plants. During the Stalinist period, Michurin was canonized as a representative of the "materialist" school of science, as opposed to the "formalist geneticists."

Supreme Soviet Presidium in connection with his transfer to other work. Appointed to replace him as deputy in charge of agriculture was Vladimir V. Matskevich.

The communication that followed I quote in full: "In the Council of Ministers: The Council of Ministers has granted Comrade Trofim D. Lysenko's wish to be relieved of his responsibilities as president of the All-Union Lenin Academy of Agricultural Sciences. Comrade Pavel P. Lobanov has been named to head the Lenin Academy."

That was all. No transfer to a new job for Lysenko, no nothing. Even today, let alone in the fifties, an announcement like that means a person has suffered a total defeat.

The unusual presentation of these announcements (normally they would have been published on the extreme right corner of the last page, in small type) meant that they were very significant, that this was not just a transfer but a change in policy.

I was staggered; I could barely wait for Father to return from work before I bombarded him with questions. I don't remember the details of our conversation, but his answers came down to this: Lysenko had been mixed up in some bad business (the word "repression" was not yet in currency), and many scholars were challenging the accuracy of his teachings. For that reason, they had decided to curtail his omnipotence. People who were more objective should be in charge. Let Lysenko work if he wanted to; let him prove his case in scholarly arguments for a change.

Father didn't know much about the essence of the dispute between Lysenko and the geneticists. I don't think he'd given it much thought. I have to admit that the labels "idealist" and "bourgeois" were firmly attached in my mind as well as in my father's to the word "genetics." For me, "genetics" was simply a term of abuse.

As for Lysenko, he faded into the shadows, but he didn't give up. He bided his time, worked to strengthen his position, and lobbied for support both in the Central Committee and the Ministry of Agriculture. I must admit he did a professional job of it. He recruited both Father's assistant for agriculture, Andrei S. Shevchenko, and Vasily I. Polyakov, who later became Central Committee secretary in charge of agriculture. Both men became passionate champions of Lysenko. They used every possible opportunity to put in a good word for him.

As is well known, Father viewed the widespread introduction of corn as one way to solve the grain problem and the problem of animal feed.[23] Corn, of course, reigns supreme in the United States of America. They know how to cultivate it, and the most productive varieties are grown there. Father knew that. That's why he dispatched an agricultural delegation there in the mid-fifties, to familiarize themselves with the most up-to-date practices. Upon their return, they reported at length to Father; among other things, they noted that hybrid seeds offered the highest yields. The order to start buying such seeds in the United States quickly followed, along with another one to launch a similar project in the USSR.

The Lysenkoites were dismayed. Their opponents had used the success of hybrid corn as an argument against them. So they decided to lobby Khrushchev.

"Your disputes about theory don't interest me," Father answered. "Hybrid seeds give a good harvest in America. They'll serve us well, too, so let the scholars worry about theory."

The battle was lost, but Lysenko wasn't about to yield. He awaited his chance, and it came.

Chairman Smirnov of the Leningrad province soviet, himself an agronomist by training, returned from a trip to Austria. In those days, foreign travel was still a rarity, so Father asked him with great interest about all the latest technical innovations.

Smirnov described vividly how the Austrians were planting vegetable seedlings in boxes of soil consisting of humus and peat. The planting process could then be mechanized, so as to increase the productivity of labor; without damaging the seedlings, the yield could be raised.

With characteristic enthusiasm, Father began to push the idea in our country. When the campaign had picked up steam, either Shevchenko or Polyakov, I don't recall who, came to see him. It was on a Sunday at the dacha. They often drove by on Sundays to have a look at Father's plantings, and decided various business matters while they

---

23. The main criticism against Father in connection with corn is that he allegedly insisted on planting it everywhere, even in the north, in the conviction that it would solve the livestock feed problem. Like any measure propagated from above, this one provoked powerful resistance, including ridicule raining down on Khrushchev himself. Jokes of all sorts appeared. Nowadays, specialists think that his proposals were basically correct. But his methods proved that even a good idea encounters great difficulty when introduced from above. Exactly the same thing happened when potatoes were introduced to Russia at the order of Catherine the Great. The result was so-called potato riots all across the country.

were there. On this occasion, as they strolled across the field discussing other issues, the guest tossed off the following as if by chance:

"Nikita Sergeyevich, we've completely neglected our own Trofim Denisovich. The Weismannist-Morganists[24] won't let him lift his head off the ground. They're interfering with his work. They themselves have nothing to offer, so they vent their anger on a real scientist who has contributed so much to agriculture. They don't recognize, they don't want to recognize, our own domestic accomplishments. The only thing they appreciate is what comes from abroad."

Father nodded his head in agreement.

"Here's a fresh example," his visitor continued, "those pots of humus and peat. Everyone is praising them, everyone knows they offer substantial gains. Why, Trofim Denisovich came by just the other day. He had a lot to say, and it was interesting, too. He's got some good suggestions as to how to raise yields, and increase milk production."

The conversation was approaching its main target, which Father's visitor had been aiming at all along. All he had to do was to keep Khrushchev from getting distracted.

"He brought me a curious article. Complained about it, too. Several years ago he proposed the practice of growing vegetables in humus-peat pots. But everywhere he took the idea, they turned him down. They even laughed at him. But when the same idea arrives from abroad, everyone grasps it with both hands. We don't appreciate our own scientists; everyone wants to tail along after bourgeois science. They're all busy with fruit flies; they don't have a clue as to how to increase yields and feed our people."

The visitor took a copy of an article out of his briefcase. It was indeed about humus-peat pots, complete with photographs. Ours were the spitting image of the Austrian ones. Father muttered something about our worship for things foreign, and about the need to support Soviet scientists, and on the spot ordered that Lysenko be given what he needed to do his work, and that he be protected from unjustified attacks.

"It's one thing to argue," he concluded. "Let them argue if they want to. But everyone should have what he needs to work."

That was all they had asked for. The rest would be easy. The ap-

24. *Editor's note:* When genetics was rejected by Lysenko and his associates, they damned it with eponymic labels such as Mendelism (after Gregor Mendel, the founder of genetics) and Weismannism-Morganism (after turn-of-the-century cell biologist August Weismann and the early giant of Mendelian genetics, T. H. Morgan).

parat had mastered the art of inflating instructions that suited it while undermining even the most urgent directives that went against the grain. Not immediately, but gradually, Lysenko regained his lost positions; he wrote memoranda to the Central Committee promising quick results and again appeared as an official orator at conferences. His Central Committee supporters expertly covered up his errors, but let a single claim of his be confirmed and the praise knew no bounds. They vied with one another to report his successes to Father, repeating them over and over again. As for doubters, let alone critics, they were simply not heard.

At this point, yet another development favorable to Lysenko turned up. It was a small thing, but it shows how even a trivial event can have a big psychological impact, provided that you know how to prepare the ground for it and sell it well. Lysenko had begun arguing with another academician, Nikolai V. Tsytsin, as to whose wheat produced higher yields. Father had always been interested in plant breeding. He knew by heart the basic parameters for new varieties, took pleasure in inspecting experimental farms, and was acquainted with breeders who had come up with new varieties of wheat, sunflowers, and potatoes. In this case, he showed a lively interest, and even invited the two competitors to his dacha.

Each of them cited a mass of arguments in defense of his position. There was no way of knowing who was right and who wrong, so Father decided on a ploy. "Not far from here, by the Moscow River, there's a field," he said. "I'll get the collective farm chairman to turn it over to you. Each of you will seed half of it and cultivate it as you wish, and then we'll see. The harvest will show who's right."

So it was settled. They plowed, they fertilized, they sowed. After that, on days off when the weather was warm, Father would take the oars of our rowboat on the Moscow River, we would find a seat where we could, and off we would go to inspect the experimental field. Father loved these outings. It wasn't far from Usovo, where Father's dacha was at the time (he moved to Gorki-2 in 1959), to Ilyinskoe, where the experimental field was located; it took forty minutes or so to get there. The security boat followed along behind us with the chief duty officer seated in the stern, intently surveying the scene. It kept a polite distance, for Father wouldn't allow them to get too close, and would tell them where to go in a few crude words.

"Why are you hanging on my back? What are you sniffing around for? Leave a little space and enjoy some fresh air."

Finally we'd arrive and clamber ashore on the left bank. Usually Lysenko or Tsytsin was waiting. Not far away on a knoll was Ilyinskoe, the Moscow party committee's country retreat. Moscow party leaders would spend their days off there. Father often did too after his return to Moscow from Kiev in 1949. He would gather together some friends, and the whole company would stroll across the fields, talking business or simply, in Father's expression, "goofing off." Nor did he abandon this practice even after moving into the Central Committee.

In sum, inspecting the experimental field at times became a mass activity, and everyone was eager to see who would turn out victorious. Tsytsin took the early lead: the plants on his half of the field were sturdier and greener. But at this point, Lysenko carried the day psychologically. On one Sunday inspection, Father needled Lysenko: "Tsytsin's wheat looks better, you know."

Without a word, Lysenko walked off among the plants, first on his side of the field, then on his opponent's. He tore out several along with their roots and examined them closely.

"I can't agree. My yield will be what I promised, but his won't amount to anything at all. His plants are overfed. There won't be any grain."

The autumn confirmed this prediction. As a result, Lysenko's authority rose immeasurably in Father's eyes.

Of course, these are only fragments, and not very significant ones at that, that I happen to remember. And in fact, everything was much more complicated. (Lysenko operated through other channels as well, particularly through the Central Committee apparat, in which he had many supporters.) Now Lysenko could have at his adversaries, and the complaints about an "idealist-Weismannist" clampdown on "real" scientists really rang out. Ever more insistently Lysenko's successes were contrasted with the "barrenness of bourgeois pseudoscience." Even Father threw himself into the battle in defense of the "real" scientists. And so, Lysenko once more became all-powerful. In August 1961, Lysenko again became President of the Lenin Academy of Agricultural Sciences.

I must say that as Father came more and more to believe in Lysenko, I began to have my doubts. I wondered how a theory could be called idealist if it had to do with strictly material objects like genes and chromosomes, the carriers of heredity. On several occasions I tried to start a conversation with Father along these lines. But it was a waste of time. He had come to believe in Lysenko and had no need for my arguments. And not just for mine. Academicians Igor Kurchatov (head of the Soviet nuclear program), Mikhail Lavrentiev (founder of the Siberian branch of the USSR Academy of Sciences), Pyotr Kapitsa (Nobel laureate in physics), and others tried to convince him. But it was an unequal struggle.

On one side, the "agricultural experts" stood foursquare behind Lysenko. They promised quick results; they had already seen them with their own eyes and touched them with their own hands, and they had shown them to Khrushchev. Their opponents were mathematicians and physicists, nonexperts on agriculture in Father's eyes. He didn't want to reckon with their arguments. After several huge disagreements, they gave way one by one.

I remember ending up next to academician Lavrentiev at a Kremlin reception in 1962 or 1963. By that time I understood who was right and who was lying. I had no doubts, and so I sallied forth into battle. I knew Lavrentiev's views, and also my father's deep respect for him. They knew each other well from Kiev days in the thirties, and after Lavrentiev had organized the Siberian branch of the academy, Father had raved about him. I thought I had found an ally, and so I uttered some general phrases to the effect that truth was on the side of genetics and Lysenko's position was mistaken.

Lavrentiev looked at me as if I were a provocateur and muttered, "I no longer concern myself with this matter." Then he walked away, and I just stood there as if in disgrace.

Not long after that I got hold of Zhores Medvedev's book that describes the whole (by now familiar) history of Lysenko's rise and the destruction of biology in the Soviet Union. It was a typewritten copy, and to this day I have it in my library. When I read it, it made my hair stand on end. I decided I had to open Father's eyes at any cost, to show him the truth, to save him from putting himself to shame. I turned the arguments over and over in my mind, trying to find irrefutable ones, waiting for a propitious moment.

Several times I began a conversation with what I considered an incontrovertible premise: "Why are you interfering?" I asked him. "Let the scientists look into it themselves. After all, documented results confirm the existence of genes."

But nothing came of it. Father scowled, grew angry, and cut me off. "You're an engineer. You'll never understand any of this. They've got you to repeat someone else's words like a parrot. Experts, knowledgeable people, say just the opposite."

His argument had its own logic and was all the more painful to me for that reason. But still, I couldn't understand him. I realized that he was being deceived. What I couldn't understand was his stubborn unwillingness to hear the other side. I guess he just trusted his advisers, who were all in Lysenko's camp, while he thought we simply weren't qualified in this field. He supported the spirit of competition in other branches of science and technology. Engineers made their proposals and then entered into competition; it was the results themselves that defined whose was best. But on this issue, Father was adamant. His final, immovable argument was to accuse someone of "idealism," to refer to the way bourgeois ideology had penetrated our society.

Father often came into conflict with scientists; they all brought their problems to the Central Committee. The fact that it was he who had to make the decision in favor of one side or the other, thus allocating substantial resources to the realization of its proposals, worried him. He didn't like deciding things with his eyes closed, and he looked around for a scientist on whose objectivity he could rely.

Most of all, he feared becoming an instrument for the attainment of someone else's aims, even when they were strictly scientific aims. He considered possible candidates for a long time. Finally, in 1960, he settled on Igor Vasilievich Kurchatov, with whom he first came into close contact in April 1956, during his visit to Great Britain. They spent a lot of time together on the cruiser that took them there and back.

Igor Vasilievich successfully combined a scholar's mind with a statesman's wisdom. His interests extended not only to military and peaceful uses of atomic energy, but seemingly to fields far from his own, like philosophy, biology, and cosmology. His lecture on the peaceful uses of thermonuclear energy given at the British atomic center at Harwell in 1956 evoked tremendous interest. He was the first to talk about research then going on in the Soviet Union. Until then, such information had been kept under tight lock and key.

Nor did the academician's black, shovel-sized beard attract any less attention. In those distant days, when we and the West had only begun to get acquainted, a beard was an inevitable part of the Western image of a Russian. Yet, with the exception of Bulganin, who wore a small professor's goatee, everyone else in the delegation was clean shaven. And suddenly along comes this big black beard. All Kurchatov had to do was appear on the street and a whole crowd would follow him.

Relations between Father and Kurchatov became very close after they returned home. They would meet at Father's office, and Kurchatov was a frequent guest at the dacha. Their ideas seemed to coincide. Igor

Vasilievich had long been concerned about the future development of science, and his irrepressible nature sought more elbowroom. During one of his visits to the dacha, he made a suggestion: "Nikita Serge-yevich, you're spending more and more time making decisions on scientific matters. These not only take deep and specialized knowledge, but a sense of how scientists really work. You yourself are very busy. You need a scientific adviser. If you'll allow me, I'll make so bold as to propose myself for this thankless position. I beg you not to doubt my sincerity."

It was obvious that this was not done spontaneously; he was carrying out a carefully conceived idea. Father didn't like it when people tried to lobby him for one thing or another, and especially when they thrust themselves upon him. I expected him to answer Kurchatov politely but to decline his offer. But that's not what happened. Father was silent for a while, obviously pondering his answer.

"Comrade Kurchatov, you're right on target. I myself have been thinking about this for a long time, and — I won't hide it — I've thought about you more than once. Two circumstances give me pause: One is that our whole atomic energy program depends on you, and that's one thing that we can't possibly neglect. The second is that you're a scientist, an academician, but you'd be serving as a consultant, a bureaucrat. Would that be proper?"

"I've thought about that," Kurchatov replied. "I would volunteer my services," he grinned, "free of charge, while continuing to work in my institute."

Father liked that answer, and the decision was made to proceed. They agreed that Igor Vasilievich would rest a bit before taking on his new responsibilities.

Unfortunately, fate decreed otherwise. Kurchatov never returned from his vacation. Instead, he died suddenly. Father got the news on the phone at the dacha. He gave the order for a Red Square funeral and then, putting down the phone, said pensively, "He was an excellent man. It's a pity we didn't get to work together. I was counting on him a lot."

Might-have-beens are unreliable in such matters. But if this plan had been realized, I think Lysenko would have found it difficult if not impossible to dupe Khrushchev any longer. Now, however, his path was clear. My sister Rada Nikitichna Adzhubei is a biologist by training and a graduate of the Moscow University journalism school. (Nowadays she is deputy editor of the popular journal *Nauka i zhizn — Science and*

Life.) She and I tried many times to get the truth across to Father, but it was like coming up against a brick wall.

The last confrontation took place in the summer of 1964. I remember it very well. It was a warm evening. We were sitting on the terrace overlooking the Moscow River. Father had spread his papers out on a small wicker table and was taking stock of what he had still to do that day. He looked tired. Rada, her husband, Aleksei Ivanovich Adzhubei (who was the chief editor of the official government newspaper, *Izvestia,* and a member of a group of advisers to Father), and I had settled ourselves around him, each of us occupied with our own affairs. Suddenly, Father broke off from his reading and, addressing no one in particular, uttered something about Lysenko's achievements and the machinations of the "antiscientific Weismannist-Morganist idealists."

We had no idea why he had said it, but we had no choice but to respond. Rada and I started to point out carefully that genetics was a science like other sciences, and that there was nothing idealistic about it. Lysenko's argument that no one had actually seen a gene was absurd; no one had seen an atom either, but the atomic bomb was a reality. This last argument seemed devastating to me. Now and then Adzhubei stuck in a word or two.

The conversation really angered Father. He never shouted at his family, never cursed or raised his voice. (Charges that he did so at work seem groundless to me, but then I don't know what went on there.) But this time he flared up and in a raised voice repeated his old arguments: that unscrupulous people were using us for their own purposes, and that we, ignorant in this matter, were echoing their words. Finally he lost his temper altogether and declared that he wouldn't tolerate carriers of an alien ideology in his own home, and that if we persisted, we'd better not darken his door again. In sum, it was a real brawl. Instead of taking our usual stroll before retiring, we parted angry and upset. Rada and Adzhubei drove home.

How to explain what had happened? It turned out that certain agricultural "experts" had dropped by just as Father was about to leave his office. They brought a whole pile of complaints that the "idealists" weren't allowing real scientists to live and work, especially Lysenko. Nor did they forget to mention us: Rada and Sergei, they said, were joining in the chorus, not out of any evil intent, of course, but unthinkingly.

Recently, certain people in Father's inner circle had been exploiting times when he was particularly tired to sling mud at "ideological degenerates" who were leading us astray. What these intriguers counted on doing, and not without real prospects of success, was irritating Father, provoking an explosive reaction, and then using it accordingly.[25] Alas, they often succeeded. In this case, Father was too exhausted to react immediately. He heard them out in silence and then went home upset. His anger had built up steam all evening and then boiled over on us.

In the morning, no one mentioned the previous evening's incident. It was clear that Father was ashamed of himself for losing control. But Lysenko had achieved his goal.

For a long time after that, we abandoned our attempts to engage Father in conversations about genetics. The subject was out of the question. After October, there was nothing to be gained by continuing the dispute.

In the years that followed, I didn't raise the subject of Lysenko with Father. I didn't want to cause him any unnecessary unpleasantness, and anyway, he was no longer in a position to have any influence. Nonetheless, I noticed that he was not about to change his basic view. From time to time visitors would ask the awkward question, and Father would defend Lysenko. Calmly and without further cursing the "Weismannist-Morganists," he would reply that Trofim Denisovich was an applied scientist who had done a lot for our agriculture.

LET us return to the Central Committee plenum of February 1964. Besides the minister of agriculture's report, there were several others on various agricultural issues. Father, too, spoke at the plenum. It was his last appearance of this kind. Many witnesses are no longer alive, and others aren't talking, but if one pulls together scraps of information from various people connected with the events of the period, the following can be said with assurance: Sometime between January and March 1964 the opposition to Khrushchev took shape in the Central Committee Secretariat. It united Podgorny, Brezhnev, Shelepin, and Polyansky. Their goals were not fully clear, nor were their roles yet distributed, but the work had begun. They were very different people, but they couldn't do without one another.

25. *Editor's note:* Asked to name names and cite other instances, Sergei Khrushchev replied: "It's hard to name names. After all, I wasn't present on these occasions and there are no transcripts of the conversations. I have no witnesses and some of the people involved are still alive. Under those circumstances, I don't consider it possible to provide names."

They had to discern the mood of Central Committee members, province party secretaries, and military leaders. The lesson of 1957 was fresh in their memory. They recalled how the June 1957 Central Committee plenum had come to Khrushchev's rescue after he had seemingly suffered a full and final defeat in the Presidium.[26] Ahead of them lay painstaking, secret work — dangerous too, if, God forbid, even the slightest hint of what they were up to got out.

A few participants and witnesses have recently recounted what went on in 1964. One of them is former KGB chairman Vladimir Yefimovich Semichastny. In an interview with a journalist, he revealed that preparations for Khrushchev's ouster began about eight months before October. He claims to have known about it from the very beginning, since without him no one would have dared to begin.[27]

Pyotr Yefimovich Shelest, former Presidium member and party leader of the Ukraine, is another witness. He dates the beginning of the conspiracy precisely — March 14, 1964.[28]

> It was my birthday. I was at home. . . . Podgorny and Brezhnev had driven over to congratulate me. We plunked ourselves down at the table and had a fair amount to drink. The talk circled mainly around the situation in the country. . . . Podgorny and Brezhnev didn't seem very self-assured; you could feel they were anxious about something. They talked

26. The Stalinists in the Presidium had proposed removing Father as first secretary and appointing him minister of agriculture. They had a majority, and the vote went against Khrushchev. But he and his supporters, among them Minister of Defense Georgy K. Zhukov and KGB chairman Ivan A. Serov, notified other Central Committee members of what was happening. When the full committee gathered in Moscow, they backed Khrushchev. They particularly feared a return to Stalinist methods of administration. Molotov, Malenkov, Kaganovich, and Central Committee secretary Dmitry V. Shepilov, who joined them in the move against Father, were ousted from the Central Committee. Among those who took their places was Nikolai G. Ignatov, whose career took off at that time but who, as will be seen in the next chapter, ended up playing a key role in the 1964 conspiracy against Khrushchev.

27. Semichastny was interviewed by the chief editor of *Argumenty i fakty*, Vladislav A. Starkov. The published version of the interview appears in *Argumenty i fakty*, May 20–26, 1989, pp. 5–6.

28. The following information, as well as citations from Shelest later in this chapter, are taken from unpublished transcripts of an interview conducted by Vladislav A. Starkov. The published version appears in *Argumenty i fakty*, January 14–20, 1989, pp. 5–6.

about how difficult interrelations were at the top, about the lack of teamwork in the central apparat. . . . Their complaints about their hard fate were the main theme of our conversation.

Even back then, I began to feel anxious, a certain unease if you will. But over the next months, I wasn't sure what lay behind it. . . . What would be my role in the change of party and state leadership? I never put the question that way; I just felt anxious, without admitting it to myself. It was scarcely perceptible, but I had a premonition. . . . They didn't quite trust me. They were sounding me out.

Taking soundings — that was the key task during those months. The work was proceeding imperceptibly but intensively through trips and conversations. Simultaneously, there was an inordinate inflation of the cult of my father: the big portraits of him on the streets of Moscow and other cities got bigger; he was constantly quoted, cited as the authority on any and every issue. The film *Our Nikita Sergeyevich* opened. It had been made in the "best tradition" of the not-so-distant past, going into fulsome raptures and heaping endless encomiums on the leader. When they showed the film to Father, he sat through it in silence; he didn't praise it, but he didn't ban it either. They prepared a series of colorful albums: Khrushchev Before the War, Khrushchev at War, Khrushchev After the War. Some were published, others were not.

Every speech mentioned Khrushchev, whether he was relevant or not. Brezhnev, Podgorny, and Shelepin set the tone for the campaign, and others tagged along.

For his part, Father committed one error after another. He resisted the unfolding campaign of flattery too weakly. He didn't find the strength to demand an end to it. Of course, all this had not begun suddenly. I remember back in the summer of 1962 or 1963 Father decided for nostalgia's sake to travel around the Ukraine on his way south for vacation. He'd have a look at the fields before the harvest, and visit a few industrial enterprises. This kind of thing had become a habit. More than that, he was just drawn to the vast expanses of the Ukraine. He had spent the best years of his life there. This time the schedule included an inspection of the recently completed Kremenchug Hydroelectric Station. Next to it a whole city had grown up with the awful-sounding name KremGES. We set out by car from Kiev. Up ahead was Khrushchev with Podgorny and other Ukrainian leaders, behind them a whole "tail" of automobiles. I was way in the back. It was a hot, sunny day.

We approached the city. It was all bathed in green. Suddenly it hit me — the road sign identifying the city read, in Ukrainian, "Khrushchev."

Several years before, Father had banned the naming of cities after living political leaders. Many of his colleagues had been opposed, especially Kliment Voroshilov, but the decision went through. Often we had heard Father recall the prewar practice indignantly: "In those days there was a mania for 'collecting' cities and towns with your name attached. They competed to see who'd get the most: Molotov, Molotovsk, Voroshilovgrad, Kirovobad. What didn't they think of?"

Our motorcade stopped at city party headquarters. I pushed closer and could see from the surrounding faces that Father had not yet said anything about the road sign. Their tense faces had broken into smiles. We had a look around the city, drove out to the dam, and sat and talked awhile at the party committee. It was as if Father had not seen the sign.

Finally, we arrived at the wharf where we would catch a steamer to Dnepropetrovsk. The boat cast off. Everyone stood around in the forward salon, waiting for lunch. Father expressed his gratitude for the great honor they had done him by naming the city after him.

Everyone nodded, vying with one another to praise Khrushchev's services, saying how much he had done for the country and the people, and how much everyone loved him.

I gave up trying to understand anything. From the moment we arrived in the city, the awkwardness and tactlessness of it all had haunted me. I had expected that Father would complain. What was happening instead made me despair. But Father was not done yet.

"Don't you read Central Committee resolutions?" he continued. "Or don't you think them obligatory? I insisted on a ban on naming cities after leaders. And what do I find here but my name!!! Do you realize what kind of situation you've put me in?"

A real blowup followed. The next day the newspapers reported First Secretary N. S. Khrushchev's visit to the city of KremGES.

Unfortunately, things did not always turn out that way.

Misfortune in affairs of state gives rise to discontent and a search for guilty parties. Father, too, was subject to this infection. It's difficult today for us to judge the causes and justifications for personnel transfers undertaken back then. But one thing is clear: they set upper-echelon teeth on edge; the higher-ups were hardly in sympathy with Khrushchev. On December 14, 1963, a Central Committee plenum had adopted a broad program for applying chemical fertilizers to agriculture; according to Father, the only way to resolve the food problem was to follow the American example. Having done so, the plenum made several personnel decisions without any discussion. It dropped Ukrainian premier Vladimir V. Shcherbitsky from his nonvoting membership in the Presidium, appointing Shelest in his place. Father didn't even know Shelest; it was Podgorny, the former Ukrainian party leader, who pushed him forward. Since being transferred from Kiev to Moscow, Podgorny had been gaining power, and at the most recent celebration of the revolution he had delivered the major speech. That said a lot.

We didn't know the true reason for Shcherbitsky's ouster. It was said that Father was very dissatisfied with Shcherbitsky's report on agriculture delivered during Father's last visit to Kiev. But no one could figure out exactly what the premier had done wrong. Many said that his deputies had played a big part in his fall. Father knew all of them from his time in the Ukraine, and he heeded their views.

Shcherbitsky didn't head the Ukrainian Council of Ministers for long, but was soon demoted to the rank of province secretary. The unhappiness with this decision was almost overt. Shcherbitsky was considered a good manager and a capable leader.

After Shcherbitsky, it was Kiril T. Mazurov's turn. On January 6, 1964, he accompanied Father to Poland on an unofficial visit at the invitation of Polish party leader Wladislaw Gomulka and Prime Minister Józef Cyrankiewicz. At his doctors' urging, Father usually took a ten-day vacation in midwinter. The Poles had invited him to go hunting for several days, but as usual he wanted to combine business with pleasure. He grabbed Mazurov, the Byelorussian party leader, and took him along to help establish closer economic ties between Byelorussia and Poland. In general he liked and respected Mazurov.

In the middle of January, I took a vacation and met them at the border. Father meant to spend a couple of days in Byelorussia at the dacha in the Byelovezhsky Forest. During one of their walks, Mazurov described at length his vision of Byelorussia's economic future. I couldn't hear exactly what was said even though I walked beside them the whole time. Many such conversations took place in my presence.

All I recall is that Father didn't like Mazurov's ideas and began correcting him. Mazurov didn't agree, and they quarreled. They were upset with each other but nonetheless parted on seemingly friendly terms. When we arrived in Moscow at the Byelorussia station, I was stunned to hear Father suddenly tell the Presidium members who had met him, "I didn't like the way Mazurov behaved at all. We had a long talk. His proposals won't stand up to criticism. We'll have to think about replacing him."

These words were a surprise to everyone — although no one entered any objection.

What happened after that I don't know. Evidently Father cooled down, reflected on his conversation with Mazurov, and changed his mind. In any event, there was no further talk of dismissing Mazurov. Doubtless, Mazurov immediately learned what Father had said, and after that could hardly be counted among the first secretary's supporters. Steps like this did not add to Father's popularity in the party and government apparat.

MEANWHILE, life took its usual course. As always, meetings, receptions, and trips were laid on in connection with pressing economic and political questions.

In the winter and spring of 1964, Father spent time in Hungary, the Ukraine, and Leningrad.

He spent less and less time in Moscow. He would rest there awhile and then head off to do some more inspecting, more organizing people and telling them what to do. The threads of overall leadership increasingly fell into the hands of Brezhnev and Deputy Prime Minister Aleksei N. Kosygin. During Father's absences they felt freer and more self-assured. They grew less eager to see him return. He prevented them from implementing their own policies. Father injected himself into all matters large and small, and they were irritated by this kind of tutelage.

As Father rushed about accomplishing relatively little, important projects in which he had once invested great hope fell by the wayside. Several of them dated back to his meeting with President John F. Kennedy in Vienna in June 1961, a meeting that I think historians have underestimated. Many of them contend that Father preached at the young American president and that they spent the entire time in fruitless argument; they also describe how Kennedy beat back Khrushchev's attacks.

The main thing I recall happening at Vienna was that the two men got acquainted. Father returned to Moscow after the summit with a very high opinion of Kennedy. He saw him as a worthy partner and strong statesman, as well as a simple, charming man to whom he took a real liking. He considered Kennedy a sensible politician with whom one could do business.

In one of their Vienna conversations they discussed an idea that was daring for its time, the idea of a joint Soviet-American flight to Mars. The world was then agog with space travel; we and the Americans were competing to be first to the moon. Khrushchev and Kennedy both thought a joint spaceflight would do a lot to increase trust between their two countries. They both approved the idea, but it never went anywhere. The ground wasn't ready for it, either in our country or Kennedy's.

In the years that followed, Father thought many times about trying to implement the plan, but he came up against resistance on the part of the military: they would have to reveal our military secrets to the Americans; they would have to show them rockets whose technical characteristics were identical in their civilian and military versions. Father wasn't ready to overcome this barrier if it meant pressing the military; the inertia of established conceptions was too strong. Evidently Kennedy confronted the same sort of situation.

I recall strolling around the house on Lenin Hills with Father not long before the tragic events in Dallas. Again and again he returned to this alluring idea. I had the feeling that he was getting close to making a positive decision.

But Kennedy's life was cut short, and Father didn't want to take up the issue with his successor. He trusted Kennedy and felt real human sympathy toward him, and such likes and dislikes played a big part in Father's life. As a politician he could overcome them, but as a man he remained in thrall to his predilections.

That's how he took such a liking to Van Cliburn — to his openness, his talent, his charming smile. Father attended several of his concerts, and invited the pianist to spend a Sunday at our dacha. He always had the warmest memories of this attractive young American.

The spring of 1964 arrived and with it the sowing season. A good harvest was an absolute must. The failures of previous years had forced us to purchase grain abroad; the quality of baked products had fallen. As far as Father was concerned, these purchases were an extraordinary, onetime measure that must never be repeated. In the last analysis, we had to learn to grow our own grain.

He never accepted excuses that blamed poor harvests on bad weather. "That's for bureaucrats. It's the kind of excuse they can put in their reports. There are always droughts or floods somewhere in a huge country like ours, but there are good harvests every year, too. You can always blame your own incompetence on the sun or the rain. Don't come to me with explanations like that. The harvest depends on us and how well we work."

Of course, there were other problems as well. Nonetheless, in the midst of them all, April arrived, and on April 17, Father's seventieth birthday.

It was a joyous day, like all anniversaries, but tragic, too, for the shameless Khrushchev cult reached unbelievable heights. Mama reacted especially sharply to all the hyperbole but kept silent. We noticed that the tumultuous glorification was not to Father's liking, but he too kept silent so as not to spoil the celebration.

The ceremonies began in the morning. A din on the first floor awakened the whole house. Security men were lugging a huge radio-television console, made by a factory in Riga, into the dining room. On its side was a small metal plate with a gift inscription: "From your comrades at work in the Central Committee and the Council of Ministers."

This gift was the exception. Father had categorically refused to accept any gifts, especially from official agencies. "Don't waste the people's money. No presents!" He even arranged for the Central Committee to issue a special directive allowing only congratulations to be sent to him. In addition to not wanting to waste money, Father felt he had everything he needed. The taboo extended to members of the family, but of course we paid no attention. Nor did members of the Presidium.

The spring morning was bright and sunny, and the guests began arriving before nine o'clock: relatives, Presidium members, secretaries of the Central Committee. There was no other time in the day; the rest of it was given over to official events that were scheduled down to the minute.

The residence where we lived was a two-story house that accommodated small receptions as well as day-to-day family life. Before 1953, Father, Malenkov, Bulganin, and several other Presidium members had lived with their families in a big apartment house on Granovsky Street. Voroshilov, Mikoyan, and Molotov lived in the Kremlin. But Father found living in the multistory apartment house oppressive. In Kiev we had occupied a one-story home (until the revolution it had belonged to a prosperous druggist) surrounded by a large garden. There you could take a walk in the evening, or sit on a bench under a lilac bush reading or resting.

Father didn't change his habit of taking a walk after work even when we moved to Moscow. Often he would drag Malenkov, who lived in the apartment under us, along with him. They would walk along Kalinin Street, down to Red Square, and around the Kremlin. Sometimes they would drop into the Aleksandrov Gardens or, taking a different route, return home by Gorky Street. Security men would follow along, of course, trying to remain inconspicuous.

After Stalin's death, Malenkov ordered designs drafted for a series of government residences at the very edge of the city in the Lenin Hills above the Moscow River. When Malenkov showed him the designs, Father at first hesitated — wasn't it too expensive? — but then agreed. The idea was that all Presidium members would move into the new houses, but not all of them did. Molotov, Voroshilov, and a few others took up residence on Granovsky Street.

Formal rooms were located on the first floor of our residence: a large dining room and a living room. There were also two separate two-room apartments on the first floor. The master bedroom was on the second floor, along with a study.

More and more people arrived to congratulate Father. The new arrivals gathered in small bunches in the living room, exchanging bits of news and joshing each other. No one smoked. Father couldn't abide tobacco smoke.

The hero of the occasion was late. Finally he appeared on the sunlit oaken staircase, smiling and elegantly decked out. The guests flowed toward him. There were handshakes, and best wishes for health and happiness — all the usual greetings that accompany birthdays regardless of the rank of the guest of honor. Brezhnev smothered Father with the ritual kisses. Little by little the bustle died down. Father invited everyone into the dining room where the big table was covered with delicacies. In the past we had rarely had enough guests to go round half the table, but this time there weren't enough places; people crowded together and squeezed in at the corners.

This room had witnessed many important events — both in our family, and involving affairs of state. It was precisely here, late at night after returning from the Kremlin, that Presidium members discussed the developing events of the Cuban missile crisis. It was from here that Father dictated his messages to President Kennedy. But at the climactic moment, Father spent the night in his Kremlin study.

It was here that Father got a call from Andrei Andreyevich Gromyko in the fall of 1963 reporting the attempt on the life of the president of the United States. Greatly disturbed, Father asked Foreign Minister Gromyko to contact the American ambassador to obtain a detailed account.

For a long time, there was no further word. Father impatiently called back Gromyko, who said that he had put in a call to Washington.

"But I told you to call the American ambassador here. Isn't that faster?" Father set him straight.

Several minutes later, the news arrived that President Kennedy was dead. It was decided immediately to send to the United States a delegation of the highest level possible. Mikoyan would head it.

But today there was a birthday party in the room.

As chairman of the USSR Supreme Soviet Presidium, Brezhnev spoke first, reading the congratulatory greeting signed by all the Presidium members and Central Committee secretaries there assembled:

"Dear Nikita Sergeyevich! We, your close comrades in arms, members and candidate members of the Presidium and secretaries of the Central Committee, extend special greetings and fervently congratulate you, our closest personal friend and comrade, on your seventieth birthday. [They all broke into applause.]

"Like our whole party, and all Soviet people, we consider you, Nikita Sergeyevich, an outstanding Marxist-Leninist, the most distinguished statesman of the Communist party, the Soviet state, and the international Communist and workers' movement, and a courageous fighter against imperialism and colonialism and for peace, democracy, and socialism. [Applause]

"Your ebullient political activity, your wisdom and vast experience in life, your inexhaustible energy and revolutionary will, your staunchness and unyielding devotion to principle — all have won you profound respect and the love of all Communists and Soviet people. [Applause]

"We are happy to work hand in hand with you, and to follow your example of a Leninist approach to the resolution of party and state issues: to be always on the side of the people, to give one's all to them, to march ever forward to the great ideal — the construction of a Communist society.

"With all our heart, Nikita Sergeyevich, we wish you good health, many more years of life, and new successes in your far-reaching and truly miraculous activities. [Stormy applause]

"We think that you, our dear friend, have lived out but half your life. We wish you at least as many more years and hope that you will live them as brilliantly and fruitfully as you have those already passed.

We warmly embrace you on this special day. You will find here the signatures of your devoted friends and comrades in arms sitting at this table; and their sentiments are shared by innumerable people all across our country."

Leonid Ilyich seemed deeply moved. He wiped away a tear and embraced Father. Everyone came up, clinked glasses, and uttered the appropriate phrases. Finally, after all had their turn, Brezhnev presented the guest of honor a handsome document case with the just-read speech in it, signed in accordance with the Cyrillic alphabet and with the table of rank [which listed full members of the Presidium first, then candidate members, and then Central Committee secretaries who were not Presidium members — ed.]:

L. Brezhnev	L. Yefremov
G. Voronov	K. Mazurov
A. Kirilenko	V. Mzhavanadze
F. Kozlov	Sh. Rashidov
A. Kosygin	P. Shelest
O. Kuusinen	Yu. Andropov
A. Mikoyan	P. Demichev
N. Podgorny	L. Ilyichev
D. Polyansky	V. Polyakov
M. Suslov	A. Rudakov
N. Shvernik	V. Titov
V. Grishin	A. Shelepin

This document gave its authors no peace until the very day of Khrushchev's death.

Reading it today (in a newspaper clipping), one recalls that back then full members of the Presidium were listed in strict alphabetical order without exception. As a result, Khrushchev always came toward the end. Today's practice of listing the general secretary first, like that title itself, was introduced later by Brezhnev.

The delivery of the address disposed of the official congratulations. At this point, the usual routine associated with such occasions began. Father's comrades in arms each rose in turn. Congratulations and best wishes flowed along with the toasts.

In a couple of hours, it was time to go. Still ahead were official congratulations in the Kremlin, and then a grand reception in the evening. Leaders of all the socialist countries and secretaries of their Communist parties had arrived for the birthday celebration. President Urkho Kekkonen of Finland was there too. Father's friendship with him went way back; they had met often in the course of establishing friendly relations between their two countries over the previous decade, and they liked each other a lot.

Many of the leaders brought medals to present to Father. By the end of the evening ceremony, he was not only weary from speeches and handshakes but had "put on" quite a bit of weight.

The next day everything was back in the usual workaday rut. The holiday was a thing of the past, and it was time to think about the future.

A POLISH delegation headed by Gomulka was in Moscow. It departed for home on April 19, to be succeeded on April 25 by an Algerian delegation led by President Ahmed Ben Bella.

After the May Day holidays, Father departed for the Crimea with Ben Bella. Having seen off his guest, he wanted to have a rest, so he debarked from Yalta by ship for an official visit to Egypt. He had been invited to be an honored guest at the inauguration of the Aswan High Dam.

Father considered our friendly relations with the Arab countries to be extremely important. Our alliance with the Arab world seemed solidly grounded in a foreign policy maneuver Khrushchev had carried out during the Suez crisis of 1956. He had managed to bring the Western powers' military attack on the young Egyptian republic to a halt.

Father took pride in his success. He loved to recall his negotiations with the then-leaders of Britain and France, Sir Anthony Eden and Guy Mollet, which led to a lightninglike end to the war and a pullout of troops from the Suez canal zone.[29]

The events of 1956 turned the Arab world around. Until then, these

29. *Editor's note:* The last two paragraphs probably exaggerate Khrushchev's role in the Suez crisis. Most Western historians contend that it was Washington's decision not to support its allies that brought an end to the invasion. Sergei Khrushchev's reply: "It's hard for me to comment on these events. My intention has been to present my father's point of view. He saw things as I have described them, and I think he had some basis for doing so. Without pressure from Khrushchev, President Eisenhower's position might have been very different. Let's be frank: Western historiography, too, has been far from objective."

countries had oriented themselves toward Western Europe. They knew as little about the Soviet Union as we did of them. The failure of the punitive action mounted against the young officers ruling Egypt altered the orientation of most countries in the region.

Father further developed the success already attained. At first Czechoslovakian, and then Soviet, weapons arrived in the Arab countries, and economic assistance was expanded as well. The armed forces of the Soviet state were mobilized for all to see when threats arose to our allies in the Near East.

It was with great reluctance that Father sanctioned the breach in Soviet-Israeli relations, which were only just beginning to develop. But there really was no choice. He preferred to befriend the many millions of the Arab world. (Although he opted for the Arabs, he looked back nostalgically on his meetings with Golda Meir in Moscow.) I must say that he kept thinking about possible ways to reconcile the two hostile peoples; he talked about this many times with Egypt's Gamal Abdel Nasser. But neither side was at all ready to accept his advice to live together in peace on God's earth.

"Someday peace will come to the Near East," he said philosophically. "Then everything will change."

Soviet-Arab friendship reached its peak in our agreement to build the Aswan High Dam and the Kheluan metallurgical combine. These steps showed the Arabs who their real friends were. True, not everyone in our country approved of Father's Near Eastern policy. There were charges of squandering our resources on the Arabs, and extending economic and military aid without justification.

The opposition that was forming in the Central Committee knew how to make use of this critical mood. When he heard about complaints that we were throwing away millions in aid to less developed neighbors, Father liked to cite the case of Afghanistan.

"We give the king tens of millions, we help him to build roads and factories and to develop their agriculture. What do we get in return? A peaceful border. You'd have to spend tens of billions to get that in other ways. So — helping them is directly beneficial to us."

Unfortunately, these obvious arguments were far from obvious to everyone else.

Toward the end of the fifties and beginning of the sixties, Nasser mounted an attempt to unite all the Arabs into one state — the United Arab Republic. Father was skeptical about the merger. He cautioned

Nasser against hasty integration with Syria, because he thought their different levels of political freedom and economic development would quickly lead to conflict.

Father prided himself on our achievements in the Middle East and took a large share of credit for them, and now he wanted to see it all himself.

However, there had long been one serious obstacle to a trip to the Near East. In the majority of Arab countries Communist parties were outlawed; they operated underground and many Communists were in prison. Our side repeatedly raised this issue during preparations for the official visit. We put forward a condition: absent a resolution of the problem of Communists languishing in torture chambers, there could be no visit.

Nasser finally gave assurances that the prisoners would be released. Father pretended to be satisfied, and the last obstacle was removed.

Father decided to take me along on the visit, but I couldn't go to the Crimea with him since I was held up by work. I flew down just before the delegation was due to depart. The whole group was there: Gromyko, Adzhubei, Secretary of the Supreme Soviet Presidium Mikhail P. Georgadze, First Deputy Defense Minister Andrei A. Grechko, *Pravda* chief editor Pavel A. Satyukov, and others.

The delegation boarded the small steamer *Armenia,* which was already at the Yalta pier. Khrushchev's departure on this state visit differed little from any other, except that there was a warm southern sun and blue sky. Brezhnev saw us off.

In the predeparture bustle, I was struck by an inexplicable change in Brezhnev's behavior. Ordinarily, he'd be smiling broadly with a ready joke, but this time he was gloomy. He even answered Father curtly, almost rudely, and he paid no attention to the others. Yet when I had seen him several weeks ago, he had been blooming; he'd given me a big hug and kisses accompanied by the odor of expensive cognac and eau de cologne.

I didn't know what to think. Finally, I came up with an explanation: Brezhnev was offended by Father's proposal that he give up his post as president and move over to the Central Committee. He couldn't refuse, and now he was upset. For many years I naively believed this. Only recently, as we've learned much of what happened in those years, has everything begun to look different.

Obviously, the decision to get rid of Khrushchev had already taken shape in May. True, they had yet to decide how and when to do it. Nonetheless, Leonid Ilyich couldn't hide his true attitude toward Father at Yalta. He tried to take himself in hand, to be his normal self, but he couldn't.

Of course, on that sunny day I wasn't thinking much about the reasons for Brezhnev's foul mood. But his unusual behavior lodged in my memory, to be dredged up half a year later as I desperately tried to make sense of the events of the intervening months.

The ship sailed away from the pier and the voyage began. Father and his aides busied themselves with official papers, while other members of the delegation basked in the sun of a May morning or otherwise did as they wished. Games of any kind were frowned on. The others were afraid of Father, who didn't like games and considered them a waste of time. He never had any time for soccer, dominoes, or cards.

With rare exceptions, his colleagues likewise displayed no interest in such diversions in his presence. They preferred to talk about construction, agriculture, or military matters, depending on the circumstances and who was taking part in the conversation. It was another matter when Father retired to his private quarters.

I couldn't help remembering a recent incident. Father had been observing maneuvers of the Black Sea fleet. Our design bureau was showing off its wares, and I was among those present.

Everyone observed the launchings attentively, and lively discussions followed the reports of civilian and military experts. When they announced a two-hour break, Father picked up his capacious brown folder, summoned an aide, and headed for his cabin. "I'm going to read some of the mail and work on the resolution concerning the navy," he said over his shoulder.

He left. Brezhnev, Podgorny, Grechko, Presidium member Andrei P. Kirilenko, and Dmitry F. Ustinov, first deputy chairman of the Council of Ministers, remained on deck, along with various ministers, admirals, and scientists. Leonid Ilyich's tense, attentive expression disappeared and his eyes brightened.

"What do you say, Kolya," he said to Podgorny, "shall we butt heads?"

Dominoes appeared. Brezhnev, Podgorny, Kirilenko, and Grechko devoted themselves to a favorite diversion, but by the time Father returned, the table had been cleared.

The *Armenia* plowed through the Black Sea on its way to Egypt.

Everyone except Father took it easy. Toward evening, as we approached The Straits, the ships of the Black Sea fleet that were accompanying us saluted and reversed course for home.

Father spent the whole next day preparing for the upcoming meetings. Delegation members, advisers, and aides gathered on deck around a flimsy little summer table. They discussed many issues, but the main topic was not so much the Egyptians' erratic payments for materials we supplied but their total lack of order and efficiency. Our ships were tied up for weeks in their ports waiting to unload. And that wasn't the worst of it. Our military people worried about the battle readiness of the Egyptian army, which remained at an extremely low level despite the modern weapons we had sent them.

Finally the voyage came to an end. President Nasser and other high-ranking leaders met us at the pier in Alexandria, and crowds of Egyptians lined up along the whole long route to Cairo to greet us with delight.

Father admired Nasser's energy and his sincere desire to transform his country. But he was uneasy about the incoherence of Arab socialism, the forcefully expressed aspiration to destroy neighboring Israel, and the plans to create one gigantic Arab state.

The negotiations were difficult, even stormy. Meetings dragged on; protocol fell by the wayside. To give but one example: Nasser asked for more weapons; Father agreed to satisfy his request on the condition that he pursue a policy of peaceful coexistence with his neighbors.[30] More than once they seemed to have reached agreement and needed only to dot the *i*'s and cross the *t*'s — but then had to start all over again.

The disagreements didn't affect the friendly atmosphere, and when the conference room doors opened, the leaders of both countries appeared with dazzling smiles on their faces. Finally, the disagreements had been overcome.

From Cairo our route took us to Aswan. Nasser and Khrushchev were to press the button generating an explosion that would release the Aswan High Dam's floodgates. The leaders of friendly Arab countries had assembled for the triumphal opening of the dam, and Father

---

30. *Editor's note:* I asked the author if he could identify any particular steps that Khrushchev demanded. His reply: "I was present at Khrushchev's negotiations with Nasser. But no minutes were taken. Khrushchev conducted them very carefully. He didn't try to pressure Nasser."

wanted to use the favorable occasion to discuss the political and economic development of the region. Finally, the long-awaited event took place. Nasser and Khrushchev simultaneously pressed the button, there was an explosion, and the Nile waters gushed through the trench. All the dignitaries present received commemorative gold medals. On the day of our arrival, the president had announced that Father would be decorated with the highest award of the United Arab Republic, the Necklace of the Nile. This medal was bestowed extremely rarely, and only for extraordinary achievements.

The events surrounding this award spawned many conflicting interpretations in our country. Since they were directly related to what followed, I will dwell on them in some detail.

In accordance with accepted international etiquette, and as a sign of the particularly friendly relations between the two countries, it was necessary for Father to respond in kind. The question was, which Soviet medal should be awarded to President Nasser, and to his vice president and commander in chief of the armed forces, Marshal Hakim Amer?

The problem had arisen before. But it was simpler where leaders of fraternal countries were concerned. Because they followed the socialist line, and stood on common ideological ground, it was easy to find equivalents for the Order of Karl Marx, or the Order of Georgy Dmitrov.

Everything was more complicated in the case of capitalist or developing countries. Neither we nor they wanted them to be honored with an award reflecting our Communist ideological principles. Several times in the past, Father had broached the idea of establishing a new medal for service in the cause of strengthening peace among peoples and states. But the matter never occupied his attention for long. He was against proliferating the number of medals, so that each time the problem of what to award to a particular statesman was resolved, he lost interest in establishing the new medal.

Once when Emperor Haile Selassie of Ethiopia paid us a state visit, he awarded a high imperial medal to Voroshilov, chairman of the USSR Supreme Soviet Presidium. That put us in a quandary. You don't bedeck a monarch with the Order of Lenin or the Order of the Red Banner. Finally they found a way out. Recalling that the august visitor had led his people's struggle against the Italian fascists, they awarded him the Order of Suvorov, First Class.

Now Father wanted to know which of our medals corresponded to the Necklace of the Nile. The Supreme Soviet Presidium provided the answer: "the highest." In our case, that was Hero of the Soviet Union, an award that didn't carry any ideological freight.

Without much further thought, Father decided to present it to President Nasser and, at Marshal Grechko's urging, to Marshal Amer, too. Andrei Gromyko, a meticulous man sensitive to the slightest nuances in international relations, approved the decision.

Off went a coded cable to Moscow. Soon we received a positive response in the form of a Supreme Soviet Presidium decree over Brezhnev's signature. They flew over the seals and sealing wax along with the medals themselves.

Father presented the awards to Nasser and Amer in a festive ceremony. Problem solved. International parity and ritual observed. Or so it seemed.

All sorts of unpleasant commentary unexpectedly began. In sum, it came down to this: "Khrushchev goes gallivanting around overseas distributing medals arbitrarily on the principle 'You give me one and I'll give you one back.' No one pays any attention to the Central Committee Presidium or the Presidium of the Supreme Soviet."

In addition, there were rumors about expensive gifts that Father allegedly received from the government of the UAR. I gave a lot of thought to whether I should touch on this episode in my memoirs. This is the kind of case where you can't prove anything, and any attempt to justify and refute is going to look more than suspicious even to friendly readers. It would be easier to keep silent. Nonetheless, I decided not to pass over these false rumors in silence. Today I am convinced that they were part of a carefully calibrated plan to discredit Father, to prepare public opinion, and to test the balance of forces. I believe these rumors were put about intentionally by the KGB as one of a number of actions undertaken in 1964. I don't think Father understood that until the Presidium met to oust him in October.

In essence, the first part of the indictment came down to two points: Khrushchev had publicly announced the awards without waiting for approval from the Presidium of the Central Committee, and anyway, President Nasser didn't deserve the honor. It's difficult to evaluate the first charge. Many years have passed, and one can't reconstruct what happened hour by hour. After a quarter of a century, eyewitnesses can support one version or another with equal ease, depending on their sympathies; memory is obliging. To me, the whole issue seems contrived. First of all, there were precedents, and second, the minister of foreign affairs and his protocol officer, on the scene in Egypt, confirmed the suitability of the award. All the rest was details, strictly bureaucratic procedures. As I have said, the requisite decree authorizing the award followed without any objections being raised.

In my view, debating whether the head of a friendly state does or does not merit an award corresponding to his rank is an exercise for Philistines. International relations are based not on personal likes and dislikes but on vital national interests. The question, therefore, is not whether Nasser and Amer merited the title Hero of the Soviet Union, but whether the Soviet Middle Eastern policy of supporting Arab countries was correct. Having answered that question, it's easy to decide whether it made sense to bestow an award on the then-recognized leader of the Arab world in response to the medal that the Soviet prime minister received from the country in which he was a guest.

But logic is logic, and rumors are spread around in accordance with other laws. There is no denying either the wit or the cunning of the author of the anti-Khrushchev rumors. A professional hand was at work here.

The question of valuable gifts is rather more complicated. On this issue everyone is an expert; everyone thinks, "It's the way of the world: everyone's on the take, and if someone isn't that's because he's already collected so much he's got no place to shove it. Those who don't play the game — well, they're not normal."

In the light of subsequent events, this subject is worth lingering over. Neither then nor previously did we ever keep the valuable gifts that Father received. It just wasn't done; Mama saw to that. All such gifts were turned over to the Central Committee, often without even opening them, or after a quick inspection by Father. He himself was totally indifferent to valuable things and adornments. In this, he differed drastically from Brezhnev and Kirichenko, who delighted in beautiful trinkets. Where these gifts ended up, I don't know. At one point, a museum was suggested, but remembering the museum that housed gifts to Stalin, Father categorically rejected the idea. Everything was logged in and stowed away somewhere. Among my mother's papers I found a list of things we turned in, although naturally it's far from complete.

I remember an occasion involving the same emperor of Ethiopia. As was his imperial wont, he placed a gold bracelet on my niece's wrist at a reception.[31]

---

31. *Editor's note:* The author refers here to Yulia Leonidovna Khrushcheva. Her father, Nikita Khrushchev's son by his first wife, was killed during the war. After Leonid

After the reception was over Father snapped: "Give that up."

Tears welled up in Yulia's eyes, but without a word she started to take it off.

Voroshilov, who was standing right there, made an impassioned plea to let her keep it. Finally, and reluctantly, Father agreed.

Mama's position on such matters was even stricter. It was impossible to change her mind. Of course, there were all sorts of knickknacks, souvenirs, lacquer cases, and drawings around our house, and especially models of miners' lamps. Remembering that my father had worked at a coal mine, people gave him these models at the slightest excuse. Even today, a dozen of them sit on the shelves in our home.

On the first floor of the Lenin Hills residence stood two large display cupboards, with mirrored rear walls, for souvenirs. They and their contents remained there after his dismissal.

The rumor that Khrushchev's hands were unclean was unquestionably useful to those who were preparing the change at the top. It was entrusted to professionals who carefully shored it up, cultivated it, and refurbished it with new "facts" as soon as old ones ceased to work. Moreover, they kept at it even after Father's retirement.

I recall a time shortly after his dismissal. The most painful events had already receded. Father was living in another dacha, at Petrovo-Dalneye, about twenty-five kilometers west of Moscow. A car from the Kremlin motor pool had been assigned for his private use. It was a ZIM, an old model, the only such automobile in the whole garage. Other Politburo members' cars were also kept there — ZILs, Chaikas, Volgas. People said that a few Mercedes, Cadillacs, and other imported prestige items later made an appearance, but I myself never saw them. By that time, they were no longer letting me in.

The drivers complained about the ZIM: "It's old, it breaks down,

---

Khrushchev's death and his widow's arrest (both mentioned later in this book in greater detail), Yulia was raised by Nikita Sergeyevich and Nina Petrovna Khrushcheva. Since she was about the same age as their own children, including Sergei Khrushchev, she has often been identified as Sergei's sister rather than his niece. He himself occasionally refers to her as his sister. Confusing matters further is the fact that she is not the only Yulia Khrushcheva. Nikita Khrushchev's daughter by his first wife, that is, Leonid Khrushchev's sister, was also named Yulia. Yulia Nikitichna Khrushcheva-Gontar lived most of her life in Kiev and died there in 1981. Yulia Leonidovna Khrushcheva graduated from the Moscow University journalism school and now works for the Vakhtangov Theater in Moscow as head of its literary section.

and there aren't any spare parts. You have to look all over the country for them."

Well, this ZIM had a private license plate. There were all sorts of plates in that garage, temporary and permanent, but all of them were government plates, and Khrushchev's was the only private plate. The ZIM wasn't much of a luxury; Khrushchev could have bought it himself. It's interesting how they worked such trifles into the rumors.[32]

To return to the trip to Egypt: After the Aswan ceremonies, Nasser invited Father to do some "fishing" in the Red Sea. The fishing party gathered on May 14, 1964, on the presidential yacht, *El Humkhuriya*, at Ras-Benas. Besides President Nasser, Vice President Amer, Father, and members of the Soviet delegation, also present were President Ben Bella of Algeria, President Abdul Salen Aref of Iraq, the president of Yemen, Marshal as-Salyal, and other "fishermen."

Far from the shore, and from journalists' and strangers' ears, they talked frankly about peace and war in the region, about the need to concert their policies, and about the future of the Arab world, including the plan to form an Arab federation. A great Arab state, which would unite all Arabs, was already beckoning on the horizon. I've mentioned that Father regarded this idea skeptically. Nor did he conceal his apprehensions now, but he promised the Soviet Union's full support to the new progressive regimes.

The fish had nothing to worry about. Lines were cast no more than a couple of times to show the guest from the north a little Red Sea exotica. We returned to Aswan on May 16, and the visit rolled along uneventfully in accordance with the well-prepared schedule.

Finally, on Monday, May 25, Father returned to Moscow by plane. On June 15, he set off on another trip abroad, this time to Scandinavia.

BY coincidence, June 15 was Central Committee secretary Yuri Andropov's fiftieth birthday. He was awarded an Order of Lenin. Again Khrushchev was absent. Those who were preparing his ouster had a free hand; all the threads of party and state administration were coming together.

---

32. *Editor's note:* The point of this story, or so I assume, is that the combination of the old car and the private plates made it appear that the vehicle was the personal property of Khrushchev.

The fourth session of the USSR Supreme Soviet, sixth convocation, was set for the middle of July. Two questions were on the agenda, and an innocent observer would never have expected either of them to produce the drama that was already being readied behind the scenes.

The first question dealt with measures to carry out the Communist party's pledge, contained in the program it had adopted in 1961, to raise the standard of living: a) pensions and assistance to collective farmers; b) wage increases for workers in education, public health, housing and municipal services, trade, food service, and other branches of the economy directly serving the population; c) the shift to a five-day work week. This set of issues was put forward by the CPSU Central Committee and the USSR Council of Ministers on Khrushchev's initiative, and he gave the report.

The second question concerned ratification of decrees of the Presidium of the Supreme Soviet. This item was a nomad that showed up on the agenda at every Supreme Soviet session; its very wording made it seem a minor matter. This time, however, deep passions erupted over it. Father had chosen this session as the moment finally to resolve an issue I've previously mentioned, namely, transferring Brezhnev from his chairmanship of the Supreme Soviet Presidium to the Central Committee.

I'll try to reconstruct the sequence of events as it appears to me today. Naturally, my suppositions may be mistaken, and I will be grateful to anyone who can correct my account.

I've already mentioned Kozlov's stroke of April 1963, and Father's initial hope that he would eventually be able to return to work as party second secretary. However, so much needed doing that in June 1963 Brezhnev was again named a Central Committee secretary (he had previously been one in 1952–1953 and from 1956 to 1960) in charge of several areas — including the defense industry — that had been formerly entrusted to Kozlov. Brezhnev kept his job as Presidium chairman; he was to provide temporary assistance on certain concrete matters, pending Kozlov's recovery. But apparently it was at this time that the Brezhnev-Podgorny bloc (or shall I call it the Podgorny-Brezhnev bloc?) began to take shape. For the moment they had no plans or even intentions; they were just a couple of old pals who were now Presidium members and Central Committee secretaries and thus had vast power.[33]

33. *Editor's note:* One might have expected that Brezhnev's transfer would have provoked Podgorny's envy. Indeed, Western Sovietologists have speculated that Khru-

Meanwhile, Shelepin was in charge of personnel matters in the Central Committee, and as far as I know, still had nothing to do with Brezhnev or Podgorny. In fact, he had no love for either of these Ukrainian "workers-become-leaders" of Khrushchev's.

It was late in 1963 that Khrushchev became convinced that Kozlov would never return to work and that he had to find a successor for him. After the long hesitation that I've previously described, his choice fell on Brezhnev. So it was that Leonid Ilyich concentrated enormous power in his hands while still serving as chairman of the Supreme Soviet Presidium. It was evidently in this period, in early 1964, that the idea of ousting Khrushchev was born. He was seventy years old, they about sixty.

The alliance with Shelepin probably took shape around this time. Each had his own aims, but they couldn't achieve them without each other. Then they began sounding out other members of the Presidium, for example, in the conversation Podgorny and Brezhnev had with Shelest in March 1964. However, in my opinion, Brezhnev was still wavering. He liked being chairman of the Presidium of the Supreme Soviet of the USSR, and the uncertainties involved in trying to overthrow Khrushchev frightened him.

In the spring, in April apparently, Father declared his firm intention to seek a new Supreme Soviet Presidium chairman. He had no ulterior motive; it was just that two such positions were too much for one man, so Brezhnev should devote all his energy to his Central Committee work. Father had no candidate in mind yet. The position was mainly a ceremonial one, and it was a pity to use a capable man who might be better employed elsewhere. On the other hand, the chairman was the head of state. The occupant of the post must be a man of unimpeachable authority, well known both in the party and among the people.

Finally, he chose Mikoyan. He had been well known since the revolution, and the next year he would turn seventy. His strength wasn't what it used to be, so this was just the right place for him.

When Father made his view known, Brezhnev cast off his last doubt. From now on, he would take an active role in preparing Khrushchev's ouster.

The question of replacing Brezhnev with Mikoyan was to be settled at the July session. Information now available suggests that Brezhnev

---

shchev created two rival heirs so as to buttress his own position. Sergei Khrushchev's reaction: "I think Sovietologists are mistaken."

feverishly sought to rid himself of Khrushchev right then and there, before the session could take place. The years that followed show how important and attractive the title of chairman of the Supreme Soviet Presidium was for Brezhnev. As soon as he accumulated sufficient power, he sacrificed his own chief ally, Podgorny (who replaced Mikoyan in 1965), and had himself named chairman again.

The actual "organizing body" was formed at the beginning of the summer. One of its main members was Shelepin's old friend KGB chairman Semichastny, without whom everything would have broken down. The 1957 coup against Khrushchev had failed in no small part because the then–KGB chairman, General Ivan Serov, had stayed loyal to the Central Committee and its first secretary. This time, Semichastny was in on everything from the start.

In June, on the eve of the Supreme Soviet session, Brezhnev bedeviled him with various suggestions for getting rid of Khrushchev. As attested to by Semichastny, they were far from gentlemanly.

Before Khrushchev's return from the United Arab Republic, Brezhnev was obsessed by the idea of poisoning him. This notion wasn't to Semichastny's liking. He took part willingly in the plot to oust Khrushchev. It promised a rapid rise to the very top. But he wasn't going to get involved in criminal activity. Semichastny resisted Brezhnev and tried to find all sorts of counterarguments. This is how Semichastny himself remembers it:

> Brezhnev put it to me this way: "Can we poison him?" I answered: "Only over my dead body. No way. I'd never have anything to do with such a thing. I'm not a plotter, and I'm not a murderer. . . . The situation in the country is different [from Stalin's time] and those methods just won't fly."
>
> Interviewer: How was he to be poisoned?
>
> Semichastny: Someone would have had to do it. I was supposed to give the order to my people . . . cooks. . . .
>
> Interviewer: But you would have put yourself in danger, wouldn't you?
>
> Semichastny: Yes, it was a crazy idea. So I came in and objected. . . . In the end Brezhnev agreed that poisoning Khrushchev wasn't feasible.[34]

---

34. This and other citations from Semichastny later in the chapter are from the unpublished transcript of his interview with V. A. Starkov.

It is said, but there is no documentary evidence to prove it, that several days later Brezhnev came up with a new project — to arrange for the plane carrying Khrushchev from Cairo to Moscow to crash.

"The plane has been waiting at a foreign airport in a foreign country," he is supposed to have argued. "So foreign intelligence services will get the blame."

"But the crew is devoted to him," was the reply. "The chief pilot, General Tsybin, began flying him as a colonel in 'forty-one, you know. He went through the entire war with him. What about all that? It's peacetime. And Khrushchev isn't the only one on the plane. Besides him, there's Gromyko, Grechko, the crew, and — don't forget — our men on the plane. This scheme is an absolute nonstarter." In short, Brezhnev's interlocutor refused point-blank.

Brezhnev didn't insist on his plan. The Soviet delegation returned safely to Moscow and no one knew about the conversation.[35]

Father was going to Leningrad early in June. A one-day meeting with Yugoslav president Tito had been scheduled there for June 9. Father set off a day earlier in order to prepare himself for the meeting; he also wanted to see how housing construction was going, and he particularly wanted to take a look at the newly restored fountains at Peter the Great's summer palace on the Gulf of Finland.

Rumor has it that Brezhnev came up with the idea of arranging an automobile accident. But obviously, no one would support him on this scheme, either.

Nikita Sergeyevich returned from his mid-month trip to Scandinavia just a week before the session opened. Leonid Ilyich was running out of time. Under these circumstances, one last, desperate proposal made its appearance — to arrest Khrushchev upon his arrival from Sweden, and detain him at the hunting lodge in Zavidovo, not far from Kalinin. Brezhnev didn't dare bring his formidable prisoner to Moscow.

However, neither Semichastny nor anyone else would agree to the plan. They preferred a more reliable and less adventurous way of doing things. Unfortunately, Semichastny's testimony on this point is laconic:

35. *Editor's note:* Is this report about a potential conspiracy to assassinate Khrushchev plausible? Is Semichastny, who now has good reason to polish his own image by tarnishing Brezhnev's, a reliable source? Sergei Khrushchev comments: "The evidence is only now being gathered. One may believe Semichastny or choose not to do so. In any event, all I am doing is citing his interview. I, too, am not sure how serious Brezhnev was in raising the issue, but I think he was psychologically capable of doing so. Shelest has orally confirmed the fact that such conversations took place."

"It dragged on a long time. . . . We considered an option, you know, when he came back from Sweden . . . to stop his train somewhere near Zavidovo, arrest him, and bring him down here. Yes, there was such an option."

It was at this time that they began active talks with members of the Presidium, province party secretaries, ministers, and the military. Some of them were approached openly, others were sounded out cautiously. Still others were left in ignorance for the time being, because they were considered too principled or too close to Father, or just to be safe. If any information were to leak out, the whole thing would go down the drain. No date for a final decision was set. But they all agreed on one thing — that the deed had to be done by the end of the year.

One other circumstance caused a lot of anxiety. Khrushchev had to be discredited, deprived of the last remnants of his popularity among the people. In regions whose leaders had already joined the conspiracy, products including household staples were disappearing from store shelves, while huge lines of people waited for hours to buy everything, including bread.[36] All it took to refill the shelves was the fall of "the source of all our troubles."

It was in this connection that the agenda for the upcoming session, which was to open on Monday, July 13, was cause for apprehension.

Father had long been developing a plan for providing collective farmers with pensions. Until this time, collective farmers were treated as a lesser breed. In addition to being ineligible for pensions, they were denied many other goods and social services. Providing them with pensions constituted yet another step away from the Stalinist policy of developing industry at the expense of the countryside. This was not only an economic but a huge political step forward. It would give them a status equal to that of workers; they would no longer be viewed as people of a different, "unsocialist" kind.

At the same time, Father wanted to resolve another burning issue by raising the miserable salaries paid to teachers, physicians, and others employed in providing services to the public. Both the pensions and the raises were very small, especially by today's standards. But even so, it was hard to find the money to pay for them. Father had spent a lot of

36. *Editor's note:* The parallel between this situation and that which developed under Gorbachev is striking. But although rumors of similar sabotage accompany Gorbachev-era shortages, relatively few people think that is the main reason for economic disarray. Were the 1964 shortages in fact deliberately induced? Sergei Khrushchev: "Yes, indeed. In that sense, 1964 and 1989 are very different."

time since the beginning of the year talking to specialists and agency heads. As a result, some money had been scraped together, and he was preparing a detailed presentation, laying out all the figures and arguments, for the upcoming session.

It was too late to reverse or obstruct the decision-making process. The issue had been under consideration too long. A suitable pretext could not be found. Brezhnev and his comrades were getting nervous. Their reasoning was simple: "Khrushchev's plan will once again link his name with measures meant to improve the lot of many people. His reputation was damaged by the recent food price rises, but this will increase his popularity. It's hard to say how people will react to his removal from power after this."

These fears were not very well grounded, but they did exist. Nonetheless, nothing could be changed. The issue remained on the agenda. It was a different story with Father's proposal to reduce the work week from six days to five without decreasing the total number of working hours. This issue too had been carefully worked through since the start of the year. At first, there were no serious objections; after all, virtually the whole world worked a five-day week.

But as early as June, seemingly insurmountable difficulties began to crop up. Opponents tried to prove to Father that switching to a five-day week would disrupt many branches of the economy. The supposedly clinching argument was that factories with a round-the-clock production process, such as those in the metallurgical, chemical, and petrochemical industries, would encounter especially serious problems. To tell the truth, I still don't understand why it's fine to interrupt the noninterruptible for one day but not for two.

Although the work week was to be cut, the work day would increase from seven to eight hours. Nonetheless, fears were expressed that the total volume of production would fall. Still another argument was that ways of switching high schools and colleges to a five-day week hadn't yet been worked out.

Father was systematically pressured from all sides — by agencies and departments, by the Council of Ministers apparat and the Central Committee Secretariat. He resisted, and put forward counterarguments; they couldn't get him to waver. The most zealous opponent of the new work week was the Central Committee secretary in charge of industry, Aleksandr Petrovich Rudakov.

Upon returning from Scandinavia, Father had sat down to put the finishing touches on his upcoming report. This was not a matter he entrusted to his aides. During the first phase of preparing a speech, Father would usually dictate a rough, often haphazard draft to stenographers. Next his aides would iron out the deciphered text. Depending on the subject, they would solicit the advice of specialists on international relations, or on industrial, military, or agricultural matters.

Next, the text would go back to Father and the editing would begin. He would reshape it, dictating new sections and discarding old ones, until it expressed his ideas precisely. That was the end of his active participation in the process. It was now up to the aides and experts to select appropriate examples and quotations before presenting the final version to Father. He then read it closely and either approved it or made last-minute changes. At that point, the text was ready.

True, there was another aspect to his speechmaking. He frequently didn't feel like sticking to "those little scraps of paper," and sometimes he left the written text behind altogether. Father liked to repeat Peter the Great's commandment against reading speeches as written "lest one's stupidity be visible." As a result, his speeches were vivid and full of graphic images, as well as sensitive to the situation and the reaction of his audience.

In all fairness, I must admit that he sometimes was carried away in the heat of a speech. Thoughts that hadn't quite ripened had a way of being expressed. When that happened, Father had to eliminate the blemishes in the course of preparing the text for publication.

Of course, so-called protocol speeches were another matter entirely: those made while greeting and seeing off foreign delegations, and at formal receptions and other such ceremonies. As is the case everywhere else in the world, these were prepared by the appropriate agencies and presented to Father in final form for his approval.

That's what he was doing — polishing his report to the upcoming Supreme Soviet session — when Rudakov decided to undertake a flanking maneuver. He managed to talk Adzhubei into trying to influence Father. I don't know which arguments convinced Aleksei Ivanovich, but he agreed.[37]

That summer Father often stayed overnight at the Gorki-2 dacha, which was in a pine forest on the bank of the Moscow River. Also known as the "ninth dacha" (this is the way it was listed in the files of

37. As the son-in-law of Khrushchev, chief editor of *Izvestia,* and an adviser to Nikita Sergeyevich, Adzhubei had a great deal of influence in official circles between 1962 and 1964.

the KGB, which managed it), the house was reserved for the chairman of the Council of Ministers. Molotov had been the previous occupant, having kept it even when Stalin became premier, because the latter had no need for it. It had originally been built for Aleksei Ivanovich Rykov, a fact that people mentioned in a muffled half whisper.[38]

Father liked the spacious grounds, which included a long path along the fence without the noticeable ups and downs that now caused him some difficulty. Every evening upon returning from work, he would circle the grounds on this path. He would walk as far as the meadow that separated the main grounds from the river.

The dacha at Usovo also looked out on the Moscow River. But between the fence and the river there was an open area where crowds of Muscovites would come on sunny days to swim and bask in the sun. At Molotov's dacha, the way to the meadow was fenced off on both sides with barbed wire. The fencing was not in the best of shape though; here and there you could see wide yawning holes in it.

Security men regularly patrolled the perimeter of the dacha along this strip. The torn barbed wire, and the seemingly secluded space beyond it, attracted couples wandering in the woods. Just at the most interesting moment, a man in a uniform would come tearing out of the bushes demanding their internal passports. Usually the scene would end peacefully, with the "perpetrators" disappointed, but with a great story for the guard to tell back at the guardhouse.

It was here in the bushes by the very edge of the river that security men once stumbled on an unusual pair. The young man refused for a long time to produce any type of ID, but when he realized there was no alternative, identified himself as a British military attaché.

Both sides went into shock. The frightened guards detained the couple, even after they explained quite reasonably that they had set out by boat from the beach at Nikolina Gora, where foreign diplomats often went swimming in the summer. Not knowing what to do next, the chief duty officer quickly reported to Father that the two detainees might have intended to "reconnoiter the approaches to the object."

Father smiled. "How about your spy's fellow traveler? Is she good-looking?"

"That's affirmative," the officer snapped.

---

38. Aleksei Ivanovich Rykov was Lenin's immediate successor as chairman of the Council of People's Commissars. He was replaced by Vyacheslav Molotov. Rykov was arrested and executed during the Stalinist terror in the late thirties.

"Let them swim where they want. Let people have a good time. I think your spy is more interested in her than in me." Father brushed it off, thus averting an international incident.

When we first moved there, the meadow had been covered with thick grass. On the right was a little swamp. In the summer a corncrake lived there. Having first heard its song when he was a child, Father would stop and listen, and his face would break into a smile. The bird was our local attraction.

In the meadow at the edge of the forest stood a green gazebo outfitted with a wicker table and armchairs. On summer Sundays Father would sit there reading his documents or the newspapers.

There, too, our frequent visitors would gather. I remember Fidel Castro's staying with us at the dacha on one of his trips to the USSR. He took snapshots of our whole family.

Father decided to construct his own experimental minifarm on the same meadow. Along the path were transplanted snowball berry bushes. Father liked them very much, with their white flowers in the spring and clusters of red berries. Rows of vegetables were planted on both sides of the path: carrots, cucumbers, tomatoes, squash, lettuce — everything that ought to be growing in a good garden.

There were separate sections for crops that particularly interested Father. In the beginning, as I recall, there were millet and Chinese millet. Father remembered the latter from the Donbas, and decided to verify for himself the rumors that this Chinese visitor produced very high yields. We had been planting Chinese millet for several years. Porridge made from it became a staple at our table. But the predictions as to its yield didn't prove out. Our climate turned out to be too severe for it.

Corn was next. Rows of various depths were dug, seeds were planted at various intervals, and different methods of cultivation were employed. Father kept careful track of the plants' growth. He was not just amusing himself. He wanted to see for himself and feel the results with his own hands.

He didn't trust reports very much, and he had developed the habit back in the Ukraine of inspecting the fields so as to see with his own eyes first the sowing and then the harvest. But whenever he visited a province capital, the local bosses tried to start things off with a luncheon; the idea was that after a good meal he would be warmer and more mellow. In those days, he would travel around the Ukraine in an open car. It was easier to see what was going on in the fields, and he could stop wherever he liked to talk to the peasants and find out what they were thinking. What they had to say often turned out to be more valuable than official reports. (By the way, he never used the armored ZIS-110 to which he was entitled as a member of the Politburo. It was gathering dust in the Central Committee garage.)

Having experienced enough warm receptions arranged by local officials, Father thought of a countermove. He bought a huge cast-iron skillet. To keep it from getting dirty in the trunk of the car, he ordered a tin container for it. Now there was no reason to hurry on to the province center. Instead, he would stop at some cozy spot by the side of the road. It didn't take long to make a fire, get out the soon-to-be-legendary skillet, and fry up some eggs with bacon and tomatoes — enough for everyone, including the aides and the driver.

Father loved to act out his meetings with province party secretaries:

"Welcome, Nikita Sergeyevich. Won't you please join us for lunch?"

Father would smile slyly. "Thank you, but we've just had lunch. Why don't we get right down to business. Let's drive out to the fields, and on the way you can fill me in."

Of course, the trick soon became common knowledge. But Father wasn't going to keep it a secret anyway. He had achieved his main goal: from then on, when he arrived at the province party committee, they worked first and dined late in the evening.

BUT to return to the events of July 1964, to an evening during the last week before the Supreme Soviet session. Father, Adzhubei, and I were strolling in the meadow. Someone else was with us, but I don't recall who.

Adzhubei argued with all his customary eloquence and conviction that the transition to a five-day work week was premature; it had not been sufficiently prepared and might lead to some serious negative consequences.

Father listened without saying anything. I remember the conversation well, because I was young and wanted those two days off something awful. Gradually I noticed that Father was beginning to waver. Aleksei Ivanovich had some effective arguments. I decided to say something and timidly began to object. What came out sounded clumsy, and Father just waved me away.

"Don't interfere!"

In the end, he gave in. Adzhubei beamed. The third part of the first item on the agenda was removed. The reform establishing a five-day work week would be credited to the post-Khrushchev era.

The Supreme Soviet session went off without incident. On July 15, after adoption of the law "On Pensions and Assistance to Collective Farms," Father took the floor.

"Comrade deputies.

"You all know that Comrade Leonid Ilyich Brezhnev was elected a secretary of the Central Committee in June 1963. The Central Committee now deems it expedient for Comrade Brezhnev to concentrate his energy on his duties at the Central Committee. In this connection, the Central Committee moves that he be relieved of his responsibilities as chairman of the Presidium of the USSR Supreme Soviet.

"The Central Committee recommends that this session consider Comrade Anastas Ivanovich Mikoyan for the post of Supreme Soviet Presidium chairman. It is assumed that he would be relieved of his duties as first deputy chairman of the USSR Council of Ministers. I think there is no need to provide a reference for Comrade Mikoyan. You all know what a great contribution Anastas Ivanovich has made and is continuing to make to the political life of our party and the Soviet state. His record as a devoted Leninist and an active fighter for the cause of communism speaks for itself. Our people have known him well for decades, and his record is known abroad as well.

"The Central Committee is confident that Comrade Mikoyan is worthy of being entrusted with such an important and responsible post as chairman of the Supreme Soviet Presidium."

That was it. The deputies voted quickly and unanimously for Mikoyan and adopted the necessary resolution. The long-ripening decision was at last made official.

When Mikoyan took office, he didn't at all like the atmosphere he found in the Supreme Soviet Presidium. Having decided to set things right, he began with personnel. A certain K. U. Chernenko, then serving as head of administration, was given his walking papers.

"We don't need people like that in the party," said Mikoyan with uncharacteristic sharpness. But he didn't go into detail, and at the time no one was particularly interested in Chernenko. Brezhnev was forced to find a position for Chernenko in the Central Committee, which wasn't too hard to do.

After the session was over and he had finally assumed his new position, Brezhnev must have been torn by conflicting feelings. On the one hand, he must have been reassured: having to abandon his Presidium

chairmanship was extremely unpleasant, but the number of his supporters was growing, and the hour of triumph seemed to be near. However, he couldn't help worrying. What would happen if Khrushchev
suddenly became suspicious?

But preparations for the transfer of power were now entering the
decisive stage. They required meetings, conversations, the inclusion of
new people. There was no going back.

With the session over, the traditional July–August vacations began.
Life slowed down. Brezhnev set off for the Crimea.

As for Father, he had to forget about his summer vacation. At the
end of July, fraternal Poland would be celebrating the twentieth anniversary of its founding as a people's state. Gomulka had telephoned
several times asking Father to attend, saying he attached special significance to Khrushchev's visit. Father couldn't turn down his old friend
Wladislaw.

After that, he would have to undertake an eastern inspection tour,
to find out for himself how preparations for the harvest were proceeding
in the virgin lands.[39]

Once again Father was leaving Moscow. Since Brezhnev was on
vacation, Central Committee secretary Podgorny was left holding the
fort. Everything was turning out extremely favorably for them.

It was important to take advantage of the summer months. Another
such opportunity would be unlikely. Province party secretaries and soviet chairmen would be taking their vacations at spas in the Crimea and
the Caucasus. They could be sounded out there without attracting too
much attention. That would be very convenient. Visiting them in their
home provinces or republics might attract someone's attention.

In any case, Brezhnev's new position as second secretary gave him
plenty of opportunities, since he was in charge of working with pro-
vincial party leaders. But it was one thing to talk in an office, and quite
another over a glass of fine cognac down south. If something went
wrong, one could easily turn it into a joke, or hide behind a barrage of
anecdotes. What didn't people jabber about while on vacation?

39. *Editor's note:* The virgin lands are the vast areas of steppe in northern Kazakhstan, western Siberia, and southeastern European Russia that Khrushchev took the
lead in opening up for cultivation in the mid-fifties. At a time when agriculture in European Russia required extensive long-term investment to produce higher yields, he tried
for a "quick fix" by cultivating the virgin lands. The gamble paid off handsomely in the
late fifties, but by the early sixties harvests were disappointing and the land subject to
serious erosion.

Brezhnev managed to talk to a lot of people in the Crimea. The general situation looked good; it seemed everyone was unhappy with Khrushchev. Party secretaries were irritated by the decision to split province organizations into industrial and agricultural branches, and by the new limits on terms in office. The military didn't like the continuing cuts in the armed forces. The introduction of regional economic councils had forced many economic planners to leave Moscow and disperse themselves among faraway and not-so-faraway regions. A solid majority was being built. Khrushchev would apparently have no support either in the Presidium or at a plenum.

All one had to do now was tie up a few loose ends and it would be time to act.

Brezhnev must have felt he already had won. Two or three years ago, could he have imagined anything like this? Out of impatience, he sometimes lost his self-control, behaving as if the deed had already been done. Then suddenly he would be overcome by doubt. At these moments, he would zealously demonstrate his loyalty, his selfless devotion to Khrushchev — either so as to obtain mercy if the whole thing failed, or to dull Father's vigilance. Glorification of Khrushchev in speeches by Brezhnev, Podgorny, and others was at its most brazen during this period.

It was at this time that another conversation between Brezhnev and Ukrainian party leader Shelest took place. Obviously, Leonid Ilyich wanted to confide in Shelest, but he took fright and became cautious and distant.

Shelest remembers it this way:[40]

> I was vacationing in the Crimea when he unexpectedly came by. It was July 1964.
>
> He didn't try to persuade me. He just sobbed, actually burst into tears. The man was an actor, a great actor. It sometimes got to the point, when he'd downed a few drinks, that he'd climb up on a chair and declaim something or other. Not Mayakovsky, of course, or Esenin, but some pun he'd thought up.
>
> . . . So he comes over.

---

40. *Editor's note:* I asked Sergei Khrushchev why the reader should credit Shelest's recollection when it is so clearly in his current interest to depict himself as resistant to Brezhnev's plans. Sergei Khrushchev's answer: "We have no other sources. Nor do I have any reason to think he is lying. Furthermore, my book is a memoir. It is not a piece of scholarly research based on extensive investigation of all possible documents."

"How are things?" he says. "How's it going?"

"How are things?" I answer. "The work is hard."

"Are you, uh, getting the support you need?"

"If not, I wouldn't be able to do a thing. I'd have to pack up and beat it. Demyan Sergeyevich Korotchenko helps a lot.[41] He's an experienced guy. So do the province secretaries."

"How are you getting along with Khrushchev?"

"He's like an older brother to me. But why ask a question like that anyway? You're closer to him than I am. You work right there in Moscow."

"He swears at us, says we don't do a damn thing." Brezhnev sounded hurt, and there were tears in his eyes.

"What if he's right?"

"No, he's impossible to work with."

"So why did you talk that way on his seventieth birthday: 'Our comrade, our beloved, our *vozhd*, leader, Leninist,' and all the rest? Why didn't you get up and say: 'Nikita, you're impossible to work with!'?"

"We just don't know what to do with him."

I decided to keep my distance.

"Well, you people up there, you straighten it out yourselves. We toil among the lower classes. Whatever orders we get, we carry out. . . . But by the way, what do you want to do?"

I permitted myself that last bit of guarded curiosity.

"We're thinking of calling a plenum and criticizing him a little."

"So what's the problem? Count me in favor."

That's how the conversation, or rather, the very gentle sounding out of Shelest, ended. Brezhnev wound up the chat and left. Something in Shelest's manner had put him on guard.

Father soon left for Poland. This time Brezhnev, who was still vacationing in the Crimea, was in charge.

As I've already indicated, when Father vacationed in the Crimea or the Caucasus, he often arranged for our leadership to meet with leaders of other socialist countries and Communist parties who were also

---

41. *Editor's note:* Korotchenko was chairman of the Presidium of the Ukrainian Supreme Soviet. When Khrushchev arrived from Moscow to become Stalin's viceroy in the Ukraine in 1938, Korotchenko was one of his top assistants.

vacationing there. Our own top scientists, engineers, and members of the government also took holidays nearby. All these gatherings were relaxed and informal. They all had their families with them; after all, they were on vacation. Usually, the occasions took place in the former palace of Alexander III in the mountains above Yalta.

Before the war, this and other palaces had been used as spas. Toward the end of the war, the Livadia and Alupka palaces were quickly fixed up in preparation for the Yalta conference of the heads of state of the Grand Alliance. After the delegations left, the palaces remained in the hands of the NKVD (the People's Commissariat of Internal Affairs, predecessor to the KGB). No one remembered the old slogan: "The palaces must belong to the people."

The Livadia palace became Stalin's dacha, although he spent only one vacation in it. The Vorontsov palace in Alupka was Molotov's. None of the other leaders had a personal palace.

After Stalin's death, Father remembered the earlier decree that transferred the palaces of the tsar and nobility for use by the people. He saw to it that the government adopted a resolution turning them into trade union resorts. But the palaces turned out to be ill suited for crowds of vacationers, so most of them were soon made into museums. Only Alexander's palace remained a state dacha. It was turned into a residence for honored foreign guests. Most of the time it stood empty.

Father would drive over sometimes when he was taking his holiday in the Crimea. He would stroll along the deserted avenues in the park. It was apparently during these walks that he came up with the idea of the social gatherings I've just mentioned. Usually the guests would arrive in the morning; everyone would stroll about, play *gorodki* [similar to skittles — ed.] or volleyball, or just sit around on benches chatting. The gathering would end with dinner in the open air.

When Father wasn't there, these gatherings didn't take place. In the beginning, that was because they were his idea. Later, apparently, none of the other leaders dared to take his place as host. That summer was the first time Brezhnev took the initiative. I should add that despite the general informality of these occasions, etiquette was strictly maintained. Guests brought their families, but families vacationing alone — that is, wives and children without the head of the household — were never invited.

That summer my older half sister, Yulia Nikitichna, was vacationing in one of the Yalta spas. She was stunned to be invited to the gathering arranged by Brezhnev. Apparently, two opposite emotions played a role in this unusual gesture. On the one hand, Leonid Ilyich very much wanted to prove, first of all to himself, that he was already boss, if only for five minutes. On the other hand, still fearing Khrushchev, he demonstrated his true devotion by inviting Yulia Nikitichna: like a faithful dog seeking its master's approval, he was ingratiatingly wagging his tail. May the reader forgive this anatomical imprecision!

Yulia Nikitichna was struck by Brezhnev's behavior at the reception. Her reaction is all the more interesting since she recounted it before rather than after October 1964. According to her, Leonid Ilyich was riding high. He behaved liked an omnipotent host. He was unusually, even aggressively, affable with everyone. She had never seen him like this. Toward the end of the evening he climbed up on a chair and began to declaim his own verses. He was obviously very pleased with himself.

No one had seen anything like this before. Many people were puzzled by the drastic change in Brezhnev's behavior, but no one could figure out the real reason. They gossiped about it a bit and then wrote it off to excessive tippling.

A little later, in August, a similar incident involved me. Father wasn't in Moscow; he had left for the virgin lands, where the harvest was about to begin.

I had gone on business to the Cosmonaut Training Center, where I received a cordial reception. We walked around, looked at the simulators, and chatted with the cosmonauts. Our host was General Nikolai P. Kamanin, the director of the center. Toward the end of the visit, we dropped by one of the laboratories to see a simulator for the first manned spacecraft, the *Vostok*. Suddenly, one of Kamanin's aides ran panting into the room.

"Comrade General! Comrade Khrushchev is asked to phone Comrade Brezhnev. They just called from the Central Committee."

I was amazed; Leonid Ilyich had never phoned me before. The distance between us on the bureaucratic ladder was too great. Accompanied by the adjutant, I walked quickly into the director's office and dialed Brezhnev's number at the Central Committee.

He picked up the phone himself.

"Listen," he said, "Nikita Sergeyevich is away, but tomorrow is the start of the duck hunting season. We're all driving out to Zavidovo, and I wanted to invite you. Will you come?"

"Of course. Thank you, Leonid Ilyich. I'll be there Saturday evening," I answered, still stunned.

I never expected a member of the Central Committee Presidium to invite me to go duck hunting! Father had often taken me along as a "complementary supplement." Dmitry Stepanovich Polyansky sometimes took his son with him. But it was one thing to go along with Father, and another to be invited on my own as an equal. I won't deny that I was greatly flattered.

When I returned to the laboratory, Kamanin looked at me with love in his eyes.

"I guess Leonid Ilyich often calls you, right?" he asked.

I didn't know how to reply, so I muttered: "Yes . . . No . . . Not very often."

At the time, I didn't think much about the call. I just took it as a straightforward sign of sympathy and kindness.

When I got back to Moscow, Father said, "So you did a little hunting, eh? How did it go? Brezhnev told me on the phone that he hadn't forgotten you, and had invited you to Zavidovo."

However, the ducks were far from the main game that Brezhnev, Podgorny, Polyansky, and the others were hunting at Zavidovo. In comfortable little cottages, far from prying eyes and ears, they worked on their colleagues, ultimately convincing those to whom, after long hesitation, they now entrusted their secret.

Gennady Ivanovich Voronov, then a Presidium member and chairman of the Russian Republic Council of Ministers, describes what happened this way:

> Everything had been under preparation for about a year. The threads led to Zavidovo, where Brezhnev usually went hunting. Brezhnev himself would put down a plus (next to the names of those who were ready to support him in the fight against Khrushchev) or minus. Each man would be worked on individually.
>
> Interviewer: Including you?
> Voronov: Yes, all night long![42]

The threads of the conspiracy led not only to Zavidovo but to the Crimea, the Caucasus, and other regions of our country.

Naturally, I did not understand that fate had prepared a role for me, not as a participant, but as an active observer of the approaching events.

42. R. Lynev's interview with Voronov was published in *Izvestia*, November 17, 1988, p. 3.

OCTOBER[1]

S UMMER had departed. It was cooler, and the leaves on the trees had turned yellow. Worries about the 1964 harvest were over, as were the inspection trips to agricultural regions. Foreign trips planned for 1964 were finished, too.

Father planned to rest some that fall, to gather his thoughts and begin planning for the future. The next Central Committee plenum, scheduled for November–December, would be making some important decisions. The agricultural situation was central. Output had grown over the previous decade, but productivity was far from the level to which Father aspired.

No less important was the personnel problem. The Central Committee Presidium was aging — most members were nearly sixty, and Father himself had just celebrated his seventieth birthday. More and more frequently, he returned to the questions: Who will take our place? Into whose hands will we transfer management of the country and party? When Stalin died, quarrels and disagreements broke out, ending in an open fight. That must not happen again, Father insisted. The only way to avoid it was to establish a formal and open process of leadership succession. If each Presidium member knew that he could have, say,

---

1. In comparison with the version published in *Ogonyok* (October 1–8, 8–15, 15–22, and 22–29, 1988), this chapter contains corrections as well as important new facts that became available after *Ogonyok* appeared.

two terms of four years each, then he would be more likely to get down to business, act decisively, and spend less time looking over his shoulder. Moreover, the upcoming generation in the Central Committee and the province committees would see a greater chance of advancement.

The Twenty-second Congress (1961) had already decided to regularize the leadership succession process, but this was just a first step. These principles would have to be enshrined in the constitution. The decision to prepare a new constitution had been taken long ago, and a commission to do so had been created, but Father hadn't had the time to come to grips with it. He was constantly distracted by more pressing matters requiring immediate decisions.

Vacation was the best time to work on the new constitution. At Cape Pitsunda there would be fewer "fires" to put out. Of course, you couldn't turn off the phone, and the papers sent down would take up time, but that couldn't be compared with the hurly-burly of Moscow. Moreover, one could think better under the pine trees.

I had heard about Father's plans. At the plenum, they were going to expand the membership of the Presidium. In recent years, a group of younger men had developed — Shelepin, Andropov, Ilyichev, Polyakov, Satyukov, Adzhubei, and Mikhail A. Kharlamov, head of the Foreign Ministry press department and later chairman of the State Committee for Radio and Television. Very enterprising comrades. They responded vigorously to new suggestions, caught on to ideas quickly, developed and immediately turned out proposals. Working with them was more interesting, more lively. In essence, they played as great a role in deciding many party and government matters as did Presidium members, and it would be useful to codify that reality by revising the composition of the Presidium. What's more, they were young people, and would one day take over. But all this must be given a great deal of thought.

Unfortunately, he couldn't leave until October. An inspection of missile technology had been delayed since the spring, and Marshal Rodion Malinovsky, the defense minister, was demanding that a decision be made about the new generation of intercontinental missiles. An inspection of the new types of strategic weaponry at one of the test sites had been finally set for September after numerous postponements.

Together with Father, members of the government responsible for defense industry would be going: Brezhnev, Kirilenko, Ustinov. Ministers, military district commanders, and rocket designers would be awaiting them at the test site.

All the arrangements had been made by September, and the final details were being settled — who would accompany the top brass. Since the number of those wanting to go greatly exceeded the available places, the lists were scrutinized critically at the Central Committee, with the Defense Industry Department chief, Ivan Dmitrievich Serbin, mercilessly crossing out superfluous names.

I very much wanted to be among the lucky ones; after all, I had attended all the previous inspections on one of the teams demonstrating new technology. Work on a new ICBM had just been completed. Now its fate would be decided. Proponents and opponents would get a hearing, and then the final decision would be made on whether to start production.[2]

To my delight, I remained on the list. Next came the predeparture preparations. But fate decreed otherwise. Several days before departure, my leg began to ache. At first I paid no attention. But a couple of days later, I could hardly walk and was forced to see a doctor.

"A business trip is quite out of the question," he said emphatically. "We'll have to put you in the hospital." After some wrangling, the idea of hospitalization was dropped, and they decided to treat me at home. By now I had already realized that there was no point in going to the test site in my condition.

My colleagues flew off after wishing me a quick recovery, and a couple of days later Father followed them. I lay in bed reading books and sadly looking out the window. It was a clear, sunny autumn. The phone rang occasionally, and somehow I managed to hobble over to it. Several days passed, and there was no news from the test site; nor could there be. I began to feel better and decided to go back to work in a few days.

In our house on Lenin Hills, my family and I occupied two rooms with a bath on the first floor; they constituted a separate apartment with a door opening onto the corridor. Opposite was the dining room.

The whole extended family rarely sat down at the table together. We were all busy with our own affairs and ate when it was convenient. Only in the evening, when Father returned from work, did we all gather for tea and to swap news. After that, Father would take his papers, move to a place from which dishes had been cleared, and begin to read. Teatime was over, the evening work time had begun. Everyone dispersed to his or her room quietly, so as not to disturb him, or settled

2. The missile whose fate was being decided was a follow-on version of the R-16. The fact that it was designed for above-ground launches was its main shortcoming.

down silently on the couch or in an armchair with newspapers or books.

I had my own regular, city telephone, as well as a local phone connected to the duty officer at the guardhouse. The telephones Father used were on a special table in the corner of the living room near the dining room. They consisted of special government phones, both city and intercity, and also a regular city line, plus a direct line to the guard duty room. Father rarely used them, and only for urgent business, believing that when the working day was over you should let people rest. He didn't approve when established working hours were not observed and people were forced to stay up late. It reminded him of the nocturnal vigils of Stalin's time.

"The fact that you stay late is not a sign of your zeal, but of your inability to organize properly," he would often say. "The working day ends at seven o'clock. After seven, go to the theater, enjoy yourself, and don't wear out your pants in the office. Otherwise, you won't be able to function properly the next day."

Knowing this was his view, people very rarely called him at home, and only in emergencies. Each time the government phone rang in our house was an event, and everyone present strained their ears, trying to make out from the scraps of conversation what had happened.

So when the *vertushka* [special phone linking top Kremlin leaders — ed.] rang one evening while I was ill, I was amazed. Everyone knew Father was not in Moscow. The voice at the other end was unfamiliar.

"May I speak to Nikita Sergeyevich?"

"He's not in Moscow," I replied, at a loss as to who it could be. Anyone who had access to this phone knew perfectly well where Father was.

"To whom am I speaking?" I was asked. I could hear the disappointment in the voice on the other end.

"This is his son."

"How do you do, Sergei Nikitich," the voice said hurriedly. "This is Vasily Ivanovich Galyukov, former chief of security for Nikolai Grigorievich Ignatov [former member of the Central Committee Presidium, then chairman of the Russian Republic Supreme Soviet]. I've been trying to get through to Nikita Sergeyevich since the summer; I have some very important information for him. But I haven't been successful. Finally I got to a *vertushka* and decided to call him at home, but again it hasn't worked out."

I was even more surprised. What could Ignatov's former chief of security have to say to Khrushchev? What did they have in common? The situation was highly unusual.

"Please hear me out," said Galyukov quickly, obviously worried, and quite rightly, that I would hang up on him. "I've found out that there is a plot against Nikita Sergeyevich! I wanted to tell him about it in person. There are many people involved."

It was getting worse and worse, I thought. The man must be mad. What kind of plot could there be nowadays? It was nonsense.

"Vasily Ivanovich," I said. "You'd better call Semichastny at the KGB. Especially since you work there. This is a matter for them to handle. They'll check it out and inform Nikita Sergeyevich if necessary." I was pleased to have found a way out. But I rejoiced too soon.

"I can't go to Semichastny. He's actively involved in the plot himself, along with Shelepin, Podgorny, and others. I wanted to tell Nikita Sergeyevich about this in person. He's in great danger. Now that you've told me he's not in Moscow, I don't know what to do!"

"Call back in a few days. He'll be back soon." I tried to calm him.

"I may not be able to. It was pure luck that I got to this government phone and managed to be alone in the room. That may not happen again, and it's very important. We're talking about the security of our state," the voice insisted. "Perhaps you could listen to what I have to say and then tell Nikita Sergeyevich about our conversation."

"Well, actually, you know . . . I'm not very well," I mumbled, trying to stall for time. I didn't know what to do. Why did I have to get mixed up in something like this? If he was crazy, he would torment me with his wild talk, groundless suspicions, and phone calls. Why had I answered the phone?

But what if he was not crazy? What if there was even a grain of truth in what he said? I would be brushing him off for my own peace and quiet. Obviously, I'd have to meet him and find out whether his story was true, or the fantasy of a sick imagination. Of course, Father couldn't stand it when members of his family poked their noses into government business. If I repeated this conversation, I might enrage him, even though he was well disposed toward me. If it were a question of new missiles, or fertilizers, or steel furnaces, it would be all right. But in this case I would be interfering in the holiest of holies — relations among the top leaders of the party and state! That area was completely off limits.

A decision had to be made. At the other end of the line, Galyukov was waiting for an answer. I hesitated for another moment and finally made up my mind.

"All right. Give me your address. I'll come by this evening, and you can tell me everything."

"No, no! You can't come to my place. It's dangerous to talk here. Let's talk outside somewhere. Do you know the Central Committee apartment building on Kutuzovsky Prospekt? It's the one where your sister Yulia lives. Tell me what your car looks like, and I'll be waiting at the corner."

"My car is black. License number 02-32. I'll be there in half an hour," I said.

I went to change my clothes, anxiously trying to convince myself that the whole conversation was the fruit of a sick imagination and that when I came back I would merely regret the loss of a few hours. But deep down I was worried. Dressing quickly, I headed for my car in the garage by the gate.

The duty officer opened wide the high, green gates separating the yard from the street. Everything seemed normal. The only unusual thing was the trip itself, and the reason for it. I didn't have far to go, only about fifteen minutes, and I began to collect myself, preparing for the conversation ahead.

I didn't know at the time that word of the developing events had already reached my sister Rada. In the summer of 1964 she had received a phone call from a woman whose name she couldn't remember later. The woman had insistently asked to meet her, declaring that she had some sort of important information. Rada made all sorts of excuses until, in desperation, the woman told her on the phone that she knew of an apartment where members of a conspiracy to oust Khrushchev had met and discussed plans.

"Why are you telling me this?" Rada had replied. "This is a matter for the KGB. They are the ones you should call."

"How can I call them if Semichastny, the chairman of the KGB, himself is involved! That's just what I wanted to talk to you about. It is a real conspiracy!"

In those days, Semichastny was friendly with Aleksei Adzhubei, Rada's husband, and was often a guest at their home.[3]

---

3. Adzhubei belonged to the younger generation of people who had worked for the Komsomol when Semichastny headed the organization. There was a whole group of them who were quite close.

Rada didn't take this information seriously. Not wanting to waste her time on an unpleasant meeting, she answered that, unfortunately, she could do nothing. She was just a private individual, and this was a matter for state organs. She therefore asked the woman not to call her again.

She didn't receive any more calls from the woman after that. But a similar warning came from Valentin Vasilievich Pivovarov, the former business manager of the Central Committee.[4] His phone call led Rada to consult with an old family friend, Professor Aleksandr Mikhailovich Markov, who at the time headed the Fourth Chief Administration of the Ministry of Health.[5] Markov wrote Pivovarov's information off to hypersuspiciousness, and advised her to ignore it. Rada put the matter out of her mind in accordance with his authoritative advice.

We now know that similar information also reached the Central Committee. Several years afterward, the former head of Nikita Serge-yevich's security detail, Colonel Litovchenko, recounted the incident. The information was received by Father's principal assistant, Grigory T. Shuisky, who conveniently buried it. By that time Shuisky had been working for Khrushchev for about thirty years, ever since the Battle of Stalingrad, but evidently he had now changed his allegiance.[6]

I drove along the Berezhkovsky Embankment of the Moscow River. The sky was covered with clouds, and from time to time a few drops of rain fell.

I reached the traffic circle by the Ukraine Hotel. Several minutes later the big cream-tiled Central Committee house came into view. On the corner stood the solitary figure of a man in a dark coat with a hat pulled down over his face. I stopped the car.

"Are you Vasily Ivanovich Galyukov?"

4. The business manager is in charge of all internal economic affairs, including Central Committee finances, publishing, apartment houses, and vacation retreats. The position is considered to be very important, and its occupant is usually someone quite close to the party first secretary.

5. The Fourth Administration controlled all hospitals and clinics serving the top ranks of the bureaucracy. Its chief was usually a very well known physician whom the first secretary was likely to consult. That's how Markov had become a close friend of the Khrushchevs.

6. Father had two assistants who worked on general political issues and ran his office — Shuisky and Vladimir S. Lebedev. Their duties included briefing him on documents, coordination with Central Committee line departments, and much more. Besides them, there were other assistants for fields such as construction, agriculture, foreign policy, and so forth.

The man nodded and glanced around. He looked about fifty years old.

"I'm Khrushchev. Get in." He carefully sat down on the front seat next to me. I drove off. "What is it you wanted to tell me? I'm listening."

My passenger was jittery. Several times he looked around, peering intently out the back window, then hesitantly suggested: "Let's drive somewhere out of town. To the woods. It's quieter there."

I glanced involuntarily out in the mirror but noticed nothing suspicious. As usual, Kutuzovsky Prospekt was full of cars. "All right. If it's out of town you want to go, we'll go out of town. We'll head onto the ring road and then we'll think of something."

We were both silent. Ahead of us was the overpass over the ring road. When we turned right and drove under the bridge, forests began to flash past on both sides. Head-spinning scenes from detective thrillers came to mind. I never had expected to take part in anything similar. On the left, a big parking lot came into view, occupied by several cars and a large truck with a trailer. The truck driver had obviously decided to spend the night there. I exchanged glances with Galyukov. No, there were too many people there. We needed solitude. We drove on. About half an hour had passed. Soon we would reach the Vnukovo Highway.

On the right was a country lane leading into a small pine grove. We turned into it. One more turn and a large glade appeared. It was getting dark, and the low clouds gave the surrounding innocent and peaceful landscape a certain mysteriousness.

Finally, I stopped the car. We got out on the grass and began walking along a path. It was too narrow to walk side by side, and our feet kept slipping into overgrown potholes.

Galyukov began the conversation.

"When Nikolai Grigorievich Ignatov was a member of the Presidium I was his chief of security. You probably don't remember me, but I know you well. I used to go with the boss to Nikita Sergeyevich's dacha, and I saw you there.

"In fact, I first met up with Ignatov quite a while ago. I began working as a special messenger for him as early as 1949. In 1957, when Nikolai Grigorievich was elected a Central Committee secretary and member of the Presidium, I became his security chief. Our relationship hasn't been just official. I've accompanied him on business trips, and I've been a kind of companion, someone to talk to, if you will. He got used to letting down his hair with me, sometimes telling me things he wouldn't tell anyone else. And I was devoted to him.

"When Nikolai Grigorievich wasn't reelected to the Presidium at the Twenty-second Congress, in 1961, he and I suffered through this unpleasant — to put it mildly — event together. On top of everything else, he was no longer entitled to a security chief, and I had gotten attached to him after all these years.

" 'Don't take it so hard,' Ignatov reassured me. 'I'll set you up somewhere. Leave the organs [KGB]. You've served long enough to get your pension. I still have friends, and we'll find you a good job.'

"I retired in 1961 and took a job as a senior assessor at the Supply Committee.[7] Later, when I had to look for another job, I called Nikolai Grigorievich and he promised to help. At that time, Ignatov was Russian Republic Supreme Soviet chairman, and he quickly found me a place in his economic department. There wasn't much work to do there, and when Nikolai Grigorievich went on vacation or business, I usually traveled with him. He liked taking part of his leave in the spring, when it was still cold and snowy in Moscow; we would go to Central Asia, where it was already summer. Local leaders gave us VIP treatment for old time's sake, and this really flattered Ignatov. He would nudge me and say: 'See how they value me, Vasya.'

"If we didn't go to Central Asia, we went to the Caucasus, which he also liked a lot.

"I also went with him on vacation in the summer, usually in August. My job was to look after his personal comfort. Nikolai Grigorievich attached great significance to where, how, and with whom he spent his time. He wanted things to be just as they had been when he vacationed as a Central Committee secretary in government dachas.

"That's the way it was this year. He called me to his office on August third. When I came in, he was sitting at his desk looking pleased, as if he had just returned from vacation.

"He told me he had decided to go to the Caucasus on the eighth, and asked, somewhat doubtfully it seemed, 'Would you like to come with me, perhaps?'

"I already knew he was going on leave, because he had assigned me to make all the arrangements. I didn't reply to his suggestion that I

---

7. The Supply Committee, which oversees the purchase and storage of agricultural production, is the equivalent of a government ministry.

accompany him. That was for him to decide. I merely said that all the arrangements had been made, and that I had negotiated with the director of the Rossiya Sanatorium in Sochi for a separate dacha for him. We usually stayed there.

"This time Nikolai Grigorievich suddenly exploded.

" 'You settled this, you negotiated that! What good is all your talking?'

"I didn't understand: 'Perhaps I shouldn't come with you, then.'

" 'We'll see about that later,' Ignatov muttered. 'You can go now.'

"Our conversation ended on this note; we said good-bye more stiffly than usual, and I left not knowing what had caused this reaction. It wasn't my fault — everything had been arranged as usual.

"Several days later, on August sixth, the head of Ignatov's secretariat called to ask me to phone Nikolai Grigorievich. I called him on the morning of the seventh, and he said, as if nothing had happened, 'Are you ready? We fly to Sochi tomorrow.'

"I was used to such departures. I quickly packed my things, and on the morning of the eighth called at Ignatov's apartment. He lives on the same block as I do. I picked up his suitcases, and the two of us drove to Vnukovo airport in his Chaika. Later the same day, we were in Sochi.

"We unpacked in the dacha assigned to us — it was in the park, some distance from the main buildings. After dinner, we went for a stroll around the sanatorium grounds. Nikolai Grigorievich was in a good mood, cracking jokes. He liked the dacha.

" 'Not bad at all, this little dacha, right on the money,' he said to me, and following some train of thought of his own, added: 'Actually, before we left, Brezhnev and Podgorny suggested I take the fourth state dacha.'

" 'So, shall I say that we're taking this dacha after all?' I asked. 'Did they tell Nikita Sergeyevich? These dachas are supposed to be only for Presidium members, you know. If he were to find out, wouldn't there be trouble?'

"Ignatov didn't answer, and set off down the path in silence. When Nikolai Grigorievich turned back, I followed a half step behind him.

"As if deep in thought, Ignatov muttered: 'There's a right time for everything. But they don't pay any attention to old Khrushch.'

"He often cursed Nikita Sergeyevich, especially recently, after he had been dropped from the Presidium, but usually when he'd been drinking heavily and concerning some specific decision. Ignatov believed that he would do everything differently if he were in Nikita Sergeyevich's place. Whatever he said about Khrushchev, you still had the feeling that he was afraid of him. But here he was hinting that Khrushchev could be ignored altogether, and that was new.

" 'We have to decide about food and the motor launch,' I said, changing the subject. 'What are your instructions? You didn't give me any in Moscow.'

" 'That's all taken care of. I've already agreed with Semichastny about both the boat and the food, and about installing a *V.Ch.* [another kind of government phone linking party and state officials — ed.] in our dacha. Ask the duty officer: they've already received their orders.' Ignatov laughed, seeing me stare with amazement.

"Ignatov had nothing to do with Semichastny before. In fact, he couldn't stand Semichastny and sneered at him for making all sorts of blunders, even though at the same time he was afraid of Semichastny, aware of his good relations with Khrushchev, and especially his friendship with Adzhubei. As recently as a year ago, there could be no question of his making such a request of Semichastny.

"What's going on? I wondered. I called the sanatorium duty officer and the KGB duty officer, too, and both confirmed that all instructions concerning the food and launch had been received.

"When I informed Ignatov of this, he was very pleased.

" 'They're great guys, Shelepin and Semichastny. They never refuse me anything.'

"This change in relations between these people was incomprehensible. Why had their barely concealed hostility been replaced by such cordiality? Clearly, something wasn't quite right. Then Ignatov asked me which Presidium members were staying nearby.

"From the dacha I phoned the Sochi city party committee secretary and told him that Nikolai Grigorievich Ignatov was vacationing in the Rossiya Sanatorium and wanted to know which comrades were on holiday in Sochi. There was nothing unusual about this inquiry. The first thing every new arrival did was to find out who his neighbors were.

"The city party secretary was always on top of things. He immediately told me that in neighboring sanatoria there were several first secretaries of province committees, including Kamchatka, Belgorod, and Volyn. The last's name was [Fyodor I.] Kalita. I passed all this along to Ignatov.

" 'Thanks. No need to call the city committee anymore. We'll figure things out for ourselves,' he replied.

"Several days passed. Ignatov took no further interest in anyone. We each kept busy with our own pursuits. I tried not to make a pest of myself.

"Suddenly they told me that he was looking for me urgently. It took me only a few minutes to get there.

" 'You know what, I thought I saw Titov, secretary of the Checheno-Ingush committee. True, he was a long way off, and I might have been mistaken. Call up the reception desk and find out whether it was he or not. If they want to know who's asking, say you're from the province committee.'

"As it happened, Titov really was staying next door. I called his room and was told that he had gone out. I asked them to say that Ignatov would like Comrade Titov to give him a call.

"The next day, Ignatov informed me in a satisfied voice that Titov had called, and he had invited him over.

" 'You get everything organized,' he said.

"Organizing dinners for guests was one of my responsibilities during our joint vacations. The guests arrived. The table had been set on the veranda. There was brandy, sturgeon, caviar, and kebab — everything as usual.

"Besides Titov, there was [Nikolai I.] Chmutov, chairman of the Volgograd province executive committee, and several other people, exactly who I don't recall. They invited me to join them at the table.

"In the intervals between toasts, Ignatov reminisced at length about his work in Leningrad. Chmutov and the others told jokes about Khrushchev. Everyone laughed loudly. There was nothing suspicious about the gathering — they just drank, gossiped, and then left.

"Ignatov was pleased with the meeting. He returned to the subject of his conversation with Titov several times during our walks. 'He's a very good man, Titov. We need a valuable man like him,' Ignatov would say.

"August was drawing to a close. On the twenty-ninth, Brezhnev suddenly called Ignatov. I was present during their conversation.

"Brezhnev said that as long as Ignatov was staying in Sochi, he should come over to Krasnodar for a couple of days to take part in celebrations connected with the presentation of an award to the Krasnodar oil and gas combine of the North Caucasus regional economic council.

"Ignatov readily agreed.

" 'I'll sound out Georgy at the same time,' he promised Brezhnev.

(Georgy Vorobyev, secretary of the Krasnodar rural regional committee of the party, was an old acquaintance of Ignatov's.) 'Titov and Chmutov were here, Lyonya. They drank a bit and it loosened their tongues. Their words speak for themselves. They reflect the general mood. But Georgia worries me. I'm getting back from vacation on about September ninth, and I'm thinking about making a quick trip to Tbilisi. Some work needs to be done there.'

"Evidently Brezhnev asked why Ignatov was worried about Georgia, for Nikolai Grigorievich explained, 'I read in the papers a letter from some hundred-and-twenty-year-old collective farm woman to Nikita Sergeyevich. That was no accident. Apparently, they don't understand the situation.'

"Brezhnev's answer must have been reassuring. 'So you'll take care of that?' Ignatov replied. 'Fine, that's a different matter,' he added delightedly. 'But there's something else. I spoke to [Zakov N.] Zarubyan [first secretary of Armenia]. He's well disposed. He's our man, Lyonya, but one thing I do ask you — everything must be done before November.'

"They talked a bit more about the weather, about Leonid Ilyich's hunting successes, and then Ignatov hung up. He was smiling happily. Clearly, the conversation had gone very well.

"I forgot to say," Galyukov suddenly remembered, "that just after we arrived at the sanatorium, Nikolai Grigorievich warned me that during his holiday he planned to go to Georgia, Armenia, Ordzhonikidze, and somewhere else.

" 'It's boring sitting in one place all the time,' he explained.

"But the journey kept being postponed.

" 'Wait a bit, it's not the right time yet.' He would shrug when I reminded him that we had to do something about the tickets.

"We left for Krasnodar on the thirtieth, the day after the conversation with Brezhnev. We were staying in a regional committee guesthouse. That evening we had visitors over — [Nikolai K.] Baibakov [head of the State Committee on Chemical and Petroleum Products], [Aleksandr I.] Kachanov [first secretary of the Krasnodar party industrial committee], [Albert N.] Churkin [chairman of the Krasnodar regional industrial executive committee], and some other leaders.

"We sat down to supper. The conversation concerned the next day's ceremonies, which were discussed in detail. Eventually, they all left. Ignatov was not pleased with the supper. Vorobyev's absence clearly upset him.

" 'He's proud. That's why he hasn't come . . . ,' he muttered.

" 'What's so special about his not coming? It's harvest time, and they're likely to come up short of their grain quota. He's probably rushing around the farms.' I tried to reassure Ignatov, but he only shook his head.

"On August thirty-first, the meeting took place at which Nikolai Grigorievich, as Russian Republic Supreme Soviet chairman, presented the award. As usual, there was a large banquet afterward for local party and government activists. From there we returned to the house where we were staying. Kachanov and Churkin drove back with us. They accompanied Nikolai Grigorievich to the door, said good-bye, and drove away.

"Soon afterward Trubilin, the chairman of the regional executive committee, drove up. He and Ignatov now waited for Vorobyev, who was seeing off [Aleksei I.] Shibaev, the Saratov province committee secretary, who was leaving that day. It was almost eleven when Vorobyev arrived. The three of them sat in the house for several minutes, and then Ignatov and Vorobyev went for a walk in the park next to the house. Trubilin didn't go with them but stayed in the house, just sitting there, looking upset. Clearly, he too wanted to take part in the conversation. The two of us waited for Ignatov and Vorobyev to come back. We had a glass of brandy. I tried to start a conversation about his region's successes and awards, but he hardly replied. His thoughts were obviously elsewhere. Time dragged on slowly. An hour passed, then another, but Ignatov and Vorobyev were still strolling. This was most unusual for Ignatov: as a rule, he went to bed around eleven; something extraordinary must have happened.

"At one o'clock in the morning, Trubilin began to get irritable. Several times he went to the door, trying to catch a glimpse of Ignatov and Vorobyev. Finally he couldn't stand it any longer and set off in search of them, but he soon came back, more gloomy than ever.

" 'They're still walking. I've got to work tomorrow. I'm going home to get some sleep. I've said good-bye to them,' he replied to my unasked question.

"Trubilin called for his car and drove off. I too went to sleep; I'd had trouble keeping my eyes open ever since the banquet. Ignatov and Vorobyev were still wandering around in the park. What they were talking about, I don't know.

The next morning, Vorobyev drove over again. We had just gotten up. He brought a new visitor with him, Mironov from Rostov. Baibakov appeared a bit later. All of them sat down to breakfast together. After breakfast, Baibakov hurried off on business, while the others stayed to stroll in the park. They were talking animatedly. I could see that Ignatov was trying to prove some point, and the rest were listening in silence.

"Before they had gone very far, the duty officer announced that Brezhnev was on the *V.Ch.* and wanted to speak with Ignatov. Vorobyev and Kachanov, who had just arrived, went into the room with him.

"I stayed outside, but the conversation could be heard clearly through the door. They were talking about the award ceremony.

"The first voice I heard was Ignatov's.

" 'Thank you, Lyonya. Everything went off well. Thanks for your help. Without you, it would have been tough.'

"The point was that Brezhnev had helped to provide money for the banquet. It was forbidden to hold banquets at state expense, and the ban was strictly enforced. Only Brezhnev, as second secretary of the Central Committee, could grant permission.

" 'I've got Vorobyev here,' Ignatov went on. 'He and I have talked everything over. I've also spoken to the Saratov secretary, Shibaev. At first, we didn't understand each other, but then we found a common language. Everything's all right with him, too. I got him to come around.'

"They said good-bye, wished each other success, and then Vorobyev took the receiver. At first they talked about the award, Vorobyev thanking Brezhnev for valuing their work so highly, and earnestly promising to achieve new successes. Then Kachanov took the phone and said more or less the same thing.

"After the conversation, they all went out on the porch and began an animated discussion of what to do next. They decided to drop in at the regional committee, and then to do some fishing in the Primorsko-Akhtarsky district.

"On the way, Vorobyev stayed behind at the regional committee office, while Kachanov and Churkin came with us. Everything had been well organized. A table had been laid for us, and fish soup was bubbling on an open fire. The first order of business was to drink and eat a bit. That took several hours. Everyone was trying to outdo everyone else at the table with fishing and hunting stories; each one was more improbable than the one before, and the catches got bigger with each toast.

"After a brief rest, we headed off into the sunset — some of us to shoot ducks, others with fishing rod in hand.

"The next day the pattern was repeated, and we returned to Krasnodar only on the evening of September second.

"Vorobyev was waiting at the house. After a word with Ignatov, he left quickly. He returned for supper, and afterward it was the same old story — the two of them again went for a walk and stayed out until one in the morning deep in conversation.

"The next day we got ready to leave. Vorobyev, Kachanov, Churkin, and Trubilin came to see us off. As they said good-bye, Ignatov invited them all to come to Sochi the next Sunday, September sixth, to have dinner with him. He specially emphasized that they should not bring their wives.

"On September sixth, about twenty people gathered at our place. There was Baibakov, [Aleksei I.] Popov (the Russian Republic minister of culture), various people from Krasnodar, and others. Kachanov and Trubilin were late, having been delayed on the road.

"The dinner dragged on until very late; there were lots of toasts. Vorobyev reminisced about Leningrad, and about the correct and principled position taken by Ignatov when he was Leningrad province secretary.

"When Ignatov was Leningrad secretary, he became famous for being tough on the intelligentsia. Many people talked, back then, about his coarseness and lack of self-control. A collective complaint, signed by many in literature and the arts, was sent to the Central Committee. As a result, Ignatov was relieved of this job and appointed first secretary of Voronezh, where people are a bit simpler and the work easier.

"About ten o'clock the dinner came to an end. The most steadfast guests stayed on to eat and drink some more, but the rest went their separate ways. At one point when he was alone, Ignatov called me in and ordered me to get Podgorny's dacha in Yalta on the *V.Ch.*

"While waiting for Podgorny to come to the phone, he put his hand over the speaker and said: 'Get Georgy in here quick, but do it so that the others don't notice.'

"I asked Vorobyev to come into the study. Titov was already there.

"While I was getting Vorobyev, Podgorny had come on the line. What they talked about, I don't know. Evidently, Podgorny wished Ignatov success. In reply, Ignatov said significantly: 'The main success depends on you, not us.'

"At this point, Ignatov noticed that I was still in the room and indicated that I should leave.

"I tiptoed out quietly and closed the door so as not to disturb the conversation.

"Everything that had happened over the last few days — the whispering until late at night, the innuendos and hints — all this had aroused my curiosity and put me on guard. Now they'd sent me out. It was impossible to make anything out through the door, and I didn't want to seem to be eavesdropping. These things are none of my business, I decided, and after marking time in the hallway a bit longer, I went out on the porch.

"On my right was the lighted window of the study, and through the glass I could see men's figures standing around the telephone. I saw Titov holding the receiver. I could hear his voice pretty well, though it was hard to make out the words.

"I really wanted to hear what they were talking about with Podgorny, to find out what this conspiracy was all about. Usually, Ignatov liked to show off that he was on close terms with members of the Presidium, and would boom loudly into the receiver: 'Hello Lyonya!' or 'How goes it, Kolya?'

"I had just stepped off the porch when I noticed a figure coming up the path.

" 'Vasya, where's Nikolai Grigorievich?' the stranger asked me.

"It was Trubilin. He hadn't noticed where Ignatov, Titov, and Vorobyev had gone, and had been looking for them in the park.

" 'They're in there.' I pointed Trubilin toward the lighted study window.

"He hurried into the house, but almost immediately came out again. 'They keep hiding. They know everything, and I don't know a thing.'

" 'Who are you talking about?'

"Trubilin gave a start. 'I won't say, damn them. Even without them, I know everything. All the instructions go through me.'

"Muttering something under his breath, he disappeared into the darkness.

"Ignatov, Titov, and Vorobyev emerged from the study. As they walked by, they were talking quietly about something, apparently their conversation with Podgorny.

"Noticing me on the porch, they stopped talking and began to bid each other good-bye. The Krasnodar people stayed on to spend the night in the dacha, while the rest went home.

"In the morning, having seen off the Krasnodar contingent, Nikolai Grigorievich invited me to go for a walk. The conversation revolved around yesterday's dinner.

" 'You see, no one proposed a toast to him. That's good!' Ignatov declared happily.

" 'Who's "him"?' I asked.

" 'To Nikita.'

"Without any obvious connection with what had gone before, he added: 'Titov's a good man.'

"This was his usual way of assessing the people around him. Those who agreed with him and supported him were good men. The rest were bad guys of various hues.

" 'Never mind, Vasya,' he reassured me. 'Just wait a little. There are good things ahead for you, too. Don't worry!'

"I didn't ask him what he meant, and the conversation turned to fishing.

"Nothing further of interest occurred in Sochi. As the vacation came to an end, I reminded Nikolai Grigorievich several times that he had planned to go to Armenia.

" 'I won't be going. Zarubyan will be seeing Brezhnev in Moscow. It's time to go home,' he said.

"We returned to Moscow on September ninth. On Monday I was out at his dacha making various domestic arrangements. Ignatov often used me as a secretary, and, catching sight of me, he asked me to put a call through to Kirilenko, who was vacationing in Novy Afon. The duty officer answered and, when he heard who was calling, said Andrei Pavlovich was bathing in the sea and could not come to the phone. To my amazement, this ordinary reply greatly upset Ignatov.

" 'Is he really bathing, or doesn't he want to talk to me?' he muttered to no one in particular.

"Still agitated, Nikolai Grigorievich began trying to get Brezhnev on the phone at the Central Committee. Brezhnev's secretary answered the *vertushka*.

" 'Leonid Ilyich isn't at work and won't be today. He's sick.'

"This really upset Ignatov. Pacing up and down, he muttered to himself: 'Is he ill or isn't he? What's wrong with him? Is this illness real or not?'

"Feeling out of place, I left. When I returned to his study an hour later, Ignatov was sitting in a leather easy chair and smiling contentedly.

" 'It was nothing. Everything is all right. He just has the flu. Everything is normal.'

"I couldn't understand why Brezhnev's flu was a good thing. So I added this conversation to the list of strange events that had taken place over the last month.

"If you take all of them together, they add up to a suspicious picture. Innuendos, hints, tête-à-têtes with province secretaries, the unexpected friendship with Shelepin and Semichastny, the frequent calls to Brezhnev, Podgorny, and Kirilenko. Why the reference to November? What is it that must be done before November?"

Galyukov then recounted various episodes that revealed Ignatov's attitude toward my father; some of them had occurred in previous years, others quite recently.

Ignatov's nasty character was well known. Nor was his dislike for Khrushchev a secret. He could never accept not having been reelected to the Presidium after the Twenty-second Party Congress. Having been relieved of his post as a Central Committee secretary, he found himself at a significantly lower level, where he had no influence on policymaking. But even before that, Ignatov had been fond of telling friends, after a few drinks, that he was doing all the work in the Central Committee, that the rest were idlers and that Khrushchev merely rubber-stamped decisions that he (Ignatov) had prepared.

Everything Galyukov had told me had to be weighed carefully before I took any action. This was no time to act rashly.

I glanced at my watch — we'd been walking for almost two hours. By now it was completely dark. We turned back to the car.

I thanked Galyukov for the information and assured him that I regarded what he had said with the utmost seriousness. I promised to tell Father about it as soon as he came back. I asked for his phone number, just in case I suddenly needed it. Vasily Ivanovich gave it to me reluctantly.

"Call me only in an emergency," he said hesitantly. "And I beg you, don't say anything on the telephone except to arrange a meeting. My phone is bugged; I'm sure of it. I even checked: I didn't pay my phone bill for a long time. By law, it should have been disconnected, but it wasn't. That means it's tapped," Galyukov concluded.

Once again I felt like a character in a detective story. Shadowing, tapping of telephones, conspiracies — all of it was strange, terrifying, and unreal. Until then I had been used to thinking of the KGB and other services as allies. You could trust and rely on them. As far back as I could remember, officers in blue service caps had stood guard around our house. I had always regarded them as friends, people who would talk to me and even join in my childhood games.

Now suddenly the KGB had shown its other face. Instead of protecting, it was shadowing; it knew my every step. Thoughts like this sent shivers down my spine.

Deep down, I was hoping that this bad dream would pass, that everything would be cleared up and life would roll along again as before. Yet something kept telling me that it wouldn't, that this was very serious, and that no matter how events unfolded, things would never be the same again.

As it turned out, Galyukov and I were equally naive in assessing our situation. His fears that his phone was tapped were well founded, but only part of the truth. The government phone in the Khrushchev apartment was also tapped, and our meeting had been tracked right from the start. After that, we couldn't take a step without the knowledge of the appropriate organs.

But at that moment, as we arranged our own "conspiracy," we naturally knew nothing about this. Or rather, Galyukov was worried, and I, while pretending to agree with him, was actually amused at how his fears were getting the better of him. Still, I thought, it wouldn't do any harm to be careful. And he would feel better, whether or not his story was true; after all, he certainly meant well.

It was time to go back. We reached the main road without any adventures and looked around: there was no tail to be seen. Ignorance is bliss!

Half an hour later I dropped Galyukov off across from his house, after promising to phone him if the need arose. I thanked him once again for his information. A few minutes later I drove into our yard. The duty officer closed the gate, and there I was, fenced off from the outside world. Here, inside, everything was familiar, calm, stable. What went on outside the gates seemed quite unreal and harmless from here.

Father wouldn't be back for several days, and in the meantime I could get on with other things. The "conspiracy" would have to wait. Once Father got back, he would sort it all out and put everything in its place.

*   *   *

THE first news arrived from the test range. The demonstration of military technology was ending, but for Vladimir Chelomei's design team, for whom I worked, the results were not good. The ICBM that we had just finished designing and testing had lost out to a similar missile produced by Mikhail Kuzmich Yangel's group. The two missiles had been produced in parallel and had similar missions.

Military men at the test range had already begun to show a preference for the Yangel missile. They were actively backed by Dmitry Ustinov. Although he was not directly involved in defense matters at the time, as one of the fathers of missilery in our country [he had been in charge of the armaments industry from 1941 to 1963 — ed.], he had extraordinary authority and his word meant a lot. As second secretary, Brezhnev was responsible for supervising the defense industry, but typically — with his softness of character — he had not expressed a definite opinion. Chelomei had managed to get through to him several months before. With his usual eloquence, he persuaded Brezhnev of his brainchild's superiority, and he received assurances of Brezhnev's full support.

However, misfortune struck in August. Ustinov saw Brezhnev, they talked for several hours behind closed doors, and Brezhnev did a complete about-face. It could be felt in certain innuendos, and in the general attitude toward our design team of people in the Central Committee apparatus who were quick to sense any change in the leadership's likes and dislikes.

Brezhnev and Ustinov had known each other for a long time. Their paths crossed right after the war when Brezhnev was Dnepropetrovsk province secretary. The persistent young minister and the likable young party secretary met at construction sites in Dnepropetrovsk, which was then undergoing reconstruction. From that time on, they had been linked, if not by personal friendship, then by unfailing mutual regard. Their paths had diverged, they had not seen each other for years, but when they did meet they enjoyed reminiscing together about the late forties. The energetic and single-minded Ustinov dominated the pliable Brezhnev.

What did Ustinov and Brezhnev talk about that August? There were no witnesses. It would appear that the main subject was neither Chelomei's nor Yangel's missiles, but rather Khrushchev. They may have touched on missilery in passing, but for the time being they had to concentrate on the main game.

Not suspecting what they had discussed, we racked our brains trying to figure out how Ustinov had won Brezhnev over. (As it turned out, we guessed wrong: this time, Brezhnev had won Ustinov over.) Where would Leonid Ilyich come down now? Chelomei kept repeating nervously: "I know Leonid Ilyich's character. He'll agree with anything Ustinov tells him. Ustinov can order him around as he likes. Brezhnev's completely under his thumb."

Technically, the rockets were almost identical, so that the most insubstantial argument could tip the scales either way.

But now Khrushchev had come out against us. Although our team had recently gotten a huge order and the future looked rosy, the likely failure of our first attempt to create a ballistic missile depressed us. However, this was only preliminary information. Both Khrushchev and Chelomei were still at the test range, and we impatiently awaited their return so as to get the whole story firsthand.

All these developments pushed aside the problems Galyukov had raised. Everything he had said was dubious, whereas here and now the fate of our brainchild, the fruit of dogged work over the last several years, was being decided.

Father had gotten a tan from the autumn sun in the desert and looked refreshed. He was pleased with what he had seen and, as usual, was quick to share his impressions. Father talked with colleagues over lunch in the Kremlin, but at home I was his interlocutor. Working on a design team, I was well versed in technology, and Father would test his impressions on me, as well as ask me about details.

At the range he had been shown the new, three-stage *Voskhod*, which would soon be launching a spacecraft into orbit, and had met its crew — [V.M.] Komarov, [Konstantin P.] Feokistov, and [Boris B.] Yegorov. Father was bursting with pride for our country, which had overtaken the United States in space. The people around him "yessed" him on everything, trying to support the illusion that the United States would continue to trail behind, and that the first land of socialism would become the world's leading technological power.

Father didn't stop at home on his first day back from the test site but headed straight for the Kremlin. He got home after five, dropped his briefcase full of papers in the dining room, and called me: "Let's go for a walk."

Recently, Father had replaced the leather folder which he had used for so long with a black briefcase with a monogram on the lock. This briefcase had been given him by a foreign visitor. For some reason, he took a liking to it. Instead of giving it as usual to one of his assistants, he kept it himself, and in fact was never parted from it until his retirement.

The ritual of the evening walk was repeated daily — from the house to the gate, a slight nod to the saluting guard officer, a left turn down the narrow asphalt path leading to the high brick wall. The path was lined on both sides with young birch trees. In the corner was a little glade with a stand of young birches in the middle. Here a short stop: one couldn't but admire them. That, too, had become a custom. Then another left turn. On the right, beyond the wall, was the neighboring house, an exact copy of the one in which we lived. Malenkov had once lived there, and after him Kirichenko. Now it was empty. There was a green gate in the wall, and if you wanted to, you could walk through the neighboring yard to Voronov's, and then farther to Mikoyan's house.

Today we passed the gate and walked around the house, which was now on our right. The birches gave way to cherry trees. In the spring, they overflowed with white blossoms, but now there were only a few lonely red leaves on the thin branches — it was autumn.

The house was behind us now, and the path began to loop down toward the Moscow River. You could follow it down to the riverbank itself and then come back in a full circle. Just the two of us were walking along — we had developed this habit quite a while ago. Day after day the pattern was repeated. Sometimes Rada or Adzhubei came along, more rarely Mama. But the two of us never missed the walk.

Part of the way we walked in silence. Obviously, Father was tired and didn't feel like talking. I walked beside him, wondering whether to start a conversation about the meeting with Galyukov or to put it off. I didn't want to broach the topic; it might provoke a crude "Don't stick your nose into what isn't your business." That had already happened when I tried to talk to him about Lysenko and genetics. Now my situation was even more ticklish — no one ever interfered in questions relating to the highest leadership echelons. That subject was taboo. Father never even allowed himself to talk about his colleagues in our presence.

Not only would I have to violate this taboo, I was intending to accuse his closest associates and comrades in arms of conspiracy. Moreover, I was loath to do it for simple human reasons. Brezhnev, Podgorny, and Polyansky — all were frequent guests at our house, all joked with Father and went for walks with him. I remembered many of them from my childhood in Kiev. If Galyukov's whole story turned out to be nonsense, the invention of a nonentity, which I kept trying to convince myself it was, then how could I look them in the eye, and what would they think of me?

In short, I decided to postpone the conversation. Instead, I asked about his impressions of the missile demonstration. Father began to talk, at first reluctantly, then more and more excitedly. His eyes burned brightly, his face no longer looked tired. Missiles were his pride and joy. He kept track of the various types, compared their characteristics, recalled his conversations with rocket designers and military men. Father was particularly proud that our military might was now comparable to America's. President Kennedy himself had recognized the equality of Soviet and American military might. And all this in only ten years! That was something to be proud of.[8]

Choosing a convenient moment, I asked: "How did you like our missile?"

He clearly didn't want to discuss the issue, having already done so endlessly at the test range.

"It's a good missile," Father replied, "but Yangel's is better. That's the one we're going to put into production. We discussed it all and decided. Don't raise the issue again."

I said nothing. I felt sorry for our team, which had put so much effort into the job. As if sensing my feeling, Father added: "Your group made many good suggestions. We approved the work program. [Leonid V.] Smirnov [a deputy prime minister] is drawing up the necessary instructions."

The week was coming to an end. On Saturday evening, we all gathered at the dacha as usual. After Sunday morning breakfast, Father looked through the papers, noted articles that interested him, and then went for a walk.

Once again, the two of us were taking a stroll. The path wound its way through a thick pine forest. We walked along silently, as I waited

8. *Editor's note:* Does "equality" really describe the strategic nuclear balance at the time? Didn't Khrushchev know better than Kennedy just how far the USSR still lagged behind the United States in the early 1960s? Sergei Khrushchev replied: "In contrast to many contemporary military men, both Soviet and American, Khrushchev considered nuclear weapons so terrifying that the existence of even a small quantity of warheads and the means to deliver them made war unacceptable for both sides. He knew, he often said, that the United States surpassed us, but added that those who perished in nuclear war would not care whether they had been killed several times over."

for a suitable moment, still putting off starting the conversation. We reached the gate and walked through it into the meadow that led down to the Moscow River.

The meadow had been dug up. Everywhere there were cement posts, troughs, and pipes. An agricultural delegation had brought something new back from France — an irrigation system in which water flowed through concrete troughs supported by small above-ground posts. Father liked the idea a lot: this way water wasn't lost in the soil, and irrigation canals didn't take up sowing space. He decided to test it at his own dacha. No sooner said than done. The order was given, and within a week the work crew appeared. The meadow was turned into a construction site.

We were now walking along the edge of the forest, Father observing his creation with pleasure. In his mind's eye, he could already see even rows of troughs, raised a meter and a half above the ground and full of softly murmuring water. The necessary amount of water for each bed would drop through measuring apertures — no more, no less, no waste.

After circling the meadow, we turned back. The walk was coming to an end. The unpleasant conversation could be postponed no longer. When we got back to the dacha, Father would get down to his papers, and then would come lunch. Most important, there would be people all over the place, and I didn't want to start this conversation in the presence of witnesses.

"You know," I began, "an unusual thing happened. I must tell you about it. Maybe it's nonsense, but I don't have the right to keep it to myself."

Then I told him briefly about the strange phone call from Galyukov and my meeting with him. Father heard me out without saying anything. Toward the middle of my story, we reached the gate leading back to the house. After hesitating for a second, he turned back toward the meadow.

I finished my story and fell silent.

"You've done the right thing to tell me," he said finally, breaking the silence.

We walked several steps farther.

"Tell me again, whom did this man mention by name?" he asked.

"Ignatov, Podgorny, Brezhnev, Shelepin . . ." I began to repeat them, trying to be as precise as possible.

Father thought for a moment.

"No, it's incredible. Brezhnev, Podgorny, Shelepin — they're completely different people. It can't be," he said thoughtfully. "Ignatov — that's possible. He's very dissatisfied, and he's not a good man anyway. But what can he have in common with the others?"

He didn't expect me to answer. I had done my duty; what happened now was beyond me. Again we turned toward the dacha, walking in silence. Just before we reached the house, he asked me: "Have you told anyone else about your meeting?"

"Of course not. How could I chatter about something like that?"

"That's right," he said approvingly. "Don't tell anyone."

We dropped the subject.

On Monday, I went to work for the first time after my illness. Given the news from the test range, I completely forgot about Galyukov.

I was already home that evening when Father returned from the Kremlin. Seeing his car approaching, I went out to meet him.

As if continuing the previous day's conversation, he began again without any preliminaries.

"Evidently, what you told me is nonsense. I was leaving the Council of Ministers with Mikoyan and Podgorny, and I summarized your story in a couple of words. Podgorny simply laughed at me. 'How can you think such a thing, Nikita Sergeyevich?' Those were his actual words."

My heart sank. That's all I needed — to make an enemy in the Presidium. If it was all nonsense, then Podgorny and anyone else he felt like telling would never forgive me. They would take everything I had said as a provocation against them.

I had worried something like this might happen when I first told Father about it. I had feared the information might get out, but had never expected anything like this.

To be sure, similar leaks had occurred before. A while back, Father had questioned me at length about the comparative characteristics of various missile systems. I told him everything I knew as objectively as I could. I didn't want to be an apologist for my "firm." The army must have the very best; as for who produced it, that was another matter. We had paid for our subjectivism too dearly in 1941 to forget those bloody lessons. Yet, several days later, presenting his views on the development of the arms industry at the Defense Council, Father suddenly blurted out: "Well, Sergei told me this and that . . ."

When this was reported to me, I nearly died! I had to go and shoot my mouth off. I could have just said that I didn't know enough about it. Instead, I had to demonstrate my erudition and zeal to defend the state's interests. Now people I worked with would never forgive me for any critical remarks Father made about them.

Since then, I had decided never to get into such a position again. And here I was, up to my neck in an even worse situation, and involving none other than members of the Presidium of the Central Committee!

"I'm leaving for Pitsunda on Wednesday, as planned," Father continued. "I'll stop in the Crimea on the way and have a look at farms in the Krasnodar region. I've asked Mikoyan to have a talk with that man you met. He'll be calling you. Let him check it out. He's coming down to Pitsunda, too, but he'll delay his departure a bit so as to clarify matters, and then he'll tell me about it when he arrives."

I was very upset. If it was all nonsense, then why talk about it? And if it wasn't, then how could Father let matters out of his own hands? If the investigation was going to be turned over to Mikoyan, why had that been done so casually, in the presence of Podgorny, who had been mentioned as a participant in the plot? The matter hadn't been treated seriously; it had all been done stupidly. And whatever happened, I was in the most absurd position.

Still, the thing was done; it was a little late to worry. I could no longer influence the course of events.

"Perhaps you could delay your departure and talk to the man yourself?" I suggested timidly.

Father grimaced. Obviously, he wasn't about to take on the matter himself.

"No, Mikoyan's an experienced man. He'll take care of everything. I'm tired, I want to rest. And anyway . . . let's not talk about this anymore."

"May I come down to Pitsunda, too? I haven't had a vacation this year. I could stay there with you." I changed the subject. After all, he knew better how to proceed in a situation like this.

"Of course! It will be much nicer for me," he said delightedly. "Get this security officer together with Mikoyan, take a leave yourself, and come on down."

Father flew off to Kiev, where he spent a couple of days, and then, after a stop in the Krasnodar region, arrived in Pitsunda. I stayed in Moscow, having decided not to take any further initiative. The usual troubles at work kept me busy for several days. No one phoned me.

Now and then a premonition of danger swept over me, but I fought it off. There was no point in panicking. I had done my duty; the rest was not my responsibility.

Then suddenly, a day or so before my departure, the phone on my desk rang. I picked up the receiver.

"Give me Khrushchev," a demanding voice rang out. The tone was unusual, to say the least, and I was somewhat taken aback.

"Speaking."

"This is Mikoyan," continued the voice on the other end. "You told Nikita Sergeyevich about a conversation with a certain person. Can you bring him by my place?"

"Of course, Anastas Ivanovich. Just set a time, and I'll call him and bring him wherever you say," I replied.

"Don't bring him to the office. Come by the house today at seven this evening. Bring him yourself, and try not to attract attention," Anastas Ivanovich asked, or shall I say ordered.

"I'm not sure I'll be able to find him right away. I have only his home phone number, and he might not be there," I said doubtfully.

"If you don't find him today, bring him by tomorrow. Just warn me in advance," Anastas Ivanovich concluded.

I immediately dialed Galyukov's number. Fortunately, he was home and picked up the phone.

"Vasily Ivanovich, it's Sergei Nikitich calling," I began, deliberately not naming last names. "Anastas Ivanovich would like to speak with you. We have to be at his place at seven this evening. I'll pick you up at twenty to seven."

Galyukov didn't sound overjoyed to hear from me, and when I mentioned Mikoyan, he got downright frightened.

"I don't want anyone to recognize me. [Nikolai S.] Zakharov [a top KGB official in October 1964, who had previously headed the section in charge of security for the leaders] knows me well. This could get very unpleasant," he muttered.

"Don't worry. We'll drive straight to his door in my car. I'll do the driving myself. It's already dark at seven o'clock. The security men know my face quite well; I go there often since Mikoyan's son, Sergo, is a friend of mine. They won't try to find out who's in the car with me," I reassured him. I don't know whether my explanations had an effect, or whether he understood that he had no alternative, but in any case he stopped objecting.

At five minutes to seven we were at the gate to Mikoyan's house. As I anticipated, the guard at the gate looked out, recognized me, and opened it without any questions. We drove up to the entrance and quickly went in through the unlocked door. The driveway up to the house curved slightly so that we couldn't be seen from the gates.

The hall was empty. That didn't bother me, since I knew the layout well. We took off our coats, climbed to the second floor, and knocked on the study door.

"Come in," boomed Anastas Ivanovich's voice.

Mikoyan met us in the middle of the room and greeted us dryly. He was wearing an austere dark suit but had on house slippers. I introduced Galyukov.

Usually, Mikoyan welcomed me cordially, inquired about my affairs, and joked a bit. This time, he was coldly official, his whole demeanor emphasizing how unpleasant he found our visit. This reception completely undid me. Here was the first result of my not minding my own business. What would be next?

All the houses in the Lenin Hills leadership compound resembled one another. Even the furniture in the rooms was identical. Just as in our house, the study walls were covered with walnut paneling. One wall was completely taken up with a large bookshelf filled with the works of Lenin, Marx, and Engels, and documents from party congresses.

In the corner by the window stood a big red wooden desk with two leather chairs in front of it. Four telephones were bunched on the desk top — the massive white *V.Ch.*, the streamlined *vertushka*, with the kind of coiled cord that had just made its appearance, a simpler black city phone, and one without any dial, for reaching the security duty officer. A little to one side on a small separate table was a large photograph of a dashing Cossack junior officer with a twirled black mustache and wearing a prerevolutionary uniform and four St. George medals on his chest. It was a gift from Semyon Budyonny, the famous cavalry commander during the civil war and afterward.

Mikoyan invited us to sit down in the leather chairs. He settled himself at the desk. The situation was strictly official.

"Do you have a pen?" he asked me.

"Of course." I wasn't sure why he asked, but reached in my pocket and pulled out my fountain pen.

Mikoyan pointed to a pile of paper lying on his desk. "You'll record our conversation. Then you'll decipher your notes and give me the record."

After this, he addressed Galyukov in somewhat more friendly fashion.

"Repeat to me what you told Sergei. Try to be as accurate as possible. Tell me only what you actually know. Keep your conjectures and suppositions to yourself. Do you understand the responsibility you are taking on yourself by making these statements?"

By this time Galyukov was completely in control of himself. He was anxious, of course, but it didn't show.

"Yes, Anastas Ivanovich, I'm fully aware of my responsibility, and I answer for my words. Permit me to recount only the facts."

Galyukov repeated almost word for word what he had told me during our meeting in the forest.

I wrote quickly, trying not to miss a word.

As Galyukov spoke, Mikoyan nodded his head from time to time, as if in encouragement, and occasionally frowned slightly. But gradually he began to show more interest.

Vasily Ivanovich finished his account of the events known to me and looked inquiringly at Mikoyan.

"Have you worked for Ignatov for a long time? Tell me about him. Was there anything, perhaps, that put you on your guard earlier?" Mikoyan asked.

Galyukov began to recall things that had happened many years before that unexpectedly fit the pattern of recent events.

"I have to say that Ignatov's attitude toward Khrushchev changed as Nikolai Grigorievich moved up and down the career ladder. And his ups and downs kept alternating. When he was falling, he would curse Khrushchev something awful.

"When they transferred us from the Leningrad party committee to Voronezh in 1955, Ignatov was very displeased; he had been dumped from the 'second capital' to a run-of-the-mill province.

"I remember that Nikita Sergeyevich once came to Voronezh for a conference on agriculture. He was traveling around the main farming regions, checking preparations for sowing, talking to the activists. Khrushchev got out of the train; it was an ordinary one, not special. People were scurrying about everywhere, all busy with their own affairs: some were kissing or embracing, others lugging their things to the exit. No one paid any attention to Khrushchev. Only if someone barged into him did his bodyguard in civilian clothes politely point the way around him.

"All this didn't last long. The local bosses had naturally come to welcome Khrushchev — the province committee, the city committee, the military, as expected. As soon as we approached, a crowd began to gather, curious to find out who was being met. When they recognized Khrushchev, they began to applaud and shout greetings. Ignatov noticed it, and after we had escorted Khrushchev to where he was staying and got back in the car, he said in a satisfied voice, 'They don't like him. Did you see what a bad reception he got?'

"The conference was stormy. Besides people from Voronezh, there were leaders from neighboring provinces. Nikita Sergeyevich kept interrupting them, asking questions, making caustic remarks. The other provinces really got it, but he actually praised Voronezh.

"During the break, I congratulated Ignatov as he came off the stage: 'Congratulations on your success, Nikolai Grigorievich. We're the only ones Nikita Sergeyevich praised.'

" 'Well, I've worked hard enough for it, haven't I?' Ignatov snapped.

" 'Sometimes you work as hard as you can, and the bosses come and pull you to pieces anyway.'

" 'Hm, just let him try that! I'd take him apart myself,' he retorted and walked away.

"Or take that same autumn. We were vacationing in Sochi as usual. I heard that Khrushchev was coming down. I informed Ignatov and suggested going to the Adler airport to meet him.

"Ignatov swore at me: 'To meet old Khrushch? You go . . . Meet him yourself if you want to.'

"When he was irritated, he never pronounced the name properly, but always shortened it contemptuously to 'Khrushch.'

"From Voronezh we moved to Gorky province in 1957. There too Ignatov couldn't forget that he had been thrown out of Leningrad, and he used any excuse to express his unhappiness.

"He recalled that Khrushchev had switched from being just a secretary of the Central Committee to first secretary back in 1953: 'So he gave himself a prefix. Never mind, he won't last long. Five years at most. At his age, he's already heading downhill.'

"As for the plenums and meetings on agriculture, Ignatov reacted with unchanging contempt: 'Nothing will come of them. Just a lot of chatter.'

"Then everything turned around. Khrushchev came to Gorky and proposed postponing bond payments.[9] They spent a long time talking, and Ignatov was a changed man. He started praising Khrushchev on every street corner. I think they talked about transferring Ignatov to Moscow.

"In early June 1957, Khrushchev invited Ignatov (who was then still in Gorky) and Mylarshchikov (head of the Central Committee Agriculture Department) to his dacha to see some crops he was growing. He started showing us rows of Chinese millet and corn.

"When Khrushchev and Mylarshchikov walked some distance off, Nikolai Grigorievich beckoned to me: 'Tell Mylarshchikov to get going, and not hang around. I need to talk with Khrushchev alone.'

"Mylarshchikov soon left.

"This was the time when the antiparty group was moving against Khrushchev. Ignatov was on Khrushchev's side.

"Khrushchev went for a long walk with Ignatov, telling him something, apparently, about the situation in the Presidium, and about the position taken by Molotov, Kaganovich, Malenkov, and others.

"I followed a bit behind them with Khrushchev's security chief and, naturally, couldn't hear the conversation. Only toward the end, we caught a phrase of Ignatov's: '. . . It's an important matter. It must be solved.'

"He was probably referring to the Central Committee plenum that was about to convene to discuss the differences that had arisen in the Presidium. It was at this plenum, at which the antiparty group was condemned, that Ignatov was named to the Presidium. He was in seventh heaven but tried not to show it, as if it were entirely to have been expected.

"Not long afterward, Pivovarov told Ignatov: 'I've sounded out Khrushchev. You're going to be named a secretary of the Central Committee.'

"Ignatov was overjoyed. He was counting on the post of second secretary; he was as sure as he could be that he would get it. But then came the disappointment: Aleksei Illarionovich Kirichenko was elected

---

9. *Editor's note:* For many years, Soviet citizens had been required to "lend" money to the state by having the cost of state "bonds" deducted from their wages. Instead of returning the principal with interest, the state offered a partial payback at irregular intervals. When Khrushchev canceled these payments in 1957 (claiming that the Gorky automobile factory had suggested this step in response to the state's straitened financial circumstances), people were deeply disappointed.

Khrushchev with other Soviet leaders at a celebration in the 1930s. Left to right: Mikhail Kalinin, Khrushchev, Andrei Zhdanov, Anastas Mikoyan, Vyacheslav Molotov, Lazar Kaganovich, Kliment Voroshilov, Joseph Stalin.

Khrushchev with Stalin in 1936.

With state security official Ivan Serov (later head of the KGB under Khrushchev) in 1945.

Nikita and Nina Petrovna Khrushchev with Anastas Mikoyan at Cape Pitsunda in the Caucasus, 1961.

Nikita Khrushchev (third from left) with local officials at the Bratsk Hydroelectric Station in Siberia, 1959.

Visiting with a group of miners, 1962.

Inspecting the Soviet corn crop.

Khrushchev dons a gas mask as Aleksei I. Kirichenko and KGB bodyguard
Litovchenko look on.

Greeting Anastas Mikoyan at Vnukovo airport, 1960. Others present include
Andrei Gromyko (center).

Khrushchev, Nikolai G. Ignatov, Frol R. Kozlov, and Aleksei Kosygin at the Bolshoi Theater, 1958. Barely visible in the second row are (from left) Leonid Brezhnev and Nuritdin A. Mukhitdinov.

Khrushchev with Nikolai V. Podgorny in Poland, probably 1962.

Khrushchev with the two men who would lead the plot to oust him, Leonid Brezhnev (left) and Nikolai Podgorny, Moscow, 1963.

A winter hike at Zavidovo, 1962. From front: Khrushchev, Brezhnev, Kosygin, Dmitry S. Polyansky, Andrei P. Kirilenko, Sergei Khrushchev.

Conversing with cosmonauts in space, 1962. Brezhnev is at left.

Honoring returning cosmonaut Yuri Gagarin in Red Square ceremony, 1961.

Khrushchev greeting returning cosmonaut German Titov at Vnukovo airport, 1961. Behind them Nikolai Podgorny (left) and Dmitry Polyansky look on, holding flowers.

With visiting U.S. vice president Richard M. Nixon and his interpreter, Alexander Akalovsky, at dacha outside Moscow, summer 1959.

Below: Greeting President Kennedy in Vienna, June 1961.

Right: With Fidel Castro in the Caucasus, May 1964.

Members of the Central Committee Presidium celebrating Khrushchev's seventieth birthday at his Lenin Hills residence. Khrushchev, his wife, and their daughter Yelena have their backs to the camera. Other Presidium members present include Anastas Mikoyan, Leonid Brezhnev, and Aleksei Kosygin at near left, and Nikolai Podgorny and Mikhail Suslov at near right. Sergei Khrushchev sits at the end of the table in the far right corner.

Above: Khrushchev offers a toast at his seventieth birthday celebration. Looking on are (left to right) Nina Petrovna, Yelena, Mikoyan, and Brezhnev. *Right:* Nikita and Nina Petrovna Khrushchev at the Gorki-2 dacha, outside Moscow, in 1959. (Courtesy of *Paris MATCH*, photograph by Walter Carrone.)

Khrushchev with Yelena and her dog Arbat at the Gorki-2 dacha, 1959. (Courtesy of *Paris MATCH*, photograph by Walter Carrone.)

Strolling through the Kremlin grounds with other Soviet leaders in 1960. From left: Nuritdin A. Mukhitdinov (waving), Frol R. Kozlov, Nikolai G. Ignatov, Yekaterina A. Furtseva, Khrushchev, Nikolai Podgorny, Vasily P. Mzhavanadze, A. B. Aristov, Mikhail Suslov, Dmitry S. Polyansky.

Khrushchev offers a toast at a meeting with artists and writers, July 1960. Listening (left to right) are Yekaterina Furtseva, Mikoyan, Brezhnev, Kliment Voroshilov, Suslov, and Kozlov.

At the meeting with artists and writers, the Soviet leader shows his skill at one of his favorite sports.

Being embraced by
the writer Mikhail
Sholokhov, July 1960.

At the gathering of artists and writers. From left: Voroshilov, Khrushchev, Ilya
Ehrenburg, Furtseva. Brezhnev is second from right.

second secretary and Ignatov became an ordinary secretary in charge of agriculture.

"His rage knew no bounds. 'How am I worse than Kirichenko? What am I, dumber than he is?'

"Once again, his positive attitude toward Khrushchev turned into barely concealed hatred.

"Khrushchev became a kind of obsession for him. Every now and then he would look at me and suddenly say: 'Look at the mug on you. You're a lout just like Khrushch.'

"Another time, he was sitting in a chair, not saying anything, and suddenly he muttered as if to himself: 'He's the biggest fool of them all . . .'

" 'Who's that, Nikolai Grigorievich?' I asked.

" 'Khrushch, of course, who else? I could do it, too. They told me I should take the leadership. And I should have.'

" 'But that would be awfully difficult . . .' I objected cautiously."

That episode attracted Mikoyan's attention, and he asked: "When was that?"

"I can't say exactly, but I remember it was in 1959. I think his attitude must have reflected his talks with his friends: Doronin, Kiselyov, Zhegalin, Dinisov, Khvorostukhin, Lebedev, Patolichev." These were all veterans of Stalin's time, high functionaries, province party secretaries, and government ministers.

"Comrade Galyukov." Mikoyan interrupted him again. "You yourself say that Ignatov's dislike for Khrushchev goes way back, yet you've come to us only now. Why is that? Why did you start having doubts? When did that happen?"

Vasily Ivanovich was ready for this question. He had obviously thought about it a great deal.

"My doubts, my suspicion that something was going on, began in Sochi this year. Before that, I didn't attach any great significance to Ignatov's conversations. So the man jabbers to himself, I thought, so what? We'd go for a walk and he couldn't stop cursing Khrushchev. He couldn't forgive the fact that he wasn't appointed to the Presidium at the Twenty-second Congress.

" 'The 1957 was my plenum,' he would say. 'They couldn't have managed without me. And "the twenty" were my doing, too.[10] All the

10. Ignatov refers to the defeat of the antiparty group of Molotov, Malenkov, Kaganovich, and others. "The twenty" were a group of twenty members of the Central

work I did! Then what does he do? He neglects agriculture. I'd have
fixed things in two or three years, but all he does is blather.'

"In the summer, the conversations became more single-minded.
What's more, his relations with many people changed suddenly and
sharply. Until last summer, Ignatov thought badly of Shelepin, Semichastny, Brezhnev, Podgorny, and others. He didn't have a good word
to say for them, and then suddenly they all became his friends. Ignatov
himself hadn't changed, so it was the circumstances; something har-
nessed them together. From 1957 until very recently, Ignatov used every
opportunity to say something nasty about Brezhnev.

" 'He got the job, but what has he done? He can't even address a
meeting. Lazar [Kaganovich] raised his voice at him and he fainted from
fear. Some "hero." ' [11]

"After that, Ignatov's attitude toward Brezhnev evened out a bit.
But he still followed his every move jealously, because Nikolai Grigorievich kept hoping to get back into the Presidium, and move up to
chairman of the Supreme Soviet of the USSR.

"At the beginning of the year, when word got out that Brezhnev
would soon concentrate entirely on work in the Central Committee
Secretariat, Ignatov began calling around to see who was going to take
the chairmanship and whether he had a chance to get it. At the time,
Khrushchev was in the Ukraine. Nikolai Grigorievich didn't want to

---

Committee who supported Khrushchev against the antiparty group in 1957 by demanding the calling of the plenum at which he proved victorious.

11. Shortly after the Nineteenth Party Congress, in 1952, when Stalin drastically
expanded the Presidium and Secretariat of the Central Committee, Brezhnev was made
a Central Committee secretary. After Stalin's death, when the membership of these bodies was reduced to its former size, positions had to be found for the "unemployed."
Brezhnev was made head of the navy's political administration, certainly no great honor
for him. Leonid Ilyich took this stroke of fate very badly. When the situation eased,
Khrushchev remembered his old comrade in arms, and Brezhnev was again made a
secretary of the Central Committee. He was among the minority who supported Khrushchev at the June 1957 sessions of the Presidium and the Secretariat, where the debates
were stormy.

When it was Brezhnev's turn to speak, he started to defend his position, but Kaganovich cut him off rudely: "Where do you think you're crawling? You're too young
to tell us what to do. No one's asking your opinion. Didn't you do enough time in the
navy? If you're not careful, we'll run you right back there, and this time you won't
get out."

The balance of forces at these meetings was not favorable to Khrushchev, so this
threat was a perfectly real one. Brezhnev was so frightened that he fainted. A doctor
had to be called to bring him to.

call Brezhnev, but he was forever on the phone with Podgorny, who gave him hope. Podgorny recounted a conversation he had with Khrushchev in the Ukraine. They evidently touched on the question of a Supreme Soviet chairman, but Khrushchev didn't yet have definite views about a possible candidate. When Podgorny asked who was in line for the job, Khrushchev didn't answer.

"Then, as Podgorny told Ignatov, he decided to ask him straight out: 'Perhaps Ignatov would be suitable?'

"Khrushchev answered vaguely: 'We'll look around, we'll confer about it.'

"Based on this chance conversation, Podgorny assured Ignatov that he had convinced Khrushchev. 'Nikita Sergeyevich agreed with me and plans to deal with the question of your appointment.'

"Ignatov couldn't contain himself: 'Just suppose it's true!'

"He both believed and didn't believe that his long-cherished dream would come true. So he kept after Podgorny, trying to find out what Khrushchev had said and how accurate it all was.

"Naturally, Podgorny couldn't add anything; it had been a passing conversation and they hadn't returned to the subject during the rest of the trip. But he inspired Ignatov with hope, so his disappointment was all the more bitter. For it was you, Anastas Ivanovich, who became chairman. On hearing the news, Nikolai Grigorievich spent the whole evening cursing you and Nikita Sergeyevich. This year, after returning home, Nikolai Grigorievich remarked several times, as if by chance: 'Nikolai and I had a nice long talk today,' followed by a meaningful pause. And sometimes he let drop: 'I went to see Brezhnev today. We had a useful talk. He assured me that everything would be all right.'

"After Podgorny was sharply criticized at the Central Committee Presidium, he and Ignatov became very close. Before that, their relations had been cool. Take the trip to the one hundred fiftieth anniversary celebration of Azerbaijan's becoming part of Russia [in 1963]. Ignatov very much wanted to head the Moscow delegation. It looked as if he would, but at the last moment Podgorny did. Again, the endless conversations: 'Why the hell is he going there? We'll have to play second fiddle again . . .' Ignatov ranted on. Nothing was to his liking in Baku, especially Akhundov's speech [Veli Y. Akhundov, Azerbaijani party first secretary] at the anniversary meeting. Akhundov kept quoting Khrushchev. Ignatov was indignant: 'Why does Akhundov need to do that? Why repeat everything he says like a parrot? He doesn't understand the situation at all.'

"In Baku, we were put up in the same house as Podgorny, but Ignatov had practically nothing to do with him. They would greet each other and then go their separate ways. Podgorny was busy preparing his speech, but Ignatov had nothing to do, so he spent days walking around outside the house to kill time.

"He needed an audience, and I was with him all the time. Whatever we started talking about, gradually he would get back to Podgorny. It was as if he couldn't think of anything else. He was afraid of something, and often repeated pensively: 'The man's dangerous. V-e-r-y dangerous. What do his boys say about him, his security guards?'

"I remember I avoided giving him a direct answer. 'We don't talk about that, Nikolai Grigorievich. We don't touch on subjects like that among ourselves.'

" 'Okay. Perhaps that's right. But he is a dangerous man. Very dangerous.' On this the conversation ended.

"Nikolai Grigorievich kept to the house in Baku, obviously feeling offended. He met only with Zarubyan; they sat and talked for about an hour, but about what, I don't know."

Galyukov paused, obviously to collect his thoughts.

"I also remember isolated episodes. I can't give concrete examples, but Ignatov often talked about the dissatisfaction of the military. 'They're sick and tired of Khrushch,' he'd say. 'His troop cuts stick in their craw. They're just waiting for a chance to . . .'

"Ignatov didn't finish his sentence but merely picked at his thumb with great relish."

Mikoyan was interested in this.

"Whom do you think he had in mind?"

Galyukov stopped short.

"I don't know. He didn't name any names. But he often met with Marshal Konev [Ivan Konev, commander in chief of Warsaw Pact forces and first deputy defense minister]. They were in Czechoslovakia together for [President] Antonín Zápotocký's funeral and got quite close there. They remained close after Konev retired. They would call and wish each other well on holidays, but there was no real friendship. I don't know any others . . . But there was one other occasion. Before going to Bulgaria, Brezhnev called Ignatov. What the reason was, I don't know, but one phrase stuck in my mind.

"As they were saying good-bye, Ignatov warned him: 'Remember, Lyonya, I was there in 1960 and had a long talk with Zhivkov [Todor Zhivkov, the Bulgarian Communist leader] alone. He's disposed to be critical. He even said to me: "He's behaving strangely, your . . ." but didn't finish.'

"And here's another fact. When [Sarvepalli] Radhakrishnan [the president of India] was here, Vysotin called from the USSR Supreme Soviet protocol office to say that Ignatov would be taking the VIP around the country. Nikolai Grigorievich liked these trips. They were a sign that people remembered him and couldn't do without him. But things misfired. That evening Ignatov got a call at home from Georgadze, who apologized and said he was calling at Mikoyan's behest.

" 'We had planned for you to go with Radhakrishnan. But today the itinerary was discussed and Anastas Ivanovich suggested a trip to Armenia. If you don't mind, Anastas Ivanovich himself would like to make the trip with the Indians. The King of Afghanistan will be coming soon, and you can accompany him.'

"Ignatov didn't object, but he was very upset. The next morning I went to see him. They were all sitting at the table having breakfast. There was a pile of newspapers on the table that they obviously had been reading.

"Ignatov's son, Lev, continued a conversation that my arrival had interrupted: 'It doesn't say in the papers that Mikoyan is accompanying the delegation,' he said unhappily. 'They just didn't want you to. It's a question of politics, see?'

"Ignatov frowned over his plate and nodded: 'Yes, it means something. They want to keep me in the shadows.' "

Galyukov shifted in his chair and looked inquiringly at Mikoyan.

"You asked me to tell you everything, even trifles. This may be a trifle, but I think it illustrates Ignatov's general mood."

Anastas Ivanovich nodded. "Tell me everything."

Galyukov continued: "And there's this, too. Every day, Ignatov counts up how many times Khrushchev is mentioned in the newspapers. If there's a picture, he examines it intently. He stares at it, stares at it some more, and then grunts with pleasure. 'I don't care what you say, his face looks worse and worse each day.'

"Recently, Ignatov has been seeming very tense, and he often blows up. He's particularly worried about why Nikita Sergeyevich hasn't gone on vacation. The other day he swore, 'Why the hell doesn't he go take a rest?' I think this heightened interest in Khrushchev's leave is somehow connected with all the other things," Galyukov added.

"You tell us the facts, and we'll draw the conclusions," Anastas Ivanovich repeated.

"I have to say," Galyukov went on, "that Ignatov doesn't speak in very flattering terms about the other members of the Presidium either. For example, he never refers to Polyansky as anything but a rogue. Voronov he regards as narrow. And Kosygin he's nicknamed Kerensky. He often says that Kosygin doesn't know what he's doing and that whatever he undertakes is sure to fail. And he talks about many others in the same way."

Seeing that Anastas Ivanovich was not showing much interest in this, Galyukov changed the subject. "Over the last few days, Ignatov's attitude toward me has changed. I think he's learned about my conversation with Sergei Nikitich. Obviously, we were followed and Ignatov was warned. Nikolai Grigorievich has become very guarded. He avoids frank conversations with me and tries to keep me at a distance. I can't cite anything concrete, but I sense that he doesn't trust me anymore.

"A few days ago, Nikolai Grigorievich was about to go to an anniversary meeting celebrating the centenary of the First International, and he phoned me. It was four o'clock, and I wasn't at my desk. I got home at seven P.M., and when I heard he had been looking for me, I immediately called him at work. He answered and began to inquire how I was doing, what was new.

"I told him everything was fine.

" 'I just got back from the anniversary celebration. Nikita Sergeyevich gave a speech. He spoke brilliantly,' Ignatov cooed.

"Those words really grated on my ears. I hadn't heard anything like that for a long time. He always referred to him as Khrushch, and now it was, 'Nikita Sergeyevich spoke brilliantly.' I didn't like this turn of events at all. I phoned Ignatov again on September thirtieth. Nikolai Grigorievich answered the phone himself.

" 'What do you want?' he asked.

" 'I saw a light in your window and decided to check. Just in case someone had broken in. May I come by?'

" 'All right, all right. Tomorrow, you can . . .' Ignatov hung up without finishing the sentence. He clearly wanted to get rid of me.

"Well, actually, that's about all . . ." Galyukov took out a handkerchief and wiped his perspiring forehead.

I put down my pen and began to flex my numb fingers. In front of me lay a pile of sheets covered with abbreviations and half-written words. I had written quickly, trying not to leave out a single word.

A heavy silence had fallen over the room. Mikoyan sat there thinking, taking no notice of either of us. His thoughts were far away. Finally, he turned toward us, his expression determined, his eyes shining.

"Thank you for your report, Comrade . . ." Anastas Ivanovich hesitated and looked at me.

"Galyukov, Vasily Ivanovich Galyukov," I hastily prompted him in a semiwhisper.

". . . Galyukov," Mikoyan finished. "Everything you've told us is most important. You've shown yourself to be a genuine Communist. I trust you are aware that you have made this report to me officially, and have thereby taken a great responsibility on yourself."

"I understand the full extent of my responsibility. Before I came to you with this report, I thought for a long time, testing and retesting myself, and I am absolutely convinced that what I have told you is the truth. As a Communist and as a security officer, I could not have acted otherwise," Galyukov replied firmly.

"Well, that's good. I don't doubt that you conveyed this information with good intentions, and I thank you. I just want to say that we know Nikolai Viktorovich Podgorny and Leonid Ilyich Brezhnev and Aleksandr Nikolayevich Shelepin and other comrades to be honest Communists who for many years have selflessly devoted all their strength to the good of the Communist party, and we continue to regard them as comrades in arms in the common struggle."

Seeing that I had put down my pen, Mikoyan snapped: "Write down what I just said."

I was taken aback. For whom was such a bombastic declaration intended? Galyukov had been spilling out his suspicions, but these words canceled out everything he had said. Vasily Ivanovich looked at Mikoyan in bewilderment. Fear flashed in his eyes. For the umpteenth time, I regretted getting myself mixed up in this business.

Anastas Ivanovich got up, indicating that the conversation was at an end.

"If you have any additional information or news, telephone Sergei. We'll get in touch with you when necessary." Turning to me, Mikoyan concluded, "Write up your notes on the conversation and send them to me. I'm leaving for Pitsunda on the third."

"I'm going there too. I want to take the rest of my vacation," I said.

"Then bring the report there. Don't show it to anyone — not a single soul. I'll tell Nikita Sergeyevich all about it, and we'll discuss what to do."

Anastas Ivanovich held out his hand to Galyukov. "Sergei will take you home."

We went down the brightly lit staircase to the empty hall and put on our coats quickly so that no one would see us. But the house was empty. Galyukov was tense. He tried to hide his nervousness, but that made him more nervous still.

We got into the car.

"Anastas Ivanovich didn't believe me. We came here in vain," said Galyukov miserably.

I tried to reassure him.

"Your behavior was perfectly correct. His last words were just a general declaration. Anastas Ivanovich didn't want to cast doubt on members of the Presidium until everything is verified."

Vasily Ivanovich didn't argue with me, but it was obvious that he was depressed. We parted after agreeing to get in touch by phone if necessary.

I DID not see Galyukov again. Events began to move at a gallop, and there was no time for a meeting.

I worried a lot about what would happen to him. Ignatov must have known everything and would be sure to make short shrift of the "traitor." Was he in fact arrested? I later found out in a roundabout way that Vasily Ivanovich did have some trouble, but they didn't give him a serious going over and soon left him alone.[12]

The next morning I went to work as usual. I had several things to do before leaving on vacation. As always, many matters had piled up; some projects were almost completed, others just beginning. Most important, I had to find time to write up the record of the talk.

I could decipher my notes all right. But what then? I can't type, and there could be no question of entrusting the secret to any outsider. We had a typing pool, of course, where they type highly secret documents. Could I have given it to them? No — too risky. I would have to write it out by hand. My handwriting is awful, but I had no choice.

I spread out the sheets of paper and set to work. I wrote legibly, almost printing. It went very slowly. I tried to recall every phrase and

12. After the publication of this chapter in *Ogonyok*, Galyukov phoned the editorial office, and he and I had a meeting. He is alive and well and works on the staff of the USSR Council of Ministers.

not omit a word. Gradually, I became absorbed in it. The conversation etched itself deep into my memory. Page after page was covered with my large letters. From nowhere the feeling came over me that I was important, that I was involved in solving matters of state. The anxiety of the last few days receded. I had played my part. Mikoyan was already in Pitsunda. They would sort it out there and do what was necessary.

I reached the last page. I left out Mikoyan's statement. Somehow its tone didn't fit with the dry enumeration of facts. After all, it was a memorandum of record, not a declaration.

I gathered up all the sheets of paper and put them together neatly. It had turned out well: it read easily, and the writing was perfectly legible. It flashed through my mind that I should have made a carbon copy. But why? The document was too sensitive. Who knew whose hands it might get into! At that moment, I couldn't imagine the actual fate of the report.[13] Later I had to reconstruct everything from my notes, which fortunately I had the wit not to burn.

Now all I had to do was say good-bye to Chelomei, and then I could be on my way. Vladimir Nikolayevich saw me right away. He was obsessed with the recent meetings at the test site and very upset about our failure. He blamed the latter mostly on Ustinov, for whom he found some choice epithets. Gradually he calmed down and the conversation turned to everyday matters.

"You must help me more," Vladimir Nikolayevich said unexpectedly.

I was taken aback and began talking about our projects, proposals we were considering, and my own thoughts.

Chelomei interrupted me: "No, I have something else in mind. You've sat around long enough as deputy head in Samoilov's design unit. You should be in charge of it yourself. It would be better for the work, and you could help me more. It's time you moved up."

I was flattered by his suggestion, as anyone would be. Praise is always pleasant. But I wasn't ready to give him an answer. I liked my job and hadn't been thinking about a promotion, particularly since I considered my superiors to be worthy and knowledgeable people.

Instead, I asked him a question: "Where are you thinking of moving Samoilov?"

"We'll find something for him." Chelomei brushed aside my question. "Don't let that worry you."

---

13. The report disappeared. Evidently Mikoyan destroyed it.

But I tried to insist. It was obvious that Vladimir Nikolayevich hadn't made any decision and was improvising on the fly.

"We'll appoint him head of instrument production. Then he can put your ideas into practice. Anyway, why should you worry about him? I'm not happy with his work; it's time for change. You're much better suited for that job."

I couldn't accept such an outcome. Valery Samoilov had been head of the design unit for many years, he was no worse at his job than the others, and he happened to be my friend. I didn't want to take his place.

But I wasn't about to argue. Whatever I was saying or doing, subconsciously the conversation with Galyukov and his warnings still kept nagging at me.

I thought to myself: I wonder what Chelomei would say if he knew what I know. Would he continue this conversation? Common sense, along with knowledge of how personal relations in our design bureau worked, told me he would not.

"Vladimir Nikolayevich, what's the sense of discussing all this just before my leave? We can continue the conversation when I return, if you don't change your mind," I said.

"I've already thought it through and made my decision. So consider it done. When you get back, we'll issue the necessary orders," Chelomei cut me off. We never returned to the subject again.

Next — vacation. After a short flight, a car brought me to the familiar green gates of the Pitsunda dacha. Inside, everything was as usual. Father was busy with the afternoon mail.

We greeted each other briefly.

"You have some lunch, and in the meantime I'll finish reading this. Then we'll go for a walk," he said, returning to the thin sheets of paper with the red printed heading — decoded ambassadorial reports.

An hour or so later, we went out for a walk along the path by the beach. But first we dropped by the neighboring house to pick up Mikoyan.

I couldn't wait to learn what was going on, but I didn't ask any questions. If I needed to know, they would tell me. Still, I couldn't help interrupting their conversation to say: "I brought the report, Anastas Ivanovich. What should I do with it?"

"Give it to Anastas when we get back," Father answered for him. "Yesterday Vorobyev came down, the secretary of the Krasnodar regional committee. We asked him about all these conversations with Ignatov. He flatly denied everything. It turns out nothing of the sort happened. He assured us that the information from that man — I've forgotten his name — was sheer fantasy. He spent the whole day here. Brought a couple of turkeys as a present, fine-looking ones, too. Drop by the kitchen and take a look."

Considering the matter closed, Father turned to the business of the moment. I was thunderstruck. So all this time they had not only done nothing, but had not even tried to find out whether the information was true or not?!

They'd had a word with Vorobyev. But if he really had been treating with Ignatov, and knew something, he certainly wouldn't tell them anything. What had they expected? A confession that Khrushchev's ouster was being prepared? What was this? Naïveté? How could they be so casual?

Only much later did I understand the sources of my father's behavior. He did not believe, he did not want to believe, that such a turn of events was possible. After all, the people accused had been his friends for decades! If he couldn't trust them, whom could he trust? What's more, my seventy-year-old father was tired, tired beyond measure, both morally and physically. He had neither the strength nor the desire to fight for power. Let everything take its course, I won't interfere, he had obviously decided.

The path was too narrow for the three of us to walk abreast. I dropped back a bit and gave myself over to my gloomy thoughts. It was getting dark and beginning to drizzle.

When we returned to the dacha, Mikoyan said he would go back to his place and would come by after supper. Father had invited him to watch a new film sent down from Moscow.

While they were talking, I ran up to my room and got the folder with the report — even though I no longer knew whether anyone in Pitsunda needed it. Without opening it, Mikoyan tucked it under his arm and went home.

So I had played my part to the end. Now I had to await further developments — if, of course, there were any.

As it turned out, however, one more episode was in store for me that day, although not a very significant one. That evening, after the film, Anastas Ivanovich asked me over to his place. Not knowing what to expect, I followed him there.

Mikoyan was living alone at the dacha. We went up to the second floor and he beckoned me into the bedroom. There he opened a three-drawer wardrobe and, bending down, poked his hand under a large pile of bed linen on the bottom shelf. After searching around for a bit, he pulled my file out from under the linen.

"Everything's recorded correctly. Just add at the end what I said about fully trusting Comrades Podgorny, Brezhnev, and the others — that we have no doubts about their integrity and that we can't conceive of their undertaking separatist action of any sort."

Mikoyan said "we" out of habit, in the name of the Central Committee Presidium. I wasn't surprised.

We went from the bedroom into the dining room, which was just like the one in our dacha. Even the furniture and slipcovers were identical.

"Sit down and write."

I sat down and began to write. Anastas Ivanovich stood next to me, occasionally glancing over my shoulder.

When I had finished, I handed him the document. He read the last paragraph carefully and nodded his approval. He thought for a moment and then gave the sheets back to me.

"Now sign it."

I was astonished, because it wasn't an official document.

"Why?"

"It's better this way. After all, you're the one who recorded the conversation."

I had no grounds for objecting. On the numerous memoranda of conversations which I had read aloud to Father, there was always a note at the bottom saying, "Conversation recorded by so-and-so."

I took the last page and signed.

"Now everything's fine." Anastas Ivanovich neatly put the pages together, placed them in the folder, and silently walked back to the bedroom. I wasn't sure what to do, and after hesitating for a moment, I followed him, also in silence. Mikoyan opened the wardrobe and shoved the folder under a pile of shirts.

Turning around, he caught my look of bewilderment.

"It will be safer here," he explained, somewhat embarrassed. "Besides, that man of yours obviously made up a great deal. Vorobyev denied everything completely yesterday. Some people's suspicions work overtime."

I tried to suggest tactfully that if what Galyukov had said was true, it was not likely that Vorobyev, being deeply involved, would confess at once in the absence of any proof.

"All right, you'd better go home now," replied Mikoyan, clearly not wanting to discuss the matter further.

When I got back, Father had already gone to his room to finish reading the evening batch of official papers.

The morning of October 12 greeted us with clear weather. Low in the sky, the sun radiated a faint warmth. Bright-capped dahlias stood out and other flowers flashed red in the massive stone urns surrounding the house — the last flowers of the retreating summer season.

Galyukov and his warnings weren't mentioned. Mikoyan didn't appear, and after breakfast and a massage, Father settled down comfortably in an armchair on the open terrace of the swimming pool, which was just by the water's edge. Next to him was the wicker worktable with a *V.Ch.* on it.

I sat down next to him. I couldn't help gazing at the sea. The silvery waves lapped against the beach with a slight murmur. We were about ten meters from the edge of the water.

"What have we got there?" Father asked the assistant, who was holding a thick pile of documents from Moscow in one hand. The other hand held a briefcase bulging with papers also waiting their turn — material concerning the new constitution, notes for reports, and draft resolutions needing study.

"Nothing urgent, Nikita Sergeyevich," replied Vladimir Semyonovich Lebedev. Today was his turn to brief Father on the mail.

"All right, we'll have a look in a minute. What's happening with the material on the constitution?"

"We'll be working on your comments in the next few days and then we'll present them." Lebedev smiled politely as usual.

"We've made use of this free time to work on preparing the text of the new constitution," Father explained to me. "They've dragged it out too long. I wanted to have a draft ready for discussion at the November plenum. I've dictated my thoughts, and they're working on them now."

No reply was required from me. I was allowed to listen to the briefing until they got to the secret documents. Then Father would usually say curtly, "Go take a walk."

"Tomorrow you're receiving the French minister of state, Gaston Palevsky. He's flying in this evening," Lebedev reminded him. "Here's the information about him."

"Good, put it down here. Here's how we'll organize it: Bring him over at two o'clock. He and I will have a talk, go for a walk in the park, and then have lunch together," Father said.

Lebedev put the thin paper folder with the information in it on the table. Next to it lay some thick files: a green one with clippings from the foreign press, a red one with decoded ambassadors' reports, and a grayish blue one with papers from various agencies. Vladimir Semyonovich sat down on a chair next to Father and got ready to begin the briefing. Recently, the aides had tended increasingly to read the papers aloud, because Father's sight had worsened and his eyes soon tired. The only documents he read himself were those requiring special attention.

Today Father was in no hurry to get to the mail. It was not an ordinary day. In the morning they were supposed to launch the spaceship *Voskhod* into orbit with a crew of three. Father followed every launching closely. Missile and space technology were his favorites, and he rooted with heart and soul for the success of each new step. He rejoiced with childlike spontaneity when things worked out well, and suffered bitterly through the setbacks. No launchings with cosmonauts on board had ended disastrously, but no one was insured against failures. For this reason, he had forbidden launchings to be scheduled for public holidays, lest an accident should suddenly happen.

"Work calmly, without hurrying. Don't rush to get it done for special celebrations. People should be sent up only after careful preparation," he was always saying to Sergei Korolyov, the head of the Soviet space program.

Father knew the scheduled launch time, and kept glancing at the small rectangular pocket watch given him by the well-known American physicist Leo Szilard. Father prized the watch and took pleasure in demonstrating it to anyone who was willing. The watch was set in a steel case consisting of two halves that could be opened up to reveal the dial. Opening and closing the case wound the watch. Father particularly liked that; he was fond of ingenious technical solutions. He was also flattered that it had been given to him by a world-class celebrity like Szilard.

Father liked to quote what Szilard said as he presented the watch: "I wanted to give you a souvenir that would give you pleasure. It's not a formal gift. The watch is very convenient; I have the same sort myself. It's in a case so it can't be broken, and you don't need to wind it in the morning. It's hard for us older people to wear wristwatches, because they can interfere with the circulation. I hope you will use it."

This warm sincerity really touched Father. It went straight to his heart. Now, sitting in the armchair, he played with the watch, opening and closing the top.

"The launch must have taken place by now," he declared, and looked over at the telephone. It was silent. "It's probably too early for them to have gotten the information."

Immediately after a launch, Leonid Smirnov, the deputy chairman of the Council of Ministers in charge of missile technology, usually telephoned to report the result, followed by Korolyov, and sometimes by Defense Minister Malinovsky. Each wanted to be the first to convey the good news and receive his share of the compliments.

Father himself never called to ask how things were going.

"Let them work in peace. I can't help them, and phone calls from on top only make people nervous; then they begin to hurry, and they might make mistakes. In something like this, there can be no mistakes," he explained.

This time the telephone remained silent for a long time. Father busied himself with his papers but couldn't concentrate. Now and then he glanced at the big white phone. Half an hour passed, forty minutes — the silence became ever more strange.

If everything had gone well, the cosmonauts would have been in orbit long ago. If there had been a delay or an accident, they should have informed him of it.

I felt awful. It was as if they had forgotten Khrushchev, ceased taking him into account, as if no one were interested in his opinion or instructions anymore. There was something sinister about the silent telephone. It gave me a sick feeling in the pit of my stomach. I couldn't help thinking again of Galyukov and the events of the last few weeks.

No, there must be something behind this, I thought.

Apparently the thought had also occurred to Father, for he ordered Lebedev, "Get me Smirnov."

"Smirnov's on the line," Vladimir Semyonovich announced a moment later.

The connection was perfect. Father took the receiver.

"Comrade Smirnov," he began, restraining himself, "what's going on with Korolyov's launch? Why haven't you informed me?"

The irritation could be heard in his voice. Smirnov must have answered that the launch had gone as planned, the cosmonauts were already in orbit and feeling fine.

"Then why didn't you inform me?" The irritation was turning into anger. "You are obliged to report the results to me immediately."

Smirnov must have said that he hadn't had time to call. Of course, he already knew everything and was in no hurry to telephone Father. For him, the change in power had already taken effect. Undoubtedly, such unusual behavior could have put Father on his guard, but what could he do here in Pitsunda?

"What do you mean, you haven't had time? I don't understand you! Your behavior is disgraceful!" raged Father.

Judging from the reaction, Smirnov was half-heartedly trying to justify himself.

"Comrade Smirnov, bear in mind that I demand more efficiency from you! It's your fault that things are getting resolved so slowly!" Father was changing the subject. "At the test range, you were asked to prepare proposals on Korolyov's new missile. The deadline passed long ago, and there are still no proposals! Bear in mind that I am displeased with you!"

Father slammed down the phone. Gradually his anger cooled down. He asked to be put through to Korolyov, whom he congratulated on the latest triumph, wishing his team new successes in the future. Having calmed down, he began to deal with current business.

"Why are you sitting there doing nothing?" he said to me with a grin. "Why don't you read the Tass reports and let Lebedev have a rest."

I opened the thick green file and began reading the Tass summaries of the foreign press. Lebedev tiptoed out. Half an hour later, he returned to say there would soon be a direct link with the spacecraft.

"Nikita Sergeyevich, will you be greeting the cosmonauts?"

"Of course. It will be nice for them and for me, too. Alert Mikoyan. Let him get on the line, too."

"It would be better to arrange the link from the small study, then there's no need to go upstairs. The journalists want to take pictures. Is that all right?" Lebedev asked for formal permission, knowing in advance what the answer would be.

"Of course. Let me know when everything's ready."

Father adored these telephone conversations with the cosmonauts. With childlike ingenuousness, he was enraptured by the technology that made it so easy to talk to a spacecraft from his dacha study. He was proud of these achievements and regarded them as partly his work.

"Let them enjoy themselves up there, let them feel that we're paying attention. It's not so easy to be up there," Father would say when asked to talk to the cosmonauts in space, or to greet them at a celebratory reception in Red Square.

Mikoyan arrived and started discussing some business matter with Father as they waited to be called to the phone. At last, Lebedev appeared and said that everything was ready.

The small study, a room of about fifteen square meters, was next to the dining room on the first floor. The walls were paneled with mahogany. In the corner was a desk, also of mahogany, covered with green baize, and with a battery of phones on it. There were also some leather-upholstered chairs and a sofa with a curved back. The furniture made the room seem cramped. The study doors opened straight onto a large veranda facing the sea.

Previously, the room had been used only to pass through. Recently, it had gotten hard for Father to climb the stairs, but all the phones had been in his study on the second floor. This room had been turned into a small study so that Father could talk to Moscow more conveniently when he was working on the terrace.

In fact, Father didn't like using the new study, preferring to settle down with his papers at the end of the big table in the dining room upstairs, or downstairs in the fresh air. But most of all he liked the open terrace by the pool.

Now the room was packed with newspaper and movie cameramen. Special lights in the corners flooded the room with bright light, and heavy cables extended across the floor. Father and Mikoyan came in through the balcony door. Shutters clicked and the usual pushing and shoving began.

Then the telecommunications officer on duty announced that they would be connected in a minute or two, and without handing over the receiver, stood aside to let Father sit down in an armchair by the desk. Mikoyan sat next to him. Armed with a camera, Lebedev joined the correspondents. I stayed by the door, trying to avoid having my picture taken. The room was packed by now.

"We've got a connection," the communications man announced solemnly.

Father picked up the receiver. Cameras clicked and flashbulbs popped even more brightly. The filming began. The conversation was like all the other conversations with cosmonauts in orbit — mutual congratulations and good wishes mixed with wisecracks.

"I've got Mikoyan next to me here trying to grab the receiver," Father finished.

Anastas Ivanovich picked up the receiver. More congratulations and best wishes for a successful return.

"The spacecraft is moving out of contact," warned the communications man. The greetings were over. Everyone left.

It was time for lunch. We all ate together. After lunch Father stayed in the dining room with his papers and Lebedev sat down next to him. I perched on the sofa with a book.

Something Lebedev said while passing Father a document caught my attention: "This is the explanation Adzhubei wrote."

I put my book down and began listening. Father read the typewritten text silently and then put it to one side.

I wondered what had happened. Not long ago, Adzhubei had visited West Germany as Khrushchev's personal representative. The Adenauer era was over and both countries were cautiously testing the waters for a rapprochement. Adzhubei's trip to Bonn was to serve as one of the steps in this process. He was a convenient figure: a newspaper editor rather than a government official, but still, the premier's son-in-law. Anything said to him was sure to reach the ears of the man for whom the information was intended. Father had high hopes for the visit. If it was successful, he himself planned to pay the West Germans a visit.

Curiosity got the upper hand, and I asked aloud: "What's happened?"

Father raised his head.

"I don't know myself. Word came through intelligence channels that Aleksei talked too much in Bonn. I asked him to write an explanation for the Presidium. Could it be some sort of provocation?"

This, it transpired, is what happened. The results of Soviet soundings aimed at establishing direct contacts between the two countries were of interest to everyone; after all, a détente between the USSR and the Federal Republic of Germany was bound to change the political climate in Europe. Adzhubei's visit attracted particularly intense interest in certain fraternal countries — for them a great deal depended on how relations developed between the USSR and West Germany.

Although leaders of the socialist countries continually exchanged political information, intelligence services in friendly countries followed Adzhubei's every step in Bonn, trying not to miss a single word.

Their diligence was repaid with interest. One of their informants reported that in response to a cautious feeler as to whether or not improved relations between Russia and West Germany would affect the Berlin Wall, Adzhubei allegedly said that when Khrushchev came and saw for himself what good guys the Germans were, the wall would disappear without a trace.

The story sounded suspicious, but our friends reported that the conversation had been recorded. It was a very delicate situation.

Semichastny informed the Presidium about it.

In his explanation, Adzhubei flatly denied everything. Of course, it was conceivable that West German intelligence had fabricated the tape in an effort to drive a wedge between us and East Germany. But if Galyukov's information was accurate, then the notorious tape had arrived just in time. After all, the issue was no longer Adzhubei but Khrushchev, who had entrusted him with such an important and delicate mission.

The truth about this story never came out; after Father's retirement, no one bothered with it anymore. Evidently, the game had been played, and no one had any further need for the Bonn episode.

Evening came on. Another day was drawing peacefully to a close. Father and Mikoyan were strolling leisurely along the path by the sea. Nine hundred meters there, and nine hundred meters back. Behind them, trying not to catch the bosses' eye, followed the security man. It grew dark. The first stars appeared in the gaps between the clouds.

The walk was interrupted by a duty officer who ran up. "Nikita Sergeyevich, Comrade Suslov would like to speak with you on the phone."

They all turned back to the dacha. Father and Mikoyan went into the study where the *V.Ch.* was. I followed them, while the security men stayed outside the house.

Father picked up the receiver. "Yes, Comrade Suslov."

A long pause followed as Mikhail Andreyevich said something.

"I don't understand. What questions? Go ahead and deal with them without me," Father said.

Another pause.

"I'm on vacation. What could be so urgent? I'll be back in two weeks, and we'll discuss it then."

Father's nerves were beginning to show.

"I don't understand any of this! What do you mean, you all 'got together'? We'll be discussing agricultural questions at the November plenum. There'll be plenty of time to talk about everything!"

Suslov continued to insist.

"All right." Father finally gave in. "If it's so urgent, I'll come back tomorrow. But I'll have to find out whether there is a plane. Goodbye." He put down the receiver.

"That was Suslov," he said to Mikoyan. "He claims that all the members of the Presidium have gathered, and that they have some urgent questions concerning agriculture that must be discussed before the plenum. They insist I fly back to Moscow tomorrow. You heard, I wanted to put it off until the end of my vacation, but they don't agree. I'll have to go. Will you come too?"

"Of course."

"Oh well. We'll have to decide what to do about tomorrow's meetings and ask them to get a plane ready. Security!" Father called through the open balcony door.

The security chief appeared.

"We're flying back to Moscow tomorrow. Anastas Ivanovich is coming too. Get in touch with Tsybin" — N. I. Tsybin was Father's personal pilot — "and ask him to get a plane ready. We'll move the meeting with the Frenchman to the morning, talk to him for a half hour, and call off the lunch. After the talk, we'll have a bite to eat and catch the plane. Order the takeoff for about twelve o'clock if the pilots can manage it. That's all."

The security chief turned and disappeared into the trees.

We went back to the path and continued the walk. A painful silence hung in the air.

Father was the first to break it. "You know, Anastas, they haven't got any urgent agricultural problems. I think that call is connected with what Sergei was telling us."

Father sighed, turned around, and noticed that I was behind them. "I wish you'd go and get on with your own business," he said to me.

I dropped back and didn't hear the rest of the conversation. Only later did I learn that Father had told Mikoyan more or less the following: "If I'm the issue, I won't make a fight."

As for me, left alone with my thoughts, I couldn't help thinking: It's begun . . .

WHAT was happening at this moment in Moscow? Firsthand accounts by participants in these events have recently become available. Using the recollections of Semichastny and Shelest, for example, one can reconstruct the activity in Moscow with a reasonable degree of accuracy.[14]

Semichastny was vacationing that autumn in Zheleznovodsk. Pyotr N. Demichev, Central Committee secretary and candidate member of the Presidium, was staying in the same sanatorium, and Shelepin was in nearby Kislovodsk.

They got together quite often, traveled to Dombai and other places, and didn't forget to get in some hunting either.

After spending a whole week together, Shelepin and Demichev hurried back to Moscow, while Semichastny stayed on alone.

Several days later, Shelepin called on the *V.Ch.*, insisting that Semichastny fly back to Moscow immediately.

Vladimir Yefimovich didn't want to break off his vacation, especially since this wasn't the first time he had been summoned, yet the previous times nothing had happened. Brezhnev feared to take the decisive step; and when he learned that Father had gotten word of what was going on, Brezhnev panicked.

Nikolai Grigorievich Yegorychev, who in those years was first secretary of the Moscow city party committee, remembers it this way: "At the beginning of October, Brezhnev himself got scared. He was heading a USSR Supreme Soviet delegation in East Germany when he heard that Khrushchev had some sort of information about the plot. The last thing he wanted to do was return."[15]

Brezhnev managed to come home after all, but he couldn't force himself to act. Endless conversations ensued, and all sorts of scenarios were sorted through, but the result was zero.

That's why Semichastny wanted to know whether this summons was the real thing. Shelepin was adamant: "This time it's on," he snapped.

"Good," replied Semichastny, hesitating no longer, "I'll be in Moscow tomorrow."

The day after this conversation, all the players met at Brezhnev's apartment. Virtually all Presidium members and Central Committee secretaries were present, along with Semichastny. They decided to

---

14. The citations from Shelest on the next few pages are from the unpublished transcript of his interview with V. A. Starkov, the published version of which appears in *Argumenty i fakty*, January 14–20, 1989. Semichastny's recollections as they appear in the remainder of this chapter are taken from the unpublished version of his interview with Starkov published in *Argumenty i fakty*, May 20–26, 1989.

15. See his account in *Ogonyok*, February 4–11, 1989.

contact Khrushchev in Pitsunda and call him back to Moscow; the pretext would be that questions to be taken up at the next Central Committee plenum had to be discussed.

Brezhnev was supposed to make the call, but once again he couldn't bring himself to do it.

"It wasn't easy to talk him into it," says Semichastny, "we practically had to drag him to the phone."

Even so, at the last second Brezhnev balked and Suslov had to make the call. It must be said that Suslov wasn't involved in the plot until the very last minute. Evidently, this was because he belonged neither to the Brezhnev-Podgorny "Ukrainian" group, nor to Shelepin's "youth" faction.

Pyotr Shelest on this point: "Suslov didn't know about it until the very end. When they told him about it, he pursed his lips until they turned blue and sucked in his cheeks.

" 'What are you talking about? That means civil war.' That was all he could say."

Nonetheless, Suslov quickly regained his footing and was calm and unbending in his phone conversation with Father.

Suslov was not the only one to be informed at the very last minute. Kosygin was included at the same time. According to Semichastny:

> When they came to Kosygin about a week before, his first question was: "Where does the KGB stand?"
>
> When they told him that we were on board, he said: "It's fine with me."
>
> As for Malinovsky, he was told with two days to go. By that time, I had already called in the heads of [KGB — ed.] special departments of the Moscow military district. I didn't tell them what was going on; I just warned them: "In the next few days, if as much as one armed soldier on a motorcycle leaves his barracks, whether with a machine gun or anything else . . . , keep in mind, it will cost you your head. . . . You are not to allow anyone to undertake anything without reporting to me."
>
> . . . The minister of defense still knew nothing about it, nor did the military district commander. Yet despite that, everything was ready to go. With only two days to go . . . !!! Can you imagine that?

Back in Pitsunda, we knew nothing about any of this. Father and Mikoyan kept themselves occupied strolling the paths under the pines. I kept to those along the beach.

I glanced at the sea. The silhouette of a warship on the horizon caught my attention. A KGB border-guard patrol boat, I thought to myself automatically. When father was on vacation, his residence was guarded from the sea as well. To the left, a few kilometers from the dacha, a border-guard motor launch was always on duty by the pier of a fish cannery, just in case someone decided to disembark from the sea. No one paid any attention to the launch. We were all used to its being there — it was part of the landscape.

Preoccupied with the telephone conversation, I gazed distractedly at the approaching ship. The swiftly moving contours of warships have always drawn my eye. This time, the patrol boat's behavior was out of the ordinary. Instead of making a wide arc around the bay and then a sharp turn toward the pier, it hugged the coast at a distance of several hundred meters and came to a stop right opposite the dacha. It was too deep to cast anchor there, so the light wind kept turning its bow to the shore. There was no one to be seen on deck. In the evening silence, you could hear the hollow grinding of some sort of machinery.

All this was very unusual, and in the light of recent events — Galyukov's warning and Suslov's phone call — it even looked rather ominous. The head of Father's personal security detail was standing nearby. He presumably would know everything.

I went up to him and pointed to the black silhouette. "What's it doing there?"

"I don't know. We asked the border guard, and they said the ship had come on orders from Semichastny. I demanded that they move it to its usual place. It's not supposed to be here. It's supposed to be by the pier."

It grew dark quickly. The blackness of the night swallowed up the sinister silhouette. Only the yellowish dots of the portholes shone brightly.

A little later the ship came to life, some commands were shouted out, and there was a ringing and banging. Gradually, as if against its will, the patrol boat moved off toward the pier. But instead of mooring there, it stopped a little way off, its bow turned seaward.

Why this ship arrived in the first place we never found out. No one cared about this minor detail in the turbulent stream of events that ensued. Surely no one could have thought that Father would decide to swim to Turkey, or descend with a landing force on Sukhumi.

Still, the grimness of the black silhouette against the serenity of the sea etched itself on my mind. It fit perfectly with the feeling of all-pervasive anxiety. "Everything is in our hands," it seemed to say.

Whether Father noticed the ship or not no one knows. Naturally, it didn't occur to anyone to ask him.

After walking for about an hour, Father and Mikoyan each went back to his house. I returned to the dacha too. Father was standing by a small table in the corner of the dining room, drinking mineral water. He looked tired and distraught.

"Don't pester me," he warned, seeing that I was about to ask a question.

Finishing his drink, he stood for a while with the glass in his hand, then put it down carefully on the table, turned, and walked slowly toward his bedroom. "Good night," he said, without turning around.

I very much wanted to talk to someone about what had happened, to ask advice. I couldn't keep everything I knew bottled up in my mind any longer. Something had to be done. Obviously, no one but Father could take any action, least of all me. I was connected with none of the political actors. But I needed to have at least the illusion of doing something.

Father didn't want to talk to me, nor did I expect him to. In his eyes, I was a boy, and on matters of this importance you don't ask a boy's advice. I knew my place. I had turned twenty-nine that year, clearly too young to aspire to the role of adviser to the head of government. At least, too young by our standards.

I didn't want to talk with the assistants or with security. I had no idea how much they knew or what role they were playing in all this. All the more so since Lebedev had a long-standing reputation as a right-winger and Suslov's man.[16]

I began roaming around the rooms of the dacha. I wandered into

16. As I've mentioned, this turned out not to be true. When the crunch came, Lebedev showed himself to be sincerely dedicated to Khrushchev's cause, and to Father personally. He didn't yield on anything and as a result was fired from the Central Committee. He soon fell gravely ill, and died shortly thereafter. Shuisky, on the other hand, whom no one had doubted, turned out (as I've already indicated) to have been informed, but kept the information from Father. He was rewarded for this by being allowed to keep his job at the Central Committee, where he survived peacefully until it was time to retire.

Lebedev's room. He was silently packing papers into large briefcases. He looked dismayed. We exchanged a few meaningless phrases: It was very inconvenient to leave now, Nikita Sergeyevich hadn't had time to get a good rest, and he was very tired. As if by prearrangement, we avoided the real subject. I hesitated by the door for a bit, but then left.

The idea of phoning Sergo Mikoyan flashed through my mind. He was my old friend — him I could tell everything. All the more so, because Anastas Ivanovich was directly involved. I should warn Sergo about what was going on.

I realized that Sergo couldn't do anything. He was as helpless as I. But two heads are better than one. I went into the small study, picked up the *V.Ch.*, and asked to be connected with Mikoyan's apartment in Moscow. Sergo turned out to be home. I told him that Father and Anastas Ivanovich were flying to Moscow the next day on some urgent business that had arisen.

"I hope very much you can meet me," I said. "I've got to talk to you." Obviously, I was afraid to give him the slightest scrap of information over the phone.

Sergo promised, but that didn't mean anything. Eternally busy, he was always late for meetings, if indeed he turned up at all. We were all used to it.

I repeated: "You've got to meet me."

"Yes, yes, of course," he said gaily.

I put down the receiver and went to bed.

I was not the only one whom Suslov's call had upset. As Semichastny's account reveals, Brezhnev, too, had trouble finding his footing.

> Brezhnev kept calling me every hour. "What's happening?" he kept asking.
>
> Why me? Because Khrushchev was supposed to order his plane through me, through my people.
>
> It wasn't until twelve o'clock at night that the duty officer called me and said that Pitsunda had ordered a plane for six the next morning.[17] The plane had to be there at six.

17. *Editor's note:* If the plane was ordered early in the evening, as recounted by Sergei Khrushchev, then why did Semichastny learn of it only at midnight? Was there a delay in giving the order, or in reporting it to Semichastny? If the former, did Khrushchev have second thoughts about returning to Moscow the next day? Sergei Khrushchev's reply: "I too am amazed that it took so long for the information to reach Semichastny.

I called him [Brezhnev] immediately and told him. Only then did we all feel somewhat relieved.

Yes, relieved. Because all of them — the cowardly Brezhnev, the dry, cautious Suslov, the sensible Kosygin, and the self-assured Shelepin — all feared Khrushchev, each in his own way.

Semichastny again: "He had crushed the likes of Malenkov and Molotov — all of them. As the saying goes, nature and his mama provided him with everything he needed: firmness of will, quick-wittedness, . . . a capacity for fast, careful thinking. When I went in to brief him, I had to be prepared for anything. With Lyonya, I could do it with my eyes closed. All I had to do was tell a couple of jokes and that was it."

They all expected Khrushchev to take fast and determined retaliatory action. The silence from Pitsunda scared them. It never occurred to them that Father had gone to bed.

They kept demanding detailed information from Semichastny, along with guarantees. But he didn't have much to report.

"I . . . was told," Semichastny recalls, "that Mikoyan would be flying with Khrushchev. Fine . . . I took that in. I . . . didn't know how much security he would have with him. If he thought it through, he might think up something new. Malinovsky had already been spoken to, so that he [Khrushchev] would be in no position to command the troops as commander in chief. Therefore, even if the worst happened, we'd be able to drag him back to Moscow."

Such were the dramatic goings-on that night of October 12 in Moscow on Kutuzovsky Prospekt [where Brezhnev's apartment was located — ed.] and at Lubyanka.

The morning of October 13 — the last morning of "the glorious Khrushchev decade" — dawned warm and calm. The sun shone through a light mist, the sea lapped against the shore, and the garden was bright with flowers.

The daily routine was not broken either. Outwardly, Father was absolutely calm. At breakfast, he joked as usual with the woman waiting on table, and complained about his diet. Then he started to confer with his assistants about the day's business.

After breakfast, Father looked through his papers, although this was no longer necessary either for him or for those who had sent them.

Perhaps there was a delay in transmitting it. The delay was not at Khrushchev's end. He had no intention of delaying his departure."

But the habit of many years demanded that the ritual be performed. Only one thing was out of the ordinary — the telephone was silent.

The security chief reported that the plane was ready, with takeoff scheduled for 1:00 P.M. Father merely nodded.

Meanwhile, the wicker chairs were being arranged on the open terrace by the pool, and fruits and mineral water set out — all to be ready for the French guest's arrival.

I had nothing to do, and I couldn't sit still, so I went down to the sea. The beach was empty. In the distance, yesterday's patrol boat loomed by the pier.

Father was sitting on the terrace by the pool, where the reception would take place, lazily leafing through some papers. His assistants were off to one side, meaningless phrases wafting back and forth between them.

At last, a group of unfamiliar people appeared on the path. Father had already noticed them. He rose unhurriedly, took his jacket, which was draped over the back of a chair, and set off to meet them with the smile of a cordial host.

Usually, before the start of official talks, he would introduce the guests to family members vacationing with him, show them the grounds, and only then invite them to get down to business. Now he didn't even look in my direction.

Continuing to smile, he shook hands with the guest, the interpreter, and others who were accompanying Palevsky, and with a gesture, invited them onto the terrace. Lebedev moved among them, making sure that everything was in order, then sat down in case he should be needed.

The conversation was a short one. Less than half an hour later, the guests had left and Father had gone into the dacha.

The last official reception of his life was over. It was time to get ready to leave for Moscow. The luggage had already been taken to the airport.

A light lunch was served — vegetable soup and boiled perch. Father had recently been keeping to his diet on doctors' orders.[18] We ate in silence, joined at the table by the assistants and Father's personal physician, Vladimir Grigorievich Bezzubik.

It was a farewell lunch, farewell to the dacha that Father loved so much, to the pine trees and the sea. All farewells are sad, and in this

18. Khrushchev's diet had been prescribed in connection with his age, rather than any illness. It emphasized light, boiled food.

case the future was completely uncertain as well. When lunch ended, it was time to go.

As usual, the linen-keeper whom we referred to as the "owner" of the dacha was waiting on the porch with a big bouquet of autumn flowers. She always met and bade good-bye to her high-ranking guests in this way. We were used to it, but today it all seemed different, more meaningful.

"Good-bye, Nikita Sergeyevich. What a pity you had such a short rest. Come again." Pronouncing the customary phrase, she handed him the bouquet.

Father thanked her for the flowers and, passing them to his security chief, who was standing beside him, sat down in the front seat of the ZIL. The car moved off, then stopped at the gates. The sentry on the left snapped to attention. Outside the gate, a man rushed up to the car.

"Stop the car," Father ordered.

His bodyguard opened the back door.

"Commander of the Transcaucasian military district," the somewhat out of breath general introduced himself. "May I accompany you, Nikita Sergeyevich?"

"Have a seat," said Father indifferently.

The corpulent general squeezed into the fold-down seat in the back. "Please excuse me, Nikita Sergeyevich. Vasily Pavlovich Mzhavanadze is in Moscow, on vacation in Barvikha, and Comrade Dzhavakhishvili is on a district inspection tour. We didn't expect you to leave and were unable to inform him in time," the general began apologizing.

"And a good thing, too. Let him do his work. There was no need for you to come, either," Father growled. "But as long as you did, you might as well stay." He stopped the general, who was about to get out, and the car drove off.

When Father came down on vacation, he was usually met and seen off by the Georgian first secretary, Mzhavanadze, and the chairman of the Georgian Council of Ministers, Givi D. Dzhavakhishvili. Father always muttered at them: "I'm the one who's on vacation, but you're just wasting working time. We'll write you up for absenteeism." But he wasn't really angry, and the tradition of meeting and seeing him off was preserved.

Mzhavanadze used to joke back: "We'll work it off by doing overtime."

This time they were not there. It had nothing to do with the suddenness of the departure, but that explanation looked convincing enough. Both of them — Mzhavanadze and Dzhavakhishvili — had evidently already gone to Moscow to take part in events to come. The general was to compensate for the awkwardness of the situation, and at the same time make sure that Father and Mikoyan actually left.

On the way, the general informed the visitors as to the state of agriculture in Georgia. Father was silent; it wasn't clear whether he was listening or was preoccupied with his own thoughts.

Finally, we arrived at the airport. The ZIL rolled up to the aircraft. The crew lined up along the stairway leading up to the plane, and Father's personal pilot, General Tsybin, reported as usual: "The aircraft is ready for takeoff! There are no anomalies. Weather en route is good."

His broad face broke into a smile. Father shook his hand and walked lightly up the stairway. Mikoyan followed him.

They both went into the rear cabin. In the government version, the rear cabin of the IL-18 had no passenger seats; they had been replaced by a small table, a sofa, and two broad chairs. This was the quietest place on the plane.

Father didn't like to be alone, and during flights his traveling companions always gathered round in the tail. He would discuss some matter with his assistants, edit the stenographic accounts of his speeches, or just talk.

This time it was different. "Leave the two of us alone," he ordered curtly.

We were now in the air. The plane was half empty. In the forward cabin were aides to both the premier and the president, along with security men and stenographers. The businesslike Lebedev opened his immense briefcase and dug around among the numerous folders. You needed an exceptional memory to find your way around the morass of papers.

The stewardess took a tray with Armenian cognac, mineral water, and snacks to the rear cabin but returned a minute later. It was no time for that.

Everyone was busy with his own affairs. For most of them, it was a routine flight. They'd often traveled with Father, both all over our country and abroad.

Back in the rear cabin, closed off from all the others, the two men worked out their course of action, weighing their options, trying to guess what awaited them at Vnukovo 2 airport.

A warm reception? Hardly . . .

A ring of troops around the airport? Even less likely. Those times had passed. But something awaited them, that was for certain.

The future depended on decisions reached here and now in the vibrating cabin. Not only their personal future, but the future of the country, the future of the cause to which these two elderly men had dedicated their whole lives.

The plane began its descent. You could already make out individual trees on the ground. At last, a gentle bump. A perfect landing, as usual. How many years had Nikolai Ivanovich Tsybin been flying Father? Someday one would have to count them. During the war in the Douglases, in any kind of weather, then in the Ukraine, and from Moscow to all corners of the planet.

The plane taxied up to the government pavilion at Vnukovo 2. A final roar from the engines, then silence. Down below there was nobody. The tarmac in front of the plane was empty except for two small figures looming up in the distance. You couldn't make out who they were from the plane. Not a good sign.

In recent years the whole gang of Presidium members had come to see off and meet Father. He would feign a frown and dismiss them as "idlers," muttering, "Do you think I don't know the way without you?" but it was clear that these meetings pleased him.

Now there was nobody down there.

The stairway was rolled up slowly. The mysterious figures also approached behind it. Now you could make them out — KGB chairman Semichastny and the head of the security administration, Vladimir Chekalov. Behind them Mikhail Georgadze, secretary of the USSR Supreme Soviet Presidium, was hurrying toward the plane.

Father thanked the stewardess for a pleasant flight and was the first to descend the stairs. The others trooped after him.

Semichastny approached and greeted Father politely but coolly: "Glad you've arrived safely, Nikita Sergeyevich."

Then he shook hands with Mikoyan.

Chekalov was two paces to the rear, standing stiffly at attention. On duty. His face was tense.

Semichastny leaned over to Father and said quietly, as if in confidence: "They've all gathered at the Kremlin. They're waiting for you." Obviously, the parts had been written down to the last detail.

Father turned to Mikoyan and said calmly, almost lightheartedly, "Let's go, Anastas."

He stopped for a moment, looking around for someone. He didn't notice me. Catching sight of Tsybin, he smiled, stepped toward him, and shook his hand, thanking him for the flight. The ritual had been completed.

Finally, after a nod to his fellow passengers, he and Mikoyan walked quickly toward the pavilion. Semichastny followed a bit behind them, then I, with Chekalov completing the procession. He walked a few meters behind, as if cutting us off from everything left on the plane.

We walked through the empty glass-walled pavilion, our footsteps echoing. Security men stood at attention in the far corners. The duty officer obligingly opened the large glass door.

Opposite the door on the pavement stood a long ZIL-111, Father's limousine. More black cars were drawn up in the square: the bodyguards' ZIL, Mikoyan's and Semichastny's Chaikas, and some Volgas.

Khrushchev and Mikoyan got into one car. The head of security slammed the door and got in the front seat. The car sped off and disappeared around the bend. The other cars took off after it. Semichastny ran up and leapt into his braking Chaika. Chekalov dashed past me.

"Can I give you a lift?"

"No thanks. Someone should be meeting me."

"Good-bye, then."

He literally dove into his Volga and was carried away to the sound of screaming brakes as they hurtled round the curve.

Here's what Semichastny himself has to say about the airport arrival:

> In the morning I call Leonid Ilyich. "Who's going to go to meet him?" I ask.
>
> "No one. You go by yourself," he replies.
>
> "How can that be?" I stammer.
>
> "Under the current circumstances," he said slowly, "why should everyone go?" On the whole, he was right. . . .
>
> "But won't he catch on?" I asked a little worriedly.
>
> "Just take some security and go," said Brezhnev, ending the conversation.
>
> I took a fellow from the Ninth [Directorate]. I took my pistol and so did he.
>
> Interviewer: Were you worried?
>
> Semichastny: No. . . . Knowing Khrushchev, I was convinced that he wouldn't opt for a confrontation. You have to

understand: crazy moves weren't his style. I was just taking extra precautions.[19]

The plane landed, and he comes out frowning. He gets in a car with Mikoyan. I follow the security car. There's one bodyguard sitting up front next to my driver. . . . The others [Khrushchev's bodyguards in the car up ahead] keep turning their heads around: the fact that I also had a security man sitting up front with me was unusual and put them on guard.

Halfway from Vnukovo to Moscow, I tell my driver: "Slow down. Stop by the edge of the road. Let them go ahead." I had a phone in the car. I called in and said. . . ."

So much for Semichastny's recollection. Meanwhile, I was alone at the airport. Everything had happened very fast.

Sergo was nowhere to be seen. Not on the tarmac, nor here. All my emphatic requests hadn't had the slightest effect. I was hurt. I really needed him now. I hoped he was at home.

I got into a car, and the excitement of the last few minutes eased a bit. It was as if nothing had happened.

We drove along familiar streets. The sidewalks were full of people, all lapping up the last warm days. Vorobyovskoe Highway was straight ahead. On the right, our massive yellow stone wall appeared. I asked the driver to stop at Mikoyan's gateway. I just had to find Sergo.

I was lucky. He was tinkering with something on the second floor. Smiling his familiar, slightly guilty smile, Sergo said: "I forgot, you see. And then it was too late. I knew you'd have a car. So everything's all right, isn't it?"

"Put down what you're doing. I've got something important to tell you. Let's go outside," I said.

Everyone knows that the walls have ears and that you mustn't talk inside. As a matter of fact, at that moment I wasn't thinking about being

---

19. *Editor's note:* This statement seems to clash with Semichastny's testimony quoted earlier, from which Sergei Khrushchev draws the conclusion that "they all expected Khrushchev to take fast and determined retaliatory action." When I put the contradiction to Sergei Khrushchev, he replied: "I'm simply quoting Semichastny. All I can do is provide some commentary. He believed that Khrushchev might take lawful measures, or make use of his authority as commander in chief, but would not do anything stupid, such as employing his personal security men (though I can't really imagine for what)."

overheard; the idea didn't enter my mind. It would just be better to talk out in the fresh air.

"Let's go," he agreed readily.

The houses stood one behind the other. Mikoyan's was number 34, ours number 40. You could walk through the yards, bypassing the street, but then you had to get the keys to the gate. It was easier to go along the street.

I began my account with the conversation with Galyukov, and finished with the arrival at Vnukovo, trying not to omit any details. Gradually, I got carried away, and even began to feel as if I were talking about some stranger who had nothing to do with me. The anxiety that had built up over the last few days seemed less sharp. Now we both knew the painful chain of events.

But what was happening now? We could only guess. No one knew what was going on in the Kremlin.

Walking along, we sorted out the possibilities. I suddenly thought of calling Adzhubei. After all, he was chief editor of *Izvestia*. Perhaps he knew something. In any case, it would give us the illusion of doing something. We decided not to go into the house, so as not to involve our families. There was no need to trigger a panic unnecessarily. We went into the guardhouse and dialed Adzhubei's number. We were calling on a government phone, and he answered it himself.

When he heard it was I, Adzhubei said he was very busy and couldn't possibly come over.

I tried to persuade him. Adzhubei replied ever more sharply and irritably.

I didn't want to tell him on the phone what was the matter, especially with the duty officer hearing every word. Nevertheless, I said: "Father and Anastas Ivanovich have been called back from Pitsunda to an emergency meeting in the Kremlin. Sergo and I are worried. We don't know what's going on. We wanted to ask you."

Adzhubei didn't know anything.

"Call back in ten minutes," he said. "I'll try to find out."

Ten minutes later, his voice had changed beyond recognition. No one had told him anything. All the Kremlin duty officer said was that a Presidium meeting was indeed in progress. He didn't know the agenda.

"Sergo and I don't know anything for certain, but we have some ideas. Come to the house if you can," I asked him.

Adzhubei evidently had no more important affairs of state. "I'll be right over," he muttered, and he arrived twenty minutes later.

I repeated my story once more. Adzhubei began to phone around. Dmitry Goryunov, the general director of Tass, knew nothing; Semichastny wasn't in his office at the KGB; Shelepin was at a meeting; and Grant Grigoryan, deputy business manager of the Central Committee, also didn't know anything.

Adzhubei drooped. It was clear he could be of no further use to us, that there was no point consulting with him further.

Meanwhile, Father and Mikoyan had arrived at the Kremlin without incident and had entered the Presidium meeting room. As soon as the door closed behind them, events developed with head-spinning speed.

Again, Semichastny:

> As soon as they arrived at the Kremlin and entered the room, I changed the guard in the reception area. I also replaced the security men in the apartment and the dacha. I had already managed to send [Khrushchev's] security chief off on leave.
>
> In his place I put a young kid. I grabbed him in the Kremlin corridor and told him: "Listen! A meeting of the Presidium has just begun. Anything may happen. I am speaking for the Presidium and the Central Committee. As a Communist, you must understand the situation correctly. Your future depends on it. Keep this in mind: not a single command, not a single order, not a single instruction is to be carried out without my approval. I forbid you to deviate from my instructions!!!"

Obviously, Semichastny had in mind possible orders given by Father. But none were forthcoming. The young guard did not have to choose.

As for us, we didn't even notice that the guards at the gate had been replaced. It was all done in seemingly routine fashion.

Semichastny's testimony continues:

> I didn't even close the Kremlin to visitors. People were strolling around outside, while . . . in the room the Presidium was meeting. I deployed my men around the Kremlin. Everything that was necessary was done.
>
> Brezhnev and Shelepin were nervous.

I told them: "Let's not do anything that isn't necessary.
Let's not create the appearance of a coup."

Time passed, and we learned nothing until evening. Sergo went
home. I walked aimlessly around the house, although my feet ached
with fatigue.

Father came home around eight. The car dropped him right at the
gate as usual. He set off to walk along the path by the wall — his regular route. I caught up with him. We walked several paces in silence. I
didn't ask him anything. He looked distraught and very tired.

"Everything happened just the way you said it would," he began.

"Are they demanding that you give up all your posts?" I asked.

"So far, only one of them, but that doesn't mean anything. This is
just the beginning. We should be ready for anything."

Father paused. "Don't ask any questions. I'm tired, and I have to
think."

We walked on in silence. We went all along the wall once, then
started around again. Suddenly he asked: "Are you a doctor?"

I was dumbfounded. "What do you mean, a doctor?"

"A doctor of science?"

"No, I have just a candidate's degree."

"Forget it."

Again silence. We made another round, then Father turned toward
the house. At the sound of the door closing, Adzhubei came into the
hall. His eyes posed the cold, unspoken question: What's happened?

Father nodded to him without saying anything and began to climb
the stairs to his second-floor bedroom. He asked for tea to be brought
up to him. No one dared disturb him.

We phoned Sergo. He appeared a few minutes later but had even
less information. Anastas Mikoyan had come home and had gone for
a walk with academician Anushavan Arzumanyan, director of the Academy of Sciences Institute of the World Economy. Sergo didn't know
what they were talking about.

Sergo suggested waiting until Arzumanyan left and then going to
see him. He and Mikoyan were probably talking about the events of
the day. Again we had to wait. Sergo went home. Time dragged im-
possibly slowly.

Adzhubei tried to call Shelepin at home. No one answered. He tried
his dacha. No answer there either. Attempts to call Polyansky and

someone else were also unsuccessful. Only several days later did I learn
that after Father left, all the members of the Presidium agreed not to
answer the phone, in case Khrushchev started calling around, trying to
win them over to his side.

Nonetheless, Brezhnev still felt insecure. He called Semichastny,
who was not a member of the Presidium, again in the evening: "Volodya, the meeting just ended. Khrushchev is leaving. Where is he
headed?"

"To his apartment."

"But what if he heads for his dacha?"

"Let him go to his dacha."

"What will you do in that case?"

"I've got everything ready, here, there, everywhere. We've anticipated everything."

"What if he phones? What if he calls in help?"

"He's got no place to call. The whole communications system is in
my hands! . . . I've got the Kremlin lines, and the *V.Ch*. If he wants
to use the regular city phone, let him."

Father had been effectively isolated.

Sergo arrived again at about ten o'clock with word that Arzumanyan had gone home. The three of us — Sergo, Adzhubei, and I — hurried out, jumped in my car, and raced through the gate. I crossed
Vorobyovskoe Highway at top speed and turned left. Out of the darkness of the trees, a man rushed toward the car, but I tore by him. He
didn't try to stop us, just stared intently after us. His job was to take
note of our license number.

We headed for Leninsky Prospekt. Arzumanyan lived there in a
large academy apartment house. We were too excited even to check
whether we were being followed. We arrived without incident and
parked the car. Now we had to find the right entrance. The sidewalks
were deserted, except for two men with that characteristic look about
them hanging around at the corner. We walked past them. They didn't
block our way, just looked us over carefully.

Anushavan Arzumanyan wasn't surprised by the lateness of our
visit. He, too, was upset by the news and felt a need to talk. We sat
down around the dining room table. The room was dimly lit by a lamp
with a heavy cloth shade.

No one knew where to begin. Sergo, who felt at home here, broke
the silence. He quickly recounted what we knew about what had been

going on, and said we were very anxious to know what was actually said at today's meeting.

"Anastas Ivanovich asked me to keep our conversation secret," Arzumanyan said hesitantly, "but I can tell you. The situation is very serious. Various charges have been made against Nikita Sergeyevich, and members of the Presidium are demanding his removal. The meeting had been carefully prepared: everyone but Mikoyan formed a united front. They lay various sins at Khrushchev's door: the unsatisfactory state of agriculture, disrespect for other Presidium members, contempt for their opinions, and many other things. But that isn't the main thing. Nikita Sergeyevich has made quite a few mistakes, but so has everyone else."

We all nodded in agreement. Adzhubei interrupted the silence: "Tell us, what was said at the meeting about me?"

Arzumanyan looked up in astonishment: "About you? Nothing was said about you. The issue now is not Nikita Sergeyevich's mistakes, but the line he personifies and is pursuing. If he goes, the Stalinists may come to power, and who knows what will happen then. We must fight, and not allow them to oust Khrushchev. I'm afraid it isn't going to be easy. But we can't just sit here with our hands folded; we've got to try to do something."

His words inspired hope: Father was not alone.[20] After all, in 1957 a majority in the Presidium had also demanded his removal, but the Central Committee plenum had decided otherwise. This time, however, everything suggested such hopes were in vain. The experience of 1957 had been taken into account, and the mass of Central Committee members were unhappy with many of Khrushchev's innovations.

We stayed at Arzumanyan's for more than an hour. We wanted to know as much as possible about everything, but Arzumanyan himself didn't know very much. The main charges against Father are now known. They reflected different approaches to leadership of the economy. For example, Khrushchev campaigned to get management as close to the production process as possible. To this end, he insisted on introducing a decentralized territorial system of management in the form of the regional economic councils. He proceeded from the fact that local

20. *Editor's note:* What gave Sergei Khrushchev hope if the words were just Arzumanyan's and not even Mikoyan's opinion? His answer: "In my mind I understood that nothing would change. But in his heart a man hopes against hope. In fact, Arzumanyan couldn't do anything except cheer us up a bit."

leaders knew better the needs and potential of their regions and would be able to resolve whatever questions arose more effectively. The ministries, for the most part transformed into state committees, should only see to it that basic principles of state policy were observed in their bailiwick. He proposed splitting the regional party committees into industrial and agricultural bodies because here too he felt that leaders should be closer to production, and because the economy had become more complex, and it was harder to find people who had an equally good knowledge of industry and agriculture.

A number of other controversial decisions had also been taken. Naturally, all of them were first discussed and then approved by both the Presidium and the Central Committee.[21]

But instead of expressing their views openly, the supporters of centralized administration of the economy secretly opposed the innovations. Only now had these differences burst into the open and become the subject of the most heated sort of debate.

The charge that Khrushchev had undervalued other Presidium members, behaved tactlessly toward them, and disdained their views was a serious one. All this concerned relations among people in the highest party organ, and it was hard for the uninitiated to judge how true and well founded the accusation was. All sorts of things get said in the heat of debate. Nevertheless, there was probably quite a bit of truth in the charge: I myself had frequently seen Father reprimand this or that member of the Presidium in front of other people for negligence on issues for which they were responsible.[22]

Other charges were also true but, to my mind, not really matters of principle and hence were unworthy of serious dispute. There were lots of them. I'll give only a few examples.

21. *Editor's note:* Other sources have raised questions as to how free and open such discussions actually were. It has been reported, for example, that Khrushchev usually spoke first at Presidium sessions, thus making clear his own preferences and discouraging full and frank debate. Asked about this, Sergei Khrushchev replied: "I think your sources are correct. Of course, Khrushchev dominated the others, so that the kind of open discussion that occurs today was impossible. But my point is this: that the decisions taken were not Khrushchev's alone, but were taken by the very body whose members now indicted him. They themselves had voted for these decisions."

22. *Editor's note:* Doesn't this contradict the author's recollection in chapter one that he never heard his father shout at his colleagues or aides? Sergei Khrushchev's answer: "There is no contradiction. The reprimands were delivered without raising his voice. Still, the fact that he spoke to them as one would to subordinates, and did so in front of other people, was offensive."

In his attempt to bring management closer to production, Father had persisted in trying to move the Ministry of Agriculture out of Moscow. Part of the plan was to force ministry officials to cultivate experimental plots of land virtually with their own hands.

Then there was the granting of the title Hero of the Soviet Union to President Nasser of the United Arab Republic, and Vice President Amer, which provoked great displeasure all over the country.

There are many more examples. And although all the decisions were taken collectively by the Presidium, Khrushchev was rightly considered their author. Now all these accusations rained down upon his head, as from a horn of plenty. Everyone remembered grievances, old or new.

Some of the charges were trumped up, although they look convincing enough to the uninitiated. For example, Father was accused of having taken his wife or children with him on visits abroad at state expense. However, Presidium members knew perfectly well that Khrushchev had not taken the lead in this matter. The idea came from the Ministry of Foreign Affairs, supported by an "expert on the West," Anastas Mikoyan, who had traveled all over the world before the war. The argument was that this was the way it was done in the West, and that the presence of family members made the visit less formal, the atmosphere more relaxed. It cost our state nothing since the host country paid local costs on state visits, and there were always plenty of seats on the plane. Nevertheless, the charge looked convincing, and it subsequently received a lot of publicity.

Arzumanyan told us that Shelepin and Shelest had been the most outspoken at the meeting. On behalf of those present, Shelepin had listed Father's mistakes, lumping them all together — matters of principle along with nonsense.

"Incidentally," Arzumanyan turned to me, "Shelepin said that you got a doctor of science degree without defending a thesis."

"So that was what it was all about," I exclaimed without thinking.

They turned to look at me.

"Father asked today whether I had a doctorate. I couldn't understand why he was asking. I started to explain to him that I defended my candidate's thesis three years ago, and what the difference is between a candidate and doctor of science. Now I can see where his question came from. The charge is sheer invention. I haven't even thought of writing a doctoral thesis yet."

The lie was a petty one, but it really upset me. For Shelepin had invariably demonstrated if not friendship, then a clear disposition to be friendly. Frequently, he was the first to call with best wishes on holidays, and he always took a lively interest in my successes. In this respect, he stood out among his colleagues, who treated me solely as their comrade's son and nothing more. Naturally, I was flattered by this friendly attitude from a Central Committee secretary, although deep down I felt uncomfortable and sensed a certain insincerity on his part. But I tried to repress this feeling and not let it develop. And now this undisguised treachery. He certainly was prepared to use any means.

"Voronov behaved particularly crudely," Arzumanyan went on. "He didn't hold back. When Nikita Sergeyevich referred to members of the Presidium as his friends, Voronov cut him off, shouting, 'You have no friends here.' "

This remark even drew a reproof from Viktor Grishin, a candidate member of the Presidium. "You're wrong," he said. "We're all Nikita Sergeyevich's friends."

The rest of them spoke with more restraint, and Brezhnev, Podgorny, and Kosygin didn't speak at all. Mikoyan proposed that Khrushchev be relieved of the duties of first secretary of the Central Committee while retaining the post of chairman of the Council of Ministers. But this idea was rejected.

It was late, so we took our leave. All we could do was wait for the next day. Arzumanyan's words had somewhat reassured us, while inspiring some illusory hopes.

We didn't know at the time that Father had already decided to retire without a struggle. Late that evening, he called Mikoyan and said that if they wanted to relieve him of all his positions, he would not object.

"I'm old and tired. Let them cope by themselves. I've done the main thing. Relations among us, the style of leadership, has changed drastically. Could anyone have dreamed of telling Stalin that he didn't suit us anymore, and suggesting that he retire? Not even a wet spot would have remained where we had been standing. Now everything is different. The fear's gone and we can talk as equals. That's my contribution. I won't put up a fight."

Our phone was bugged, and his words instantaneously became known to his opponents. But we knew nothing of this.

The whole morning of October 14 was spent in exhausting expectation. At last, the duty officer in Father's Kremlin reception room called to say Father was on his way home.

Normally, he never came home during the day but saved time by lunching in the Kremlin. I met the car at the gate.

Father thrust his black briefcase into my hands and sighed. "It's over . . . I'm retired . . ."

After a brief pause, he added: "Didn't want to have lunch with them."[23]

It was all over. A new stage in life had begun. What lay ahead, no one knew. Only one thing was clear: nothing depended on us. There was nothing to do but wait.

"I wrote the statement myself, asking to be relieved for reasons of health. Now the decision has to be ratified by the plenum. I said I would submit to discipline and would carry out whatever decisions the Central Committee adopts. I also said I would live where they tell me to, in Moscow or elsewhere."

Father didn't say what else happened at the meeting, and I didn't want to upset him by asking. Only years later did I learn some details.

The minutes of the Presidium meetings of October 13 and 14, 1964, are said to have disappeared. Apparently, they were destroyed to preclude examination in the future. But materials pertaining to the hastily scheduled Central Committee plenum that took place at 6:00 P.M. on October 14, 1964, have evidently been preserved.

Fortunately, fragments of notes that Pyotr Yefimovich Shelest took on the fly during the Presidium meeting have also survived.[24] "Khrushchev was dispirited and isolated," Shelest recalls. "He was helpless to undertake any action, yet still found the strength and courage to say:

" 'Thank you for at least saying something positive about my role. I'm glad for the Presidium, glad to see it manifest its maturity. I like to think that I had a tiny bit to do with developing that maturity.' "

Shelest's notes go on: "And thus speaks a man who has just endured two days of a searing indictment who finds himself in the most difficult situation one can imagine, both morally and physically."

"The party brought up and educated all of us, including me," Father continued, according to Shelest's account of his final speech.

---

23. As a rule, members of the Presidium lunched together. This had become something of a tradition. Urgent issues were often discussed during these collective lunches, and important decisions were made.

24. In his interview with Starkov, Shelest quotes directly from his notes. In the pages that follow, I quote from those passages as they appear in the unpublished transcript of the interview.

"We owe our political situation to it and it alone. You and I stand on common political and ideological ground, so I cannot fight you. I'll step down; I don't intend to fight. I ask you to forgive me if I ever offended anyone, if I allowed myself to behave rudely. All sorts of things happen in the course of one's work. I just want to say that some of the accusations made against me I categorically reject. I can't remember all the charges, nor will I try to answer them. I'll just say one thing: my main failing, my main weakness is being too good, too trusting, and perhaps also that I myself didn't notice my own failings. But you, all of you present here, didn't tell me openly and honestly about my shortcomings. Instead, you always yessed me; you supported all my proposals. You yourselves were too weak and unprincipled. You charge me with having combined the posts of first secretary of the Central Committee and chairman of the Council of Ministers. But let's be objective about it. I didn't combine them all by myself. Remember, the decision was made collectively, and many of you, including Brezhnev, insisted on the combination. I may have made a mistake in not resisting the decision, but all of you said that it should be done for the common good. And now you accuse me of combining the posts.

"Yes, I recognize that I allowed myself to behave less than tactfully toward people in the arts and sciences. You could put some of my pronouncements about the Academy of Sciences in this category. But after all, it's no secret that our science lags behind foreign science and technology in many areas. We invest vast sums of national resources into science; we're doing everything necessary to encourage scientific creativity and to apply the results in the economy. So we have to force them, we have to demand that scientific institutions get more active and pay us real returns. That's just the truth, and there's no getting around it."

Going further, according to Shelest, Khrushchev defended measures taken in connection with the Suez crisis of 1956[25] and the Caribbean crisis of October 1962. In particular, he said:

25. *Editor's note:* What specific criticism was addressed to Khrushchev in connection with Suez? Sergei Khrushchev: "I don't know. However, Father was criticized for 'excessive spending' on economic aid to Egypt in the years after 1956."

"You accuse me of pulling out our missiles. What do you mean, that we should have started a world war over them? How can you accuse me of undertaking some sort of Cuban adventure when we made all decisions relating to Cuba together?

"Or take the erection of the Berlin Wall. Back then, you all approved the decision, and now you're blaming me. For what, for goodness' sake? Anyone can talk. But to decide what to do concretely — none of you could suggest anything then, and you can't even now.[26] Or take our relations with the Chinese leadership. They're quite complex, and they'll get even more sticky. You're going to come up against great difficulties and complexities in four or five years. Don't lose your capacity for class struggle, for political and tactical maneuvering on all disputed issues.

"I understand that this is my last political speech, my swan song, so to speak. I will not appear before the plenum, but I'd like to address one request to the plenum. . . ."

He didn't manage to say [Shelest continues] what his request was before Brezhnev cut him off.

"There will be no request!"

Suslov backed up Brezhnev.

Tears appeared in Nikita Sergeyevich's eyes, and then he simply broke down and cried. It was sad to see. I think that what he wanted to say was:

"Comrades, forgive me if I am guilty of anything. We worked together. True, we didn't accomplish everything. . . ."

I don't think he would have said anything else. After all, he was all alone, and everything had been determined in advance.

But Brezhnev was afraid of what Khrushchev might ask of the plenum, that he would answer the charges, and debates would flare up. That's why he decided — no questions, no requests.

Khrushchev continued:

"Obviously, it will now be as you wish. What can I say —

26. *Editor's note:* Again, the author was unable to explain what specific criticism was addressed to his father in connection with the Berlin Wall.

I got what I deserved. I'm ready for anything. You know, I myself was thinking that it was time for me to go; we face a lot of problems, and at my age it isn't easy to cope with them all. We've got to promote younger people. Some people today lack courage and integrity. . . . But that's not the issue now. Someday, history will tell the whole, profound truth about what is happening today. . . . As for now, I ask you to write up the statement about my departure, my retirement, and I'll sign it. I'm relying on you to do this. And if you insist, I will leave Moscow [and live elsewhere]."

Someone called out: "Why should you leave?"

And everyone agreed.

Polyansky had prepared the report to the plenum. The idea was for Brezhnev to give it, or at the very least, Podgorny. But Brezhnev simply finked out. And Podgorny also refused.

"I just can't give this speech against Khrushchev. I worked side by side with him for many years. How would it look? I can't, and that's all there is to it. I'd suggest Shelepin. He's got a way with words, but he's too young."

Then it was decided this way:

"Let Mikhail Andreyevich [Suslov] give it. After all, he's our ideologist. . . ."

Another no less important witness was Semichastny. He has his own view of the situation surrounding the second day of the Presidium meeting, on October 14, even though he didn't rank high enough to attend it:

Adzhubei writes that they ousted him [Khrushchev] "in camera." What does he mean, in camera? It happened at the plenum. There wasn't much discussion, but questions like that are not put forward for discussion.[27]

I phoned Brezhnev on the second day [October 14], and

---

27. *Editor's note:* Semichastny refers to Adzhubei's article "Those Ten Years," which appeared in *Znamya,* June and July, 1988. "I can only say," adds Sergei Khrushchev, "that I agree with Semichastny that the Presidium observed its own procedures — in the sense that all its members expressed their views. There was very little discussion at the plenum, but they did vote. It's true that certain well-known supporters of Khrushchev were not invited to the plenum, but there were only two or three people in this category."

called him out of the meeting. "All this criticism is going too long," I say. "Get it over with. I couldn't stand a second night of it. At the rate you're going, Leonid Ilyich, you'll keep meeting until they arrest either you or Khrushchev. I don't need that. I've heard enough from both sides today.

"Some are upset because they want Khrushchev saved; others are calling on us to save you. Still others are asking why you're sitting around in the Central Committee doing nothing. I pretend I don't know anything."

By that time, people [i.e, Central Committee members] were summoned on phony pretexts so that they would be right at hand and the plenum could be held immediately. They were nervous. Calls were coming in to me from all sides.

Brezhnev was begging: "Dear Comrades, just wait a little longer. I've got just a little consulting to do." Thirty minutes or so later, he calls me: "Listen, reassure them. We've settled on this: Those who haven't managed to speak yet will be given three or four minutes. Full members of the Presidium have already spoken; only candidate members and [Central Committee] secretaries remain. Let each of them have his say. The plenum will start at six o'clock."

"That's fine with me," I said. "Can I announce it?"

"Go ahead."

At this point, Semichastny briefly shares his impressions of the plenum, in which he did participate.

I didn't even know there would be no discussion. . . . I was indignant about that, and I told both Shelepin and Brezhnev about it later. But I think they knew what they were doing. They didn't know where the discussion might go, and didn't want others to start getting criticized. Some sort of conversation might spring up. . . . I think the old men thought it all through, and since they were afraid for their . . . skin, did everything to avoid discussion at the plenum. Nobody clued us in as to what was going on.

A real commotion began in the hall. I sat there, observing it.

Zealots and toadies were shouting: "Exclude him from the party! Turn him over to a court!"

People who were a little calmer just sat there silent. There was no serious, critical, analytical discussion of the sort that would demonstrate the authority of the Central Committee.

The Presidium decided everything for the Central Committee, and having decided, prepared, chewed it over, and then chewed it over again, threw it to the CC, saying, "Vote!"

Much of what these witnesses have to say is obviously subjective, but I still think it is entirely credible. As to the fact that they counted on no discussion at the plenum, Yegorychev confirms it: "Now, after so many years [his interview for *Ogonyok* took place in 1989], it's clear Brezhnev had good reason to reject speeches at the plenum. In the heat of discussion, much could have been said that would have tied his hands later on. Whereas Leonid Ilyich obviously already had his own plans."

I would like to mention one more episode.

As she herself has said, Ukrainian Central Committee secretary Olga Ilyinichna Ivashchenko learned of the plot in the beginning of October and tried to reach Nikita Sergeyevich on the *V.Ch.* But she wasn't able to get through to him. Khrushchev was effectively blockaded. They didn't let her into the plenum, nor was another pro-Khrushchev Central Committee member, Zinovy Timofeyevich Serdyuk, admitted. Soon afterward, they were both relieved of their posts and sent into retirement.

But to return to that day in October: After lunch, Father went for a walk. Everything was out of the ordinary that day — this walk during working hours, and its aim, or rather, lack thereof. In the past, he would go for an hour's walk after work, to shake off the stress that had accumulated during the day, and after a short rest, he would get down to reading the evening mail. This hour was strictly observed, no more and no less.

Now his last papers — material for the next Presidium meeting, including an exposition of the McNamara doctrine [on counterforce nuclear targeting — ed.], and some Tass summaries — remained in his briefcase. They were destined to lie there unopened and forgotten until his death. He never looked into his briefcase again.

There was nothing to limit the length of our walk now. We had to kill time and release at least some of the nervous tension of the last few days.

We walked in silence. Beside us trotted Arbat, the Alsatian who lived in the house. He belonged to Lena, my sister.[28] Previously, Arbat hadn't shown much interest in Father. He would go up to him, wag his tail, and go off about his own affairs. But on that day he never left Father's side. And from that day onward, he followed Father constantly.

Finally I couldn't bear the silence, and I asked the question that interested me most.

"Whom did they appoint?"

"Brezhnev will be first secretary and Kosygin, chairman of the Council of Ministers. Kosygin's a good choice." Father's habit of assessing a candidate's suitability for a post got the upper hand. "I suggested him for the job way back when we relieved Bulganin of it. He knows the economy very well, and he'll do a good job. It's harder to say about Brezhnev; his character is too soft and he's too easily influenced. I'm not sure he'll have the strength to carry through a correct line. Still, it doesn't concern me now, I'm now retired. I'm on the sidelines." Bitter lines appeared at the corners of his mouth.

We never returned to the subject again.

That evening, Mikoyan came by. The Presidium had met after lunch, for the first time without Father. Mikoyan had been delegated to inform him of the decisions taken.

They sat down at the table in the dining room, and Father asked for tea to be brought. He liked tea and drank it out of a thin, transparent glass with a handle like a cup. He had brought this glass from the German Democratic Republic and was very fond of it, forever singing its praises to visitors, demonstrating how convenient it was to drink hot tea without burning your fingers.

"I've been asked to tell you the following," Mikoyan began hesitantly. "Your present dacha and city residence are yours for life."

"Good," said Father vaguely.

It was hard to tell whether this was an expression of gratitude or merely indicated that he had heard what was said. After a moment's thought, he repeated what he had already told me: "I'm ready to live where I am told."

"You will have bodyguards and a domestic staff, but new personnel will be assigned."

28. Yelena Nikitichna Khrushcheva, born in 1937, died in 1972 after a long illness that for all practical purposes prevented her from holding a job.

Father grunted that he understood.

"Your pension will be set at five hundred rubles a month, and you'll have a car." Mikoyan hesitated. "It was suggested that you remain a member of the Supreme Soviet Presidium, although a final decision on that hasn't been taken. I also suggested setting up the post of consultant to the Presidium for you, but that was rejected."

"There was no need to," Father said firmly. "They'd never agree to that. Why would they want me around after everything that's happened? My advice and inevitable interference would just tie their hands. And even seeing me around wouldn't exactly give them pleasure. Of course, it would be nice to have something to do. I don't know how I'll be able to live in retirement, doing nothing. But it was a mistake to propose that. Thanks anyway. It's good to know you have a friend at your side."

The conversation was over. Father saw his guest out to the small square in front of the house.

All the previous days, the weather had been warm, almost summery. Now, too, it was warm and sunny.

Anastas Ivanovich embraced Khrushchev and kissed him. In those days it was not customary for leaders to kiss, and therefore everyone found this farewell extremely touching.

Mikoyan walked quickly to the gate. His short figure disappeared around the turn. Nikita Sergeyevich watched him go. They never met again.

RETIREMENT

F ATHER was now retired. Our lives had changed fundamentally in just a few days. We would have to reorganize everything from beginning to end. The main thing was for Father to set himself a goal; after all, life hadn't ended with retirement.

Father was used to being needed by everyone, to being constantly involved. He had been the one everything depended on. No matter what his position, he had always had this feeling of indispensability. Everyone needed the battalion commissar during the civil war; no one could do without the party secretary, either at the district level or on any other step on the long hierarchical ladder to the very top posts — first secretary of the Central Committee and chairman of the Council of Ministers of a great nation.

He had never had spare time. From the very start, he was one of those leaders who try to involve themselves personally in everything, to master even the smallest, most specialized details. Once they grasp the essence of an idea or technological proposal, they charge ahead, brushing aside all obstacles to its implementation. That's the way he was with housing, the virgin lands, missiles, steel furnaces, and much more. He made mistakes, some of them flagrant, like his support for Lysenko. But here I'm not speaking of being right or wrong, I'm speaking of an attitude.

Sometimes you notice in a different person, in a different time and place, traits that are familiar. The same desire to know everything shines through the piles of telegrams, quotations, and documents in the memoirs of Sir Winston Churchill, everything about the new guns, tanks, and planes on which the fate of the British Empire depended in its terrible struggle with Hitler. When all was said and done, Churchill made the final decisions and shouldered the entire responsibility. There was no one else to blame, and errors by the experts were no excuse.

This kind of approach demands that one give completely of oneself; it doesn't leave a minute of free time. All one's thoughts are subordinate to one thing; the brain is constantly preoccupied with the main task. Finding the correct solution is the reward. All truly creative people, whether political figures, scholars, artists, or writers, know the joy of achieving this reward.

But the joy of creation comes at an enormous price. Deception, clever tricks, keeping even a small part of yourself private, is impossible; any sham is immediately perceived. You have to give yourself completely, holding nothing back, without considering the consequences.

What if something goes wrong, disappointment sets in, the Great Cause disappears, everything comes crashing down? You feel yourself in a vacuum; you don't know what to do, to what to devote your efforts. Your cause is gone, but the only thing you know is how to pursue it. Nothing is left to guide your life; you have nothing to aspire to. A man in this situation is like an ant. We've all seen these purposeful insects when some malicious hand suddenly puts an insurmountable twig in their path to the anthill. Suddenly these businesslike, industrious ants begin to rush aimlessly in all directions, circling senselessly.

After a blow like this, you need exceptional strength and enormous will power to get control of yourself, to keep yourself from coming unstrung, from indulging in self-pity or hatred of others. You have to find yourself again, to find a new goal, to destroy old patterns and create new ones. In short, you must do what we sometimes unthinkingly refer to as starting a new life. That rarely works out. It's hard to throw off the shackles of habit which you've lived with for so long that you're hardly aware of them. You turn down a new path and think that there's no returning to the past, but when you look around, you see you've been going in circles and are once again back where you started.

It's hard enough to start a new life when you're young and the years stretch endlessly before you. It's a hundred times harder when the sun is setting on your old age. You don't know which milepost will be your last, or if you'll make it down the part of the road that is clearly visible from where you stand. It's hard even to start down the road.

You don't want to move, you want to finish out life where you are. Everything has already been done. Ahead is just emptiness. All this Father now had to face.

Just yesterday, he had made the final decision as to what proposals to put before the United Nations, whether to reduce the armed forces, whether to expand the area under cultivation, whether to build hydroelectric and thermal power stations, whether to concentrate on metallurgy or the chemical industry.

And today? Whether to go for a walk or watch television. Whether to read a bit or clean his hunting rifle. Father didn't want to do anything. The shock to his nervous system caused by the events of the last few days was too great. It was one thing to talk about retirement, and to prepare for it gradually as something that would inevitably occur in the distant future. It was something else entirely to be stopped short in midstride, to suddenly feel himself useless — especially when he still was strong, still energetic, still full of new ideas.

Nothing helped — neither friends nor family who tried to distract him with conversation or coax him into some other activity, nor the tranquilizers solicitously prescribed by Dr. Bezzubik. A single thought must have kept pounding in his head: *Useless, useless, useless . . .*

ON the first morning of retirement, October 15, 1964, no one else even knew. Vague rumors were just beginning to circulate in Moscow. Congratulatory greetings from Khrushchev to cosmonauts and collective farmers had disappeared from the newspapers.

During the night between October 14 and 15, the entire security detail at Father's house was changed. Many new officers had appeared on duty during the last two days, but the familiar faces hadn't departed. Now the change could be made openly. It was all done quietly and efficiently; no one had any idea it was going on. Only in the morning did we discover strangers on duty.

So that was why the chief duty officer had said good-bye the way he did, squeezing my hand and saying in a half whisper: "I guess that's the way it is. . . . We might not see each other again. . . ." Obviously, he knew about the impending change.

Under Stalin, security men for all members of the Politburo (later renamed the Presidium of the Central Committee) were subordinate to a single commander. Only he could give them orders. This arrangement had caused great uneasiness among the leaders in 1953 as they prepared to arrest Beria. While planning their strategy, Khrushchev, Bulganin, Malenkov, and others were quite literally in Beria's hands. Because he was minister of internal affairs, their personal bodyguards got their orders only from him. He had the authority to tell them to do anything he wanted. Everyone felt trapped.

After Beria's removal, the bodyguards took orders only from those they guarded, no one else. It was the possibility of interference by Father's bodyguards that Semichastny had worried so about during the last few days. That's why his first step was to replace the contingent assigned to Father. Men who had worked with Father for many years were spirited away, disarmed, and transferred into the reserves. After a while, their lives settled down: some retired, some were assigned to other leaders after several years had gone by, and some, much later, even ended up protecting our dacha again.

At the time, the sudden appearance of unfamiliar faces on the first day of Father's retirement was alarming. All the multiple telephones fell silent. The government phone wasn't the only one disconnected. Only one of the several city phones was left on — that and the phone to the guardhouse. The silent receivers, from which the familiar bass dial tone had vanished, seemed to have died.

First thing the next morning, a car appeared at the gate, a Chaika to replace the familiar ZIL. Only three people in the country were allowed a ZIL: the first secretary of the Central Committee, the chairman of the USSR Supreme Soviet Presidium, and the chairman of the Council of Ministers.

The Chaika wasn't with us for long. That very same day it vanished as unobtrusively as it had arrived, to be replaced half an hour later by a Volga, one car lower in "rank." At the time, these changes didn't attract much attention. They just registered on our minds: a Chaika is here, the Chaika is gone, now a Volga has arrived.

The reason for this surreptitious switching of cars became clear later on. When a Chaika was allocated to my father, one of the bosses remembered his repeated attempts to eliminate, or at least reduce, the number of cars assigned to the bureaucracy. Father's "automobile initiative" had provoked enormous unhappiness among leaders of all ranks, and now it was their turn. We even heard that one of the bosses had said: "He wanted to give us Volgas. Let him try one himself." Many such petty jabs awaited Father in the future.

The first day had begun. I remember Father came down to breakfast later than usual. Today there was no need to be at his desk by nine, in accordance with the work routine he had established after Stalin's death. During the night, his face seemed to have grown thinner and grayer, and he moved more slowly. Despite the sedative brought by Dr. Bezzubik the night before, he had hardly slept at all.

After breakfast, which he barely seemed to taste, Father went out into the yard. Out of habit, he circled the house and headed toward the gate. Someone unfamiliar hurried toward him.

"Good morning, Nikita Sergeyevich," the stranger began, stopping about two steps away. His stance reflected respectful deference. Nature had not stinted on his height; he looked down at my father. His round, Russian face was impossible to dislike.

"Melnikov, Sergei Vasilievich, your new *kommendant*," he introduced himself. "You don't remember me, but I worked in the government box at the Sports Palace. I used to see you there. What are your orders?" Half turning, he motioned toward the black Volga. "Perhaps you'd like to take a drive to your dacha?"

Sergei Vasilievich fairly exuded readiness to serve and to help, without a trace of obsequious servility. Maintaining his own dignity, he managed to show respect for the retired premier.

Father extended his hand. "Hello." Melnikov's question had caught him by surprise. His thoughts had been far away. "You've got quite a tedious job cut out for you. I'm a loafer now. I don't know what to do with myself. You'll waste away from boredom with me. But you may be right. Why sit around here? Let's go."

The three of us drove off to the dacha: Father, Melnikov, and I. Nina Petrovna, my mother, had not yet returned from Karlovy Vary, where she was vacationing and taking a cure.

Familiar places flashed past the car windows. We stopped at the tightly closed gates of the dacha and signaled impatiently. Usually the guard had been alerted to Father's arrival and stood at attention next to the wide-open green gate. This time, after our signal, a stranger peered out the small window. The guards had been changed here, too.

Melnikov waved his hand. At this point, the gate opened just enough for a young fellow with a sergeant's blue epaulets to squeeze through. He looked suspiciously into the car and, recognizing Father through the window, smiled with relief. He quickly opened the gate, and the car sped down the drive, stopping near the house.

Father clambered out, but then hesitated by the front door. "Let's go for a walk in the field. What else is there for us pensioners to do? We've done our share," he announced with cheerfulness that was clearly forced.

In recent years he had walked a regular route: along the asphalt drive to the gate and then down the slope where the brook bubbled softly in its bed. Each grain of sand on the bottom was visible through the water, which was transparent in the fall. The lazy current carried along thin strands of waterweed; the bank was overgrown with thick grass. It wasn't mowed here, and the tangled grass grabbed at our feet, making it hard to get through. A small bridge, carrying the road to the dacha, crossed the brook. Behind it, on a small rise to the left, the fields of a state farm began. During the summer, the farm's corn stood like an unbroken green wall. The field was tended with particular care, for the local bosses wanted to please Khrushchev and win his favor. Photojournalists would often come calling, and the next thing you knew a picture of a horseman up to his ears in corn would appear in *Ogonyok* or some other magazine.

Now the field was bare. The stumps of cornstalks cut off just above ground level jutted up among the graying lumps of earth. The asphalt road from the gate veered off to the right toward Uspensk Highway. We turned left along a narrow path that skirted the field.

At first, Melnikov walked a bit behind us, in keeping with protocol. However, Father motioned him forward: "Come on up here. We've got no secrets."

After that we walked three abreast. Recalling the corn that stood there in the summer, Father began to talk, getting more carried away as he did so, about raising livestock, about feed, about corn and lupine. He quoted statistics from memory, comparing the yields of various crops, and immediately translating them into kilograms of meat per hectare of grain. He spoke interestingly and convincingly. He made you want to listen. It was as if the rich words and the precise comparisons issued forth by themselves. His vivid examples were right on target.

This was the old Khrushchev — except that he wasn't speaking to an all-union conference. His only audience was Captain Melnikov and me. Melnikov nodded and agreed politely, and asked questions. Father's enthusiasm awakened his interest, or perhaps his curiosity. It wasn't every day that one could attend a private lecture on agricultural development given in person by a former premier.

In the midst of the conversation, Father's energy suddenly subsided and the light in his eyes went out. "No one needs me now. What am I going to do without work? How am I going to live? I can't imagine," he said to no one in particular.

We started to object with a cheerful but false optimism. We listed the charms of leisure: walks, books, movies. Father remained gloomily silent as we came to the end of the field. At the foot of the hill, with its sparse stands of pines, the mirrorlike Moscow River glistened. We returned to the dacha by way of the meadow. Only a short time ago, I had walked here with Father, trying desperately to find a way to tell him about Galyukov's improbable report. Installation of the irrigation system had been halted, and the cement conduits strewn about the landscape gave the place the impression of a house abandoned by its owner. This project of Father's would never be completed either.

During the days that followed, walks like this would become our main occupation. I extended my leave and spent all my time with Father, not wanting to leave him alone with his gloomy thoughts. I tried as best I could to divert him.[1]

Occasionally we would watch new movies in the screening room that had been set up at the dacha, but he never got caught up by them. His thoughts were elsewhere, and the images on the screen flashed past without touching him.

One film, *The Chairman,* did seem to interest him a bit. It portrayed recent agricultural policy positively, stressing our achievements. At the time, the film was seen as a panegyric to Father, and those at the top debated at length whether to release it to the public. We all waited to see Father's reaction, but he was almost completely indifferent: "It was a good film."

As I already indicated, my mother, Nina Petrovna, had been vacationing in Karlovy Vary, in Czechoslovakia. This year, as in the past, she had gone there with Brezhnev's wife, Viktoria Petrovna. When Father came back from the plenum, he had been agitated: "We need to call your mother," he said to us. "But how can that be done now? See if you can get through to her on the phone."

The problem we faced was unprecedented. The usual government *V.Ch.* wasn't working. (How simple it had been before to pick up the receiver and ask for Nina Petrovna in Karlovy Vary!) None of us knew how to reach her on the regular long-distance line.

---

1. *Editor's note:* Did Sergei Khrushchev fear his father might contemplate harming himself or even committing suicide? "Not at all," he replied. "He had no thoughts of suicide. It was simply that I wanted to take his mind off his troubles."

We asked security to help us (the guards hadn't yet been changed) and after a while the duty officer reported that Nina Petrovna had been contacted and would fly back the next day.

"She was very upset," the guard said. "After all, they have no idea what's going on here, and we couldn't tell her anything. All we could say was that everyone was in good health, but that Nikita Sergeyevich would like her to return home at once."

The next day brought a new problem — how to meet her plane. Could we send the car assigned to Father? Melnikov assured us that everything would be taken care of. The plane arrived after dark. The whole family had gathered to await Mama. At the slightest sound outside, we would run out on the porch. At last the car drove up and Mama got out carrying a large bunch of flowers. It somehow looked out of place.

"Some Czech women presented them to me at the Prague airport," she explained, as if justifying their presence. "I already know what happened."

We went inside and sat down in the dining room where, just half a year before, on the morning of April 17, the entire Presidium had sat singing Khrushchev's praises. Their gift to him, the radio-phonograph from Riga, still stood by the wall.

Father briefly recounted what had happened. He looked depressed. "Now I'm retired. Yesterday there was a Central Committee plenum that pensioned me off. I said I was prepared to abide by any decision they made, and that I would live wherever they wanted me to. So, get ready to move." Father forced a smile, obviously recalling his itinerant existence and all the trouble each move had caused Mama.

As usual, Mama was upbeat. She didn't even hint at her feelings, holding them inside her and remaining outwardly calm. She said that the Czech women, including President Antonín Novotny's wife, who had seen her off at the airport, had wished her and Father all the best.

After Father had gone up to his room, Mama told us about an "amusing" incident that had occurred on her last day in Karlovy Vary. "As usual," Mama said, "Viktoria Petrovna and I stayed next door to each other. We often took walks together, despite her sore feet. Zimyanin" — Mikhail V. Zimyanin was the Soviet ambassador to Czechoslovakia — "threw himself all over me, showering me with compliments and souvenirs. On the last day, the telephone rang and the operator said that Comrade Zimyanin was calling. I still didn't know what had happened and I suspected nothing, although I was worried after the call from Moscow. After saying hello, Zimyanin said he had just returned from Moscow, where the Central Committee had removed Khrushchev. Zimyanin said he had lit into Khrushchev's methods of leadership at the plenum. I said nothing. Not suspecting a thing, he congratulated me on Leonid Ilyich's appointment as first secretary. I was still silent, and that made him uneasy. He sensed something wasn't quite right. Finally he realized that he'd asked to be connected with me instead of Viktoria Petrovna. He mumbled something unintelligible and hung up." Mama finished her story on a melancholy note: "He had wanted to inform her. What a farce!"

After talking a bit more about what had happened in Moscow, and concluding yet again that there was nothing we could do to change the situation, we went to our rooms.

THE days followed one after the other with little to distinguish between them. Father paid hardly any attention to what was going on in the outside world.

The Central Committee officially announced the leadership changes. Father halfheartedly opened the newspaper, glanced through it quickly, and put it aside without reading it.

I dropped by the Mikoyans' several times. I didn't talk with Anastas Ivanovich, but discussed Father's situation with Sergo at length. We tried to guess what would come next. You could feel the anxiety in the Mikoyan household. Out of the blue, unknown workmen had shown up and begun cleaning the enormous crystal chandelier that hung in the dining room. They moved all the furniture and spent quite a while casting their mysterious spell on the ceiling. Sergo and I concluded they were planting listening devices, so from then on we did our talking outside.

The subject of my "doctorate" came up again. Mikoyan had referred to it at one of the Presidium meetings.

"Comrade Shelepin has told us that Sergei was awarded a doctorate without defending a dissertation. I asked Sergei about it. He was surprised; he said the idea of a doctorate never came up."

Mikoyan's remark created a bit of a stir, and Kosygin had poured fuel on the fire: "So, who's right, Aleksandr Nikolayevich [Shelepin]? What was the basis for your accusation?"

Shelepin was thrown off for a moment, and began to mumble that it wasn't important anyway, and that he would make some additional inquiries. At the next meeting, he said he had been inaccurate.

"Khrushchev's son has not been granted his degree. His work has been submitted for attestation, but we held it up."

One lie had replaced another. I never had anything to do with the attestation committee, but naturally no one was interested enough to raise further questions. I was left with a feeling of having touched something dirty.

At the same time, the Presidium was discussing something else that concerned me. My association with Galyukov had not gone unnoticed and was now the object of attention by our party's highest body. They proposed sanctions against me and Galyukov for informing Khrushchev about impending events and thus threatening to explode the whole carefully prepared plot.

This could have caused me a great deal of unpleasantness, but luckily the proposal didn't go through. The plot had come off successfully, members of the Presidium were more concerned about the future, and one of them reportedly objected to the sanctions, saying, "How can you accuse a son of warning his father? It's only natural."

The proposal fell of its own weight. Galyukov and I were spared.

While many of these stormy events were going on, the three cosmonauts continued their orbital flight. In his conversation with them, Khrushchev had promised a hero's welcome. In the meantime, they had landed and been examined and debriefed at the cosmodrome, but their triumphal reception in Moscow was put off from day to day. Finally it was announced with one day's notice that the reception would take place on Friday, October 23. The ritual was familiar — ceremonies at the airport, a motorcade through Moscow, a rally on Red Square, and a concluding reception at the Kremlin. There was one big difference: no Khrushchev.

Live television coverage began in the morning at Vnukovo airport. Mama turned on the television, which was one of our few remaining links with the outside world. Until now, Father hadn't liked watching television; in any event, he hadn't had time. Even now, he was sitting in the next room with a book. In fact, he wasn't reading; he couldn't help getting excited at the thought of the cosmonauts.

When the crew commander, Colonel V. M. Komarov, spoke at the airport, Father couldn't resist joining us in front of the set. But he didn't sit there very long, and left to go out, growling, "I don't want to watch this." He walked around the house a couple of times but couldn't calm down. By this time, the motorcade had arrived at Red Square and they were all taking their places atop Lenin's mausoleum.

Father suddenly caught sight of his car standing at our gate. Sergei Melnikov was chatting about something with the driver. "Let's take a drive to the dacha," Father said to Melnikov. They got in and drove off. Of course, no one but Melnikov knew where Khrushchev was going. As usual, the duty officer immediately reported on his special line that Khrushchev had left the house and was heading for an unknown destination.

While the car drove along the Berezhkovsky Embankment, the report quickly passed up the chain of command. A right turn at the Borodinsky Bridge would take them to Red Square. A left turn led toward the dacha. Which way would the car turn? No one could say.

Meanwhile, as we were unsuspectingly watching the scene in Red Square, we saw a security man come up behind Brezhnev and whisper something in his ear. Brezhnev's face darkened and he leaned toward the person next to him. The people on the tribune started stirring around, paying no attention to the speaker. Shelepin hurried behind the leaders into a special room on the top floor of the mausoleum. There, next to a table laden with the traditional hors d'oeuvres, was another little table full of telephones. Something had to be done to stop Khrushchev from making his way to Red Square. Who knew what that impulsive man might have taken it into his head to do!

The milling about didn't last long. Reassuring news apparently arrived quickly: Father's car had turned left. He was headed for his dacha.

Father returned toward evening with no idea of the consternation he had caused. The outing had refreshed and relaxed him. However, we didn't have to wait long for the reaction to his surprise trip. Within an hour Melnikov arrived, visibly upset: "Nikita Sergeyevich, beginning tomorrow you are requested to move to your dacha and, for the time being, not to return to your residence in the city." Sergei Vasilievich pronounced these words in a muffled tone, trying not to look directly at Father, who was sitting at the table with a glass of tea in his hand.

"All right," was Father's indifferent reply.

We were already getting used to his flat reaction to the unending jabs. It was so unlike Father; now nothing seemed to faze him. To the dacha? So be it. To Siberia? So be it. That seemed to be his attitude.

It was Mama, sitting next to him, who became agitated: "How can we pick up and leave for good tomorrow, just like that? We won't even have time to gather our things!"

Father didn't react at all to Mama's objection, but Melnikov explained: "The order applied only to Nikita Sergeyevich. The rest of the family can stay here, if you wish, until an apartment is found for you in the city."

There it was: Father had been ordered out of Moscow. It made sense. The trip from the dacha to the city took nearly an hour, so there would always be ample time to figure out where he was going and, if necessary, stop him. The chances of the former premier showing up where he wasn't wanted were sharply reduced.

The next day we moved to the dacha. Except for brief trips to the polyclinic, Father would remain there until the move to another dacha, at Petrovo-Dalneye.

THE next regularly scheduled Central Committee plenum took place in November 1964. It was at this plenum that Father had intended to discuss the new constitution. Now the meeting had a quite different agenda.

There had been no time in October to deal with all the organizational issues. Now the Central Committee dropped Adzhubei from membership, elected Shelepin to the Presidium, and adopted a number of other decisions.

It's actually quite interesting to trace what happened to several of those who played active roles in the change of leadership. Far from all of them got what they had expected.

After Father's retirement, Leonid Ilyich Brezhnev, then second secretary, automatically became first secretary of the Central Committee. The main task had been to get rid of Khrushchev, and no one wanted to sow the seeds of further conflict. Any other candidacy besides Brezhnev's would have been sure to create discord. Deep in his heart, each of them felt worthy of the highest post in the party hierarchy; that's why a clash between groups would have been inevitable. But now, in the first days and months without Khrushchev, they needed unity as much as air itself.

In this situation, the majority favored the obvious choice: the first secretary would be replaced by the second, and the chairman of the Council of Ministers (Khrushchev had held both posts simultaneously) by his first deputy, Kosygin.

However, not everyone was pleased with this procedure, particularly Aleksandr Nikolayevich Shelepin. He viewed his election to the Presidium as but the first step toward an even higher position in the party. On the surface, everything was fine. Brezhnev would be a transition figure. For the moment, there was no doing without him, but his time would soon come — all Shelepin would have to do was raise his voice a bit and Brezhnev would voluntarily turn over the top spot. That's the way Shelepin apparently saw things as 1964 came to an end.

His friends and supporters had been placed in key government posts: Semichastny controlled the KGB, and the Russian Republic Ministry for the Preservation of Public Order was in the hands of Vadim Stepanovich Tikunov. Shelepin's men were spread around in other, somewhat lesser, positions as well, just waiting to receive their marching orders.

However, Shelepin had miscalculated on the main point. His role in October 1964 was well known, nor was his ultimate aim a secret to anyone. His colleagues feared him, and that in itself practically guaranteed his defeat. His fellow Presidium members watched his every step, and quickly combined against him. Any attempt at a further change in the leadership was doomed, but Shelepin apparently didn't understand that. For the time being, he looked to the future with high hope.

Gradually, the ground beneath his feet began to shake. One after another, his supporters were dislodged. But in the beginning, it seemed nothing untoward was happening. Immediately after October, Shelepin's close supporter KGB chairman Semichastny substantially strengthened his position: he was awarded the rank of colonel general in appreciation of his role in the conspiracy. Many of his associates were promoted to general as well. However, this was but the promising prelude to the doleful finale.

It was not very long before Semichastny was replaced at the KGB by Yuri Andropov. It was done quietly, almost without attracting attention. One day in 1967 Presidium member Comrade Suslov arrived at KGB headquarters on Dzerzhinsky Square.[2] He was accompanied by Yuri Andropov, the Central Committee secretary in charge of relations with socialist countries. The ostensible purpose for their visit was to meet with KGB party activists. Nothing hinted that something extraor-

---

2. The following description is based on information that circulated in Moscow at the time. More up-to-date sources generally confirm this account. Nonetheless, I would be grateful for any corrections or clarifications.

dinary was about to take place. But in fact the Presidium had just completed a meeting at which Semichastny had been fired as KGB chairman. According to Pyotr Shelest, the formal excuse had to do with the defection of Svetlana Alliluyeva (Stalin's daughter) to the West. Semichastny had defended himself by insisting that he had categorically opposed giving her permission to travel to India, and that it was Kosygin who had decided the matter. But no one was listening.

As for Suslov, he was about to perform a not-so-simple mission — to announce the Presidium's decision to the KGB apparatus and to introduce their new chairman to them.

Both at Central Committee headquarters and at the KGB, those in the know were nervous. Who knew what Semichastny might try? He still had enormous power. The situation duplicated in miniature that which had occurred when Beria was ousted. This time, to be sure, the KGB chief possessed no troops of his own. That limited his options, but he still controlled the security forces protecting the Kremlin and the Central Committee itself. Just in case, the troops of the Moscow garrison were raised to a higher state of readiness on orders from the Central Committee.

The applause was less than overwhelming when Mikhail Andreyevich Suslov took the floor at the KGB meeting. At first, he spoke generally about the complex international and internal situation, about the need for constant vigilance. The words were familiar and they flowed smoothly. Then Suslov started talking about the great significance that the Central Committee attached to the state security organs.

"The Central Committee has decided to strengthen the leadership of state security by appointing candidate member of the Presidium Yuri Andropov as chairman of the KGB."

For a split second he hesitated and looked around the hall. The response was a cautious silence. His audience was digesting the news; they should have been expecting it, but nonetheless it came as a surprise. They could remain on the fence only so long. Somewhere in the depths of the hall, timid applause began and then swelled into an avalanche as each person hastened to outdo the one seated next to him.

Suslov sighed with relief. The sigh was picked up by the sensitive microphone and broadcast throughout the hall, but few heard it since it was drowned out by the applause. Andropov spoke next, and after him someone else, but none of it meant anything. The mission had been accomplished.

Semichastny was made deputy chairman of the Ukrainian Council of Ministers. From that distance, he could no longer exert any influence in Moscow.

There was another interesting sequel: for the first time since Beria, the new KGB chairman became first a candidate member and later a full, voting member of the Politburo.[3]

In 1953, on Father's initiative, it had been decided to change the role of the Ministry of Internal Affairs, to circumscribe its functions, limit its capabilities, and render it more manageable. Father wanted to reduce the authority of the all-powerful security organs, so that they could no longer rise above party and state.

The Ministry of State Security (MGB) was therefore detached from the Ministry of Internal Affairs and given somewhat lesser status as the Committee for State Security (KGB). General Ivan Serov was appointed chairman. Neither he nor his successors Shelepin and Semichastny could have imagined moving into the top political leadership while still heading the KGB. However, that didn't mean the KGB itself lost power.

Meanwhile, the same rule was applied to the Ministry of Defense and the Ministry of Foreign Affairs: their leaders, too, could no longer enter the top party synod.

Father had put his argument simply: the minister of defense and the chairman of the KGB had vast power concentrated in their hands. They must use it in strict accordance with decisions taken by the Presidium and the government. Their job was to implement those decisions. They should therefore be subordinate to the Presidium. Otherwise, in the event of divisions in the leadership, they could use their power to advance the parochial interests of this or that group.

Semichastny refers to this in his memoir:

> Then he [Brezhnev] shoved Andropov into the Politburo and made him a full member. It hadn't been that way before, and it was a mistake. These organs have to be kept under control. Otherwise, Malinovsky or Gromyko or their agencies could become the subject of a "report," and after that, no one would be able to check up on it.
>
> Up until then, a Central Committee department could call in my deputy. But now they couldn't, because the KGB chairman was a full member of the Politburo.

3. *Editor's note:* As noted in my foreword, the Central Committee Presidium regained its old name, Politburo, after Khrushchev's ouster. Sergei Khrushchev uses the two terms interchangeably in the pages that follow.

In essence, he didn't have to answer; all he needed to say was, "I got my orders from the chairman, a member of the Politburo" . . . and that was that — he was beyond criticism.[4]

In this way, Brezhnev was returning to a Stalinist tradition.

Of course, this question is extremely complicated and delicate, and arguments can be mustered on either side. However, I wanted to recall Father's arguments put forward many years before.

Semichastny's transfer didn't exhaust the changes in the KGB. The fate of Colonel Chekalov, in charge of security for party and government leaders, was particularly strange. He had met us at the airport on October 13. After that, he had just enough time to sew on the epaulets of a major general before he was demoted to deputy chief of the Tambov province KGB administration. Nor did he work there very long. A misfortune occurred. This robust, young-looking fellow took ill one day during morning exercises at the local stadium. Semichastny describes what happened next: "A nurse came up and gave him a shot. After that the guy died."

After moving up rapidly, many other KGB officers were either retired or transferred to the personnel departments of various ministries. These transfers came gradually, rather than as a bolt from the blue, but no one was spared who did not enjoy the new leadership's absolute trust.

Father had also broken up what was left of the Ministry of Internal Affairs after the KGB was detached from it. He had reduced its status from an all-union (i.e., federal) ministry, and changed its name, leaving several ministries for the protection of public order at the republic level. As we approached communism, their functions were supposed to be performed more and more by society itself.

For a short time after Father's dismissal, this structure remained untouched, and with it the position of Tikunov, the Russian Republic's minister for the protection of public order. Like Semichastny, he was a former Komsomol official. But his fate differed a bit from his mentor's. One day in 1966 Tikunov was called to the Central Committee, where his interlocutors made several points: errors had been made and it was necessary to correct them; the ministry should play a bigger role; it had

---

4. In this chapter, except as otherwise noted, Semichastny's recollections are taken from the unpublished transcript of his interview with V. A. Starkov of *Argumenty i fakty*.

been proposed that the old name and the former structure of the All-Union Ministry of Internal Affairs be restored.

Tikunov readily agreed, the proposal impressed him.

"Very well," said his interlocutors approvingly, "prepare a draft for the Central Committee. By the way, if a unified, all-union ministry is created, your ministry will be redundant. We hardly need two ministries in Moscow. If you don't object, then please note that in your draft, too."

In a few days the draft reorganization was ready. As he waited for the decision, Tikunov had no doubt he would head the new ministry. His only cause for concern was that as time went by there was no response, no further summons to the Central Committee. It seemed they had lost all interest in the issue.

Clarification came in an unexpected way. Tikunov one morning read in the newspaper an edict of the Presidium of the USSR Supreme Soviet abolishing the Russian Republic Ministry for the Protection of Public Order (MOOP RSFSR) and reestablishing the All-Union Ministry of Internal Affairs (MVD USSR). "Nikolai Anisimovich Shchelokov has been named minister of internal affairs of the USSR," the paper reported.

Tikunov rushed to the Central Committee. This time his reception was quite a bit cooler: "You yourself made the proposal," they said. "You said the state interest required creating MVD USSR and eliminating MOOP RSFSR. The decision was based on your report."

It was impossible to object. How could he say that he wanted to run the new ministry? In any case, the appointment had already been made.

"The Central Committee Presidium attaches great importance to the work of the new ministry," his interlocutors continued. "The country needs order. Possible candidates for minister were thoroughly discussed. Your previous work speaks well for you, but the ministry's scope is being substantially broadened. We need a man with extensive experience in party work. The Central Committee settled on Comrade Shchelokov."

"What will happen to me?"

"For now you'll be in reserve. We'll find something for you." It was clear that further conversation would be useless.

According to Semichastny, he and Shelepin "raised a ruckus" about Shchelokov's candidacy, but it was too late. Brezhnev put the issue to a vote at a meeting of the Presidium and it passed, although not unanimously.[5]

The rearrangements continued. One after another, Shelepin's brothers in arms, the *Komsomoltsy,* as they were then known, were relieved of the Moscow posts that they had attained with such effort under Khrushchev, and scattered around the world. Many received the high rank of "extraordinary and plenipotentiary" ambassador to some distant country.

Aleksandr Nikolayevich Shelepin understood that events would soon leave him isolated, a general without an army, but he was powerless to reverse or even halt the process.

Soon it was Shelepin's own turn. At the time, he was in charge of personnel. All appointments in the party, government, and army passed through his hands. That didn't suit Brezhnev. Then an opportune moment arose. Yet another *Komsomolets,* Nikolai Yegorychev, the former Moscow province party leader, had been sent to Denmark as ambassador. The chairman of the All-Union Central Trade Unions Council, Viktor Vasilievich Grishin, took his place.

Thus a vacancy appeared. By tradition, the trade union chairman was either a full member or a nonvoting member of the Presidium. The post was offered to Shelepin in 1966. From his new office on Leninsky Prospekt, it would be much harder to influence decisions being prepared at Central Committee headquarters on Staraya Ploshchad. He understood that this was another defeat but couldn't do anything about it. All his Presidium colleagues unanimously favored the change, and a direct refusal could bring even worse consequences.

However, Shelepin didn't give up hope. After all, he was the youngest member of the Presidium; time was on his side, and all he had to do was to be patient, to wait until the situation improved. For the moment, he would start preparing the ground anew.

Just as in 1964, he began to look for an influential ally, someone he could get to knock together an opposition — this time to Brezhnev — while he himself stayed in the shadows. In 1964 Ignatov had been such a man; now his gaze fell on Mikoyan. Mikoyan apparently seemed the ideal candidate because he was no longer a member of the Politburo. Shelepin probably assumed that Mikoyan's removal had left

5. During both Khrushchev's and Brezhnev's time, the Politburo almost always operated by consensus. When disagreements arose, my impression is that the issue was usually deferred for further consideration at a later date.

him unhappy and hostile to the new leadership. It was this animus that Shelepin was going to play upon. Besides, Mikoyan was well known in the party and in the country, and people would listen to him. In case of failure, it would be easy to hide behind him.

For him to approach Mikoyan would be dangerous. How would Anastas Ivanovich react? He might kick him out or even turn him in, informing the wrong people about Shelepin's visit. The conversation itself could hardly remain a secret. His own or Mikoyan's security detail would doubtless report such a strange rendezvous.

He had to find an intermediary and then prepare arguments that would impress Mikoyan. Knowing Anastas Ivanovich's personal unpretentiousness, he decided to prime the pump by referring to the recent repair of Brezhnev's dacha, which had cost several million rubles. If Mikoyan took the bait, then he could move on to political questions, get a feel for his mood, and after that act accordingly.

But the plan broke down right at the start. Mikoyan was experienced and cautious; he immediately sensed trouble and was on his guard. He didn't approve of the expensive remodeling of the dacha, but he flatly rejected any attempt to discuss or criticize Brezhnev's policies.

As recounted by Sergo Mikoyan, his father answered, "Of course, it's too bad that Leonid Ilyich is spending so much on his dacha. It's excessive and I don't approve of it. But it's a matter for his conscience. On the whole, he and I have no fundamental differences on internal and foreign policy. In general, I consider his policies correct."

Mikoyan summed up, "I'm no longer young, and I've been at it long enough. I'm not active in politics anymore, and I don't intend to get active again."

Shelepin had made a big mistake. Mikoyan might have been offended by his dismissal, but he was not about to undertake a career as a conspirator. He no longer dreamed of returning to the Politburo, and was even less inclined to become a weapon in someone else's hands. The conversations remained secret. Mikoyan didn't tell anyone about it at the time.[6]

It's quite possible that Shelepin approached not just Mikoyan but others as well. It's unlikely he gave up his plans just because Mikoyan refused to cooperate. But whatever he did remains a mystery. Only one thing is certain — his efforts were unsuccessful.

6. I found out about these talks from Sergo Mikoyan, who served as one of the intermediaries between Shelepin and Mikoyan.

As the years passed, the coalition of *Komsomoltsy,* which seemed so strong in 1964, disintegrated. Their dreams of obtaining high party and government posts became dimmer and more uncertain. Shelepin's trade union work wasn't going well; the fact that it didn't lead anywhere irritated him no end.

"Iron Shurik," as they had once called him, didn't want to give in. He decided on a desperate step — a personal conversation with Brezhnev. Shelepin wanted at any cost to return to the Central Committee. So that the conversation would be on record (rather than disappearing without a trace), he prepared a written statement addressed to the Politburo. In essence, it said the following: Lacking any specialized economic training, he couldn't be as useful as trade union chairman as he could be in another job. He therefore requested the Politburo to relieve him of his current duties and transfer him back to the Central Committee. Naturally, as a member of the Politburo, he'd have to be made nothing less than a secretary of the Central Committee.

Leonid Ilyich listened carefully to all his arguments and promised to think about it. He put Shelepin's statement into his folder, but the meeting produced no results.

Nonetheless, it wasn't long before hope revived once more. Brezhnev fell ill. Rumors spread that he would not be able to return to work again. Aleksandr Nikolayevich decided to have a chat with Suslov. He seemed a natural ally in possible encounters with Kirilenko, who was then serving unofficially as second secretary. If Brezhnev had moved into Khrushchev's place from just this post in 1964, doubtless Kirilenko was preparing himself to move up as well.

Shelepin paid Suslov a visit. It would have been better, of course, to hold this sensitive conversation in an informal setting, but such a situation didn't present itself. Shelepin had to be satisfied with an official meeting in the office of a secretary of the Central Committee.

Quickly dispensing with the ostensible reason for the meeting, Shelepin cautiously approached the real issue. He said that he, like Suslov, was concerned about the fate of the party and the future of the country. Much depended on who headed the Central Committee. Yet, Leonid Ilyich was seriously ill, and no one knew whether he would be able to return to duties in the near future. Moreover, we were all mortal. Didn't it behoove them to think of a possible replacement?

"If you're referring to Leonid Ilyich's illness, then your information is incorrect. He feels much better. The issue you bring up is, to say the least, inappropriate." Suslov cut him off coldly.

Shelepin saw yet another of his schemes fail. His only hope now was that Suslov would keep their meeting to himself. However, that hope was in vain. The very next day, Suslov visited the ailing Brezhnev and told him everything. Leonid Ilyich said nothing, but he didn't forget, and waited for an opportune moment.

He didn't have long to wait. A world forum of trade union leaders was scheduled to take place in Great Britain. It was decided that Shelepin would head the Soviet delegation. Was it by chance that no one noticed that the chairman of the Trade Unions Council was a former head of the KGB, that no one thought to ask how the English public would react?

The visit immediately created a scandal in England. The British press set the tone. How could a former secret policeman lead the trade union movement? The tune was played over and over. Demonstrations broke out demanding Shelepin's ouster from Britain. The situation heated up, and finally Shelepin was called home before the tour officially ended.

His reception at the airport was cold, but no one in Moscow seemed to take the scandal as seriously as our London embassy did. In the Moscow hurly-burly, the trip to England seemed distant and almost unreal. Shelepin hoped no one would remember it.

A call from the Central Committee brought him back to reality. He was informed that one of the issues on the agenda at the next session of the Politburo would be his report on his trip to England. The session began in the usual way. Brezhnev presided. According to eyewitnesses, there were many issues on the agenda. Some draft decisions were adopted without discussion, others were briefly discussed.

Finally, it was Shelepin's turn. Aleksandr Nikolayevich briefly outlined events at the trade union congress and stressed that the fuss raised by the British press had been inspired by "certain circles intent on a provocation."

When discussion began, everyone spoke in turn, but there was this common core: the leader of the Soviet delegation had not coped with his assignment and had failed in an important international undertaking. When the discussion ended, a resolution was passed; it established that there had been a failure and that as head of the delegation, Shelepin was to blame. The vote was unanimous, Shelepin himself included.

But Brezhnev didn't stop there. He expressed his view that the situation in the Trade Unions Council was clearly not what it should be. The council's leadership, and particularly Comrade Shelepin, were responsible. The passage of time had shown that he was a poor manager. By the way, Brezhnev continued, Comrade Shelepin himself shared this negative opinion of his own performance. Brezhnev opened the folder lying before him. It contained Shelepin's request that the Politburo relieve him of his duties and transfer him to work in the party apparatus — the very same request that he had so carelessly handed over to Brezhnev just a while back!

Brezhnev slowly read the first half of Shelepin's appeal. Before he got to the request to be given a Central Committee post, he stopped reading and lifted his head. "Who favors granting Comrade Shelepin's request?"

He scanned the faces of those present. "The majority," declared Leonid Ilyich, and with that, the Politburo moved on to the next issue.

A few days later, Shelepin was officially relieved as trade union chairman and given an insignificant assignment as a deputy chairman of the Committee on Labor Resources. If he hadn't been one of the youngest members of the Politburo, he could have been retired forthwith. As it was, he needed employment. The Central Committee plenum dropped him from the Politburo. The year was 1975. Shelepin's political career was over.

Fate wasn't much kinder to Nikolai Grigorievich Ignatov. He was sure that all his feverish activity would be rewarded, that after Khrushchev's removal, he would rejoin the Presidium. Was it not he, Ignatov, who had carried out the difficult and dangerous mission of communicating with Central Committee members and explaining the changes being prepared? His job had been to gain virtually everyone's consent, to make sure they were unanimous if and when the matter was discussed at the plenum.

Luckily, everything had worked out. Next, after his appointment to the Presidium, he would begin the battle to become first secretary of the Central Committee. Brezhnev would be no obstacle.

Fate decreed otherwise. Ignatov's wish to play a dominant role in the party and government was widely known, as was his love of intrigue. But Ignatov had already played his part, and now it was time to get rid of him. He had been a very convenient figure indeed. His animosity toward Khrushchev was well known. Everyone knew that his hostility had grown into hatred after his removal from the Central Committee Secretariat in 1960. Coming from Ignatov, anti-Khrushchev sentiments seemed entirely natural.

In case Ignatov's activities had become known it would have been easy to portray him as a loner, the sole ringleader of an anti-Khrushchev action. Khrushchev would have been unlikely to conduct a serious investigation; that wasn't in his character. And Ignatov was too petty a figure. In the worst case, he'd be dismissed, and that would be the end of it.

In the end, everything went well, and all the conspirators' fears proved groundless. When Father was removed in October, all they decided was who would replace him as first secretary and premier. As I've indicated, other major changes were postponed until November. But Ignatov's presence at the November plenum was highly undesirable. He might start a public fight. There were enough other problems without him.

The situation resolved itself. An official delegation was to go to Thailand and Cambodia in November 1964. Ignatov was appointed to head it. He tried to object but then resigned himself to going. Nikolai Grigorievich departed under a black cloud; he still hoped against hope that he might be promoted, even while he was out of the country, but deep down he knew all was lost.

Ignatov learned the results of the plenum in Bangkok: they had elevated Shelepin to the Presidium, removed Ilyichev and Polyakov from the Secretariat, and removed Adzhubei from the Central Committee. There wasn't a word about him, as if he didn't exist.

His return to Moscow was frigid. He gloomily shook hands with those who had come to the airport to meet him. He asked no questions. As soon as the official procedure ended, he got into his waiting Chaika and drove home.

Ignatov did not have a chance to get even with his tormentors. He never recovered from the shock. One illness after another overtook him. Medicines didn't help; his body refused to fight. Ignatov died in 1966. His ashes were entombed in the Kremlin wall at Red Square.

Such were the fates of some of those who participated in those memorable events.

ALTHOUGH all of us could still feel the pain of recent events in the autumn of 1964, Father gradually began to develop new habits.

While still in office, he liked to say, "The immediate reaction to a decision isn't so important. The main thing is to know what to do when events begin to unfold. Sometimes a crisis will materialize years after the decision is made." But now he could only observe from the sidelines.

Father glanced through the morning newspapers, but he no longer made note of articles on domestic and international developments that required his study, reflection, and final decision. The newspapers set aside, he went out to walk down by the Moscow River. An endless day lay ahead.

"I've got to learn how to kill time," he would often say.

Father selected a pile of books from his extensive library. Earlier, there simply hadn't been time for them; now there was more than enough, but he didn't have the required concentration. His own recent experience rankled too much for him to empathize with others. He would mechanically leaf through the pages, lay the book aside, and set off again on one of his interminable walks.

As always, Mama ran the house. Somehow she managed everything. She saw to it that everyone was fed, made sure that Father wore his habitual clean white shirt, put everything in its proper place — all this with a warm, ready smile on her round face. She acted as if no catastrophe had occurred: the Central Committee had simply made another decision, in this case involving the dismissal of her husband, and she accepted it as she had accepted so many others in her day. After all, she wasn't just his wife, but a party member, and democratic centralism's dictates about subordination from top to bottom, of the minority to the majority, had become second nature. Once they were made, decisions had to be unconditionally carried out. Even to discuss them was fractious activity, sedition, just a step away from a political "deviation."

Moreover, Stalin's character had had a definite effect on the way of life led by Politburo members. Deep down, he seemed to hate family life, to fear that mutual trust and loyalty between husband and wife would somehow infringe on his monopoly over the thoughts of his comrades in arms. Stalin had instituted eastern traditions that kept women out of men's affairs. As far as I remember, Mama was never invited to Stalin's dacha, nor were the wives of other leaders.

This weighed heavily on our family, but it didn't ruin the relationship between my parents. They always supported each other and attentively looked after their children's upbringing. But there was an unspoken barrier that no one, not even Mama, ever crossed. It was too dangerous to discuss at home what went on at the higher levels. No one ever asked Father what went on at Stalin's dacha, and he never told anyone.

Nor did his habits change much over the years. There was a gulf between his work and his family. When politics wasn't involved, Father would willingly talk for hours about an idea that intrigued him in construction or in agriculture. But the October 1964 decision was one of those that it was taboo to discuss.

Only many years later, when Father was no longer alive, did Mama tell me something of her suffering, of the agonized nighttime monologues she had addressed at Brezhnev. Her torment was no less than ours, but she concealed it better behind an exterior of calm cordiality.

Her strength of character had manifested itself in her youth. When she was still in high school, she became a Red Army scout who sneaked way behind White Guard lines. She must have done so with a fearful heart, but with a lighthearted smile concealing her inner tension. During the tragic thirties, when every knock at the door might be fatal, when friends and comrades disappeared, she never let on how she felt; she just went about her homemaking with a smile that had a calming influence on everyone around her.

In more recent years, as the wife of the chairman of the Council of Ministers of a great power, she always knew how to act, her gentle tact putting everyone from workers to presidents at ease. So it was in those difficult days. She took control unobtrusively, without excess words, and everyone accepted this as fitting and proper.

Father had no visitors. The seemingly inexhaustible stream suddenly ceased to flow. Some people had no further reason to see Khrushchev; they needed to cultivate new contacts quickly. Others, the majority, were simply afraid, and not without reason. Every visitor was carefully scrutinized. No one asked for identification papers, but a detailed report was on Semichastny's desk the very next day — who the person was, who were his parents and friends, his occupation, his views, and whether his contact with Khrushchev might be dangerous.

One Sunday I invited my friends and co-workers Valery Samoilov, Yuri Dyatlov, and Volodya Modestov to the dacha; they had been frequent visitors in the past. I wanted to try to distract Father, to dispel his gloomy thoughts.

Father perked up a bit, and we all went for a walk. He showed off the dacha's recently built hydroponic greenhouse with his old enthusiasm. Hydroponics, the raising of vegetables without soil in a solution of nutrients, was his latest passion. When we entered the hothouse, Father's eyes lit up and he was once more his old self.

"Only hydroponics can ensure a year-round supply of vegetables to our cities," he declared. "There's no other way to solve the problem. The whole world is doing it this way. We have to create a situation where fresh vegetables in winter are no longer a delicacy."

Politely nodding agreement, the guests squeezed the green cucumbers and reddish pink tomatoes. At the height of his peroration, Nikita Sergeyevich stopped short and fell silent; the light had gone out of his eyes.

"This is no longer any of my business. And you don't understand much about it anyway. So let's go eat." He abruptly turned toward the exit.

After dinner the guests left. On Monday, the organization where we all worked received an inquiry listing the names of everyone who had visited the dacha over the weekend; the KGB demanded detailed information about them.

His former colleagues were afraid of Khrushchev. Although overthrown, he still seemed dangerous; they still expected him to do something unpredictable, to take some sort of action. No one could believe that he wasn't about to attempt anything, that he was reconciled to his fate. It was very difficult to picture the frenetically energetic Khrushchev as a pensioner uninterested in political activity. Every visitor was considered a potential "contact." What if Khrushchev linked up with his supporters, broke out of his isolation, and entered Moscow like Napoleon returning from exile?

Nothing could have been further from reality. Father was too depressed; more important, he had decided in October that if his colleagues wanted to dismiss him, he would go quietly.

Again and again he would repeat these words: "The fact that my comrades could demand my removal — whether rightly or wrongly — the removal of the first secretary of the Central Committee and the chairman of the Council of Ministers, represents the greatest achievement of my life. It means that we have succeeded in restoring Leninist principles in intraparty life. Could we have imagined anything like this in Stalin's time? Now we can speak our minds freely to each other. Even if I hadn't done anything else, it would have been worth living and fighting for this alone." Khrushchev considered even his own removal a victory, the victory of the course he had proclaimed at the Twentieth Party Congress, in 1956.

Speaking of this atmosphere of nervous suspicion, I remember an episode that occurred at the beginning of December. I had to go to Leningrad on business. I took the Red Arrow, the overnight train, along with a leading scientist, Semyon Abramovich Alperovich, and an official from an affiliated institute, Aleksei Dmitrievich Aleksandrov.

Our business in Leningrad was quickly resolved. After lunch, just a few trivial formalities remained. We put off signing the agreement until the following day and went to check into a hotel. But everywhere we received the standard answer, "Sorry, no rooms." To make matters worse, it was very cold — ten below zero Celsius, with a wet wind off the Baltic that made it feel like twenty-five below.

We were saved by our colleague Yasha Kavteladze, a gallant navy captain. Running into us on the Fontanka, he dragged us all back to his home. As a result, we dropped out of sight, creating more than a little alarm on the part of those out of whose sight one isn't supposed to drop.

Having completed our business, we returned to Moscow, where we immediately found ourselves surrounded by nervous whispering. Semyon Borisovich Puzrin, who had authorized the trip, had been punished for lack of vigilance. They tried at length to elicit from Alperovich the reasons we had gone to Leningrad: Was the trip really necessary? Why had we gone there now? And above all, had he noticed anything out of the ordinary in my behavior? The anxious Semyon immediately related everything to me. During the next few months, I didn't take any more business trips.

Life at the dacha flowed along uneventfully. Father's ties with the outside world had been cut off for good. Only his doctor, Vladimir Grigorievich Bezzubik, periodically came out, prescribed something to calm Nikita Sergeyevich, chatted about life, and related the latest news. "Time is the best healer," he would say. Before leaving, he would remind Father that he would pay him another visit in a few days.

Father's seclusion was breached by an invitation, delivered by Melnikov, to come to the Central Committee. Brezhnev wanted to speak to him. Father was still quite crushed; he simply didn't have the strength for such a discussion, but of course he went.

Brezhnev reported that it had been decided to grant Father a personal pension of five hundred rubles a month (until then he had still drawn his pay as chairman of the Council of Ministers). The decision also specified where Khrushchev was to live. He would be given an apartment in Moscow, a dacha in the country, and the use of a car from the Kremlin motor pool. The house in Lenin Hills and the dacha in Gorki-2 were to be given back to the state. Certain other household questions were also spelled out.

Having communicated this, Leonid Ilyich stood up, indicating the audience was over. Father curtly expressed his thanks, and the two men parted coldly, never to meet again. Now we faced all the problems of moving.

They quickly picked out an apartment for Father. He would henceforth live at 19 Starokonyushenny Lane. Mikhail Sholokhov, the prize-winning author of *And Quiet Flows the Don,* had once lived in the same flat. The apartment house was an old one, built in the 1930s for employees of the Central Committee of the Communist party. They put it up right after they built the "House on the Embankment."[7] There weren't even any garbage-disposal chutes.

One entered the apartment through well-constructed double doors that nicely insulated it from the stairwell. There was a spacious entrance hall of five or six square meters, off which were four rooms. Straight ahead was the largest one, which was rather dark; the window looked onto the very corner of the courtyard. This was the master bedroom. Next to it was the sitting room, with a window on the street. To the right, a glass door led to a small, bright dining room, beyond which was the combination office-library, to which they moved the books from Lenin Hills. On the left, a low-ceilinged corridor led to Nina Petrovna's bedroom, and to the right of that was a long, irregularly shaped kitchen and other necessary facilities.

The apartment wasn't very comfortable, but Father made a pro forma inspection and agreed to accept it. Besides, it wasn't clear he had any choice. He had little interest in how and where he was going to live and would have agreed to anything. Even before his fall from power, Father had been extremely undemanding when it came to clothing or food. He always wore made-in-Moscow suits. Rumors about his having an Italian tailor are untrue, and the image of him standing for hours in front of a mirror (in Peter Wright's book *Spycatcher*) is a fantasy.

The move couldn't begin immediately because some remodeling had to be done. We understood that they needed time to rig up their listening devices. Moreover, they immediately ran into complications about where to put the receivers. After all, you don't bug someone just for a day or a month — it could be years! Father was in good health.

The KGB had to requisition a room from a family that lived two

7. *Editor's note:* The House on the Embankment, where members of the party and government elite lived, is described in Yuri Trifonov's well-known novel of the same name.

floors below, the Burmistenkos. Mikhail Alekseyevich Burmistenko had been a secretary of the Ukrainian Central Committee when Father was in charge in Kiev; he perished in 1941 trying to break out of the city, which was surrounded by the fascists. The duty officer of Father's security detail was installed in the Burmistenko apartment. No one told us about the installation of the listening devices. It was done secretly. But in those days no one doubted the existence of such devices, nor was any special proof needed that they had been installed.

There was a small hitch with the dacha. Father's security was entrusted to the Ninth Directorate of the KGB, which protected members of the Presidium. State dachas were also under their authority. Father tried to decline such protection, citing his status as a pensioner and the desirability of saving the state money. But his effort failed.

The boss in charge of such matters couldn't resist needling Father: "What are you talking about, Nikita Sergeyevich? You can't get along without security. You can't imagine how many people despise you. We're responsible for your safety!"

Khrushchev waved his hand and didn't raise the subject again. But once in a while he would joke sadly: "It isn't easy to figure out who they're protecting from whom — me from the outside world, or it from me."

Since the Ninth Directorate protected Presidium members, it naturally had at its disposal the very best dachas, one of which Father was still using. But none of these dachas, in the opinion of the leadership, was suitable for the ousted Khrushchev. They had to find something a bit more modest.

Finally, it was found. Several employees of the apparat who were particularly close to Father had been dismissed from their posts. Such was the fate of Georgy Sergeyevich Stepanov, business manager of the USSR Council of Ministers. The dacha he was obliged to give up went to Father. That left only the formalities — transfer of the dacha from the Council of Ministers to the KGB, and installation of listening devices.

At the end of December, Mama, Father, and the children who were around at the time went out to Petrovo-Dalneye to see the new dacha. The move was to take place right after the New Year's holiday.

Father liked the place. The single-story, green-painted log house stood on a high, pine-covered bank of the Istra River, not far from where it flows into the Moscow River. The pines around the edge of the house had been felled long ago, and now an apple orchard stood in their place. Flanked by flower beds, paths wound among the apple trees.

Ancient, overgrown lilac and jasmine bushes grew beneath the windows, and in summer the scent of their flowers filled the house. In winter, flocks of sparrows, tomtits, and bullfinches made themselves at home in those bushes, and once in a while a nimble finch would swoop in. When it was very cold the birds would huddle all bristled up, plumelets extended, like colored balls.

From the gate, an asphalt driveway led to the house, ending in a square space next to the porch.

Accompanied by Melnikov, who had already been there in his role as guide-"owner," we entered the house and found ourselves in a tiny entrance hall. The walls were paneled in oak veneer. The house had been built in the thirties, when wood-paneled walls were considered a sign of respectability. Stalin liked such walls.

A small coatrack stood in the entryway; beside it was a simple rectangular mirror, beneath which stood a small table. The rest of the walls consisted of doors — straight ahead to the bathroom, on the right a tiny corridor to the kitchen. Yet another door led to a living room in the corner of the house whose windows opened onto the little square by the porch. And on the left was a long corridor leading to a fifteen-square-meter room with a large window that overlooked the orchard.

The house seemed spacious and yet cozy. Mama divided up the rooms among our large family. The large billiard room became the dining room where the entire family could gather — children, grandchildren, nephews, and nieces.

Having examined the house, we donned our coats and went outside. Melnikov wanted to show us the outbuildings and the rest of the property. To the left of the porch stood the greenhouse with its tall chimney. Its glass roof sloped toward the house, and blackened shelves for flowers were visible through the square glass panes. We didn't go inside.

"Behind the greenhouse there's a summer kitchen," Sergei Vasilievich said, pointing to a little shed. "But really it's just an unheated house with two rooms, one small and one a bit bigger. The little house over there by the gate is heated."

Glancing at me, Sergei Vasilievich evidently remembered that there was no room for me in the dacha. He continued, "We want to put the security duty officer in the heated house by the gate, and that will leave one room free. Sergei could have it."

We looked at this gatehouse too; it had three rooms and a small glassed-in veranda. One of the rooms would have suited me fine, but I never did get to use it. It turned out there were special circumstances that Sergei Vasilievich had naively failed to take into account.

We had begun the move, and I was lugging my goods and chattel to my new lodging, when I found Melnikov blocking the way. Blushing and stammering in embarrassment, he explained that he had consulted with his superiors. The house was reserved for service personnel, so I could not move in.

Not understanding at first what was going on, I began to insist, citing our previous conversation. But after a moment, I decided not to humiliate myself and turned back to the main house.

Later we understood. We should have guessed right away what they were up to, but at that time we didn't yet fully realize that Father was under surveillance. Naturally we anticipated microphones in the dacha, but we didn't think about receivers and tape recorders. It turned out the equipment had been installed in the little gatehouse. My regular presence there, and the prospect of my dropping in whenever I wished, would have unquestionably hindered those working there.

It's worth mentioning that the equipment was extremely mediocre, and the eavesdropping was quite careless, especially in the last years of Father's life. The guards who came on duty after Melnikov was replaced often substituted music tapes for the blank recording tapes to while away the long autumn evenings. When they did, we could just make out the faint melodies and indistinct words through the walls of Father's room; the microphones had become speakers.

A couple of times, I allowed myself to play a joke. On hearing the music, I pretended to be surprised and proposed searching for the source. A moment later, the music stopped.

After checking out the new dacha, we drove back to our old one and began preparations for the move. As usual, Mama was in charge. She had to move many times in her overburdened life, sometimes willingly, mostly against her wishes. Sometimes she joked sadly that she could become a professional packer.

Everyone packed his own things. Together we packed the books. Mama warned us sternly that we must not take along any "souvenirs" from the residence; no matter how much we might treasure them, everything was to be given back to the Central Committee. Her word was law for us. There was no need to say it twice.

The preparations took many days and a lot of energy. However, no one tried to hurry us.

I've already written that in this difficult transition to a new life, one of Father's most frequent and welcome visitors was Dr. Bezzubik. They had gotten used to each other during the preceding years. Dr. Bezzubik not only treated Father in Moscow but accompanied him on his trips around the Soviet Union and abroad. In short, they became friends.

Father had listened attentively to his numerous physicians, including a few quite famous ones, but also regarded them with some irony. As the recipient of so much advice, he'd mastered the physician's guiding rule: Always reassure your patient — whether you've diagnosed the problem or don't have a clue. That's why Father's physicians had assumed an air of erudition, and pontificated instead of speaking.

Bezzubik was smarter. He quickly realized what kind of man he was dealing with and adopted a different tone, one of friendly frankness. If he didn't fully understand the source of an illness, he openly admitted it, all the while preserving a professional distance between doctor and patient. He discussed various alternatives with Father, and didn't so much prescribe as advise.

This approach evoked candor from Father in return. Gradually, they got to be friends who discussed the most varied topics, some of them far removed from medicine. Father liked to trip Bezzubik up with a good-natured joke. Vladimir Grigorievich would answer in a humorous vein, but there was always deep meaning to his words. Father took these conversations very seriously.

Bezzubik's very presence always had a positive effect on Father, but now he really needed Vladimir Grigorievich. Bezzubik brought with him a sense of confidence that everything would be all right, and transmitted it to us. He seemed to me the embodiment of the now-forgotten family doctor — a friend, a guardian of family secrets, a man you could count on at a time of hardship.

Moreover, at no time during his many years of treating Khrushchev did Bezzubik ever try to exploit the connection for personal gain. He hadn't ever forced his way into the academy, nor had he even snagged himself a full professorship. Considering it indecent to make a career in this way, he remained an assistant professor.

During those difficult days at the end of 1964, Bezzubik made every effort to help Father recover from the shock, and to reduce the stress and tension. They conversed for hours at a time. He prescribed sleeping pills and tranquilizers. However, the medication didn't take effect; only the passage of time would bring relief. Meanwhile, Father would silently circle the dacha grounds again and again, walking along the fence that ringed the property, deeply immersed in his thoughts. Melnikov and I would walk with him, sometimes alongside him, sometimes single file.

The silence oppressed us. We tried to distract Father by attempting to strike up a conversation about some more or less neutral news from Moscow, but he didn't react. Sometimes he himself broke the silence and repeated bitterly that his life was over, that life made sense as long as people needed him, but now, when nobody needed him, life was meaningless. Sometimes tears welled up in his eyes. We were worried, of course, but Vladimir Grigorievich told us not to be afraid.

"This is one of the consequences of shock," he explained to us.

Meanwhile, the endless walks continued, and father remained withdrawn.

Nineteen sixty-five arrived and everything was ready for the move, but we had to greet the New Year in the huge, gloomy dining room of the old dacha. The only thing that had changed here since the previous owner left was that the portrait of Stalin, which used to hang beside those of Marx, Engels, and Lenin, had been taken away. One couldn't help noticing the bare patch on the wall.

Along the walls were uncomfortable couches covered with black leather, and in the middle of the room stood a huge table for thirty or forty people. The fireplace, at the end of the room, was made of gray marble; we weren't allowed to use it, for safety reasons, they said, an excuse we found somewhat farfetched.

All the members of our extended family gathered together on December 31. It was our first family New Year in several years. Father had always loved having guests. Right until the very eve of his dismissal we always had visitors on weekends — party officials of different levels, military men, engineers, and sometimes even the American ambassador.

Father put great stock in personal relations; that way he could better understand whom he was dealing with and be sure he was making himself sufficiently understood. He applied this principle to international affairs when he became head of state. He preferred a face-to-face conversation to lengthy correspondence conducted via the Ministry of Foreign Affairs.

He really liked some of the leaders he met and talked with, but after other conversations he would literally spit with disgust; he never failed to add, however, that one can't be guided in politics by sympathy or antipathy, just rationalism. But like any normal person, he preferred to deal with people he liked.

Establishing good relations with the United States was a matter of great importance to Father, a fact that needs no explanation. That's why he paid such close attention to Ambassador Llewellyn Thompson, who had replaced Charles Bohlen, a man Father valued immensely for his political wisdom.

Father also took a liking to the new ambassador's calculatedly re-strained cordiality. Thompson was good at finding mutually acceptable solutions to the stickiest problems, and his wife, Jane, was open and sincere.

After Father's first invitation to Thompson to spend the weekend at the dacha turned out well, other such weekends followed. These get-togethers weren't frequent, and they ceased during periods when relations between the two countries worsened, but they always resumed.

Business discussions in the living room alternated with walks in the woods, inspections of rows of corn, or boating on the Moscow River.

Mama imparted a special ease and naturalness to these gatherings. She made it seem as if two friendly families were getting together, rather than representatives of two great powers whose relations left a lot to be desired. She had her own items to discuss with Mrs. Thompson: problems of raising grandchildren, questions about housekeeping in the faraway United States. The main thing I remember today is the mood of those weekends. I don't remember what the discussions were about, but I still have a clear image of nice people strolling with Father around the dacha grounds.

I think these meetings made a great contribution to improved un-derstanding of the motives of leaders of our two nations. And improved understanding is the first, the most difficult, and the most essential step toward the establishment of mutual trust.

AFTER Stalin's death, Father proposed opening the Kremlin to the peo-ple. After that, one of the first big events became the New Year's Youth Ball, held in the St. George's Hall of the Kremlin Palace. Once the Pal-ace of Congresses was completed, it held the annual New Year's recep-tions that I've already described. Father was always drawn to people, to life, to movement.

One of the first acts of the post-Khrushchev leadership was to abolish the big New Year's reception. Even if they had continued it, Khrushchev certainly wouldn't have been invited.

None of us was in a holiday mood that year, but we all dressed up and tried to look merry and cheerful. By eleven o'clock we were in our places at the huge table. Even our large family couldn't fill half the table. We drank to the past year and to a happier 1965. Father sat there quietly, taking no part in the festivities, just looking on.

The dacha's telephones were in the living room next to the dining room. All except one city line were disconnected. A few people called with New Year's greetings. I answered the phone, since most of the calls were from my friends. Sometimes people from the remote past — father's colleagues from the Donbas or Mama's comrades from the Electric Lamp Factory — called to wish them well. Until 1917, Father had been a metalworker at coal mines and factories in the Ukraine. After the revolution, he worked for the party in the same region. Early in the thirties, when Father was a party secretary for one of Moscow's districts, Mama directed a political discussion circle at the Moscow Electric Lamp Factory.

But nobody asked to speak with Father, which was why I was surprised when I heard a voice that sounded familiar: "Nikita Sergeyevich, please."

My thoughts were on a different wavelength, and I had no idea who this brave caller was. I didn't think it prudent to ask who was calling so, slightly discombobulated, I shouted through the open door: "Papa, it's for you."

Father raised his head but for a moment or two didn't get up. He was apparently wondering who could be calling and trying to decide whether to come to the phone or not. But he didn't ask; instead, he slowly stood and shuffled over to the phone like an old man. He had been walking this way for a while now.

Father took the phone. "Hello." Pause. He was listening to the phone, and we were listening to the silence.

"Thank you, Anastas." His voice sounded young again, almost as it had been before. "Happy New Year to you, too. My best wishes to your family."

Again, he was listening.

"Thank you, I'm trying to keep my spirits up. My business is now retirement, I'm learning how to take it easy." He was trying to be playful. The conversation soon ended. When father appeared in the doorway, he looked younger.

"Mikoyan called," he said. "He sends his greetings to all of you."

Father took his seat. Gradually the new life in his eyes died out. His old friend's call had cheered him up, but not for long. We all rejoiced that the short call had brought a little joy into his life. Anastas Ivanovich had courage to call. Mikoyan had never lacked courage or decency.

The call didn't go unnoticed. The next day Semichastny sent a transcript of the conversation to Brezhnev. Nor did Brezhnev let it go by; he made Mikoyan aware of his extreme displeasure.

No one else who had anything to lose called Father that evening.

The clock struck midnight. We opened a bottle of champagne. At that moment, several women who worked in the house entered the room: the cook, the waitress, and the maids. They brought a cake that they had baked for the New Year and set it down in front of Father. He came to life a bit and poured them champagne. They said that they had come to say good-bye; they were going to be transferred to other places, but they would always feel warmly toward Nikita Sergeyevich, and would remember him as a good and kind person for whom they had enjoyed working.

Toward the end of the speech, tears appeared in their eyes; Father shed a few as well. To this day, our family has the warmest feelings toward these women. When Mama was alive, they occasionally dropped by to chat or to help her around the house. From time to time, we encounter those who are still alive at Father's grave at Novodevichy Cemetery.

With this farewell, our New Year's party was over. Half an hour later, everybody had departed.

Early in 1965 we finally moved to the new place. Both Father and we spent that whole year getting used to his new status as a pensioner. On top of everything else, the shock and stress triggered a serious illness. At first the doctors suspected pancreatic cancer, but it proved to be simply an inflammation. The ways of the Lord are indeed inscrutable, and one never knows where and when the body will break down. Dr. Bezzubik prescribed a cure, which Father followed diligently, and everything turned out all right, although until the end of his days he was on a strict diet, including a total ban on alcohol.

It wasn't a high price to pay. Even before then, Father had never abused alcohol. But he certainly wasn't hypocritical either, and wasn't averse to downing a couple of glasses of good brandy on a holiday. I saw him intoxicated only very rarely. He never forgot the lavish drinking bouts at Stalin's late-night suppers. Stories about my father making public appearances under the influence of alcohol I find extremely dubious.

Of course, in the company of friends, he would sometimes allow himself to sit up late into the night. At times like these, he especially liked to sing Ukrainian folk songs. He would start the song and the rest would join in. I remember many of the songs he would sing, and I still love them today.

After his illness, Father raised a glass only twice. The glass he used was a special one he had brought with him from Kiev. It was a narrow, long-stemmed goblet that held about ten grams. For his seventieth birthday, in April 1964, he had received a bottle of seventy-year-old brandy. He had tasted it then and liked it very much. But it stayed in the bar until 1971, when it was drunk at his funeral banquet.

Gradually, Father began to pull himself together. He started to show some interest in events going on around him, to look for something to occupy his time.

Fishing is considered the traditional pastime of retired people — it has the advantage of combining the maximum amount of time with minimum effort and expense. But Father never liked it. I remember going fishing a couple of times when we were living in Kiev. A big, noisy crowd emerged from our dacha on the steep right bank of the Dnieper, lugging one of those huge nets the use of which would later be forbidden by law.

You couldn't hear yourself think as they hauled the net out to the boat, cast it over the side, and then began to drag it. The catch wasn't large, but by evening there was enough for a bucket of fish soup. A bonfire was lit, and neither it, the conversation, nor the Ukrainian songs died down until very late. I'll always remember the banks of that river, the fishing net, and the fish that jumped out of the net at the last moment.

Now we were all falling over one another in an attempt to get Father to start fishing again. A tackle box with lines and lures was found in a closet; it was a gift from the East German leader Walter Ulbricht. I brought a fishing rod and bobbers. Father spent several days preparing his equipment and reading books on fishing.

Finally everything was in readiness, and he went down to the Istra River. There were a few scattered fishermen on the banks. One of them recognized Father and made a place for him. Father cast out his line and waited. As is customary, the fish weren't biting. He took the rod, checked the bait, and cast his line out again. I don't recall whether he caught anything or not, but the experiment failed. He was irritated by the endless, meaningless sitting.

"You sit there feeling like an absolute idiot! You can even hear the fish laughing at you under the water. That's not for me," was how he summarized his experience.

He never fished again. But sometimes, on his walks along the river, he would ask the fishermen, in a low voice, about their catches. The fishing rods remained unused until the end of his life. They now stand unused in my house.

Father's near total isolation from the outside world was a special problem. Previously, an abundance of information had flowed in from numerous sources: state, party, industry, the Foreign Ministry, intelligence services, the Soviet and foreign press; now only a thin and carefully filtered rivulet of news from newspapers, television, and radio reached him. This was his only link with life beyond the dacha fence.

He used to call us good-for-nothings when he found us in front of the television. Times had changed: "Now my business is retirement," he chuckled. "Let *them* make the decisions. Then I'll find out on TV whatever it is they want to reveal."

When he took a walk, he always brought along a small Falcon radio. In the morning he read newspapers, as he always had, frequently grumbling: "This is just garbage! How can they write like this? What kind of propaganda is this? Who will believe it?"

Father obviously missed his information. He found a Zenith shortwave radio that had been given to him in the fifties by the American businessman Eric Johnston and started to listen to Western Russian-language broadcasts.

What he heard didn't exactly make him rejoice. Step by step all his reforms were abolished. One of the first steps was the return to central economic management. The heads of the former regional economic councils strained at the leash, eager to return to Moscow and regain their status as ministers. There weren't enough ministries for them all, so they had to scramble to find good slots.

Kosygin picked out some new apartment houses going up on the newly created Kalinin Prospekt and gave an order to transform them into new ministry buildings. The construction was extremely expensive, since apartment houses couldn't easily be adapted to the requirements of office buildings. But the high cost didn't stop them. The reborn ministries were now claiming their share of the pie; their time had come.

Father wasn't the only one living in Petrovo-Dalneye. There were several other dachas in the village. Two vice chairmen of the Council of Ministers, Mikhail A. Lesechko and Ignaty T. Novikov, and the finance minister, Arseny G. Zverev, also lived there.

They treated Father with respect when they ran into him in the village. They didn't know how to address him or what to say, so out of habit they half reported to him, half telling him about their official activities, as if waiting for him to give them an order or some advice. These meetings oppressed Father, and he tried to avoid contacts with his former subordinates.

The dacha community had a small club with a movie theater where twice a week they showed new films. But Father practically never went there.

The dachas in the village were separated from each other by solid green fences with wooden gates opening onto the asphalt road. The gate to the village as a whole was guarded by old babushkas from the general security service, but at the entrance to our dacha stood officers of the KGB.

From the dacha's windows one could see the Istra and Moscow rivers, and the fields beyond. The slope of the hill that led to the river was punctuated by holes of various sizes which were remnants of dugouts, trenches, and gun emplacements from the last war. Positions on the hill were a great advantage, and in 1941 our troops had awaited the Germans there, but they never came.

Under the trees was a very thick layer of hazel, elder, and stinging nettle. Because of this undergrowth it wasn't easy to walk there, and you had to force your way through. Somewhere in the brambles a badger had his hole; if you were lucky, you might even encounter him. A flock of gray herons lived in the tops of the pines. Once a couple of white storks arrived and settled in as our neighbors. They were like a message from Kiev. A pair of storks had nested next to Father's dacha on the banks of the Dnieper, in a thick poplar whose top had been lopped off by lightning. Before the war there were two of them, but when we came back in 1944 we found only one. He continued to live a solitary existence. Since my childhood, I had been used to waking up to the tapping of storks' beaks. However, the latest storks didn't like Father's new dacha and failed to return the next spring.

To get to a dressing hut and a small wooden platform at the edge of the Istra you took the wooden stairs that led down the steep slope straight from the house. Or you could get there in a roundabout way by taking the asphalt path to the gates, turning right, and then passing the green hut where the guards lived. This route took you along a sloping path that skirted the whole property and then descended straight to the river.

Near the fence was a hilly meadow that once had been an apple orchard. Now only a few trees remained, scattered and mutilated by time, and with no apples on their branches. On the edge of the woods between the pines was a bench that became Father's favorite place.

Several years after moving to the new dacha, Father began using a cane. He refused to use the numerous fancy walking sticks that had been given to him as presents, because they were too heavy. He made one for himself from an aluminum tube, bending the end to form a handle, which he wrapped with blue insulating tape; this one was his favorite.

Father always carried with him a small aluminum folding chair with a striped linen seat, in case he suddenly needed to sit down or his heart began palpitating. That began happening more and more often.

Usually Arbat, the German shepherd who accompanied Father on all his walks, carried the folding chair in his teeth. But if Arbat wasn't in the mood, Father had to carry it himself. A pair of binoculars given to him by West German chancellor Konrad Adenauer always dangled on Father's chest.

From the edge of the forest you could see the nearby fields that began just beyond the fence and extended to the Moscow River. They were planted every year with either barley or oats, but the harvest was very small.

With plentiful water close at hand, and the huge Moscow market nearby as well, they should have grown vegetables. The profit would have been enormous. At any rate, that's how Father saw it. Incompetent management upset and angered him. First he talked about his idea with us; then he couldn't stand it anymore and started to keep track of the farm workers' movements in the field. He hoped to spot the local bosses. Finally, he got lucky; one of them drove out in a four-wheel-drive vehicle.

Father went out to the field and tried to reason with the man — whether he was the director of the state farm or a team leader wasn't clear, because he didn't introduce himself properly — but nothing came of it. "We get orders from above on what to plant and where," said the man, "and they check up on implementation. So we can't take any advice; we have to make sure we do as we are told." Father never butted in with advice again, although he kept complaining to us about the scandalous mismanagement.

If you wanted to know what was going on in the neighborhood, behind the tall wooden fence, you could climb "Grass Snake Hill." The grandchildren nicknamed it that because of the grass snakes that basked there in the early spring sun.

It was on Grass Snake Hill that Father was once spotted by vacationers at a nearby lodge. The lodge was a simple place; its rank-and-file guests weren't afraid to be seen with the ousted Khrushchev. At first he and they shouted to one another over the fence, but later Father asked the village authorities to cut a small gate in the fence. After that, the crowd would sit at the edge of the forest. They used to take a lot of pictures. Even today a casual visitor will now and then proudly show me a snapshot of my father in the middle of a crowd of vacationers.

Father would regale them with stories about the past: about the war, Stalin, the Twentieth Congress, or Beria's arrest. Or he'd comment on current international affairs. They all listened with bated breath; not everyone had the chance to hear a lecture on foreign and domestic policies by a man who had just recently been making those policies.

They asked a lot of questions. Father answered them willingly and expansively. But if the questions were about Brezhnev and his policies, or the people around him, Khrushchev responded jokingly: "I'm retired now. My job is to take walks and not criticize. Let them figure things out on their own." Then he would change the subject.

These encounters relieved his loneliness. He could speak freely with these people, ask them about their jobs and lives, and find grateful listeners. Soon "Khrushchev visits" became part of the "cultural program" of the lodge. I should add that there were almost no hostile questions; when someone did ask an awkward one, Father was a sufficiently experienced politician to find an appropriate response. He never took offense.

Father kept repeating the same stories, but when I once asked if he weren't bored by these occasions, he slyly screwed up his eyes and said: "I'm an old man. When I die, all this will die with me. This way, maybe someone will remember. What I'm recounting is the very history they'd like to bury as deep as possible. But you can't hide the truth, it will find its way out."

These words made me think. I'll return to them later, but for now

I've run too far ahead of our first months in the new dacha. For the moment, let me continue my description of the house, the things in it, and the thoughts they bring to mind.

To the left of the porch was a veranda covered by translucent yellow plastic. On it were a folding aluminum table (made in Germany) with a blue oilcloth on top, and several folding and wicker chairs.

It was here on the veranda, cut off from prying eyes by lilac bushes, that Father usually rested, read, or simply sat. It was a favorite place when the weather was warm. On the wall near the window hung bunches of absinthe.

In those years I liked to spend my vacations traveling by car, sleeping in a tent, stopping where I liked. Once, when I was leaving, Father asked me: "If you're in the southern Ukraine, get me some thyme. I can smell it in my dreams. I wish I could see some again before I die."

I didn't know what thyme was. But when I was driving across the fabled steppe in Askania Nova, some local people pointed out a short grass with a pungent smell, and I picked some. I brought it home carefully and proudly gave it to Father. He smelled it, thanked me, and hung it upon the wall of the veranda. After his death, I took the bunch to my home and preserved it as a keepsake until it crumbled into dust.

Recently, when I was vacationing by the Caspian Sea, somebody showed me some unfamiliar grass and said it was thyme. I immediately remembered the "thyme" I had brought: this was absolutely different. Father hadn't wanted to upset me. He never told me what I had brought him wasn't thyme.

The double oak and glass doors to the dacha led into an entry hall. To the right was the room where my sister Lena lived with her husband, Viktor Viktorovich Yevreinov, a young chemist. Unlike my other sisters, Lena got married after Father's ouster, which meant that Viktor couldn't count on him to help advance his career. Nonetheless, he received his doctorate and now works in an institute. We see each other quite frequently.

Lena's room was small and quite dark. Two beds stood near the left wall, their heads toward the wall and separated by a bedside table. In the far right corner was a dresser made of light wood, and close to the door was a three-door wardrobe. The room was pretty cramped. Next to it, another door led from the entrance hall to a small corridor. If you went through it and turned left, you'd reach a storage closet.

To the left from the entrance was another hallway. At the end of it, behind a glass door, was a small but very light room with three doors opening into it. It was too heavily traveled to live in, but infrequent houseguests occasionally spent a night on a couch in the corner. Over the couch hung a big pink and blue picture in a golden frame — *Dnieper in the Spring,* by Nikolai P. Glushchenko. It was a birthday present to Father from my half sister, Yulia Nikitichna. After 1971 Mama gave it back to Yulia; since Yulia's death, the picture has vanished.

Next to the big window, which took up the whole wall, was a huge oak table covered with letters, photographs, and other papers. This was Mama's realm.

Father received a lot of correspondence, from his countrymen and from abroad. He hardly ever dealt with it himself. Mama looked through the mail and then read aloud to him those letters she considered interesting. She left most of the letters unanswered, but to some she typed answers and gave them to Father to sign. It was a lot of work. There were many letters asking for autographs, mainly from abroad. Mama was firm on this point — she considered it improper to indulge collectors — although there were some exceptions.

The walls of the room were crammed with so-called Swedish shelves for books that wouldn't fit into the library. Mama had made sure these shelves followed us to Moscow from Kiev.

Next to this room was the one where Father spent the last seven years of his life. It wasn't big — only about fifteen square meters in size. Two walls were almost completely given over to windows that looked out onto the veranda and the garden.

In the left corner next to the door was a big safe of the sort that used to be found in prerevolutionary tsarist offices. It was painted "oak color," actually a tasteless mixture of yellow and brown stains in the best bureaucratic style. Father had asked for it, not knowing himself, I think, why he needed it. Perhaps it was just habit: there had to be a place to keep secret documents and his firearms. Now it stood empty; even his party card was kept in the desk instead, since opening the safe required too much effort.

On top of the safe was a picture of a girl, inlaid in ebony, sitting under a tree with her hand extended; behind her was a young man with a bow and arrows. It was a gift from Jawaharlal Nehru. Next to it, on the wall, hung a watercolor, a view of a river, and a picture by Borya Zhutovsky of a black bear with a red ladybird. It was his present on Father's seventy-fifth birthday.

Zhutovsky was a very well-known painter who, along with the sculptor Ernst Neizvestny, was fiercely criticized by Father at the

Manezh exhibition [to be described in chapter six — ed.]. But he didn't bear a grudge; he realized other people had put Khrushchev up to it. After Father's dismissal, Zhutovsky was one of his few regular, although infrequent, visitors.

Next to the only windowless wall was a bed. On one side of the bed was a table with a night-light, on the other an oval Indian table decorated with an inlaid ivory peacock. It too was a gift from Nehru. On the table was a tape recorder made in Kiev; when it broke it was replaced by a Uher. At first there was only one tape, with a morning exercise program; later we used this machine to tape Father's memoirs.

Also on the table was an English phonograph in a wooden African box, a present from Ghana's president Kwame Nkrumah, who at one time was a good friend of Father's. Next to it were records of Ruslanova, Zykina, Shtokolov, and others.[8] There were a lot of recorded Ukrainian songs. Father liked to listen to his favorites and always insisted that guests take in the music as well. He never knew when to stop; he kept pressing them to listen to more and more.

He actively disliked jazz and modern music. Nor did he like the idol of those times, the singing star of opera and variety shows, Muslim Magomayev, whose style Father rejected as pretentious.

In the corner by the door leading to the terrace was an ancient radio made in Minsk. All it could pick up was Moscow, and that with plenty of static. In another corner, between two windows, was a dresser made of light wood. On it lay a Braun electric razor that Father used in his last years, a bottle of eau de cologne, and some medicines.

Near the window that looked onto the garden was a yellowish red armchair, a gift from President Kekkonen of Finland. With its back lowered and footrest raised, you could recline in it and read or sleep comfortably, especially with a Siberian cat in your lap. Next to the chair was a table with bent metal legs. Both it and the long, wide windowsill were covered with books. Father read a lot in retirement, trying to catch up on what he had missed when he was in the thick of things and had no time for literature.

I took all the books that were on the table and the sill when he died and put them on a special shelf in my house. The books are quite varied: *Notes from the Steppe,* by the nineteenth-century writer Aleksandr Erter; *In the Rushes of the Balkhash,* Aleksandr Shakhov's tale

---

8. Lidia Ruslanova, Liudmila Zykina, and Boris Shtokolov were well-known Soviet singers specializing in Russian folk songs.

about the animals living near that central Asian lake; Hemingway's *Moveable Feast;* Halifman's book about ants, *The Password of Crossed Antennas; Industrial Hydroponics,* by Dr. Maxwell Bentley; and *Fascist Germany's Strategy in the War Against the USSR: Top Secret Documents and Files for Special Use Only.* Father frequently referred to this last book when dictating his recollections of the initial period of the war. And there were these other books, too: *Military Strategy,* edited by Marshal Vasily Sokolovsky; two volumes by the Ukrainian humorist Ostap Vishnya; a collection of speeches entitled *French Court Speakers of the Nineteenth Century; The Soviet Economy: Figures and Facts;* plus a brochure advertising Tupolev's airplanes.

During those years, I was friends with Aleksei Tupolev, the son of the famous aircraft designer. Father had always been interested in airplanes. He had often visited Andrei Tupolev's design bureau, where he was briefed on the latest projects. Once at the end of the sixties he said: "I wonder what's new at Tupolev's. I used to know everything. Now I'm no longer up-to-date. Ask Alyosha to let me see some pictures of their new planes."

I don't know what he expected to get, but his request made Aleksei very uneasy. He couldn't say no because of the old friendship between his father and mine, but he was afraid to comply.

Finally he found a solution. A couple of days later, I received a colorful booklet depicting Tupolev passenger planes available for export. Father already knew these very well; when I gave him the booklet, he leafed through it, looked sad, and said only "Give my thanks to Alyosha." He put the booklet on the windowsill and never touched it again.

Father read widely during these years. Most of all he preferred classics, especially *War and Peace,* by Leo Tolstoy. He read it over and over, each time finding something new in it. This was one of the few books he liked to read before going to bed even in the period when he was in power.

He liked Leskov and Kuprin very much.[9] He read Galsworthy's *Forsyte Saga,* and many other books as well. We tried to bring him

9. *Editor's note:* Nikolai S. Leskov (1831–1895) was a Russian prose writer whose stories often focused on the lives of merchants, artisans, and clergy. Aleksandr A. Kuprin (1870–1938) was a prose writer who spent many years in emigration, returning to the USSR shortly before his death. Neither Leskov nor Kuprin fits the canons of Socialist Realist "orthodoxy." Both were "racy," Leskov in language, Kuprin in his themes.

some of the latest publications, but frequently our taste and his didn't coincide. Sometimes he asked for a particular book, usually another classic.

I brought Father some "forbidden" books, too. Once I got a typewritten copy of *Doctor Zhivago*. He took a long time reading it; the type was small and the paper very thin, almost like cigarette paper. I can't say he didn't like the book, but he didn't talk about it or quote from it, as he liked to do when reading Leskov or Kuprin. Once, during a walk, he just said, "We shouldn't have banned it. I should have read it myself. There's nothing anti-Soviet in it." Included in Father's reading was Solzhenitsyn's *First Circle* and *Cancer Ward,* and also Orwell's *1984.* He didn't like them.

While I'm at it, I want to clarify the tragic history involving Boris Pasternak. In the fifties, everyone was scandalized by the fact that Pasternak handed his book over to a Western publisher. This happens all the time now. But back then it turned Father against Pasternak.

The Twentieth Congress had recently taken place. But the image of the foreigner as the enemy, and to be treated as such, was deeply rooted in everyone's mind. Once that assumption was made, the whole affair rolled along the well-beaten Stalinist path, with "ideologists" adding fuel to the fire by spreading all sorts of nonsense about Pasternak, and denouncing him left and right.

I remember certain scattered details. I recall several typewritten pages of quotations plucked out of *Doctor Zhivago* to prove its anti-Soviet character. Like any tendentiously selected set of citations, this one proved exactly what its compilers wanted. We may not be good at much else in this country, but when it comes to quotations, we sure know how to establish nonsense as truth. Father sanctioned the actions against Pasternak [i.e., the campaign that forced him to renounce the Nobel Prize in 1958 — ed.] after reading these pages.

Semichastny was one of the most active, although not the only persecutor of Pasternak. Nowadays everyone who was involved in the affair feels ashamed, and would prefer to conceal his role, to bury the speeches he made at the time.

Semichastny recalls the tragic circumstances involving *Doctor Zhivago* in a brief memoir. I don't want to comment on his account as a whole,[10] but I can't accept that Semichastny's speech attacking Paster-

10. V. Semichastny, "Ne Zabyvaemoe [Unforgettable]," in *Nikita Sergeyevich Khrushchev: Materialy k biografii* [*Khrushchev: Materials for a Biography*] (Moscow: Politizdat, 1989), pp. 47–54.

nak was dictated by Khrushchev, or that Khrushchev at least added the foul language against the poet. Just from a psychological point of view, it doesn't make sense.

We know there were people who could incite Khrushchev against someone or something; when they succeeded, a real blowup was sure to follow. However, I can't imagine Khrushchev slyly inserting paragraphs into someone else's speech.

Nor do I remember anything like that either, although frankly speaking, I don't recall much about Pasternak; at the time, I had only a vague notion of who he was. This and other events formed but a general backdrop in my mind; only later did I understand their full significance.

I do remember one episode, however, which reveals the attitude toward Pasternak in Komsomol circles. Adzhubei once drove out to the dacha after meeting Semichastny at a soccer game or something. He brought with him a new joke.

"Nikita Sergeyevich," he said after a brief burst of laughter, "have you heard the new one making rounds? There are three plagues in Moscow: *rak* ["cancer" in Russian], Spartak [a popular soccer team not doing very well that season], and Pasternak."

I can't remember my father's reaction. I know only that he never liked jokes of that sort.

Father's confession of his guilt in the Pasternak affair came many years too late. Even before that, however, when the poet had been hounded and baited, he finally put a stop to it. After receiving a letter from Boris Leonidovich, he gave the order through an assistant: "Enough. He's admitted his mistakes. Stop it."

If not for those words, there would have been yet another stain on us. Zealous activists used to seize *stilyagi* [zoot-suited young people — ed.] on the street and "correct" the cut of their trousers with scissors. Pasternak would have been thrown out of the country just as enthusiastically.

Father's relations with artists and writers were not all as one-sided as some commentators now try to suggest. At the Second Moscow International Film Festival, when the tradition of giving the first prize to a Soviet film had not yet been established, the jury awarded it to Fellini's film *8½*. The decision was natural and fair, but it sparked a violent reaction among our ideologists. Especially outraged was Leonid Ilyichev, secretary of the Central Committee in charge of propaganda. Their arguments were simple; they repeated the hackneyed formula that the film was distant from traditions of realism and contaminated our clean and healthy society with bourgeois ideology.

The next step would have been simple — to ban the film, take away its first prize, and disband the jury. It's easy to imagine what a scandal that would have caused. As usual, they would have arranged it so that Khrushchev was responsible. Ilyichev briefed him on "the provocation" and proposed that he see the film himself and give it an objective "party assessment."

Father agreed reluctantly. The jury had already made its decision, and he had no wish to discuss or argue over it. But he agreed to see the film, and it was sent to the dacha that evening. Usually the whole family was invited to watch films in the dining room turned screening room, but this time Father didn't ask anyone.

I happened to visit the dacha that day. At first, it seemed no one was home. When I asked where Father was, I was told he was watching a film sent over from the Central Committee. That meant the screening wasn't routine, for usually our films were ordered from a movie distribution agency.

I glanced into the room, looked at the screen, and was horrified. Like Ilyichev, I assumed Father's reaction to the film would be extremely negative. Movies of this sort require a degree of preparation and experience. It's difficult for an average viewer to figure out what the director is up to, and when such films are shown, movie theaters are often half empty. I won't hide the fact that I too found Fellini's film difficult.

I was in a tough spot. But I had to act. I walked into the room, sat down on the couch next to Father, waited several minutes, and then started to whisper: "Fellini is a genius. This film created a furor all over the world. It symbolizes . . ."

Here I stumbled, and Father flew into a rage: "Get out of here and don't bother me. I'm not sitting here for the fun of it," he hissed. Downcast, I beat a hasty retreat.

Soon the film was over. Father came out into the garden and we started to walk. The silence hung heavy. "How did you like the movie? He's a very famous director —" I started to say.

"I already told you, don't keep pestering me." Father stopped me again, although now he was no longer angry. "I had no choice but to see it. It got first prize at the festival. Ilyichev is against it and asked me to have a look."

"And what do you think?" I asked cautiously.

"I didn't understand a thing, but the international jury has awarded it first prize. What am I supposed to do? They understand it better than I do; that's what they're there for. Why do they always palm these things off on me? I've already called Ilyichev and told him not to intervene. Let the professionals decide."

I sighed with relief. The trick had failed. We changed the subject and never returned to Fellini.

Ilyichev's role in the development of our ideology in those years is far from monochromatic; it's actually quite puzzling. Unlike Khrushchev, Kozlov, Brezhnev, Suslov, and many others, he really knew something about art. Recently, academician Ilyichev was shown on television giving his collection of paintings to the Soviet Cultural Foundation. Socialist Realist art was but a relatively small part of it. Ilyichev is a very interesting phenomenon who should be studied before it is too late. But such a study is beyond the scope of this book.

Speaking of films, I recall that Father had very sharp words for *The Cossacks of the Kuban,* the late Stalinist classic made just after the war. He absolutely hated the way it improved on reality, showing rich and happy peasants with tables groaning with food when in fact people had been starving.

It seems strange, but Father didn't like memoirs. I kept trying to encourage a taste for this sort of literature. I brought him Churchill, de Gaulle, the diaries of the nineteenth-century Russian statesman Pyotr Valuyev, and Sergei Witte's turn-of-the-century essays.[11] But he quickly turned the pages and said: "I'll read it later."

He reacted very negatively to the memoirs of our top military officers published in those years. It was the same with the war films. It pained him to recall the horrors of the war. These books brought back the terrible devastation the country had suffered. But the main thing was that he thought the memoirs and literary works about the war (which he didn't like either) didn't tell the truth. Some authors distorted it to their own advantage, others romanticized the time.

As a veteran who had lived through both defeats and victories, who fought at Kiev and Barvenkovo, Stalingrad and Kursk, he couldn't help

11. Sergei Witte was a Russian statesman of the end of the nineteenth and beginning of the twentieth century. Like my father's memoirs, Witte's were repressed by the police and first published abroad.

remembering the war. It was very much alive in his memory until the day he died. That's why he suffered so much each time he received news about his wartime comrades' "betrayal." He repeatedly came back to this subject in conversation, and he devoted a separate section of his memoirs to it.

It all started with General Pavel Ivanovich Batov, who fought half the war side by side with my father. Somebody (Father didn't say who) told him Batov had been asked about Khrushchev's role in the war (more specifically, about whether Khrushchev had been at Stalingrad) at a meeting dedicated to the anniversary of either the victory or the foundation of the Soviet army.

The general hesitated for a second and answered vaguely that he didn't know whether Khrushchev had been at Stalingrad, or what Khrushchev had been doing during the war, for that matter!

That sort of "forgetfulness" was to be expected; after all, Khrushchev's name was being crossed out everywhere. Ivan Khristoforovich Bagramian barely summoned the courage to name Khrushchev as a member of the military councils in the places they had fought together, that is, all the way from our western border to the Volga and back.

Other wartime "witnesses" went even further; they concocted fables or half-truths about my father. Many excelled at it, even Georgy Konstantinovich Zhukov. In his massive memoir, published in the West in the early seventies, he mentioned Khrushchev just twice.[12] First, he recalls dropping in on Father to get something to eat. So much for the fact that they first met at the front in June 1941 near Lvov, and fought together at Stalingrad, Kursk, and the forced crossing of the Dnieper, until Zhukov began his advance to Berlin. By the way, he didn't keep his "promise" to Father to bring Hitler to Kiev in an iron cage at the end of the war.

Zhukov mentions Father a second time in recounting the wounding of General Ivan Fyodorovich Vatutin. According to Zhukov, Vatutin was wounded while covering my father with his own body. Zhukov succeeded Vatutin a day later as commander of the First Ukrainian Front. In fact, he knew that Father wasn't even present at that moment.

The truth is that Father had spared no effort to save his friend. He and Vatutin had been together from Kursk to Kiev. Vatutin developed

12. G. K. Zhukov, *Vospominaniya i razmyshleniya* [*Memoirs and Reflections*] (Moscow: Novosti, 1969).

blood poisoning and gangrene. He could be saved only with antibiotics, but as if out of spite, Stalin forbade treatment with American penicillin: there was no knowing what "the imperialists" could have added to the medicine. After that it was too late.

Father proposed burying Ivan Fyodorovich not in a graveyard, but in a park in the center of Kiev: "Let the people of Kiev never forget the man who led the army that liberated them."

Until his death, Father never believed that Zhukov wrote his own memoirs. He thought they were written for him. I fear the bitter truth is that Father was wrong.

General Sergei Matveyevich Shtemenko surpassed everybody else in the memoir business. In fact, Father had never liked him; he considered Shtemenko an incompetent sycophant. "The only thing he knew how to do was to carry Stalin's maps," Father used to say about him.

Let history judge these memoirists. But let me add that all the omissions of his name, and all the petty thrusts and jabs hit their target. Father pretended he didn't care, but he did. I remember only one instance when he couldn't contain himself. In 1970, not long before his death, he noticed a guard wearing an unfamiliar pin. The guard explained that it was to commemorate the twenty-fifth anniversary of victory, and had been given out to everyone who was in the army on that day.

Father didn't say a word, but the fact that he had been "forgotten" wounded him deeply. He kept coming back to it. We tried to persuade him to forget the whole thing, but our exhortations had no effect.

Father's detractors had plenty of opportunities to wound and slander him. After all, he couldn't respond in public. I've already mentioned the cock-and-bull stories that were spread about him. But their authors were never satisfied; they kept fabricating more and more "facts" and circulating them by word of mouth. Rumors flew in all directions. They could be traced back to an elaborate system for spreading smears. An experienced director was staging the show.

Recently, historian Aleksandr Nikolayevich Kolesnik told me about a lie that started circulating widely in 1965. It alleged that my half brother, Leonid, who was a military pilot, surrendered to the Germans during the war and gave away military secrets. At the end of the war, the story continued, Leonid was apprehended by our troops and awaited just and inevitable punishment. At this point, Khrushchev supposedly went to Stalin and implored him to spare his son's life.

But Stalin rejected him with contempt. "I didn't help my own son, who was a hero. Why should I spare yours, who is a traitor? Let him answer to the people."

The story portrayed the Great Leader in a noble light; in that sense it was part of the whitewashing of his reputation that had just begun. Moreover, it was a double blow at Khrushchev: his motives for debunking Stalin were depicted as personal and not very pure, and in general he didn't look very attractive in the story. Fortunately, this foul piece of disinformation never reached Father's ears.

My half brother's true story is simple and tragic, like that of millions of others who went to war in June 1941. From the very first days, Lyonya was at the front. He was twenty-three years old and a bomber pilot. At the end of 1941, he was wounded, and decorated with an Order of the Red Battle Banner. After his release from the hospital, he managed by hook or by crook to get transferred to fighter aviation. Bombers were too slow for him. He didn't have much experience in piloting fighters, but there was no time for training since the Nazis were advancing.

The sad finale is only too typical. During one of his first combat missions, he was shot down. The bog into which his plane crashed left no trace of the plane or its pilot. All that remained of him was an Order of the Great Patriotic War awarded to him posthumously.

It happened in 1943 at the Voronezh front. Instead of a standard death notice, the front commander sent Father a letter of sympathy and condolence. We still have the letter. We tried to find the place where Leonid died, but without success. His widow, Lyubov Illarionovna Khrushcheva, really *was* arrested after her husband's death, and accused of being some sort of Swedish spy. She wasn't rehabilitated until Stalin died.

My half brother's children grew up. His daughter, Yulia, graduated with a degree in journalism and after working several years for the Novosti Press Agency became the literary director of a theater. His son, Yuri, followed in his father's footsteps, becoming a test pilot. He had shown admirable stick-to-itiveness in pursuing his goal. As an officer's son, he had studied at the Suvorov Military School, but he had been injured in the eye during a soccer match there. Until then he had dreamed of the clouds and couldn't imagine himself outside the military, but the partial loss of sight drastically altered his fate.

He managed to stay in the armed forces. One way or another, he got into an academy for infantry officers. The doctors on the review committee sternly advised him to give up the idea of becoming a pilot. Yura didn't argue, and seemed to be reconciled to the situation. But whether he was learning how to handle a machine gun or practicing hand-to-hand combat, his thoughts were in the sky, not the trenches. Finally he developed a plan that we only learned about years later.

After finishing the military academy and serving in the infantry for a while, he suddenly applied to the air force military engineering academy.

"I'd just like to be a little closer to airplanes, and I've always had an interest in technology," he explained to his grandfather.

Father supported him. He had always been attracted to a career in engineering and had a high regard for people who could work with their heads as well as their hands.

While at the academy, Yura learned to fly and joined a flying club. He proved that his defective sight didn't prevent him from feeling as secure in the air as he did on the ground. Not many could match his qualifications at that time, so he was noticed. He didn't become a fighter pilot because of medical restrictions, but he got what he wanted. He became a test pilot, testing new radioelectronic devices for helicopters, both military and civilian.

His passion for flying didn't diminish with the years. The air was the place he felt he belonged. He was recently offered the rank of general but would have had to give up flying. Yura quickly turned it down.

The years flew by. At the age of fifty he retired as a colonel. Personnel reductions in the military always affect the "oldsters" first. After a few months off, he managed to find employment as a civilian test pilot. Specialists are worth their weight in gold everywhere. That's how he makes his living, as a pilot — the son of a pilot.

LET me return to the description of Father's room. It remains to note that a mahogany veneered wardrobe with three compartments containing personal items stood near the door. On top of it was a beautiful wooden box containing three pistols — a Parabellum, a Walther, and one other — gifts from the KGB on his seventieth birthday. We didn't have any bullets for them. After Father's ouster, Vasily Kondrashov, who replaced Melnikov as head of our guard detail, suggested that it might be a good idea to turn in the guns, but Father fixed such a stare on him that he never raised the matter again.

Dmitry Nalbandyan's small painting of Lenin writing in exile hung on the wall.[13] A lovely white rug covered the floor, but Father had a linen runner put on it. It was hard to clean the rug, but the runner could easily be shaken and washed if necessary.

Mama installed herself opposite Father's room. There had once been a little terrace there, through which you could go from the billiard room into the garden without passing through the house. The former occupants had closed in the terrace and put in heating, making a cozy little room with windows on two sides. Nina Petrovna's bed stood along the wall to the right of the door. There was a sofa under one of the windows, and an old chest of drawers from our Kiev days.

To get to the former billiard room that was now the dining room, you went along the hall and turned right into a dark, wide dressing area about four meters long. On the left stood a low, wide chest with oak veneer doors which Father used for storing his rifles.

With the sole exception of hunting and guns, Father had never had a hobby during his active years. Both in Kiev and in Moscow he regularly went hunting, except for a break between 1950 and 1953. Hunting was his way of relaxing, but Stalin didn't approve of his colleagues' getting together; hunting could prove costly to the hunters.

Father loved to take out his guns and examine them. He had a couple of dozen, gifts from generals who passed through Kiev after the war and from both Soviet and foreign guests. While hunting, or when he had guests who knew weapons, he loved to show off his guns and check out those of others. Every gun was critically examined, aimed, felt, turned over. Afterward they sometimes swapped weapons. Father wasn't greedy, and if he saw that a gun pleased a guest, he himself would suggest an exchange, usually to the guest's advantage.

Later he would say with a laugh, "Did you see how happy it made him to think he got the better of me?"

After his dismissal he no longer hunted, and only rarely would he take out a rifle, examine it, look down the barrel, and fondly turn it over in his hands. Having cleaned and oiled it, he would return it to the chest.

In 1968 Father decided to give his collection away: "Let some good

13. Dmitry Nalbandyan was an official Soviet artist particularly well known for his depictions of high officials attending meetings of various kinds. When such leaders fell from power, he would replace them by painting in new figures where the old ones had once appeared. Nalbandyan had presented this picture when Father was still in office. The two men hardly knew each other otherwise.

people have the guns — something to remember me by. Otherwise, they'll be stolen after I'm gone," he added in a melancholy tone, as though foreseeing the future.

He gave rifles to me, to his grandsons, to his doctor, and to the guards who, when their superiors weren't around, helped him on the sly with little everyday chores.

After Father's death, all that was left of his collection was several beautifully made rifles and carbines of various calibers from various countries. While saying good-bye, the chief of the guard detail told me: "You better get permission to keep the rifles; either that or you should turn them in. Otherwise, you could get into trouble. They'd make a perfect excuse if anyone has it in for you. It would be no problem to get you five years in prison."

When we had recovered from the funeral, I scrupulously recorded the serial numbers and prepared an application to the minister of the interior, N. A. Shchelokov, asking permission to keep the guns at home as a memento of my father. Having found out his telephone number, I called the receptionist and stated my business. Nikolai Anisimovich himself came on the line.

"Come in tomorrow a little before five o'clock," he said.

I arrived at 6 Ogaryov Street before five and went in through the "generals' " entrance. They were expecting me and escorted me inside without a pass.

Shchelokov greeted me in quite kindly fashion. He spoke warmly of Father and asked after my mother's health. Then to the business at hand. He had read my application and said he would think about it. "Call me in a week. And don't worry — we'll settle this right."

When I called a week later, the secretary informed me that Nikolai Anisimovich wished to see me again. At the designated time, I appeared and was again received right away. The minister was still amiable, but he refused my request.

"You've got nearly two dozen rifles — enough to arm a whole platoon. You have to understand that we can't let you keep them. They have to be in a safe place."

I objected that my apartment building was as secure a place as any; after all, Politburo members lived there. In effect, the guns were under constant guard.

"And anyway I can disarm them," I said. "I'll drill some holes in the barrels and they won't be weapons anymore."

Shchelokov didn't agree. "We'll put them in a museum and make you an album with photographs of them. They'll be perfectly safe."

Having said his last word, he summoned several of his associates. I was humiliated almost to tears, but there was nothing I could do. A general and a colonel entered.

"Accompany Sergei to his apartment and pick up the rifles — they're going to a museum," Shchelokov ordered. Then he added, "Make sure you do it right."

We left. I got into my car, and my companions followed in a black Volga. It's just a stone's throw from Ogaryov Street to Stanislavsky Street, and we arrived in five minutes. I reached up to where the guns were stored and started handing them down, along with the telescopic sights, in their beautiful leather cases.

"Well, that's it," I said, surrendering the last, a small-caliber American weapon with its ten-shot ammunition clip.

"All right . . . ," the general muttered. He hesitated, apparently pondering something, and added: "Take the guns out of the cases. You can keep the cases, and the scopes too."

"But why?" I was surprised, since everything was supposed to go to a museum.

"They'll get along without them," the general snapped. "It's not forbidden to have those in your possession. And they cost money." He had a somber expression on his face. Clearly, he had no stomach for what he was doing. "We'll take them down to our car, and you tell the concierge we're going hunting with you."

The general had carried out the minister's orders.

They promised to give me an itemized receipt the following day. I never received it, nor did I ever get the album of photographs Shchelokov promised.

At first, the general put off giving me an answer from one day to the next. When I called they said he wasn't at his desk, or that he'd been called away. Still later, I learned that he had been demoted; no one else knew anything about the matter. I wasn't about to call Shchelokov again.

Only later did I realize that Shchelokov simply wanted Father's guns for himself, or maybe as a gift for Brezhnev, who had feasted his eyes on them more than once. Of course, today those guns are nowhere to be found.

In a niche on the wall opposite the gun cupboard stood a huge, beautifully made oak dresser. In it was the old uniform Father had worn at the front, along with one tailored in 1958 especially for the fortieth anniversary of the Soviet army. He had strutted around in that lieutenant general's uniform at the solemn ceremonies, after which he had me join him for a commemorative photo.

"You know, this is the last time," he said rather sadly as he left to change. Indeed it was.

It was about that time that Marshal Grechko suddenly got the idea of making my father a marshal of the Soviet Union.

"You're chairman of the Defense Council, you're our boss," Andrei Antonovich said slyly, "and we military men have our own procedures. It's not right for us to be subordinates of someone we outrank. If you become a marshal, that's another matter."

Father didn't like the idea and answered a bit rudely: "It's peacetime and nobody expects war, so I can handle you even though I'm just a general. If, God forbid, war breaks out, we'll do what needs to be done about rank. So don't come slinking around again with this nonsense," he said angrily.

Grechko grinned down at Father — he was almost six feet six inches tall — and turned the whole thing into a joke. They were old friends not only from wartime but also from Kiev, where Andrei Antonovich had been commander of the military district.

In the same little hall where the gun closet was located stood a round table with a 16 millimeter sound projector. When it became obvious that Father wouldn't go to the local club, I unearthed a long-idle Yugoslav Iskra projector and a German screen and turned the room into an impromptu cinema.

It turned out to be easy to rent films, and sometimes friends would bring new foreign ones. The quality of films and projector wasn't good, but we managed. Father particularly liked a Disney film about birds and Mikhail Shatrov's historical film *July 6*, which depicts events of 1918.[14]

14. Mikhail Shatrov (Marshak) is a well-known Soviet playwright who specializes in historical dramas. In contrast to many other writers, he has tried to portray events objectively. For this reason, his plays were banned for many years, and when one of them did manage to get produced, it was always received in Moscow as a "political event." The play *July 6* depicts events connected with the murder in 1918 of the German ambassador Count Mirbach, and the mutiny of the Left Socialist revolutionaries, who until that time had been coalition partners of the Bolsheviks in the new Soviet government.

Sometime earlier, granddaughter Yulia had brought Shatrov to the dacha as a guest. Father went for a long walk with him, boasting about his garden. Having a guest whom he liked lifted his spirits, and Father treated Shatrov solicitously. Mikhail Filippovich gave him an appropriately inscribed copy of the journal *Teatr* with one of his plays, and invited him to the Sovremennik Theater to see *The Bolsheviks*.[15]

Father rarely went to the theater in those days. In earlier times, he had often attended plays, not because he was obliged to, but because he simply loved going to the theater and concerts. His usual pattern was to go out not once but twice a week. But now his hearing was failing, he couldn't always understand the actors, and this irritated him. The fact that people stared at him made him uncomfortable, as though he were some sort of weird exhibit. Thus, he didn't have much of a cultural life. Now and then he'd go to art shows at the Manezh Exhibition Hall, across from the Kremlin, and once he visited the permanent exhibit devoted to the battle with Napoleon at Borodino.

This time he accepted the invitation with pleasure, and he liked the play. We went backstage to the director's office both at intermission and after the final curtain. Father thanked all the participants for presenting the truth — a rarity in those days — and entertained them with his reminiscences.

After this visit to the theater, Father asked me to get the film version of *July 6*. He liked that, too; he said it was historically accurate. Later he read the script several times in the journal Shatrov gave him.

Roman Karmen came to visit a couple of times with his wife, Maya, and daughter, Alyona.[16] They sat with my father for a long time at the edge of the woods. Father had a lot to tell Roman. He expressed regret for his sharp words at the Manezh, and at the meetings with artists and writers that followed. He admitted that he had been egged on by the ideologists Suslov and Ilyichev.

I remember quite well that all Father had to do, when he was in power, was hint at the desirability of democratizing of ideology, and the whole harmonious choir would pipe up: "What are you saying,

15. The Sovremennik was a young theater that had gotten its start during Khrushchev's time in power. It was famous for its bold productions, which often outraged venerable practitioners of official art. Inviting Khrushchev to the theater was itself a kind of political act in those days.

16. Roman Karmen is a well-known director of Soviet documentary films. Among his films are the Soviet-American television series *The Unknown War*, as well as movies about the Spanish Civil War and the Vietnam War, and a film about Chile.

Nikita Sergeyevich? It's unthinkable to permit the slightest hint of bourgeois ideology. That's how it all started in Hungary."

In 1970 Yulia brought Vladimir Vysotsky to see Father.[17] They spent almost an entire day together. I don't know what they talked about. All I know is that Volodya didn't sing for Father; he hadn't brought his guitar. I don't think his style would have been to Father's liking.

Nor could they have discussed the outdoor exhibition of unorthodox art that Moscow authorities dispersed with bulldozers in 1974. That way of dealing with disagreeable trends in art belongs to the post-Khrushchev era; Father relied on force of conviction and his vocal cords. The idea of using bulldozers to demonstrate a preference for realism in art would never have occurred to him.

Whom else do I recall among my father's guests?

Stella and Pyotr Yakir came several times. Father had known their father, Iona Yakir, the famous military commander whom Stalin liquidated in the late thirties. Father had taken Iona's arrest and death badly. The sight of his old friend's children gladdened him. After his own rehabilitation, Pyotr Yakir had fought to unmask Stalin's crimes and to defend human rights in our country, and, as often happened in those years, he had been persecuted and arrested. Father felt deep sympathy with them but was powerless to do anything.

Vera Aleksandrovna Gostinskaya, an old Polish Communist, spent a long time as a guest at Petrovo-Dalneye. Father loved to talk to her about the past, and while he did so, he tape-recorded his recollections for his memoirs. Her questions were quite helpful; that was easier than sitting alone at a microphone.

They had a lot in common. In the late twenties, Khrushchev and the Gostinskys had lived in Kiev in a communal apartment on Olginskaya Street. Then fate separated them. Vera Aleksandrovna received her Stalinist sentence in due course and proceeded to knock about the camps.

Along with other convicts, she was freed in the fifties. They were loaded onto trains without any documents and sent to their homeland. The train was held up at the border; not a single person — neither

17. Vladimir Vysotsky was a Soviet poet, actor, and popular singer who became a kind of cult figure for young people in particular. Because his songs reacted critically to the reality of our life, as well as having a deeper meaning, Vysotsky was out of favor with the authorities at the time he met Khrushchev.

Soviets nor Poles — had a passport, much less a visa. All they had was a certificate of release. So they sat there, hungry, for several days. Only an appeal to the Central Committee of the CPSU resolved the problem, allowing these former activists of the Polish Communist party to return to Poland.

Krystyna Beirut, daughter of the late first secretary of the Polish United Workers party, was another of Father's guests for a short while.

New friends appeared, among them Professor Mikhail Aleksandrovich Zhukovsky, the well-known Soviet endocrinologist. He was treating my nephew Vanya, who was living with his grandfather at the time.[18] Brimming over with energy, Mikhail Aleksandrovich used to pepper Father with questions, listen attentively to the answers, and take some notes. After a while, he started coming to see Father just to talk, and more than once my father was a guest in his home.

Visits by my friends and my sisters' were more common. They went for walks with Father, sat with him around a bonfire for hours, and listened intently to his stories. Because they had nothing to do with politics, these guests didn't arouse the authorities' anxiety. But with other guests they sometimes dispensed with the niceties. When it became known that a former colleague intended to visit Father, he would be warned to change plans if he didn't want trouble. That's how they shut the door on Father's pilot, General Tsybin. Nor did they let his former chief bodyguard Litovchenko visit him.

Even people who couldn't be threatened managed to "forget" their fallen friend, with whom they had worked for decades. After I had written a first draft of these memoirs, Mama retyped them for me. She inserted the following at this point:

"Once Yevgraf Ivanovich Cherepov, Father's old comrade dating back to Donbas days, came to Moscow for a miners' congress. They had studied together at the Yuzovka *rabfak* [special school for workers — ed.] and worked together on its executive committee. In a word, Cherepov was a close friend. At the time he still worked in a mine. He called (the dacha at) Petrovo-Dalneye and chatted awhile but refused to come out; he said he didn't have time — he had to visit his daughter, and then hurry home; he had business to attend to. . . ."

---

18. Vanya Adzhubei, who was born in 1959, is the son of my sister Rada and her husband, Aleksei Adzhubei. Vanya wasn't well enough to go to school at the time and so lived with his grandparents. My son, Nikita, also lived with them at times when he wasn't going to school.

People often ask me, "Did Mikoyan ever visit your father?"

Because I always regarded Anastas Ivanovich with filial respect and was friendly with his family, the very question pleases me. It shows special respect for Mikoyan, alone among Father's colleagues. No one ever asks, "Did Podgorny visit your father, or Polyansky?" Yet these men worked with Father more than Mikoyan did. At one point, they were personally closer to him; their friendship with him took shape when they were young, and that sort of thing sticks in the memory.

I'll never forget Anastas Ivanovich's principled position in October 1964. He had to display more than a little courage. When Mikoyan proposed that Father be allowed to retain one of his posts, one of his opponents (Sergo says Shelepin), indifferent to Anastas Ivanovich's age, rudely shot back: "Never! You'd better keep your mouth shut or we'll take care of you, too."

The threat didn't work; Mikoyan answered with dignity: "We're not carving up a pie here, we're deciding the fate of our state, of a great country. Khrushchev's work is the party's political capital. Kindly do not threaten me."

Judging from recently published materials, Father's former Politburo colleagues didn't hate him at all. Over the years, they came to see the method in his work rather than the mistakes.

Still, people ask about Mikoyan. Alas, he didn't come to see Father. For a while they called each other on the phone, but then even the calls dried up. Why?

It's difficult to give a simple answer. As always in life, there were lots of reasons. Of course, Mikoyan, who soon found himself disgraced to only a slightly lesser degree than Father, didn't want to take any risks. Everyone tends to think first of himself and his family.

If it had come to a defense of principle, or of Khrushchev personally, Anastas Ivanovich would not have wavered. But why risk who knows what for the sake of a cup of tea with an old friend?

There are also petty, mundane explanations. Such things may not seem serious, but anything can happen in life, and quarrels often begin with trifles. Mikoyan was treated better in retirement than Father was. They allowed him to write his memoirs, and even provided a secretary to assist him. Anastas Ivanovich lived alone in his dacha. His wife had died long ago, and his sons had their own families. The new secretary gradually took over household chores, too. There's no doubt her duties included keeping an eye on the conduct of a man who had become a ward of the state.

Mikoyan's friendship with Khrushchev didn't suit those at the top. It didn't threaten anyone or anything, but the authority of each man had been too great to permit them to socialize: who knew what the two disgraced politicians would dream up? So the authorities apparently set out to break up the friendship using a simple but reliable method — gossip. They poured disinformation about Khrushchev all over Anastas Ivanovich.

Here's just one example Sergo told me about. It seems Father's chauffeur told Mikoyan's that every time Father got into the car, he started reviling Mikoyan. Could any story be more petty or stupid? For one thing, the chauffeurs couldn't even have met: Father's car was dispatched from the KGB's Kremlin motor pool, Mikoyan's from the Supreme Soviet's. Furthermore, as far back as I can recall, Father had never uttered a nasty word about Anastas Ivanovich.

Nevertheless, this hearsay had an effect. Mikoyan was offended and he practically ceased calling Khrushchev. Father himself didn't call anyone, not wanting to put the other person, or himself, in an awkward position just in case his call wasn't "advisable." There may have been other disinformation we never learned about, maybe not. Whatever the case, after his retirement, Mikoyan never saw Khrushchev.

One can understand why others didn't visit Father at Petrovo-Dalneye. After all, this was a time when people tried to forget that Father had ever existed. They even renamed the Crimean village of Nikita, home of the Nikitsky Botanical Garden, which had borne that name for centuries, so that Leonid Ilyich wouldn't be reminded of his predecessor on the way to his Black Sea dacha.

All this Father endured silently.

I want to mention two other episodes.

After Father's ouster, foreign friends, too, stopped having anything to do with him. This was to be expected, so he was all the more delighted to receive a box of Jonathan apples, together with a warm note, from Hungarian leader János Kádár and his wife, Maria. Father liked Jonathans. The Kádárs knew this and had regularly sent him a box every autumn. Kádár himself had experienced Stalinist imprisonment, and he decided to disregard the unwritten "rules of good form."

I recall one other visitor, whose visit never actually came off. Before the opening of the presidential campaign that would carry him to the Oval Office, Richard Nixon visited Moscow. He came by Starokonyushenny Lane but Father wasn't at the apartment. The regular mail, however, brought his business card and a note. He expressed regret at missing Father at the apartment, and hoped a meeting could be arranged before he departed for home. But by the time the note arrived, Nixon had already left and the question was moot. This gesture from an American political figure pleased Father, although he didn't have a very high opinion of Nixon.

As far as I know, his poor impression was formed at their first meeting. During their conversation in the model kitchen at the 1959 American exhibition in Moscow, Nixon asked an inappropriate question about the type of fuel used in Soviet rockets; this stuck in Father's head. At the time, he was indignant.

"What was I supposed to answer? He didn't act like a statesman in that kitchen but like a second-rate spy. He, the vice president of the U.S.A., asks me, chairman of the Council of Ministers of the USSR, what kind of fuel we use in our ICBMs! Obviously, I wasn't about to tell him. It wasn't his business to find out whether we used solid or liquid fuel or something else. Everybody's got special services for that sort of thing. One should think about the questions one asks."

Yet, at the same time, Father considered Nixon a rather cunning politician. In any case, the visit with Nixon that didn't take place gave Father some satisfaction.

Most of Father's visitors at the dacha were members of the family. On weekends, we would all gather around the dinner table in the large room. These dinners became a tradition that united us. As always, Mama was at the center of things. She prepared a lot of food for Sundays, trying to make sure our favorite dishes were on the table. In the evening, everyone would take home food packages that she had carefully wrapped.

In the absence of many visitors, a TV set became virtually Father's only window on the world. It was a combination television-radio console, a gift from Egypt's Nasser. The television was black-and-white, but the picture was quite sharp. In front of it stood a comfortable armchair and a little footstool; if the program got dull, you could do a little dozing. Besides the television and radio, the console included a tape recorder that Father used when he first began to dictate his memoirs. Always keen on technical improvements, he himself made a wooden pedal he could press with his foot to stop the tape while he gathered his thoughts.

*   *   *

WE always racked our brains trying to decide what to give Father on April 17. So I decided to present a color television on his birthday. Father scolded me gently for spending money foolishly, but you could see in his eyes that he was very pleased, and to the end of his days this was one of Father's favorite toys.

Especially during the first few days, he gazed with childlike delight at the multicolored test pattern rose that was shown on the screen. He would summon us to admire the different shades of color. Next to the set, on a wood-carved Indonesian screen, Father hung a large political map of the world. On it he noted the location of events described on the news.

He was especially interested in the great changes in Africa, where new independent states were coming into existence. The process had begun while he was in power, and he worried about the problems of the Congo, Guinea, Algeria, and Ghana as if they were his own. In his day he had developed warm, friendly relations with President Kwame Nkrumah of Ghana and President Ahmed Ben Bella of Algeria. For reasons I can't recall, his relations with President Sékou Touré of Guinea were worse.

Father had taken the death of Patrice Lumumba of the Congo especially hard. He had been on vacation at the time, in Kiev. The local leadership had gathered, and at one point Olga Ilyinichna Ivashchenko repeated a ditty then making the rounds: "Had Lumumba half a brain, / Moise Tshombe — down the drain!"

Father loved a good line and delighted in coming up with one himself, but this time his face tensed angrily. He said Lumumba was an intelligent leader but the time hadn't been right for him; economically and politically, the Congo was still immature. Ivashchenko's joke fell flat.

To come back again to the first months at Petrovo-Dalneye: The winter had passed. Time began to ease Father's wounds, on the surface at least. Gradually, a certain routine was established, including new habits and diversions. He arose regularly at seven o'clock, did his calisthenics according to tape-recorded instructions, and then had breakfast. In the last years he devoted his mornings — a time when no one disturbed him — to dictating his memoirs. After that, he went for a walk with Arbat, then read newspapers, journals, and books. After lunch, more dictation. In the evening — television, supper, reading, to bed.

Father didn't adjust easily to contemporary rules and customs after his dismissal. For years he had lived his government life in an ivory tower. Naturally, he knew the country's needs because he traveled around a lot, but the everyday life that stuck in his mind was that of the twenties.

Early on after his ouster, he suddenly started worrying about how to get into the city for the weekly meetings of his party cell. I didn't understand, and he repeated the question. "Can it be that the cells don't meet every week? How can they solve urgent problems?" He was astonished.

He was on the rolls of the party organization of the Central Committee apparatus, but during all those years they had apparently been afraid to invite him. He had no idea that party cells, which had met once a week in the twenties and played an active role in party life, now convened only a few times a year to rubber-stamp decisions (having to do with enrolling new members or other such things) passed down from on high.

The most ordinary things amazed him. It was difficult to know what might upset him; especially painful to him were bribery, bureaucratism, and laziness. Once a guard mentioned having bought his way out of some traffic violation by giving the policeman a three-ruble bill. The story made an indelible impression on Father. He often recalled it, told visitors about it, and concluded bitterly: "Can you imagine!! People entrusted with enforcing the law taking bribes!! How in the world can we build communism?"

When security chief Melnikov's deputy, Lodygin, carried off some materials from a nearby construction site to use at his own dacha, Father was beside himself: "How can he do that? He's a KGB officer, isn't he? What are we coming to?"

It's a good thing he didn't know what his former Kremlin comrades in arms were up to.

One of his former interests to which Father returned after his first winter of discontent was hydroponics. I think it was Lena, who had a lifelong passion for flowers and even managed to raise orchids, who bought him Maxwell Bentley's book *Industrial Hydroponics*. He studied it thoroughly. (Today it stands on my shelf, its pages speckled with underlining, check marks, and other notes in the margins.)

Having mastered the theory, Father set about building the troughs and concocting the mixture in which the plants would grow. Polyethylene plastic was just beginning to come into use; with characteristic enthusiasm Father had pushed the first factories into production on the very eve of his ouster. Therefore, there was nothing to construct a hothouse out of, and the open troughs lay on the terrace. Father improvised by filling the cement vases flanking the staircase with stones and the mixture. We all pitched in and planted cucumbers and tomatoes. The results were nothing special. Hydroponics is an industrial process, requiring precise measurements and automation. It's difficult to do at home. Father didn't stay with it long, just a couple of years. Gradually he gave it up and turned to traditional methods of raising vegetables.

That spring he decided to try photography, something he had done in his youth. Before the war he had a Leica, but only a few of his photographs from that period have been preserved. We had had to leave all our possessions in Kiev in 1941, where naturally they disappeared.

In 1947 the Kiev plant Arsenal was converted with equipment brought from Germany from making guns to cameras. They gave one of the first cameras off the production line to my father. He had just recovered from a severe bout of pneumonia and had been given leave to recuperate, his first rest in a decade. While on leave he took up photography again, but when his leave ended the camera was shelved.

Now he would try a third time. I bought the necessary accessories. Father armed himself with a Zenit and went looking for subjects. He developed the first films himself in the bathroom, and they didn't come out badly.

But he didn't like fussing with chemicals and willingly accepted my suggestion that the film be given to a shop to develop. Slides soon replaced prints, and this time Father was captivated by the idea of photographing nature. He sought out flowering branches, rowanberry clusters, and snow-covered pines; he took a long time picking just the right spot for his camera, and rejoiced in his successes. He liked to show off his trophies to his children, grandchildren, and guests. He would draw the blinds and get out a semiautomatic German slide projector. He would fool around with it mysteriously and at great length, select the slides, and at last the show would begin. I must say, his slides were of high quality. He had learned how to compose with the camera.

Nevertheless, Father wasn't really interested. Photography was just a way to pass the time. In those days, he often said sadly, "Now I've got only one job — figuring out how to kill time."

After several years passed, during which Father photographed everything around him several times, he became utterly bored and put the camera away, taking it out only when guests came. On these occasions, he took pictures of the visitors and photographed himself with them.

More than anything else, open-air bonfires gave him the greatest satisfaction. In any weather, even in the rain, Father would wrap himself up in a greenish beige cloak that made him look like a French gendarme,[19] pick up brushwood (which was always there in abundance), start a fire, and then stare at it for hours. The fire brought back to him his faraway childhood in his native Kalinovka, when he had herded horses out to pasture. Usually his sole companion was Arbat, but on weekends we all sat around with him.

Comfortably seated around the fire, we'd listen for the umpteenth time to Father's stories about the old days. He loved to tell us about his childhood. There had often not been enough to eat and he had gone hungry, but the bitter memories faded with time, so that he remembered primarily the nightingales in Kursk, the short, warm summer nights, and potatoes cooked in the embers of a fire.

Back then, village life wasn't very romantic. The primary goal was to find a way to feed yourself, and his father took Nikita, then barely ten years old, to work in the coal mines of the Donbas. My grandfather had no education or other qualifications, and he worked winters in the coal mines. He returned home to the village each spring to work in the fields.

After a few years, my father learned metalworking and stayed permanently in the town. It was here that he found friends and came into contact with revolutionary activities.

His dream was to become an engineer, to build "clever" machines himself. Before the revolution this was impossible, but afterward, in the

19. The man who gave him this cloak was Boussac, a leading French capitalist in the textile industry and the owner of the reactionary, right-wing — or so it was then reported — newspaper *Aurore*. They had met during Father's visit to France, and they took a liking to each other and kept up contact. Boussac would send holiday presents such as a bottle of wine. That's how the cloak arrived. Father liked its simple utility very much and didn't part with it until his final days.

I can't help noting that Father easily established ties with representatives of the business world. They admired his practicality, his businesslike grasp of things. "You could become a good businessman if you lived in our country," one of his foreign guests joked. The words stuck in Father's memory. The praise pleased him.

1920s, he returned to school. His life took a different turn, but for a long time he continued to take his case of metalworker's tools with him from one party job to another as if they were a thread linking him to the dreams of his youth.

When the fire died out, the stories stopped. It was time to collect more brush for the fire.

Meanwhile, the days flowed by unhurriedly, one after the other, without change. Father liked spring best, when nature renewed itself. He didn't like autumn; in fact, he dreaded it. The darkness and the howling wind weighed down on him, and the dark, gloomily swaying pines reminded him of death.

When spring came, Father was constantly occupied in the garden; the plastic sheeting arrived and he set to work on the hothouses. He gathered up some unused water pipes scattered around the dacha grounds, bent them into the proper shapes, painted them, and drove them into the ground, making the frames for the hothouses. He worked without letup; he didn't know how to do anything halfway. Everyone pitched in: children, grandchildren, guests, the young security men. Melnikov, chief of the guard, took an active role, bending pipes and digging. It was another matter with his deputy, Lodygin; he didn't help and when on duty didn't allow his subordinates to do so either.

The hothouses took shape next to the house. Excellent cucumbers and tomatoes ripened in them. Father raised them scientifically; he acquired a library of books on agriculture and kept up with the latest developments.

In open rows in the meadow below the house he grew dill, radishes, potatoes, pumpkins, sunflowers, and, of course, corn that produced good ears of a milky-waxy ripeness.

Father had problems coping with the rooks. From their colonies in the trees bordering the garden, they paid close attention to the planting. As soon as the corn and the sunflowers broke through the surface, the rooks swooped down from the trees early in the morning, plucked out the budding plants, and left the young stalks lying in neat rows.

The war against the rooks waxed and waned. Father rejected out of hand a proposal to shoot them. He felt sorry for the birds, and therefore he tried a passive defense. He erected a barrier of thorny branches over the rows of budding plants and put up a scarecrow. But the rooks paid no attention to the scarecrow and threaded their way through the branches with the cunning of a good cat.

Still, Father never considered the rooks his enemies. He loved birds.

Once he found a fledgling rook that had fallen from the nest, picked it up, and fed it. It became quite tame, flew after Father everywhere, and ate out of his hands. Now there were three of them on his walks: Father, Arbat, and the rook.

Also living in the house were a Siberian cat and a canary that belonged to the grandchildren, who later gave it to Grandfather. Lena kept some beehives in the garden.

There was more and more to do. The days weren't long enough, and Father couldn't do everything himself. His strength wasn't what it used to be. Chores piled up during the week, and Father prepared to parcel them out when his children arrived. On Saturday everyone was assigned a task, a "lesson," as he said. Not everyone was pleased. Grandson Yura, the colonel and test pilot, willingly helped with mechanical jobs but was banished forever from agricultural work after he pulled out the cucumbers, leaving the weeds themselves untouched.

Aleksei Adzhubei wasn't in the best of shape; he developed sciatica and unfortunately could no longer perform physical labor. His hearing wasn't good, either; he couldn't hear when Father called him, or when he asked a question he'd leave without waiting for Father to answer. Gradually, the Adzhubeis began to visit us less frequently, and soon they found a dacha of their own.

Lena and Vitya, her husband, managed to escape Father's "lessons" with the excuse that they had to take care of the bees from the hives that stood next to the house.

I don't remember how I got out of it. I just remember that I didn't take much delight in working in the garden. Yet today I find that hard to believe, because digging in the earth gives me a lot of satisfaction. Whereas if my own children work in the garden, it is without much interest. Everything repeats itself.

Father saw through our tricks and laughed; he wasn't offended. Whether we wanted to or not, we worked together amiably. Our brigade "foreman," proud of his former occupation as a metalworker, gave us orders.

"I'll show you how this has to be done. You call yourselves engineers but you can't even bend or twist a pipe."

Father got hold of a set of tools, some oakum and flax, and some paint, and worked like a real pipe fitter. He didn't spare himself; for days on end he dragged the pipes around and screwed them together. He decided to pipe water to the garden down by the meadow. By that time, the young security men had been forbidden to help him, so they watched from their post as Father lugged the pipes around. He never realized his dream of installing a water system. Before he could finish it, he took seriously ill and couldn't work anymore.

Immediately after his death, the dacha at Petrovo-Dalneye was torn down. They say a guesthouse was put up in its place.

MEMOIRS

MY father's memoirs have been published in sixteen languages. People around the world have been reading them for nearly two decades. But there is still no Soviet edition. Somewhere in the Soviet archives is a complete text recorded on tapes, more than two hundred hours of dictation. But for seventeen years, nobody paid any attention to it — yet another example of our long-standing thoughtless, "who cares" attitude to the history of our homeland.

The story of these memoirs, and of the high-level political intrigues that surround them, is full of the most unexpected twists and turns, from the first day Father worked on them right up to the day they were published in the West.

Talk about memoirs first started in 1966, when Father was recovering from his pancreas ailment. At the time no one, including Father, had any idea of their content or length or of the role they would play in our lives. All we wanted to do was to get him involved in some kind of project. No one could imagine the uproar that would be caused by his decision to start working on memoirs, even though he wasn't the first whose desire to address history caused anxiety. Zealous guardians from the KGB had once reported to Father that Marshal Zhukov had begun writing his memoirs. They proposed to steal them so as to prevent further work.

But Father objected. "What's wrong with it? Let him write. He has nothing else to do now. Don't do a thing, let him do what he considers necessary. It's very important for our history. Zhukov was fired for certain things he did, but that's not related in any way to his earlier activities, nor to his present work on his memoirs."

In fact, when we tried to convince Father to write his memoirs, we expected the same reaction at the top, but we were wrong.

Father didn't respond to our first suggestions. Sometimes he laughed them off. More frequently he said nothing, not even his usual "Don't bother me." As time went by and life settled into a new routine, Yulia Leonidovna's husband, journalist Lyova Petrov, raised the subject of the memoirs again. We decided to tempt Father with examples of others and to get him used to reading memoirs. I took an active part in this operation. I found and brought to him as a lure Churchill's and de Gaulle's memoirs. However, as I've already mentioned, our efforts had no effect.

Almost everyone Father met in those days, whether people he knew or those he never met before, asked him whether he was writing memoirs. They were obviously distressed by his answer, and tried to convince him that he was committing a crime, since he alone could testify to facts that should belong to history.

Finally, the project was set in motion. Lyova brought a tape recorder, and in August 1966 Father started dictating. The weather was warm. They sat together in the garden and talked.

We had no plan or schedule for the memoirs since we couldn't imagine the immensity of the work that lay ahead. In fact, it wasn't real work yet, just a trial, simply a recording of the same stories Father so willingly shared with his visitors. However, this didn't last long. The project quickly changed from amateur storytelling to a professional endeavor.

In the beginning, Father didn't want to dictate in the house because of the KGB listening devices there. As a result, his words on the early tapes are sometimes drowned out by the noise of planes flying overhead. Later he said, "The hell with the bugs," and dictated in the house. He hadn't been trying to hide the fact that he was dictating, he just didn't want to broadcast the contents to the KGB. But when he saw how working outside complicated things, he changed his mind. As to the authorities, it took them a long time to react. In the absence of any initial prohibition, reports had to be passed up the line, and decisions considered and taken. All that took several years.

The first recording was about the Cuban missile crisis. At the time, it was still recent history. Everyone wanted to know about the dramatic events that brought the two superpowers to the edge of conflict. Even today, it hasn't lost its relevance. Lyova insisted that Father tell this story in particular.

Lyova took the tape home with him, transcribed it, and brought back the edited version a week later. Father didn't like it. Lyova hadn't simply transcribed the tape; in fact, he had rewritten it. It wasn't Khrushchev anymore, it was Petrov on a theme by Khrushchev. Certain nuances disappeared, the style changed radically, and some facts were distorted beyond recognition.

I have to admit that working with Father's original texts wasn't easy. His dictation was neither a conversation nor a speech with Khrushchev setting forth ideas in an interesting, vivid way. It was the result of his sitting there for many hours one-on-one with a microphone. The spinning reels made him hurry, imposed their own pace. Unwittingly, he would start to speed up, to become agitated. As a result, useless words would appear, or he'd forget the subject, skip the predicate, or put words in a wrong order. The editor was supposed to set it straight, to preserve the meaning and nuances without distorting the text. It required a vast amount of patience and time. It was much easier and quicker to rewrite everything in your own words, which is what Petrov did.

After reading Lyova's transcript, Father rejected it outright. At this point, Mama started to assist him. She typed while editing at the same time. Things started to move faster, and the quality improved, but Father still wasn't satisfied with the pace; at this rate, he wouldn't live long enough to complete the memoirs.

It was then that the work of transcribing and editing fell upon me. Altogether I worked through fifteen hundred typed pages. It took years to achieve this. Step by step, I developed a certain rhythm. I was able to edit no more than ten pages a day, working without breaks until I got headaches. Although I tried very hard, Father considered the results just average. But before that, I had urged Father to apply to the Central Committee for a secretary and a typist.

"This isn't a private matter," I argued. "The Central Committee must be interested in your memoirs. We're talking about history."

He refused to appeal to the bosses. "I don't want to ask them for anything. If they offer assistance, I won't reject it. But they won't offer, they don't need my memoirs — they'll only get in their way."

Now I understand how naive I was. If some "appropriate agency" had lent a hand, there would have been no memoirs, but endless squabbles about what should and shouldn't be said, what did and didn't meet the requirements of "the present moment."

We decided to work on our own and not ask for help. But immediately, new problems cropped up. The first was where to find an experienced typist we could trust; we had to be sure that the materials wouldn't be lost or fall into strange hands. It wasn't easy. I confided my concerns to friends, Semyon Alperovich and Volodya Modestov. Together we found a candidate — Lora Nikiforovna Finogenova. At the time, she worked at the same organization as I did, and she frequently traveled with us to the test range. She was a competent professional, and one of the most honest people I know.

I broached the issue and Lora agreed. That left only technical questions to be decided. I bought a typewriter in a shop on Pushkin Street. And I had already bought a four-track reel-to-reel Grundig tape recorder. We needed only to adapt headphones to it. We decided to work in my apartment. I couldn't imagine letting the tapes out of my sight.

One autumn evening, I think in 1967, Lora came to my apartment at Stanislavsky Street. We spent a lot of time figuring out how to place the tape recorder and the typewriter so that Lora could turn the recorder on and off and type at the same time. Neither she nor I had any experience in this line of work.

These preparations took a lot of time, but finally everything was set up and the work began. Despite Lora's proficiency, she clearly couldn't keep up with the production of the text. The fact that some words on the tape weren't clear further complicated matters. She had to replay them over and over. Within an hour, it became apparent that this arrangement wouldn't work. At this rate a few dozen or, at best, a hundred pages would get typed, but ahead of us were hundreds or even thousands of pages. We were depressed.

By this time it was quite late. We decided that we'd had enough for our first attempt. Over tea we canvassed other possibilities. There seemed no alternative to having Lora work at home, where she would have more time. At this early juncture, "the proper authorities" were still not interested in us, so that shifting our operations to Reutovo didn't attract anybody's attention.

After that the real work started. Father dictated several hours a day. Lora typed fast but still lagged behind. I was completely exhausted. I spent every free minute editing, at home and at work, on workdays and weekends, from morning till late at night. I couldn't catch up with either of them, but still I pressed Lora to hurry. I was afraid that we weren't going to get it done in time. Something inside me kept telling me things could not keep going so smoothly.

Father dictated from memory, without any sources. The problem wasn't finding relevant materials; I could have managed that somehow. The problem was that Father was used to working on concrete issues with real people, and, as Pushkin said of Eugene Onegin, "he had not the least desire to dig in history's dusty chronicles." He relied on himself and his own memory, which was indeed phenomenal.

How could he keep so much information in his head — events, places, names, numbers — and convey all of it almost without repetition or confusion? Obviously, some names had disappeared, sometimes forever, but sometimes they just popped out a few lines later.

Gradually Father got used to working with me, and more and more often the text he dictated would include comments to me like: "When I talked about the trip to Marseilles, I forgot the name of the government official who accompanied me there. Now I've got it — Joxe. Do I pronounce it correctly? Yes, it was Joxe. When you edit this, put it in the proper place."

Or: "A member of the Romanian delegation came up to me at the congress of the Bulgarian Communist party. I forgot his name. [At this point he described what the man looked like.] You look it up and put in the name."

When Father recalled the war, I checked to make sure he referred accurately to the army units involved. I was amazed to discover how few mistakes he made. There could be but one explanation: the events of those years had cut deeply into his memory. Names, dates, figures, all were correct.

Confusion began when he tried to remember the sequence of events during an official visit to a foreign country. For example, his and Bulganin's visit to Burma in 1955: Father tried to recollect who received them and where they traveled and when. An ordinary human being doesn't remember such details, but Father recalled at least the general outline. He was utterly confused, though, about such things as in which town they were greeted by traditional rowing competitions, and in which there was an elephant parade in their honor. I had to sort it all out by checking the transcript against official reports published in the newspapers.

There was a lot of work to be done. Father labored long and hard. He dictated three to five hours a day, in the morning when no one could disturb him, and then again after the midday meal.

"It goes better when there's somebody to listen to me, when I see a live human being in front of me and not a dumb box," he frequently complained.

He was right. Whenever he had listeners, his dictation went faster and was livelier. One could hear a dialogue on the tape. Usually his visitors were old acquaintances, retired people far removed from politics who came for a week or more. However, such visits were infrequent, and when he was alone with the "box," his speech became less vivid, with many stumbles and long pauses.

Autumn and winter were the most productive time for Father. In summer the work in the garden moved to the forefront, and dictation was relegated to odd moments.

For every theme Father planned to discuss, he prepared long and carefully. During his walks he thought about what he would say and how he would say it. The most dramatic events of his life were engraved in his memory. He had recounted them many times. These included, among others, the defeat at Barvenkovo in 1942, Beria's arrest, Stalin's death, the Twentieth Party Congress. In retelling these stories, he hardly altered a single word. A story told in 1960 sounded the same in 1967, although he used to complain: "I'm getting old, my memory's starting to fail me."

As Father dictated one reel after another, he began to agonize about what would happen to his memoirs. "It's all in vain," he would say during our Sunday walks. "Our efforts are useless. Everything's going to be lost. As soon as I die, they'll take it away and destroy it, or they'll bury it so deep that there'll be no trace of it." We never talked about this in the house because of bugs in the ceiling.

I tried to reassure my father as much as I could, but deep down I was inclined to agree with him. The fact that everything was quiet now didn't mean that it would continue that way forever.

WHAT were Father's reminiscences about? He declared at the very start that he was not going to describe his life beginning with childhood. He couldn't stand chronological narratives; they depressed him.

"I want to recount the most dramatic events of our history which I witnessed. First of all, I want to talk about Stalin, about his mistakes and his crimes, particularly since they want to clean the blood off him and place him on a pedestal again. I want to tell the truth about the war. All that garbage they're cramming into people on radio and TV makes me sick. I have to tell the truth."

At first, he didn't intend to deal with his time in power. Perhaps he considered it immodest, or maybe he had other reasons. I argued that his life, and the events that occurred after Stalin, were no less interesting and important for history. Father didn't disagree, he just kept silent. However, at the time, this was an abstract issue, since he had just started working. He began with the thirties, with his work in the Ukraine and in Moscow.

Next he talked about preparations for the war, the war's tragic start, and about our retreat in the face of the German attack. His account differed substantially from the then-official version that had been repeated in innumerable publications of doubtful quality.

As a reader I found his description of the tragic and heroic events of 1941 striking. I tried not to omit a word, not to distort any of his meaning. At that time, Father's account was the only reliable source of information to which I had access. To save these memories for future generations was becoming my main aim in life.

Next came the postwar period: restoration of the Ukrainian economy, famine, political intrigues; Kaganovich's replacement of Father as Ukrainian party leader for several months in 1947, followed by his recall to Moscow; Father's own transfer to Moscow in 1949; the so-called Leningrad Affair [in which Beria and Malenkov settled accounts with followers of their late colleague Andrei Zhdanov — ed.], the Moscow Affair that didn't happen [because Khrushchev prevented a repetition of the Leningrad purge in the capital — ed.], and many other things.[1]

By this time, there was already a lot of material. We began to get confused about what had already been covered and what had yet to be told. We decided to get more organized. I spent a week drawing up a list of issues that I thought should be addressed first. On Sunday we discussed it, and Father took the list to think over at leisure.

By the next weekend, we had the first draft of a plan that we followed in subsequent years, crossing out themes as they were covered, and writing in new ones we had initially forgotten.

Our intention was to illuminate all the major aspects of the day: the virgin lands and the problems of agriculture, development of

---

1. These episodes are illuminated in detail in *Khrushchev Remembers* (Boston: Little, Brown, 1970), chapters seven and eight.

industry, ways of reorganizing the economy, questions of defense and defense industry, ways of democratizing our society, Father's relationship with the intelligentsia. Nor did we forget international affairs: the struggle for peace, the first summit with Western leaders in Geneva, further contacts and visits, problems of peaceful coexistence, disarmament.

Although Father followed the plan, he often became distracted, as was his wont, by long digressions that by a process of association took him far from the planned subject. Unfortunately, he didn't succeed in covering everything we had planned.

Among the subjects left out were Father's thoughts about how to democratize our society, including his ideas for electing government and party officials, limiting their terms and creating more openness in those jobs, and erecting constitutional guarantees of citizens' rights which would prevent a repetition of the terror of the thirties.

His chapter on the creative intelligentsia, in which he wanted to evaluate events that took place between 1962 and 1964, didn't work out, either. He wanted to explain why he had behaved the way he did. However, there wasn't enough time. His last recording, made shortly before he died, dealt with this issue, but he wasn't satisfied with it. I draw on conversations with Father when I describe these episodes at various points in this book, but I don't know what it was he wanted to say on the last tape. He was counting on dictating another whole reel. He even wanted to erase the one he had already dictated.

But although not everything was completely covered, still a lot was accomplished. The dictated material comes close to two hundred hours. In general, we worked productively and well; the three of us — Father, Lora, and I — made a good team.

One might well ask where were the numerous journalists in our family. I've already mentioned Lyova Petrov. He continued to help, although his assistance didn't last very long. He developed an incurable disease and soon died. Yulia was busy with her young daughters and wasn't inclined in the direction of political journalism anyway. Rada didn't get involved in the memoirs. She pretended that they didn't exist — not the tape recorder nor the transcripts. She was totally preoccupied with her magazine, *Nauka i zhizn,* the widely popular journal of which she was a leading editor. During her infrequent visits to Petrovo-Dalneye, she usually settled herself on the couch under the painting of the spring flood of the Dnieper and read proofs for her journal. The cat lay blissfully beside her, but Father was offended by her indifference.

By this time, I was deeply absorbed in work on the memoirs. Even though I had never done anything like it before, I considered it my own. I constantly thought about it, and pestered Father with suggestions and advice. I was haunted by a vision of beautifully produced, published volumes. I resented anyone's interference in my newly established diocese, and as a result my sister's indifference suited me just fine.

Father's attitude toward Adzhubei was very special. In the beginning, he apparently counted on him to be his main assistant. That was natural. Adzhubei had regularly accompanied Father on his travels in recent years. He and other eminent journalists composed the so-called working group attached to the first secretary, which helped Father prepare speeches, documents, and drafts of new laws. As the editor in chief of *Izvestia*, Adzhubei himself had written quite a bit and was considered an able journalist. Now they both were in disgrace, and it seemed only natural that a son-in-law would help his father-in-law with his literary work.

For a while that seemed likely to happen. Aleksei Ivanovich actively supported the idea of memoirs, and although he didn't offer to help, work was only just starting. But with time, his attitude started to change. He stopped mentioning the memoirs and avoided talking about them with Father.

Evidently he had decided to be cautious, his highly developed political instincts having alerted him to the danger of such a collaboration. At that time, in the mid-sixties, Aleksei Ivanovich still hoped to resume his political career. He had recovered somewhat from the shock of the November 1964 plenum and was looking for a way to return to active political life.

He placed all his hopes on Shelepin. Just recently he had appeared utterly defeated, but now Adzhubei squared his shoulders again. Each time he visited Petrovo-Dalneye, he would invite one of us outside and say secretively: "Everything will change soon. Lyonya [Brezhnev] won't be around long. Shelepin will soon take his place. Shurik won't forget me, he won't be able to do without me. All we have to do is wait a little."

Indeed, there were a lot of rumors of this sort, and such a scenario didn't seem at all impossible.

Adzhubei supported his words by mentioning conversations with his Komsomol friends Grigoryan and Goryunov. Once he even confided in strict secrecy that he'd met with Shelepin himself. I believed him and yet didn't believe him.

Should Aleksei Ivanovich be condemned for striving to return to the political arena? I think not. After all, he was hardly over forty, and working on the memoirs could only damage his position.

It soon became clear that Brezhnev was not a transitional figure, that he knew quite well how to hold on to power. Shelepin's cause was finished. However, at this point something else happened that prevented Adzhubei from even thinking about getting involved in work on the memoirs. All of us were affected, Aleksei Ivanovich, Father, me, along with the very future of the memoirs.

In the summer of 1967, when Khrushchev seemed almost completely forgotten, his name suddenly cropped up again. In fact, nothing special had happened; some Americans simply decided to make a biographical film about the former Soviet leader. But the Soviet side interpreted it as a provocation, a hostile anti-Soviet move.

The problem was that Brezhnev couldn't bear any mention of Khrushchev's name. People like him, who are kind and weak on the one hand, and vain on the other hand, have a peculiar way of perceiving and "processing" their bad deeds. Having committed one, they project their guilt onto their victim, trying in this way to justify their actions to themselves and to the world.

Father's name stood in the way of Brezhnev's attempt to solidify his own role in history. Many of Leonid Ilyich's "achievements" had, in fact, been launched long before he came to power. Moreover, many of them were steadily losing momentum.

Naturally, the boss's attitude spread down the hierarchical ladder. It was in this atmosphere that the Khrushchev film controversy erupted.

No one in our country had yet seen the film; they had only heard about it. It was said that the film was shot at the dacha, where Father had given several interviews, one more frightening than the next. Unfortunately, I didn't manage to see the film until after Father's death, when American journalists (alas, I can't remember their names) showed it to me at their Moscow apartment.

As could have been expected, there was nothing sensational or seditious about it. The film was mostly based on archive materials, photographs, and old documentaries. The spark that set the forest on fire was a two-to-three-minute fragment at the end of the film that showed Father sitting in Boussac's cloak beside a bonfire with Arbat by his side.

Father was recounting something. His voice was muffled by the voice of a translator who explained that Father had been speaking about his youth, and then about Cuba.

I've already mentioned that Father was frequently to be found sitting beside a bonfire. I myself was an amateur cameraman — I often carried around an 8 millimeter camera — and I shot a lot of film beside bonfires, as well as elsewhere. Many of Father's visitors also brought movie cameras with them, especially vacationers from the neighboring lodge. Anyone could easily have sent a piece of film abroad. There was no law against doing so. If someone had asked me to do it, I would have been afraid to shoot the film myself, but not because the footage was in any way reprehensible.

It's possible that the sound they used was fragments of Father's speech recorded before 1964. In those days, he often reminisced about his life in the Donbas, and about his friend Pantelei Makhino, a coal miner who wrote poetry. But it could have been a later recording as well. He liked to tell visitors about his youth. And the Cuban missile crisis was one of his favorite subjects.

The reaction to the film was immediate and fierce. Since it was so disproportionate, I could never understand whether it was designed that way at the very top, or picked up momentum lower down in the hierarchy.

In either event, it didn't touch Father directly; nobody asked him anything. Instead, the wrath descended upon those around him, with chief of guards Melnikov the first victim.

In fact, Melnikov had been out of favor for a long time. His superiors considered him pro-Khrushchev, too eager to please Father, to help him, to do everything possible to make his life a little less boring. Such behavior didn't accord with the spirit of the time, and the film was a good pretext for punishment. Melnikov was charged with lacking vigilance: how could he allow Father to give an interview to a foreign journalist? The fact that no journalist, whether foreign or Soviet, had ever been at the dacha was immaterial.

Melnikov was removed from his post and dismissed from the KGB. It wasn't until many years later that I ran into him again. He was working as a superintendent in a vacation resort. He looked old; his hair had turned gray and he could hardly see. The last time I saw him was at Father's funeral. He came to say farewell.

Melnikov was succeeded by Vasily Mikhailovich Kondrashov, an absolutely different, much more up-to-date kind of person. He tried to make Father's life difficult in all sorts of petty ways. Whenever Father asked him for anything, his standard reply was that he'd have to check with his superiors. The answer usually came a couple of days later: "No, that's not permitted in your case."

Now nobody except us helped Father with the garden. Kondrashov made sure the security detail observed this prohibition. He used to walk along the path, watching Father lugging and sawing the pipes and boards he used on his simple construction projects.

Perhaps this strictness wasn't a matter of personality; he may simply have been following orders, while keeping in mind the fate of his predecessor. In any event, the departure of Melnikov was obviously designed to show Father who was boss. But he pretended all this had nothing to do with him. He practically never mentioned what had happened even in conversations with us. It didn't affect his work on the memoirs. Instead of abandoning them, he redoubled his efforts.

The authorities became aware of those efforts in the winter of 1967–1968. By then, Brezhnev had consolidated his position and was taking pains to be sure his standing was properly reflected in the mirror of history. His books *Malaya zemlya* (*A Piece of Our Land*) and *Vozrozhdenie* (*The Rebirth*) were still far in the future, but the first shoots of a new cult of personality were springing up.

Word that Khrushchev was dictating his memoirs upset Brezhnev a great deal. But how to make Father stop work on the project? Various options were probably considered. Should they search his dacha and seize the tapes? That would trigger a scandal, leaving Brezhnev looking like a tyrant and Khrushchev a martyr.

So what was to be done? The choice was to meet with Khrushchev and convince him to cease work on his memoirs and turn over what he had written to the Central Committee. If he couldn't be convinced, he should be compelled, even scared into cooperating. After all, what was more important to him, a comfortable life in a state dacha or papers of some sort?

Brezhnev had no desire to speak to his former boss personally. He'd had it with their 1965 meeting. So he instructed his first deputy in the Central Committee, Andrei Kirilenko, a rude and high-handed man, to call Khrushchev in and to get him to drop the memoirs. Kirilenko was to give Khrushchev no quarter. Arvid Pelshe, the chief of the Party Control Commission, would attend as well; his mere presence would add pressure since everyone knew the Control Commission wasn't to be trifled with. The third man present was Pyotr Demichev, who in the past had been close to Khrushchev. If need be, he could relieve the tension, or convince Khrushchev not to do something foolish.

The decision to proceed in this way was made sometime in the spring of 1968. The next step was to implement it. That April, on the eve of Father's birthday, I arrived as usual to spend the weekend at Petrovo-Dalneye. Father wasn't inside. Mama said that he had gone to the edge of the forest to sit in the sun.

"Father is very upset. Yesterday he was summoned to the Central Committee. Kirilenko demanded that he cease work on the memoirs and hand over what's already been written. Father became infuriated, and started to shout. He made a huge scene. He'll tell you everything himself, but don't press him. He was very agitated yesterday, and he doesn't feel well."

Quite agitated myself, I went down the path. Father was sitting on the bench, watching the sun go down. Arbat was lying beside him. Father didn't notice me coming, and when I silently sat down next to him, he didn't turn his head at first. We were both silent. Father looked tired, his face seemed grayer and older.

Turning toward me, he asked, "Do you know already? Did Mama tell you?"

I nodded.

"Scoundrels! I told them what I think of them. Perhaps I went too far, but it serves them right. They thought I would crawl on my belly in front of them."

"Actually, Mama didn't tell me much," I said. "She just said that Kirilenko called you in and demanded you stop work on the memoirs."

"Right. What a scoundrel!" Father repeated, and started to recount what had happened. While he was talking, his face came to life again, and his eyes turned angry. Clearly, he was living every sentence, every retort, again.

I remembered Mama's warning and tried to change the subject so as to calm him down. Father didn't want to be distracted. He was boiling with indignation, and described the whole scene that occurred at the Central Committee. Later he would repeat his account of that day many times.

I remembered the story very well, and made some notes while it was still fresh in my mind. When Father entered Kirilenko's office, Kirilenko, Pelshe, and Demichev were already sitting there. Kirilenko skipped the usual greeting and went straight to the point: "The Central Committee has received information that you have been writing your memoirs for quite some time, and that they include many events of party and state history. Actually, you are rewriting party history. But interpreting the history of our party and state is the business of the Central Committee, and not of private individuals, let alone pensioners. The Politburo demands that you stop work on these memoirs and immediately turn over what you've already dictated to the Central Committee."

After finishing his speech, Kirilenko looked around at the others. Clearly, it hadn't been easy for him to say it. But Pelshe and Demichev kept silent. Kirilenko had worked for a long time with Khrushchev in the Ukraine, in Sverdlovsk, and here in Moscow. He had been his first deputy in the Central Committee Bureau for the Russian Federation. He knew Father's explosive temperament and understood how much he had offended the man who only four years earlier had been the first secretary of the Central Committee and the prime minister of the USSR.

But in retirement, Father was dependent for even the smallest things on the people who had given Kirilenko his assignment, and he counted on that to render Khrushchev more obliging and tractable. Whether deep in his soul Kirilenko had pangs of conscience at that moment, I don't know.

At first Father was silent. Then he looked at his former associates. He started to speak quietly, but got more and more incensed.

"I cannot understand, Comrade Kirilenko, what you and those who sent you want. A lot of people in the world write memoirs, and in our country too. There's nothing wrong with it. Memoirs aren't history, they're just a person's view of the life he's lived. Memoirs supplement history and can serve as useful material for future historians of our country and our party.

"I consider your demand to be an act of force against a Soviet citizen, and as such a violation of the constitution, and therefore I refuse to obey you.

"You can put me in prison, or you can seize this material from me by force. You can do all this today if you wish, but I categorically protest."

"Nikita Sergeyevich," Kirilenko insisted, "what I have informed you of is a decision of the Politburo, and you are obliged, as a Communist, to obey."

Father cut him off again. "You are behaving in a way no government allowed itself to behave even under the tsars. I know only one such instance. You want to treat me the way Nicholas I dealt with Taras

Shevchenko: he sent him into the army and barred him from writing or drawing while in the service.[2]

"You can take everything away from me; my pension, the dacha, my apartment. That's all within your power, and it wouldn't surprise me if you did. So what — I can still make a living. I'll go to work as a metalworker — I still remember how it's done. If that doesn't work out, I'll take my knapsack and go begging. People will give me what I need."

He looked at Kirilenko. "But no one would give you a crust of bread. You'd starve."

Seeing that Kirilenko wasn't getting anywhere, Pelshe interjected: "Nikita Sergeyevich, the Politburo's decisions are obligatory for everybody, including you. Hostile forces could make use of your memoirs; American spies could easily steal them."

That was a mistake.

"Then let the Politburo provide me with a stenographer and a typist to record what I dictate. That wouldn't be difficult. They could make two copies; one could be kept at the Central Committee, and I would work with the other." Father was calmer now, but then he remembered something that agitated him once more. "But no, you violated the constitution again when you stuck listening devices all over the dacha. Even in the bathroom — you spend the people's money to eavesdrop on my farts."

It was clear to everyone present that their mission had failed, that Father was not going to give anything up willingly, and that there was nothing more to be said.

In parting, Father said, "As a citizen of the USSR, I have the right to write my memoirs and you don't have the power to deny me that right. My notes are intended for the Central Committee, for the party, and for the whole Soviet people. I want what I write about to be of use to the Soviet people, to our Soviet leaders, and to our nation. The events I have witnessed should serve as a lesson for our future."

On that note the second, but unfortunately not the last, visit of Khrushchev to the Central Committee ended. The conversation had unsettled Father and he worried about it, playing it back in his mind over

---

2. Taras Shevchenko was a Ukrainian writer, poet, and artist of the first half of the nineteenth century. For writing poems that displeased the authorities, he was exiled to the wilderness beyond the Caspian Sea, where he was forbidden to write or paint. Since compulsory military service lasted for twenty-five years at the time, he was in effect sentenced to life imprisonment. Father knew Shevchenko's verses well and loved to read them aloud.

and over again. He quit dictating regularly and returned to it only infrequently. He didn't dictate much at all during 1968. So, in a way, Kirilenko had achieved his aim. Once again, Father took to agonizing about whether it was all worth it. During our walks away from KGB microphones, he repeated the same sentiments he had voiced earlier. "The project is senseless. They aren't going to back off. I know them too well. They won't dare do anything now, but after I'm gone they'll seize everything and destroy it. I see what's going on these days. They don't need truthful history."

I reassured him but couldn't stop worrying myself. I had to find a way to store the material safely until better times came. But there was no absolutely safe place for the tapes and transcripts inside the country. We had made copies and kept them separately in secure places, but all it would take was a concerted effort by a few professionals (of whom our country had an abundance) and all our amateur secrets would be out. As the conversation with Kirilenko had shown, Khrushchev's name provided only so much protection.

Even before the confrontation at the Central Committee, it had occurred to us to look for a safe place abroad. At first, Father had hesitated, out of fear that we'd lose control over the manuscript, and that it might be distorted and used against our state. But after lengthy weighing of the pros and cons, he asked me to find a way to get the materials out of the country. Obviously, we kept this decision strictly secret. To be honest, at the time I didn't have the foggiest idea of how to carry out this plan.

Now Father and I came back to the idea of finding a safe hiding place abroad. It was at this time that we first discussed publishing the memoirs as retaliation if they were seized, or in some other extraordinary situation.

Publication would solve once and for all the problem of preserving the memoirs and might also reduce the Central Committee's incentive to seize and destroy them in the Soviet Union. Why should they try to search for them if the book was available? What were they going to do, buy up all the copies? No amount of secret funds could pay for them all — in the West, unlike in the USSR, after all, there was no shortage of paper.

Father finally calmed down after the confrontation in the Central Committee and busied himself in the garden. May was fast approaching and it was time to get ready for the sowing season.

Meanwhile, I found what I thought was a good way to send a copy of the memoirs abroad. It turned out to be much simpler than I expected. Still, aside from the physical problem of getting the memoirs out of the country, there was a moral consideration. It was no longer 1958, but it wasn't yet 1988.

Only ten short years before, Pasternak had drawn thunder and lightning for giving his manuscript to an Italian publisher, and just recently Andrei Sinyavsky and Yuli Daniel had been put on trial.[3] Father had not approved of that travesty of a trial, but . . . My mind wandered to more distant events; I remembered Raskolnikov's letter exposing the horrors of Stalin's regime. Had it not been published in France, there was much we wouldn't have known about.[4]

And what about V. I. Lenin's letters and articles? Hadn't they, too, frequently been published abroad?

Nevertheless, my indoctrination was powerful: "No matter what the content, if it's published abroad, it's a hostile act." It was a difficult feeling to overcome, and to a certain extent we still haven't today.

Father was bolder than I. His were the memoirs of the first secretary of the Central Committee, he insisted, the confessions of one who had devoted his entire life to fighting for Soviet power, for a Communist society. The memoirs contained truth, words of warning, facts — they should be read by the people. Let them come out first abroad and at home later. The reverse would be better, but would we live that long?

In deciding to take this step, we crossed the threshold from legal to illegal activity. I felt uneasy. Where would it end? Arrest? Internal exile? It was no time to ponder the consequences; it was important to act.

Many of those who took part in the effort are still alive, and I still can't reveal details or the names of those who offered their assistance.

---

3. *Editor's note:* Writers Sinyavsky and Daniel had published abroad under the pseudonyms Abram Tertz and Nikolai Arzhak. They were convicted in 1966, under Article 70 of the Russian Republic Criminal Code, of "agitation or propaganda carried out with the purpose of subverting or weakening the Soviet regime."

4. *Editor's note:* A lieutenant in the tsarist navy before the Russian revolution, Fyodor Raskolnikov joined the Bolsheviks, headed the revolutionary committee at the key Kronstadt naval base, and rose to command the Bolshevik fleet on the Volga and in the Caspian Sea. While serving as Soviet ambassador to Bulgaria in 1939, Raskolnikov refused to return to Moscow and instead wrote a letter to Stalin accusing him of usurping power. The letter was published in an émigré Russian newspaper after Raskolnikov's death in September 1939. In the current era of *glasnost,* it was published in the popular Soviet magazine *Ogonyok.*

Many of them asked me not to, and I'm not about to violate their confidence; not everyone wanted to become a hero of this book. I would like only to express my sincere thanks to those who helped preserve and publish Father's memoirs.

Once the materials — the tapes and transcripts — had crossed several borders and found a safe harbor behind the steel doors of a vault, another issue arose. The memoirs were secure there, but if something happened to us here, it would be impossible to retrieve them, and they might lie untouched for generations.

Yet they hadn't been dictated "for future use only"; they contained reflections on our victories and defeats, on our past successes and failures, and they were aimed at our tomorrow. As such, they were a highly perishable item and not suitable for lengthy storage. What they had to say would be of use if people read them now, in today's circumstances.

That's how I saw it, but I turned out to be wrong. The Brezhnev era of stagnation erased entire decades from our lives. Recently I reread the memoirs, and there it all was: disarmament, troop reductions, shifting military industry to peaceful production — all those were on the drafting board, but in 1964 they were quietly laid to rest. Gorbachev would later speak about them all at the United Nations — ideas today that are quite in keeping with what Father wrote then.

Leasing land in the countryside — Father called it by a different name back then. I could also mention his unmasking of Stalinism, his views on housing construction, peaceful coexistence, material incentives, or other well-known principles that formed the basis of Father's foreign and domestic policies.

ON my next day off, I told Father about my concern about access to the memoirs abroad. He had been thinking along the same lines. "Anything might happen," he said. "It's possible no one would be able to get into the safe. It would be a good idea to arrange with some respected publisher to publish the book at some unspecified future date, but only after we give them the signal from here." He fell silent, and we continued strolling along the path.

"We have to be ready for anything," he said suddenly. "They're not going to leave it at this. We should expect any kind of dirty trick — they might secretly steal the memoirs, or they might seize them openly. They won't risk arresting us; they don't have the guts. But they'll try to take them."

By the end of the year, we had reached a tentative agreement with Little, Brown and Company to publish the memoirs. Removed from the text were passages that might constitute military secrets and incidental references to people then in power in the USSR, and Father agreed to delete them.[5]

With this decision behind us, the material mounted up as days, months, and years passed. Now we worked without worrying; whatever happened, the book would be safe.

I remember one amusing episode. The publisher was worried that someone might be palming off a fake. And why not? Everything certainly looked strange. They were afraid of provocateurs and decided to try to verify the authenticity of the material they were getting.

We weren't in a position to write to them ourselves; it would have been too dangerous. Our colleagues found a solution involving the use of a camera. Father received two wide-brimmed hats from Vienna, one bright scarlet and the other black. In order to verify that they were dealing with us and not some imposter, the publisher asked us to send photographs of Father wearing these two hats. When I brought the hats to Petrovo-Dalneye, they attracted everyone's attention because they were so outlandish. I explained that they were souvenirs from one of Father's foreign admirers.

Mama was amazed. "Can he really think that your father will wear them?"

When Father and I were alone, setting out for a walk, I explained the real reason for the hats. He got a big kick out of the situation. The plan appealed to him; he liked witty people. When we returned from our walk, he got into the game himself. Sitting on the bench in front of

---

5. *Editor's note:* That there were omissions in the tapes and transcripts received by Little, Brown is not new. Jerrold L. Schecter's introduction to *Khrushchev Remembers: The Last Testament* (Boston: Little, Brown, 1974, p. xiv) names "Khrushchev, his family and friends" as those who "had taken pains not to violate Soviet State secrets, or Politbureau security regulations, and not to accuse any living Soviet leaders." But other questions remain: Exactly what was removed? Who removed it? And what happened to the material that was excised? Was it preserved? If so, by whom?

I put all these questions to the author. I asked him in addition about rumors that the KGB, or elements of it, played a role in transmitting the tapes and transcripts to the West, and that in return for this help, Khrushchev and his associates agreed to certain cuts in the material.

Sergei Khrushchev replied: "I understand the interest in these questions and I agree they are important. I greatly regret that due to circumstances beyond my control, I cannot answer them."

the house, he asked me loudly, "Bring me those hats. I want to try them on and see if they fit."

Mama was horrified. "You can't really be thinking of wearing them?!"

"And why not?" he said, egging her on.

"Why, they're much too loud," she said, and shrugged.

I brought him the hats, grabbing my camera on the way. Father put one on and said, "Take my picture, let's see how I look." So I photographed him wearing one hat and holding the other in his hand.

The publisher received the picture and knew that they were not being led astray. But despite all our preparations, I still hoped very much that we would not have to take the final step and authorize publication in the West.

Summer meant farm work; it swallowed up practically all our time. There wasn't much left for dictation, and Father didn't feel like it anyway. To work on the memoirs, he had to be in the right mood; he had to want to do it. But now, whenever he thought about the memoirs all that came to mind was what Kirilenko had said.

Kirilenko and his friends were not about to accept defeat, and they decided to act. They went after his children so as to show Khrushchev that he wasn't as invulnerable to the authorities' wrath as he thought.

They started with the Adzhubeis. Aleksei Ivanovich was now heading a department of the magazine *Sovetsky Soyuz* (*Soviet Union*). They called him in and "suggested" he leave Moscow for a job with a publisher in the Soviet Far East. Aleksei Ivanovich was frightened, and he sounded all the alarms. He refused to relocate and declared that he was going to write an official complaint immediately to the secretary general of the United Nations. Surprisingly, his threat worked and he wasn't bothered again.

Apparently they also talked to him about some other matters. In any event, from that time on he had less and less to do with Father. On the few occasions the memoirs came up in conversation, his opinion turned out to have shifted 180 degrees. He now felt work on the memoirs was useless and unnecessary.

"Nikita Sergeyevich, your deeds speak for themselves. You held a worthy position in history and no additional explanations are needed. Everyone understands things without them." When Adzhubei expressed such sentiments, which he did more than once, Father didn't answer, or muttered some meaningless, neutral response. Aleksei Ivanovich also tried to get me to convince Father to give up the memoirs. I refused, saying that the memoirs were historically important, as well as important for my father. This conversation left me with an unpleasant aftertaste that has lasted to this day.

Nor did I escape the repression. I have mentioned that I worked for an organization involved in missile technology. I liked the work, and I liked my boss, academician Chelomei, a brilliant man and scholar.

At the time, I directed the department working on control systems for several different projects. Not long after Kirilenko's talk with Father, I received a phone call at my office from a stranger.

"Sergei Nikitich, I'm calling from the personnel office at the Ministry of Instrument-making. We've been informed that you will be transferring to our Institute for Electronic Control Equipment. Please come by to take care of the formalities."

I had no idea what he was talking about. "You must be mistaken," I answered. "I'm not planning on transferring anywhere."

"I don't know about that. I have your transfer documents here in front of me," the man continued. "Well, it's up to you, but please take down my phone number in case you need to contact me." He gave me the number and we hung up.

I didn't know what to think. It was an unpleasant situation. Chelomei's relationship with me had changed greatly over the last few years. He tried to be friendly, but he did everything he could to make sure I was seen as little as possible by visitors to our design bureau.

He even said to me once, in a fit of openness, "Don't let anyone catch sight of you. Just stay around here; don't drop in on any neighboring organizations."

What was going on? Did he know something and was trying to help me? Or did he want to avoid reminding the rest of the world that he had such a politically inconvenient colleague. He couldn't just dump me. That would have meant losing face in front of his fellow academicians: Korolyov, Msitislav V. Keldysh, Valentin P. Glushko, and Nikolai A. Pilyugin. They all knew how much Father had done for him, and how enthusiastic Chelomei had been about me.

The first person I met after my strange phone call was Yevgeny Lukich Zhuravlev, Chelomei's personnel director. I told him what had happened.

"I was just about to tell you what I thought of your betrayal!" said Yevgeny Lukich. "I have a request for your transfer on my desk. I thought you had cooked it up behind our backs. I told Vladimir Nikolayevich, and he told me to speak to you."

I knew that someone was lying. I just didn't know who. I later learned that a few days before all this happened, some KGB types had paid Chelomei a visit to talk about me. They said that in view of my particular circumstances I had a chip on my shoulder, and it would be a good idea to transfer me to unclassified work.

If Chelomei had said this was nonsense, and that the bureau needed me, the matter would have been dropped. At least that's what I was told later by people in a position to know. But Chelomei answered differently. He saw an opportunity to get rid of me. Otherwise, my name could slip into one of his conversations with Brezhnev or Ustinov (they knew all about me and where I worked) and cause him trouble. This way he could save face; after all, it hadn't been his decision.

At the time, I didn't know any of this, and so I told Zhuravlev that I had no intention of transferring anywhere. Then I went right up to the sixth floor to see Chelomei. Vladimir Nikolayevich listened attentively and didn't claim that he knew nothing about what had happened.

"It's all Ustinov's doing, he doesn't like you," he said, mounting his favorite hobbyhorse. He hated Ustinov, who felt exactly the same way about him.

"I got a call about you from Serbin [head of the Central Committee Defense Department], asking when you'd be leaving. You can't imagine what a lowlife he is; he's capable of the dirtiest tricks."

I didn't know whether he was referring to Ustinov or Serbin, but since he was in the habit of characterizing many people that way, I didn't pay much attention. I was quite upset and had come to him looking for help.

"What should I do? I don't want to transfer anywhere at all."

"You know," Chelomei said, "you should write a letter to Leonid Ilyich. He's the only one who can do anything. And he knows you and has always treated you well."

His advice was irreproachable, and with it he deftly stepped out of the game. If Brezhnev suddenly deigned to let me stay, that meant I had top-level blessing and Chelomei could relax. If Brezhnev refused, then there was no appeal. In that case, Chelomei was up against a situation in which he was powerless.

"If you'll excuse me, I've got an urgent appointment to see the minister. They've called me twice already." That's how Vladimir Nikolayevich ended our conversation.

Writing to Brezhnev, especially after Father's clash with Kirilenko, was the last thing I wanted to do. It would be both useless and very unpleasant. I decided to do nothing: perhaps they would forget about me.

Two weeks later, Zhuravlev phoned me. "Well, what have you decided? What are you going to do? I've been getting calls."

"Frankly, I haven't done a thing."

"That's too bad. They were giving you time to make your own decision. Now it's time to act. You need to pay a visit to the other organization."

I resolved to make one final, desperate attempt to keep my present job. "Lukich, what will you do if I refuse to go? There's no legal basis for firing me."

"You're just wasting time. You and I are old friends, but I've got to follow orders. And there are a lot of laws they might use. For instance, they might eliminate your department as no longer necessary, or as a result of reorganization. Then out you go. My advice is either take the offer or take some action. Time is working against you."

"Thanks for the advice. Can you put me in contact with whoever it is that is giving you these orders?"

"I can't answer that question. Let me call you back."

Half an hour later, Zhuravlev gave me a telephone number and a name. The prefix told me that it was a KGB number. The conversation I had with the invisible person who answered my call was short and uninformative; he could tell me nothing I didn't know already.

"What if the work you are suggesting doesn't appeal to me?" I asked. "What then? Can I go somewhere else?"

I naively supposed that I might transfer again to a job in my field in a design bureau headed by some other chief designer I knew, say Nikolai Pilyugin, Viktor Kuznetsov, or Mikhail Petelin.

"There are no other alternatives." The voice on the other end cut me off. "If you don't like our proposal, then there's nothing we can do for you."

I hung up. The only choice left was to give in or to go straight to the very top. Otherwise, I could be left with no job at all, and then no one would take me. At least that's how I understood his closing comment.

Chelomei called me that same day. "Have you contacted Leonid Ilyich yet?"

"No, not yet. I've been trying to get things sorted out without asking him for help. I really don't want to write to him."

"That's too bad, because he's the only one who can help you.

Serbin's already called me twice. I've been as vague as I could, but I think he's going to lose patience soon."

Had he really gotten a call from Serbin? Or did they just want to increase the pressure on me by adding Chelomei's advice to that of Zhuravlev?

I had no choice, so that evening I wrote a short letter to the general secretary outlining the facts and requesting him to let me remain at my present job, where I could make a contribution in my area of expertise.

I got hold of the phone number of Brezhnev's aide Andrei Aleksandrov-Agentov and called him. I wasn't up on the pecking order of Brezhnev's aides and didn't know that his specialty was foreign affairs.

Aleksandrov himself picked up the phone and after hearing me out, suggested I come by his office at my convenience. We agreed to meet the following morning.

He received me with exceptional courtesy. Aleksandrov said he would report everything to "the man himself" very soon and hoped that things would fall into place. "Call me in a couple of days," he said encouragingly as we parted.

I left feeling a bit better. I hadn't expected such quick action. Since Brezhnev had once been involved in military-technical matters, he was well acquainted with our department, and with me. Everything probably *would* fall into place.

I conveniently repressed Father's conversation with Kirilenko, and the fact that Brezhnev had changed since 1964. Two days later, Aleksandrov informed me somewhat sheepishly that he had delivered my note to Brezhnev, but Leonid Ilyich would not become involved. He had said it was Ustinov's business, and that Ustinov should decide.

"Give Dmitry Fyodorovich a call. Here's his aide's number," Aleksandrov said.

I wasn't about to call Ustinov. Brezhnev's answer was an unambiguous and scornful refusal. He knew very well that Ustinov was not on the best of terms with our organization, and hence with me. After recounting all this to Chelomei and receiving what I now understand was his less than sincere sympathy, I called the number of the director of the organization to which I was to be transferred. His name was Boris Nikolayevich Naumov.

He took my call immediately and in response to my fractured explanation said amiably, "I know all about it. I've heard a lot about you.

I think you'll like it here and will enjoy the work. Come by to get acquainted whenever you like, right now if you want to."

A couple of hours later, I arrived at my new place of employment. To tell the truth, I was as nervous as a schoolboy. I walked through the entryway into a small courtyard containing a single five-story building. After the huge organization I had worked for, with its numerous multi-story buildings spread out over a vast expanse, this place looked shabby.

On the second floor, a plump blonde gave me a welcoming smile. "Sergei Nikitich? Boris Nikolayevich is waiting for you. Go right in."

Inside the office I was greeted by a large man who seemed to consist of nothing but smiles. He radiated good humor. I began to tell him about myself, making it as short as possible.

"Just a minute," he interrupted. "If you can, please give me more details. I've heard a lot about your work." He spoke into the intercom. "Lyubochka, tea please, and hold all my calls; I don't want to talk to anyone."

We conversed over tea for a good two hours. I told him as much as I could about myself, about Chelomei, and a bit about my work. Naumov was all attention and courtesy. He asked questions clarifying certain points. He was clearly very interested in what I had to say.

Then he told me about the institute, and when he had finished, several others joined us at a long table in a meeting room. Boris Nikolayevich asked them to describe what the sections and divisions did: the distribution of electrical energy and water resources, stockpile management, library information retrieval systems, scientific and technological forecasting. Not one involved any field I had worked in during the past ten years, or anything that appealed to me.

The division heads left us. Naumov told me that he would make me a department head in whichever division I wanted. "Those were my instructions," he explained.

We decided to meet again in a few days. I gave the situation a lot of thought, trying to understand all the information I had been bombarded with. It was all so unfamiliar, so removed from my experience, and so uninteresting. Finally, I got angry. They didn't want me to work in the field where I could make a contribution. That was their business. They didn't need me, so I didn't need them. I'd take up something more general, less practical, something where I could work with as few people as possible. If they wanted me to head a department, I'd head a department.

That's how I chose a new career forecasting scientific and techno-logical progress. When I told Naumov, his eyes betrayed his surprise. He had apparently expected anything but this. "We don't have a de-partment specially for forecasting. Can I make you a senior researcher instead?" he asked.

Before coming to see Naumov a second time, I had had another long talk with Zhuravlev. Yevgeny Lukich knew the personnel game inside and out. He gave me several valuable pieces of advice.

"If they try to place you where you don't want to go, stand firm for what you've been promised. Don't agree to anything less — it's their problem. You won't have a chance later if you don't assert yourself now. I was sent to Germany once as a division head, but when I got there, I found there was no vacancy. I stupidly agreed to become a department head temporarily. Well, that's where I doodled away the rest of my time. Don't get involved in their problems."

"I was told I would get a department," I mumbled to Naumov. I was embarrassed but decided to stand my ground.

"Very well," Boris Nikolayevich agreed without objection.

I'm not going to describe the new work, since my activities are relevant only when they intersect with those of my father. I will say only that everything turned out very well. In contrast to Chelomei, nei-ther the director nor those under him were afraid of my disgraced fam-ily, at least no more than the average educated Soviet citizen.

I didn't end up doing purely scientific work. Due to my own char-acter and the circumstances around me, I found myself once again in the center of events. It was gratifying that several of my co-workers at Chelomei's design bureau joined me at the institute during my first year there. With their help I was able to pull together a top-notch group that remains together even today.

These fast-moving developments prevented me from helping Father on the memoirs, but the summer of 1968 was an unproductive one for him anyway. In the fall, however, Father took up his dictation again. It was slow going, since he had gotten out of the routine. He had for-gotten what had been already dictated, as well as what our plan called for him to cover.

We reviewed the notebook with the chapter headings. Each week-end we chose a topic for the coming week, and then on my next day off, I, like a nagging inspector, would check over what he had accom-plished.

At first Father took offense, responding to my questions with his usual "Quit pestering me!" But gradually he got involved again, approaching the work with new life.

Nineteen sixty-nine began peacefully enough. They seemed to have forgotten us "up there." The rebuff to Kirilenko had apparently had an effect, and they didn't contact Father again. Meanwhile, things went according to schedule: dictation, work in the garden, walks, picture-taking, more dictation, television, reading. So it went, day after day. By the spring, Father was working as intensively as he had two years before.

We relaxed a bit, but, as it turned out, prematurely. Deep within the bureaucracy, invisible to us, they were at work too, vigilantly monitoring progress on the memoirs. The next year, this became fully clear.

Something else happened in 1969 that seemed unrelated to the memoirs, but, combined with other developments, it interfered with work on them and had a definite effect on everything we did later. My younger sister, Lena, had long had serious health problems. While still a child, she had returned from a trip to the south with a case of systemic lupus that baffled the doctors and was apparently incurable.

My father and mother tried everything they could think of. They were both very good parents; even when he had his own troubles, Father was always solicitous of ours. They consulted the top medical specialists and employed folk medicine, too, but without results, while the illness progressively worsened.

During the latter half of the 1960s, Lena's condition took an even graver turn. She couldn't work; she could barely walk. With her courage and optimism, though, she continued to occupy herself with the flowers and the bees at the dacha. She even raised orchids in transparent plastic boxes made for her by her husband.

During the summer of 1969, after a particularly bad spell, Lena had to enter the hospital. Her illness had reached a new, more threatening stage: she had cramps in her arms and couldn't walk at all. Her situation was critical.[6] The top specialists in Moscow — academician Yevgeny Tareyev and professors Vadim Smolensky and Valentina Nasonova — had long ago been called in on the case, but she just wasn't getting any better, and they were powerless to stop the course of her illness.

6. My original notes contain a discrepancy in dates, and it is possible that these events took place in 1968 instead of 1969. I cannot remember exactly, but judging from the sequence of events, it was probably 1969.

Yulia's husband, Lyova Petrov, having spent several years as a journalist in Canada, had developed a faith in Western medicine. He suggested that a sample of Lena's blood be sent abroad for analysis. Perhaps diagnostic and treatment possibilities existed there that we had no knowledge of. Lena's doctors were skeptical but didn't object. They knew the situation was grim and felt obliged to let us explore any avenues of hope. That raised the question of how to make the necessary arrangements. At that point an opportunity presented itself.

One day I mentioned what we were trying to accomplish to a couple of friends, Volodya Baraboshkin and Revaz Gamkarelidze, who were both men of action and ready to help. Revaz said, "There's a delegation of American mathematicians in Moscow. I'll talk to them; maybe one of them can arrange for something to be done in an American hospital."

I hadn't wanted to get involved with foreigners, but there was no choice. A few days later, Gamkarelidze had the Americans to his apartment, and I was invited too.

It was there that I met Dr. Jeremy Stone [who later became director of the Federation of American Scientists — ed.], a mathematician with political interests.

"This man can help you," said Revaz.

We chatted. I got the impression that Stone had known the late President Kennedy. He spoke warmly about my father.

Revaz had already mentioned my problems to him, and he was ready not only to undertake the trouble of handling the analyses but also to find and even send to Moscow a physician who specialized in collagenitis — the scientific name for Lena's illness.

His offer stunned and even frightened me a bit. How would it look under the current circumstances for an American to show up at our door? There might be some unpleasant consequences. But I remembered my sister's condition and my doubts disappeared.

Before leaving, Dr. Stone took some blood samples with him for analysis and promised to call soon. A couple of weeks later, he informed us that one of the top American specialists — I've forgotten his name — in the field was then in Europe. Stone had persuaded him to come to Moscow if he could get a tourist visa. The matter had to be settled quickly, within a day or two. The renowned American medical specialist's European tour was coming to an end; he was about to return home from Vienna.

To be honest, until this call I hadn't taken the talk about a foreign doctor seriously. It was almost unbelievable that something like this could happen to a Soviet citizen. My first inclination was to express thanks and decline, but then I realized this might be Lena's last chance, and I agreed with gratitude.

But how could I, in my situation, arrange for a visa? And in a couple of days at that? The answer came to me unexpectedly: Go right to the top. The only person who could help was Andrei Gromyko. I didn't doubt his decency, but I had to take his extreme caution into consideration.

We lived in the same building. That wasn't the least of the factors that might make a meeting easier. Gathering my courage, I called that evening and asked permission to drop by on a very important matter.

Of course, my call caught him by surprise, and my request was hardly cause for rejoicing, but he gave no hint of his feelings. As if we had regularly spoken in recent years, he calmly and benevolently suggested I come by right away. I went down to the floor where he lived, and he met me in the hall of his large apartment; his wife, Lidia Dmitrievna, was with him.

I quickly summarized the situation. Andrei Andreyevich knew our family quite well and was aware of my sister's illness. He reacted positively to my request and in a deep voice, with his O's emphasized as usual, said: "Well now, this is a humanitarian matter. I'll try to help. Call me tomorrow."

Lidia Dmitrievna, who constantly protected him against possible unpleasantness, interjected: "Andryusha, you can't decide this by yourself — you have to coordinate this with the others."

Andrei Andreyevich didn't back off. "Call me tomorrow," he repeated. He knew better than anyone how to handle the matter, exactly what had to be run by whom. With that, the audience ended.

The next day, I telephoned him at the Foreign Ministry. I wasn't wrong about Gromyko: he had real human qualities. Even before I called, the matter had been settled favorably; a cable had gone out to Vienna authorizing a visa for the American physician.

But the doctor evidently became frightened at the prospect of a trip to Moscow. I think his apprehensions about Russians were similar to my own about *his* compatriots. In any event, he refused the visa and left Vienna for home. All this was reported to Gromyko, and when I called to thank him he said he stood ready to help in the future, should that prove necessary.

I was later told that Gromyko sent a cable on his own initiative to our ambassador in the United States, Anatoly Dobrynin, requesting him to render assistance if asked to grant a visa to an American physician. Gromyko did much more than I asked.

I called Stone in the United States to tell him what had happened. Refusing to be discouraged, he assured me he'd find another solution. "I was at your embassy," he said. "They promised favorable action. That's the main thing."

At the time we didn't know about Gromyko's cable.

A few days later Stone called again; he had found the physician we needed, a very knowledgeable man of vast experience who had long served as Nehru's personal physician. He was the world's leading specialist in collagenitis, and he was ready to go to the Soviet Union. He would come with his wife. His mother-in-law had recently died and his wife was grieving, so the change of scenery would be most welcome.

"The visa problem is settled," Stone reported. "Your embassy told me they'll issue it without delay. As a sort of honorarium, you'll have to pay for the trip and the stay in Moscow — and maybe you can arrange a bit of a cultural program for the doctor and his wife."

I gladly agreed. The problem was resolved. Rada and I split the cost of bringing the renowned specialist to Moscow.

The formalities went quickly, and at the end of October I met the short, thin Dr. A. McGehee Harvey and his wife at Sheremetyevo airport. They were not young people. It was freezing in Moscow, with snow on the ground. They checked into the National Hotel.

Difficulties unexpectedly arose in the matter of consultations: Tareyev and Smolensky at first refused to meet the American, and it took a lot to change their minds. After careful examination and analysis of all available data obtained by both Soviet and American experts, Professor Harvey came to the same conclusion as our doctors. After that, relations between the three specialists went very well.[7]

The American physician even gave us a bit of hope. He believed the situation was not as bad as might have been expected; it might still be possible to arrest the disease. Moreover, one could live a long life with it. Nonetheless, it was incurable; no one either in America or in Europe knew how to cure it.

---

7. I should perhaps make clear that there were no political reasons for the Soviet doctors' standoffishness. It was rather that they took the American's presence as a vote of no confidence in them, despite their high professional standing, and hence took offense. Since *we* had invited him, they meant to say, let *us* talk to him. They felt better about it once he had confirmed their diagnosis.

Lena didn't live a long life. She died four years later. Either the professor was mistaken or — in accordance with medical ethics — he was just trying to reassure us. We'll never know which, nor do we really need to.

After the first consultation, the doctors ordered further tests. When the results came, there was a second consultation. Harvey asked to have supplementary blood samples sent to his laboratory in the United States, which was equipped with modern technology that might give different results. But from the expression on his face, it was obvious he didn't expect anything different. It was all too clear to him.

I won't deny that I was rather disappointed and dispirited — so much trouble, fantastic efforts, and the miracle didn't happen. The professor only confirmed what we had heard earlier.

The cultural program I'd arranged for the doctor and his wife went off successfully. They visited theaters, museums, the Palace of Congresses, and the Kremlin Armory, and they went to Leningrad for a couple of days. With Baraboshkin's help, I went through the Patriarch's office and arranged an excursion to Zagorsk, complete with a viewing of church treasures and a gala dinner.

The Intourist interpreter-guide [assigned to escort the Harveys, and probably to report on their movements — ed.] simply couldn't understand who we were. Lena's husband, Vitya, and I never introduced ourselves to her, and yet we tried never to leave the guests alone and from time to time took them away somewhere. (This was for the medical consultations.) This perplexed the guide, who obviously found our behavior suspicious.

As the Harveys' stay in Moscow neared its end, Father, who appreciated their courtesy, invited them out to the dacha. Vitya and I thought the matter over and, without asking Father's opinion, decided not to take the guide. No special considerations were involved; we simply didn't want to drag a stranger along. In the light of subsequent developments, I now think we made a mistake, although it probably didn't have any influence on the general course of events.

Arriving at the hotel that morning, we told the guide she could have the day off because we were going to take care of the guests. She took offense, but we didn't attach any significance to that. As planned, we went first to Arkhangelskoye to see the palace, then had lunch in a local restaurant. Only after lunch did we tell the Harveys that Khrushchev's dacha was nearby, and that he wanted to meet them if they didn't object. They gratefully accepted the invitation.

Father put on a coat and tie for the guests. We hadn't seen him dressed like that for some time; usually he went around in a jacket. He greeted the guests heartily. Harvey clearly made a good impression, and my father was glad to welcome him into his home.

Mama invited us to the table she had set for the guests. We hadn't expected this; we had to have a second lunch. There was more to the table talk than medicine. Father first thanked Harvey for coming to Moscow, then, by well-established tradition, the Russian winter became the subject of conversation; a deep snow covered the ground. After that, the conversation turned — as might have been expected — to Soviet-American relations. Father reminisced about his visits to the United States, recalling the people and the country warmly. He spoke of his meetings with President Eisenhower. It was a relaxed conversation.

To mark the festive occasion, Father even permitted himself to drink a small glass of cognac with the guests as a toast to friendship between our peoples. He had two favorites among these ceremonial glasses: the tall, narrow one that held ten grams that I first recall seeing in Kiev, and a large, solid one. He liked to brag about the latter the way he did about his German tea glass with a handle. It was partially solid, leaving but a tiny space on the top to hold the liquid. Yet from a distance it looked filled from top to bottom. Jane Thompson, the wife of the American ambassador, had given him the glass on one of her visits to the dacha.

"You have to attend a lot of receptions," Mrs. Thompson had said with a smile. "This glass will come in handy when you've got to make a toast but don't want to drink any more."

Father frequently told this story and showed off the glass. It was no different on this occasion.

After lunch, we went out onto the porch. It was getting dark, and Harvey wanted to use the day's last light to take some more photographs; we had already taken some around the table.

Naturally, nothing had been said during the conversation about the memoirs. Harvey knew nothing at all about them, and it would never have occurred to Father to mention the subject. It was dark when we returned to the hotel. The guests were delighted at having been received by the former premier and asked us to express their most sincere gratitude.

We had no inkling of the clouds that were gathering over us.

The Harveys' visit to the Soviet Union had gone very well. Mrs. Harvey had relaxed and enjoyed herself. The November 7, 1969, holiday, the anniversary of the Bolshevik Revolution, was approaching. From the beginning, I had tried to coax the Harveys into prolonging their stay for a couple of days, and in the end they couldn't resist postponing their flight from November 6 to November 8. Intourist didn't make any trouble about changing the ticket.

It was no secret when the guests were leaving. Nor did the change in departure date seem very important. Who cared if they left a day early or a day late? In fact, someone did care: it turned out that a special event had been prepared.

We didn't manage to get tickets for the Harveys to view the parade in Red Square, but I reassured them, pointing out that their window in the National Hotel looked out on Gorky Street — they could see almost the entire spectacle without leaving the room. I planned to bring a portable television set so we could watch the events in Red Square itself; at the time, hotel rooms didn't have sets.

One had to get to the hotel early on November 7, before 7:00 A.M.; after that it would be impossible to get into the city center without a pass. I brought not only the television but two samovars, which were our gifts to the Harveys and Stone. Because of the holiday, everyone was at home, and Vitya was too busy to come. Finally, a fellow with whom I had a passing acquaintance agreed to lend me a hand.

At the last moment, I grabbed a book to take along. If the guests were still sleeping at that early hour, I would sit in the lobby and read. I am scrupulously enumerating these petty details because each would play a role in the events that followed.

The Harveys were already waiting for us. We drank coffee and had just started to have a look at the samovars when the concierge came in and warned us that no one was allowed in the room during the parade. She didn't explain [presumably this was a general security precaution, in view of the presence of political and military leaders in Red Square — ed.], but we weren't upset; we were in a festive mood. Everyone went to the hotel entrance to watch the parade.

We stood for a long time in the cold and got quite chilled. After the parade, we were permitted to reenter the room. The Harveys were quite pleased; we swapped impressions and jokes. Dr. Harvey anticipated with pleasure his friends' reaction to the interesting photos he had taken.

To warm ourselves up, we ordered a bottle of Armenian cognac and some hors d'oeuvres sent up to the room. We turned on the television. It was all cozy and peaceful. Still to come that day was Professor

Harvey's last meeting with Mama and Lena, at which he would offer a few last bits of advice. One final evening at the Bolshoi Theater, and tomorrow our guests would fly home to America.

Suddenly there was a gruff shout: "Everyone stay where you are! We've got information that you're engaged in activity harmful to the Soviet state! Don't move!"

Accompanied by the woman hotel administrator, several men thrust the double doors wide open and burst into the room. The senior man presented KGB identification in the name of Yevgeny Mikhailovich Rasskazov.[8] More calmly, he repeated, "You are suspected of antistate activity. We have to search you. Show your identification and remain where you are."

No search warrant was shown. I forgot about such necessary formalities, and the Harveys simply didn't know what our rules were. Their most sinister fears about the Soviet Union confirmed, they probably regretted ever having agreed to make the journey. Still, Professor Harvey was the first of us to regain his balance. With the rest of us still gripped by fear, he politely but firmly demanded permission to telephone the U.S. embassy.

His request was summarily rejected.

Making us face the wall, they searched us. They took all personal effects from our pockets and examined them carefully. Then they began a thorough search of the hotel room and our guests' baggage.

Once I recovered my equilibrium, I asked what they were looking for. Rasskazov didn't bother to answer.

They turned the room upside down, searching through the beds and the suitcases, rummaging through the shelves, examining the toilet bowl meticulously, leafing through my book. They took an interest in the television set and wanted to take it apart. I refused to do it, and they themselves decided against it, settling for a close inspection through the grille-like back of the set.

The self-assuredness of our uninvited guests diminished a bit, and the man who was rummaging around in the toilet bowl burst out angrily, "There's nothing! We're too late. They managed to pass it on."

The telephone rang. It could have had to do with tickets for the

8. These people are still alive. They carried out orders from superiors; if they hadn't, someone else would have. Nothing would have been different. Therefore, I have changed the names.

Bolshoi Theater, or it might have been Mama, whom the Harveys were supposed to meet.

"Don't move," Rasskazov bellowed. "Don't pick it up." He didn't go to the telephone either.

By this point, my friend had recovered his courage, and his sense of irony, too. "Is this what you're searching for?" He pointed to a piece of paper jammed into the keyhole of the door connecting the suite's bedroom and sitting room.

Rasskazov looked at him fiercely.

"I don't know what you're looking for," my friend explained. "I was just trying to help."

Finally, Rasskazov consented to answer my question.

"This man," he said portentously, pointing at Dr. Harvey, "is a CIA agent. He's engaged in spying."

The most interesting thing is that I believed him! Not totally, but I believed. That's where the stereotyped thinking that had been hammered into us over the years had led. Talk about "the image of the enemy" — here it was!

The search ended in failure, if one doesn't count the films taken from our guests, films that were precious to Dr. Harvey.

Our uninvited visitors now felt uncomfortable; as a result, their tone changed sharply. Rasskazov made excuses, saying he was only fulfilling his duty. Then he asked us to sit down at the table, and he began to write something.

It turned out to be a short statement to the effect that we, the so-and-sos and the so-and-sos, had no claims against the organs of state security in connection with the search that had been carried out.

Stunned by what had happened, and relieved that everything had ended "satisfactorily," my friend and I nodded agreement. Unwillingly, the Americans followed our lead. They didn't know how the game was played in our country.

Rasskazov asked me to recopy the statement in my own handwriting. Mechanically, I did as I was told. Everyone signed. Then Rasskazov pulled me after him into the corridor.

"You understand, we were doing our duty. These are dangerous people," he repeated.

I nodded.

"If there's nothing unlawful on the films," he said, "we'll return them developed tomorrow morning. I'll call you one of these days."

With this, his voice became even firmer. "Please don't invite these people to your home under any circumstances. Good-bye."

I returned to the room. My friend hurriedly excused himself and departed. Depressed, we took our seats around the table. I don't know who among us was most upset. Trying to calm the Harveys, I started mumbling rubbish.

"Mistakes happen in all countries. Intelligence services have to carry out their duties, but sometimes things go awry."

Obviously, my words weren't very convincing. And the look on my face left a lot to be desired.

In his turn, Harvey tried to reassure me: "Mr. Khrushchev, for several years I worked in Peru. I saw worse there. Don't be upset. I can understand you don't want any publicity. I promise you that when we get home I won't say anything to the press."

Indeed I didn't want any publicity. I smiled at him in gratitude. After a while, we all calmed down, but Harvey didn't want to remain in the room.

"I don't want to be reminded of what we just went through," he said. "Let's get out of here. And your mother and sister — it's terrible that they have to come here. Let's arrange to meet them in your apartment."

I recalled Yevgeny Mikhailovich's parting words: "under any circumstances." I didn't dare disobey.

"My place hasn't been cleaned," I mumbled. "And Mama is planning to come here. Let's not change our plans."

With a sad grin that indicated he understood everything, he replied, "All right, so be it." We sat in silence until Mama arrived, each of us lost in thought.

The final conversation with Mama and Lena was spoiled, or so it seemed to me. I was preoccupied with what had just happened. We didn't talk about that. Nor did I say anything later. Why upset them — as if they didn't have enough troubles. Father, Mama, and my sister all departed this life knowing nothing of the events of that day.[9]

9. *Editor's note:* Why did the KGB descend on Sergei Khrushchev and the Harveys in this way? Were they responding to the interpreter-guide's suspicions? Did the KGB really believe that Dr. Harvey was a spy? Were they simply seeking the memoirs? Or was the KGB trying to blackmail Sergei by linking him with a man it knew quite well was not a spy?

Sergei Khrushchev replies: "Our interpreter-guide was not the key to this affair. We didn't tell her our names, and I don't think she ever found out. I'm sure it wasn't

Before saying good-bye, Harvey reminded us that it would be advisable to do another blood analysis in his laboratory and suggested we send him another sample. Mama and Lena thanked the Harveys and left. The next morning, Vitya and I took them to the airport.

As Rasskazov had promised, the films were returned to the Harveys that morning, developed. Only one roll was spoiled; I didn't know which and whether that was intentional. If it was the one of my father at the dacha, then it was unquestionably deliberate.

The practical, punctilious Vitya had carefully packed the samovars to withstand the long journey, but it wasn't meant to be. Customs officials turned the Harveys' suitcases inside out. They made a rough check in the main hall, then took them away somewhere, evidently to search them. At the old Sheremetyevo airport, the whole examination procedure was quite visible through the grating that divided the hall into domestic and international sections. They brought the samovars back, declaring they couldn't be taken out of the country without a certificate from the Ministry of Culture. It had to be established that they had no artistic value.

Finally, the harassed and exhausted Harveys waved good-bye to us and, sighing with relief, walked to the airplane. Their Russian adventure was over. Once home, they could regale their friends with colorful stories, comparing police methods in South America to those of Russia.

As for us, we still had unfinished business: we had to find a way to get the blood to Harvey for analysis. At first, it seemed simple. In early December, Yuli Vorontsov, Sergo Mikoyan's old classmate who was now Dobrynin's deputy, flew to Washington. I knew him, although not well. Vorontsov readily agreed to my request; he was all the more

---

her report that was the real reason for the search. Nor, I believe, did the KGB really consider Harvey a spy; if they had, they wouldn't have allowed him to come to Moscow. This was just a convenient and time-tested way to cover up an illegal search for which no warrant had been issued.

"Living in a police state is simpler and less dramatic than it may appear in the West. We knew, of course, why Father was being guarded, and that our phones were tapped — that much attention we figured we had 'merited.' But we had no reason to think that the KGB was tracing our every step. I don't think I was naive about this; it's more likely that Western readers will be naive in assessing it. But, of course, that leaves the larger issue of exactly what the KGB was up to. I really don't know. I can guess which other forces were at work, but I have no hard information. Some of the people involved are still alive, and if I accuse them without proof, they could take me to court."

willing to do so because he had helped organize the Harveys' trip to Moscow.

Complications arose unexpectedly. Alarmed and astonished, Vorontsov's wife, Faina, said to me on the very eve of their departure: "It's unprecedented. They summoned us specially to the Ministry of Foreign Affairs and warned us not to take any parcels from anyone to the States. I don't know what to do."

The rule against taking third-party parcels had always existed, but the authorities had winked at violations. Unlike Faina, I immediately understood what was going on: Rasskazov had put up a new barrier. They didn't mean packages from third parties but rather from *me*. Suppose this blood analysis was only a pretext, while in reality . . .

I managed to persuade the Vorontsovs, who already had a thermos with the blood. However reluctantly, they kept their word, and the blood reached its destination.

A few days later I called Harvey. It was a bad connection, and the professor's tone was cool. He said he hadn't found anything new; he had mailed me the results. Our paths didn't cross again. Of course, I never received his report. It's obviously preserved in my dossier.

At the end of December I met Rasskazov. Yevgeny Mikhailovich warned me again that both Stone and Harvey were veteran intelligence agents. If I noticed anything suspicious I was to telephone him immediately. He gave me his number.

The canard that the cunning Khrushchev had deceived everybody, exploiting Lena's illness and the credulity of those around him to send his memoirs abroad, circulated for a long time in certain circles.

They floated the rumor, echoes of which can still be heard today, that Harvey asked for my father's memoirs as an honorarium and Father agreed. In fact, the books published in the West contain passages that relate to periods long after the Harveys' departure, but that was immaterial.

The November events brought unpleasantness not only to us but also to those who had helped with the invitation to the Harveys, and to people who had nothing whatever to do with it. Academician Gamkarelidze could no longer go abroad, nor was Stone particularly welcome in the Soviet Union. Only recently did these barriers come down. I read with satisfaction in the press that Dr. Stone was among other American guests received by Mikhail Sergeyevich Gorbachev. Times had changed, and he ceased to be a "hardened CIA agent."

My acquaintance with the Vorontsovs ended. I heard that some totally innocent people who filled out the Harveys' visa forms in our Washington embassy had suffered.

I think that even Gromyko got caught up in this; after all, he had sanctioned the invitation to the doctor. I didn't get the opportunity to explain myself to him. And that pains me a great deal.

Acquaintances of mine then serving in the organs of state security were dismissed although they had never even heard of either Stone or Harvey. To be sure, they were reassigned to pretty good places in other departments.[10]

I should like to express my belated apologies to all these people.

Thus the samovars never reached their destinations. For a long time, Vitya couldn't get the certificate from the Ministry of Culture; they bounced him from one office to another. At my next regular meeting with Rasskazov, I casually mentioned Vitya's odyssey in search of permission to send the samovars to America. His reaction was quite unexpected. Ashen-faced, he barked, "Why are you so hung up on these samovars? Why are you trying so hard to send them to your Americans?"

They obviously remained confident these were not mere samovars. I couldn't imagine what our guardians were afraid of. Maybe they suspected that some microfilm was concealed in them. I imagined Yevgeny Mikhailovich sawing the samovars into tiny pieces.

BY 1969 the memoirs had already become tangible, more than just odd pages or chapters. We had in hand about a thousand typewritten pages that I had edited; they covered the period from the beginning of the thirties to the death of Stalin and the arrest of Beria. There were also descriptions of various episodes from Father's life: the Cuban crisis, the Twentieth Party Congress, the Geneva summit, reflections on the general staff and on others' wartime memoirs, relations with China, and a few other things. All this was kept in several folders.

In the summer of 1969, Father reread these materials and made notes. There was quite a bit that he didn't like, especially the way it was written. I decided to find a professional writer to help with the

10. These people were simply acquaintances. They did their service honorably, and I never asked them for anything. From time to time, we had dinner at each other's homes. They were fired "just in case," and given new jobs in other agencies. Getting rid of them was just a routine preventive measure. Why worry that Comrade X would say something to me, or that I would ask him about something? Let the comrade work somewhere else.

rewriting. But it was a major job that not just anyone would agree to undertake: working with the fallen Khrushchev wouldn't pay either moral or material dividends.

I got lucky. I described my problem to a friend, Vadim Vasilievich Trunin, author of the screenplay for *The Byelorussian Station,* a film directed by Andrei Smirnov that caused a sensation in Moscow, and he offered to take on the literary reworking. He noted that it would indeed be an enormous job and that such work usually paid well — but he would do it for nothing.

I gave Vadim the copy I had edited. Having read it, he asked for the original text and I gave it to him. After administering a sound scolding for my editorial efforts, he said everything would have to be redone. I was slightly offended, having expended so much time and effort, but I understood that it would be hard for me to compete with a professional.

Trunin set to work. I didn't cease my own activity either, but continued to edit the pages Lora produced. When I told Father about the agreement with Trunin, he became uneasy.

"Are you sure he isn't an agent? What if everything he gets his hands on just disappears?"

I assured him I had known Vadim for a long time as an honest, reliable friend who regarded him sympathetically. Father relaxed a bit. He was willing to leave it to me. I should add that I didn't make any secret of our work; secrecy would only provoke suspicion. Since authorities were eavesdropping on the dictation anyway, there was no point in mounting a conspiracy. The reader shouldn't think of us as daring operatives jousting with counterintelligence agents. Life isn't like that at all. One lives in a country and gets used to it. I even called Lora regularly (she had meanwhile taken a new job) to discuss problems we encountered in the work.

The new year, 1970, changed nothing in Father's life. He still seemed forgotten. As part of his customary routine, he continued to dictate. To be sure, his health declined somewhat, and he became noticeably weaker. Dr. Bezzubik, who examined him regularly, warned us that he had developed a serious case of arteriosclerosis, involving some loss of memory.

"It's possible he could live many years with this — or he could die at any moment. Medicine is powerless in such cases."

In general, Father paid no attention to illness, and he tried to ignore his ailments. With the arrival of spring, he set to work as usual. He intended to lay a pipe from the house down to the meadow and so solve the problem of watering the garden. As with everything he did, he began the job enthusiastically and devoted himself to its completion. All day long he dragged pipes, painted them, wrapped them in flax, and threaded them together. The work made him happy and he joked the way he used to: "My profession as a metalworker comes in handy. None of you know how to do this. Didn't they teach you anything?"

Now that fine weather had come, the memoirs were almost completely abandoned.

July-like heat descended on us on May 29. It was hard to work, but it was time to weed. Father took a hoe, went to the garden, and busied himself there until the middle of the day. When he returned after noon, he didn't feel like eating; he complained of not feeling well, said his heart bothered him. He wandered around the house, thinking it would pass, but it didn't. We had to summon the doctor.

Vladimir Grigorievich declared he had suffered a serious heart attack. Father was immediately taken to the hospital on Granovsky Street. Days of restless, uncertain waiting began.

Dr. Bezzubik explained that Father would have to stay in the hospital a long time, perhaps several months, but the first ten days were critical. Anything could happen; death could come at any minute. He concluded with the stock phrase, "We're doing everything possible." And despite their formality, his words had a calming effect on me.

Vladimir Grigorievich didn't object to our visiting the patient. Exercising his right as chief hospital physician, he got me a pass that allowed daily visits at any hour.[11] His only caution was that Father must not be upset. Agitation could have a baneful effect on the course of the illness.

Each day I spent an hour to an hour and a half with Father, sometimes during the day and sometimes in the evening. The weather was hot, but in the air-conditioned ward it was cool. They had recently renovated the old building, which was built in the early thirties for the Kremlin Medical Department. Father lay on his back, motionless. He wasn't permitted to read; all he could do was think. I tried to distract him by relating various domestic news items and telling him how work on the memoirs was going, what Trunin and I were doing. There wasn't

11. The fact that Bezzubik was chief of the Kremlin hospital is not a sign of the authorities' special respect for my father. It was simply that Father continued to be treated by the same doctor who had attended him until 1964.

always enough news to fill the visit, so long pauses were wedged in between bits of conversation.

Tubes from an apparatus next to the bed were hooked up to the patient, and a broken green line kept running across a screen — the cardiogram. A nurse was always on duty in the room; the patient's condition was grave. Only when I came would she leave for a while. My gaze was involuntarily drawn to that running line, almost straight for a while, then a rise and fall, and so on, endlessly. If the customary pattern changed, I began to panic: should I summon the doctor, or was it a problem with the apparatus? I decided against calling the doctor, but I agonized a fair amount.

Father didn't like wasting time, which was how he regarded my visits. He'd begin to feign anger: "Why do you come so often, anyway? Don't you have anything better to do? You're wasting your own time and bothering me. I'm pretty busy here. Either they're giving me drops or shots, or the doctors are examining me, or they're taking my temperature. No time to get bored."

But the expression on his face made it clear he welcomed my visits. Of course, Mama and his daughters also came to see him. And as time passed, Father began to mend. There was no further talk about the possibility of death.

I remembered Bezzubik's warning to avoid anything that might agitate Father, so my reports to him were optimistic. But I had ample reason to be worried. A new stage of the hunt for the memoirs had obviously begun. Or, perhaps, the hunt hadn't stopped at all after the Harveys' visit.

The first warnings had sounded in early spring, when Father was still in good health. In the beginning I didn't take them seriously; it was too much like a bad movie. Toward the end of April, I learned that something was wrong. As happens so often in life, the disclosure came accidentally.

Vladimir Aleksandrovich Lisichkin, a smiling, likable young man, worked in our section. He was forever in a hurry, always running late, whether he had to prepare a new book, complete a plan, or simply clean up the hackwork. Regular mass transit was too slow for him. He got around exclusively by taxi.

Flying into our room that sunny day, Volodya looked unusually confused. Dragging me into a corner, he declared in a secretive whisper, without any preliminaries: "You know, they're following you!!!"

I didn't believe it. All that had happened ought to have taught me

Fidel Castro snaps a family portrait at the Gorki-2 dacha. Seated (left to right) are Yulia Nikitichna Khrushcheva-Gontar (Khrushchev's daughter by his first wife), Nina Petrovna Khrushcheva holding grandson Nikita Khrushchev, Khrushchev, grandson Nikita Adzhubei, and daughter Rada Adzhubei. Standing (left to right) are Yelena Khrushcheva, V. P. Gontar (husband of Yulia), G. M. Shumova, and Sergei Khrushchev.

At Livadia in the Crimea, 1956.

Father and son at Livadia, 1959.

Khrushchev with grandson Nikita Khrushchev at Livadia, August 1962.

Taking a stroll in the meadow at the Gorki-2 dacha with his son Sergei and grand-sons Nikita and Vanya Adzhubei, 1959.

Sergei Khrushchev with Yuri Andropov at Bri-juni, Yugoslavia, 1961.

The dacha at Petrovo-Dalneye, where Nikita Khrushchev lived from 1965 to 1971.

Khrushchev with "camera-gun" at Petrovo-Dalneye, 1967.

A quiet moment in the woods with Arbat and a tame rook, summer 1966.

With Hasselblad camera in a meadow at Petrovo-Dalneye, 1965.

Right: Khrushchev romping with Arbat, 1966.

Posing with guests from a neighboring lodge, 1969.

At Petrovo-Dalneye, 1966.

Khrushchev watching his daughter Rada Adzhubei and grandson Vanya Adzhubei,
1965.

The view from the bench where Khrushchev loved to sit at Petrovo-Dalneye.

Khrushchev at the Petrovo-Dalneye dacha, 1971.

At Petrovo-Dalneye, 1969, wearing the cloak he received as a gift from a French industrialist.

Khrushchev with family and guests at a bonfire.

The author with his father at Petrovo-Dalneye, January, 1971.

Showing the hats sent by Little, Brown and Company to verify authenticity of the Khrushchev memoirs. With the retired statesman is his grandson Nikita Khrushchev.

With academician R. Gamkarelidze, July 3, 1971, in the last photo taken of Khrushchev before his death.

Sculptor Ernst Neizvestny at work in his studio on the memorial for Khrushchev's grave.

Sergei Khrushchev (in glasses) with Vasily Ivanovich Galyukov (former bodyguard to Nikolai G. Ignatov) in Moscow, 1988. They are standing at the very corner where Sergei Khrushchev first met Galyukov in the autumn of 1964.

Memorial headstone of Khrushchev at Novodevichy Cemetery.

to be surprised by nothing, but this was hard to believe. They keep spies and criminals under surveillance — they're outlaws. But why follow me?

The memoirs? Without a doubt.

Volodya continued: "An hour ago, you were driving along Leninsky Prospekt, where it ends, right?"

"Yes."

"You see! I was hurrying to the editorial office in a taxi to get a manuscript from the typist. The driver was a talkative guy — he says, 'Want to see how they follow a car? Those two Volgas over there are after that Fiat.' I glanced up and was dumbfounded — it was your license plate. We were behind them, and I saw it all clearly: one car overtook you while the other remained behind. Then they changed places."

With his typical curiosity, Volodya put the question directly: "What are they after — the memoirs?"

Everyone at work knew I was devoting my spare time to editing my father's notes. There was nothing disloyal in Lisichkin's question. I didn't answer, just thanked him for the warning.

If it hadn't been for Lisichkin, it would never have occurred to me to pay attention to the cars that swarmed around me on the street. Everything would have gone on unnoticed. To be sure, my newfound knowledge didn't change anything: there was nothing to hide, and no place to run. I decided against acting any differently. Better not show my pursuers they had been found out. Who they were wasn't in doubt: Yevgeny Mikhailovich Rasskazov at work.

I did, however, decide to make sure I *was* being shadowed. My curiosity got the better of me. It didn't occur to me just how serious the situation was. The whole thing seemed like a game. It would be interesting to see how they shadowed me. Would I spot them quickly? How to sort out the pursuers from the stream of automobiles?

Episodes from detective films swirled around in my head. Before me stood the brave, slightly ironic, cool-headed Banionis and his pursuers from the hit movie *The Dead Season*.[12] With this in mind, I set off on the hunt.

---

12. Donatas Banionis, the well-known Soviet movie actor, played the role of a courageous Soviet intelligence agent in *The Dead Season*. The action takes place in an unnamed country where Soviet, American, and West European agents engage in a struggle involving former Nazi inventors of poison gas.

I drove along Leninsky Prospekt slowly, then slower still, at not more than forty kilometers an hour. There it was — a gray Volga with two antennas trailing steadily behind me. At my tortoiselike pace, everyone passed me except the Volga, which dragged along as if stuck to me. At last, unable to resist, it too passed me. I made a note of the license, braked, and pulled over to the curb. Behind me, a light blue Volga, also with two antennas and also in no apparent hurry, turned into a side street. After a moment I set off, paying almost no attention to what was ahead of me, looking mainly in the rearview mirror. There it was again — the familiar Volga creeping out of the side street.

I continued to play my childish game. I drove on slowly, looking to see when they would show. Usually I was able to identify the observers, although often there were several suspicious cars.

The trickery included disguises. One day in May, I drove to the Moscow Institute of Technology to give a lecture — I've been teaching there for twenty-five years — with a suspicious Volga behind me. At the wheel was a man with a carefully coiffed girl, wearing a blouse, next to him. Were they or weren't they? I lost them, made a left turn, crossed Hospital Bridge over the Yauza River, came to a stop in the institute parking lot, scrambled out of the car, and waited. No one in sight. Suddenly, the same car shot past. The same girl was now at the wheel, but wearing a sweater and with tousled hair. The same young man was next to her. I recognized the girl for sure. My curiosity satisfied, I set off for the lecture.

For the moment, I decided not to say anything to Father, not wanting to upset him. He couldn't do anything about it, and I didn't want to interrupt work on the memoirs, a step that would have testified to our fright.

It's a good thing I didn't say anything to him. Had I done so, I would have blamed myself for the rest of my life, for I have no doubt my words would have provoked a heart attack. Today my conscience is clear at least on that score; but at the time it was I alone against the threat.

The number of incidents increased. The ring tightened as they checked out all connections, trying to find where the material was being typed.[13] There was a search at work: I noticed that a roll of Kodak

13. *Editor's note:* Was it only now that the KGB began trying to find out where the transcripts were typed? Sergei Khrushchev had been talking to the typist on a tapped

color film taken at the dacha was missing from a drawer. No one in our country knew how to develop such film and it had been lying around for almost a year.

I decided to act as though I hadn't detected anything. Without making any fuss, I shut the drawer slowly; one of my co-workers might be an informer. Such a possibility certainly couldn't be excluded.

Suddenly some instructions came down from the director: Investigate, determine whether departmental typists are typing outside material, and report the results immediately! They had obviously decided to enlist others to check on the conspiracy at work; they hadn't counted on section heads, including me, being brought in on it.

With pure heart, I reported as follows: "No such typing going on. Necessary preventive measures taken."

Our typists really weren't doing any outside work, except for the speedy Lisichkin's verbose articles, which I was sure didn't interest the investigators. But another typist I knew told me about certain strange things that had happened to her. Halfway to the office one day, she realized she had forgotten something and turned around and went home. Certain unknown people were hanging around outside her door, but when they spotted her, they hastily went up to the next floor and started ringing the bell of the apartment above hers. On another occasion, a woman jumped out from some bushes in front of her building; the description fit the woman behind the wheel of the car that had overtaken me.

I assured her that her fears were groundless, that she was just imagining things. But I knew what was going on. They were checking, they wanted to find out whether the memoirs were in the apartment. They weren't.

My mood worsened with every passing day. So far they hadn't found anything, but they knew how to search. In our case, no special professionalism would be required. Soon they would be onto Lora, too, and everything they were looking for so persistently was right there at her place. What to do? Break off contact? That wouldn't do any good. They'd find the stuff. Besides, that would be both humiliating and

---

phone for months. Why did it take them so long? "Apparently they hadn't been eavesdropping after all," replied the author. "Either that, or some sort of foulup took place. The fact that they didn't know about Lora amazed me, and I regretted having called her on the phone."

suspicious. For the lack of any other inspiration, I decided to act as though nothing had happened.

Meanwhile, Lora fell ill and entered a hospital. Naturally, she couldn't type there. Toward the end of June, I went to visit and warn her about what was going on. The light blue Volga followed me that day; I noticed it next to the fence not far from the hospital entrance. The driver and passengers remained in the car.

Lora and I strolled through the grounds around the old hospital building. I told her about recent events, downplaying them so as not to frighten her. I ended my story by pointing out the car behind the fence: "They're following me."

"But I know that car," Lora suddenly interrupted. "I've seen it there before. A couple of days ago, we were playing Ping-Pong in the little garden near the entrance. I knew everyone there — that's why a tall, thin man in a gray raincoat and a wide-brimmed hat caught my attention. There was something odd about him — he looked like a movie detective. He whirled around, stared at us intently, and then vanished as quickly as he had appeared. I hadn't seen types like that around here before.

"I broke off the game, ran up to the fence, and glanced up the street. The man in the hat and raincoat was already in a light blue Volga. The Volga tore away and disappeared — that very car."

Lora was now quite frightened, and I had to calm her down. "It's not so bad. So what if they follow us! We're not doing anything wrong. If they want to find out who's typing the memoirs, let them find out. There's no secret about it. If instead of this stupid snooping they'd just ask me, I'd tell them. What's there to hide?"

We parted on this note. I myself wasn't as calm as I pretended. They were getting ready to do something. But what? One thing was clear: they already knew about Lora.

From this point, events developed quickly. The operation entered the final stage: seizure of the memoirs. A few days after my visit to Lora, Rasskazov called. He hadn't shown any sign of life since returning the things seized during the Harvey search.

Yevgeny Mikhailovich politely asked me to meet him; some details needed clearing up, he said, and having no objection, I readily agreed.

"It would be more convenient not to meet here," he said, referring to the KGB's Lubyanka headquarters. "If you don't mind, we'll wait for you at the Moskva Hotel."

He named a floor and a room. Curious and also a bit frightened, I went up to the floor; the concierge showed me where to go. With a bedroom and a sitting room, the suite was no different from other luxury suites I had seen in this hotel. In the sitting room there was a round table surrounded by several chairs and covered with a velvet cloth with an ashtray on it. A sofa stood against one wall, a buffet table against another. All quite ordinary and prosaic.

There was another man with Rasskazov; he introduced himself as Vladimir Vasilievich. During the conversation, he observed my every movement closely. The questions turned out to be humdrum, and my answers didn't especially interest my interlocutors. I don't remember everything, but there was one thing that seemed significant: "Do you have any new information about Stone and Harvey? Aren't you still in contact with Harvey?"

It was Yevgeny Mikhailovich who began putting the questions.

I wasn't about to conceal anything. "No news from Stone. I think he's got enough to do without me. As we agreed in Moscow, I sent Harvey a sample of my sister's blood for analysis. I tried to call him, but it was a bad connection — the only thing I could make out was that he was going to send the results of the analysis by mail. We're very worried that we haven't received anything. Lena's health is at stake."

Yevgeny Mikhailovich expressed sympathy but didn't offer to help.

"Tell me, Sergei Nikitich," his colleague interjected, "do you know a man named Armitage. Have you ever met him?"

"I once met someone by that name, although it's hard to say, of course, whether he's the one you're interested in. When I went to the U.S.A. with my father eleven years ago, a State Department representative in New York named Armitage went to Brooklyn with me. A collector of butterflies whom I wanted very much to see lived there. Butterflies are my hobby. Since that time, I haven't seen or heard of him."

I was amazed. What was this all about? They asked me about Armitage again later. I don't know why his connection with me interested them so much. Even if he worked for U.S. intelligence, which wouldn't have been unusual, his dealings with me were strictly within the confines of protocol. To be sure, in the old days such a connection would have been more than enough to get you in deep trouble. In any case, I never met Armitage after 1959.

"He's working in Moscow now," my interlocutor continued, "in the embassy, an out-and-out spy just like Stone. Both are active CIA agents. If he suddenly appears, inform us immediately."

I agreed.

"Have journalists taken any interest in you?" asked Rasskazov.

"No."

"If they do, let us know."

"All right."

And that was just about the entire conversation, except that as I was leaving they offhandedly put the main question.

"By the way, how's Nikita Sergeyevich coming along with his memoirs?" Rasskazov asked while the other man fixed his eyes on me.

"So-so, thanks. He's ill now, in the hospital. Can't do any work there."

With that we parted. Why did they need this meeting? To take my measure? To feel me out? To gauge my future reaction? Probably all of these. You see, the real action was about to begin.[14]

About two weeks passed. On Saturday, July 11, 1970, my wife and I were invited to a dinner. Evening was approaching when the telephone rang. I lifted the receiver. Again it was Rasskazov.

"Hello, Sergei Nikitich. This is Yevgeny Mikhailovich. It's urgent that we talk to you. Can you meet us?"

I didn't like the idea of a meeting at all. And anyway we had just recently had a talk, essentially about nothing. "Yevgeny Mikhailovich, it's my day off. You just barely caught me. I was on my way out the door. We're invited to dinner. Let's meet next week."

"No, no," he said hurriedly, "it's extremely important. Something's happened that I can't talk about on the telephone. Please do as I ask."

Who the hell knew what had happened? Maybe it really was important; why else would he be sitting there working on Saturday evening? I could be a little late. I can handle this, I thought as I answered, "All right, I'll come right away."[15]

"Thanks," Rasskazov rejoiced. "Come right to the entrance — someone will meet you there."

I spoke briefly to my wife, told her I had to go to "the ministry"

14. Of all the motives behind this conversation, I think the primary one was probably to convince me that the spies existed, as a way to raise the issue of the memoirs. It was a primitive device, to be sure.

15. *Editor's note:* Why did Sergei Khrushchev agree to go? His answer: "From the very beginning, I had considered it useless to try to resist the KGB openly. I could have refused to come in on a Saturday, but that wouldn't have changed anything except to put my adversaries on guard."

on urgent business (I didn't say which ministry), and promised to return as soon as I could.

Rasskazov's colleague from the Moskva Hotel was indeed waiting for me at the huge, oddly molded metal door of the massive Lubyanka building that all Soviet people know so well.

He took me past all the security checkpoints to the right floor, and we entered Yevgeny Mikhailovich's small office. I had already been there, after the episode with the Harveys.

Rasskazov stood up from behind his desk, his face beaming with cordiality. We shook hands and sat down. The man who had accompanied me sat opposite; the whole routine was by now familiar.

Only recently have I asked myself, Was I close to being arrested? Apparently not. Yevgeny Mikhailovich struck up the old song we had just been through. Again Stone, again Armitage. How was Nikita Sergeyevich's health? He also asked something about the memoirs.

I was puzzled: What was so urgent? What had happened? Didn't he have anything else to do? I didn't say this out loud. Quietly answering their questions, I waited to see what would come next.[16]

"Sergei Nikitich, our boss wants to talk to you. Do you have any objection?"

"Of course not. But who is it?"

"The deputy chief of the directorate."

We left the office and went up several flights of stairs. After knocking at a tightly closed door, Yevgeny Mikhailovich opened it and let me go ahead. This office was bigger but not really large. On the right, a desk stood by the window; on the left, along the wall, was a long walnut conference table covered in the center with green felt. It was all done in Stalinist style.

A wiry man of forty-five or fifty rose from behind the table. He had the look of an intellectual.

16. *Editor's note:* Why didn't the author voice his anger and resentment? "But what did I have to gain?" Sergei Khrushchev replied. "The bulk of the manuscript was already in the West and safely beyond their reach. Nor was it clear where more active resistance would lead. The key fact was that they had their orders. Until they did, they didn't act. Once they had Brezhnev's decision in hand, they had no choice but to carry it out." This response leaves several points unclear: How much of the manuscript (and which version of it) was in the West, and how long had it been there? How did the version already sent abroad differ from the one Trunin was editing and Lora Finogenova was typing? When these and other questions relating to the manuscript were put to the author, he declined to answer.

"Hello, I'm Viktor Nikolayevich. Please sit down."

We sat down at the long table. Yevgeny Mikhailovich was now the third man. Yet another genteel conversation about life and work began. I remarked that two years ago I had been transferred against my will from my design bureau to an institute.

"And how's your work going in the new place?" the boss asked with interest. I had the feeling that he knew everything about me, and that my transfer had not taken place without his participation.

By that time I felt comfortable in the new job; I liked the work and the people, too. Therefore, I answered that I didn't hold any grudges and was in a certain sense even glad I had changed jobs. I didn't get more specific.

My answer suited him. It would be more difficult to reach a mutual understanding with a dissatisfied, embittered man. Finally he switched to the main subject.

"Tell me, Sergei Nikitich, where are Nikita Sergeyevich's memoirs kept these days?"

I pricked up my ears. It had begun. Earlier, pondering how to act, I had decided not to lie. When you get all tangled up in lies it makes things worse. Moreover, the role of a naive simpleton was more in keeping with my physiognomy. Above all, I had nothing to hide.

"Part of the memoirs are at my place, and part are in Nikita Sergeyevich's safe."

"You know," said Viktor Nikolayevich, lowering his voice and with a secretive expression on his face, "we've received information that foreign intelligence agents want to steal the materials. How are you safeguarding them?"

Everything was now clear. The only thing that surprised me was how primitive their approach was. All right, let him take me for a fool.

"I keep them in a locked bookcase," I said. "But of course that's not the main thing. My apartment's in the same building where Politburo members live. The KGB guards it carefully. There's a guard post at the entrance, and a sentry patrols the building. Foreign agents would find it as difficult to get in to steal the materials as they would to break into this building of yours," I added, permitting myself a joke.

He was momentarily confused. Then Viktor Nikolayevich regained his composure.

"Ah . . . you see, for professionals, guards and locks don't exist. I can't even guarantee my own safe one hundred percent."

At this point, his benevolent expression disappeared, and he continued in an official tone. "The Central Committee has asked me to speak to you. The Central Committee has decided that when Nikita Sergeyevich recovers, a secretary and a typist will be assigned to him for the remainder of the work.

"You're to be commended for helping your father with this work, but we must ask you now, in the name of the Central Committee, to turn the material in your possession over to us.

"As you know, the state security organs are the Central Committee's right hand. Your father often put it that way himself. Everything we do is done with the Central Committee's sanction and on its instructions. The material will be quite safe here, and we'll feel secure knowing it won't fall into the hands of foreign intelligence. I speak absolutely officially, as the representative of a Central Committee organ. The material will be returned to your father complete and intact."

What to do now? I couldn't possibly surrender the material without Father's permission. He had refused Kirilenko's request for the manuscript just two years before.

"You put me in a difficult situation," I replied. "Nikita Sergeyevich is ill. He's had a heart attack and he's in the hospital. I can't consult with him — doctors categorically forbid anyone to upset him. The memoirs are his property, and I can't give them up without his permission."

They had counted on my not dashing to my sick father; they thought that if they approached me alone they could get me to give in.

"I understand your predicament very well," Viktor Nikolayevich insisted, "but this isn't a matter of giving anything up. We're asking that you let us have the material for temporary safekeeping, pending your father's recovery."

"This is an extremely important matter for me," I said, continuing to defend myself. "I've already told you I have no right to dispose of the material. If the Central Committee attaches such importance to the matter, then I'd like to request a meeting with Yuri Vladimirovich Andropov. I'd like to get the guarantee from him, the more so since we're well acquainted. His word would carry enormous weight."

I had always held Andropov in great esteem, respecting him as a wise and intelligent man. I was convinced he wouldn't go back on his word. I first met Andropov when he went to work at the Central Committee after the events in Hungary in 1956. As ambassador there, he had struck Father as an intelligent man with an analytical bent. It wasn't long before he entered the inner circle of Father's aides and advisers. And there, too, he stood out with his intelligence, clarity of judgment, and lack of the self-abasing servility that is so widespread in Russia.

Later he became a secretary of the Central Committee. Although I didn't see him very often, I liked him. Sometimes, trivial episodes turn out to determine whom we like and dislike. I remember an event that took place in 1961, on President Tito's yacht, that involved Andropov and two other top leaders of ours. I happened to witness a conversation that was distressing, amusing, and disgusting all at the same time. The Leningrad party leader, Vasily S. Tolstikov, was discussing the fate of our Charlie Chaplin, the great Soviet comic actor Arkady Raikin, with Nikolai Yegorychev, who headed the Moscow party organization.

Tolstikov didn't like Raikin; he considered him capricious and demanding because he was constantly requesting things — a new apartment, help in buying a car. If the petitioner had been a district party secretary or local soviet chairman, that would have been different, but an artist-comedian? Come on!

Yegorychev heard his colleague's complaint and offered this suggestion: "Let Raikin move to Moscow. He's already broached the idea to me and asked my help."

Tolstikov frowned for a moment but then broke out in a wide grin: "Good riddance! It'll be easier for us without him. We'll find a new young guy and develop him."

His words horrified me. He couldn't possibly be serious, but he wasn't joking. It was as if a great artist was a carrot or a cabbage. And if so, what was Tolstikov, the gardener? But he was quite serious.

I hadn't noticed that Andropov had come up and was standing nearby listening to the conversation. When there was a pause, he let drop just one sentence: "Be careful. Keep talking like that and you'll end up in deep trouble." After that, he leisurely set off down the deck.

I wasn't so much struck by what he said, as by an inner kindness in his tone, and by the gentleness of his smile. It was then that I began to feel a sort of trust in him that didn't disappear even when he became head of the KGB. As a matter of fact, there were a lot of stories going round about how he was supposedly trying to restrain the growing repression. It was hard to judge whether this was true, but I want to believe it was.

It turned out my request to meet with Andropov had been anticipated. Viktor Nikolayevich was ready with an answer. "There's no possibility of seeing Yuri Vladimirovich. He's away at a meeting with the voters."[17]

A lengthy, oppressive silence hung in the air. We sipped coffee without speaking. I was thinking frantically: of course, I didn't believe Viktor Nikolayevich, but I couldn't brush aside what he'd said. Suppose I refused; suppose, although it was highly unlikely, they went along with my refusal. The material could still be "stolen" any minute by "foreign intelligence." Then I'd have nothing, and on top of that, they'd slap some charge on me. Then I'd really look like a fool.

On the other hand, the offer of Central Committee help was tempting. Father and I had discussed that possibility more than once, and he had spoken to Kirilenko about it. That's probably where the idea came from. Still, I couldn't decide something like this without his permission; I couldn't take the responsibility. After all, Father had turned Kirilenko down. Who would give guarantees?

Yevgeny Mikhailovich broke the extended silence.

"Why so quiet?" he asked sullenly.

"I'm considering what to do."

"You don't have any choice!" The words burst out of him. Viktor Nikolayevich shot his aide a look of reproach. I smiled stiffly.

"Well, there *is* a choice," I said with some effort, pointing to the door.

Viktor Nikolayevich looked worried. "Sergei Nikitich, it's up to you. We're just warning you about the situation and the possible consequences."

Both men now looked very anxious. Changing the subject, Viktor Nikolayevich began to talk about the United States, where he had worked for many years and from which he had recently returned. His impressions came down to this: life was worse in America than in the Soviet Union. And the food wasn't as tasty — everything was frozen.

I nodded mechanically and stirred my coffee, which by now was quite cold. If I don't give them the material, I thought to myself, they'll keep searching and God knows where it will end. They won't let me work. They know about Lora. They'll see to it I don't find another typist. If I give in, they'll likely stop searching. They'll shadow me a little while longer and then calm down. That way I can let things blow

---

17. *Editor's note:* Even when elections to the USSR Supreme Soviet were virtually meaningless, as in the period before 1989, when there was only one party-chosen candidate for each seat, the top party leaders went through the motions of appearing in their electoral districts and addressing "the voters."

over and then get back to work. Meanwhile, we'll have to give the signal for publication abroad. But not right now, no hurry, I'll have to think that through carefully. If only I could talk to Father. No, I'll have to make a decision right now. If I give them the material, they'll be satisfied; they'll be the winners. They can report immediately. I can explain everything to Father.

Having decided to take the difficult step, I felt better immediately. Ever on the alert, Viktor Nikolayevich noticed the change in my expression and looked at me quizzically.

"All right," I muttered, "I've thought it over. If foreign intelligence is hunting for the material, let it be in your hands. That really would be safer."

Now, I thought, I'll have to go home — where my wife was waiting for me to go out to dinner — for the files and tapes. I'll have to explain, and I don't feel like doing that.

"Let's do it tomorrow," I suggested naively. "I'm late for dinner." But of course they insisted on today, lest the all-powerful enemy implement his notorious plans to seize the material that very night.

Because I had given up, it was now easy to press me further.

"All right, we'll do it today, but part of the material is with the typist, Lora Nikiforovna Finogenova." I had decided to be totally open so as to show we were now in complete accord.

"We've already collected that," Viktor Nikolayevich said. "We went to her and asked her to give us everything she had."

"That's dishonest," I burst out. "You didn't have the right. You should have asked me."

Viktor Nikolayevich tried to smooth things over.

"I understand your indignation," he said. "You're right, but we were in a great hurry. Every minute was precious. You see, we had reliable information that foreign agents were on the point of stealing that material."

This argument "convinced" me and I continued to "spill" what I knew. "My friend Trunin has another part of the material in his home. He's a screenwriter — he's doing the editing."

It turned out they didn't know about Trunin. He and I had rarely seen each other in recent months.

Once again Rasskazov and Viktor Nikolayevich looked worried. "Where does he live?"

Trunin rented apartments first in one place, then in another, wherever fortune took him. He had recently moved, and I hadn't been to see him. He'd found something near the Warsaw Highway. "I don't have his address. I can give you his phone number — you can easily get the address."

Yevgeny Mikhailovich noted down the number and left the office. He returned a few moments later.

"Trunin isn't in Moscow. He'll be back next week. Did you give him the material a long time ago?"

"In the fall of 1969."

"Let's proceed this way," Viktor Nikolayevich said, taking the initiative into his own hands. "We'll put a guard on the building where Comrade Trunin lives. As soon as he returns, you yourself will get the material from him and pass it on to us."

I agreed. One final operation remained: to turn over the material I had and to get a receipt.

"Yevgeny Mikhailovich will go with you," Viktor Nikolayevich announced.

"All right, we can go up to my apartment and he can help pack the tapes and files," I said, playing the fool.

My interlocutors couldn't conceal their delight. They had expected more stubborn resistance. Their quick, complete victory had put them in a good mood. The operation had gone successfully.

We reached my house in ten minutes and I went up to the sixth floor. I told my wife I had one more errand to run and would soon return. I opened the bookcase doors and my heart sank. So much feeling, effort, and time had gone into those folders. I was mortified to be on the verge of surrendering them. Don't give them up, hold some back! a voice in my head insisted. Perhaps I could have hidden some tapes and files. Probably no one had sorted through them, let alone read and listened to them, so that their absence would not have been noticed. But reason triumphed over emotion: I began to fill two large bags with files and tapes.

When we returned to Viktor Nikolayevich, the material taken from Finogenova lay on his desk. There, among the big audio tapes with my father's memoirs, I noticed another, smaller one that I had quite forgotten.

About a year earlier, I had dictated a rough draft of an account of the events of October 1964 to which I had been a witness. Now that tape, too, lay on Viktor Nikolayevich's table. How could I have forgotten about it? In the beginning, I hadn't expected Father's memoirs to provoke such a negative reaction from the authorities. His story was about bygone days, and current leaders weren't even mentioned in passing. But my own tape was another matter. It covered events from the recent past, included today's top leaders, and concluded that what had happened in October 1964 didn't involve principled party politics at all but was a simple palace coup.

At that moment, I naively thought Father's tapes would be transcribed and examined attentively, if not in the Central Committee, then at least by someone in the KGB. If so, they'd listen to my tape too. Frantically, I tried to decide what to do. All I could hope for was a miracle.

"This little tape doesn't belong with the rest. It contains my own notes. I'd like it back."

No one had any intention of returning it to me, and I had no choice but to give in. My own blunder had drawn their attention to the tape. Out of that entire mass of material, the only thing they ended up examining was my tape. I came to that conclusion much later.

Meanwhile, the three of us sorted through the material — the edited text, the rough copies, and the tapes I had numbered according to chronological sequence. They counted the number of pages and the tapes.

Tired, I made a proposal: "Write out a receipt, we'll sign it, and then we'll say good-bye."

"No, no," Yevgeny Mikhailovich objected brusquely, "write it in your own hand."

Here, as in the Harvey case, they had to have proof of my voluntary cooperation.

"All right," I agreed, "what'll we write? Let's begin this way, just the way it was: 'To guarantee safekeeping of the memoirs of my father, Nikita Sergeyevich Khrushchev, and to prevent their theft by foreign intelligence agencies, the organs of state security approached me and requested that I turn the memoirs over to them —'"

"No, no," Yevgeny Mikhailovich interrupted hurriedly, "we're not going to put it that way. We need a different formulation."

"Such as?"

The final version stated: "On July 11, 1970, at the request of representatives of State Security, which aims to ensure the security and safety of tape recordings and typewritten text containing materials for the memoirs of Nikita Sergeyevich Khrushchev, Sergei Nikitich Khrushchev turned over the following materials to Viktor Nikolayevich Popov and Yevgeny Mikhailovich Rasskazov [names changed]: 18 tapes with 13 cm. spools, 10 tapes with 18 cm. spools, and 16 folders of typewritten materials containing 2,810 pages. Further, Lora Nikiforovna Finogenova, who worked on the memoirs at my request, has given the KGB 6 large tapes together with 929 typewritten pages of dictated text. In the fall of 1969 I gave part of the memoirs, 10 folders of typed text, to the writer Vadim Vasilievich Trunin for editing. On his return to Moscow, these materials will also be turned over to the KGB for safekeeping. No material was given to anyone other than the persons named above. All materials enumerated here will be returned to the author upon his recovery. July 11, 1970. Signed: V. Popov, Ye. Rasskazov, S. Khrushchev."

"All right," I said indifferently. "I'll write it the way you want."

Following his dictation, I wrote out the receipt. After we signed under the handwritten text, Popov summoned a secretary and ordered her to type it up. While we waited, we drank coffee and talked about this and that. Viktor Nikolayevich couldn't conceal his satisfaction, and Yevgeny Mikhailovich was obviously overjoyed.

We talked about the memoirs, agreeing that they were of great historical and political interest. Viktor Nikolayevich again emphasized that the KGB acted only on the instructions of the Central Committee and that all its activities were fully coordinated with the Central Committee. He repeated that Nikita Sergeyevich himself had seen the KGB as the right hand of the Central Committee.

At one point, we started talking about the United States. Viktor Nikolayevich again lamented the poor quality of American food, and added that working there was difficult — constant surveillance, never-ending tension.

"Surveillance isn't so bad," I joked. "You just have to get used to it. You've been following me and I survived."

They didn't find that funny! "What are you talking about? We haven't had you followed. You're imagining things."

"Let's not argue about it," I said. "To each his own opinion."

Time passed. The text was still being typed. I touched on a painful topic, the defection to the United States of KGB officer (and the son of a former minister of shipbuilding) Yuri Nosenko. There had been a lot of noise about this. I asked how it could have happened, and what Nosenko was doing now.

"Nosenko's a corrupt character." Viktor Nikolayevich frowned.

"He broke the law for personal gain, thinking that as an employee of the organs he couldn't be touched. And now he's gone as far as treason." [18]

"There's no justification for treason," I said. "But lawbreaking in the interests of the state can also be a slippery slope. You never know where to stop."

My implication that their own operation was far from legal hung in the air; the conversation languished. Then the typed text of the receipt arrived. We signed a second time. The meeting ended. They accompanied me to the door of the building and we parted.

Each of us went about his own business. Viktor Nikolayevich evidently hurried off to report the successful conclusion of an important operation. Galloping home to get my wife, I at long last drove to our friends'. We were hopelessly late, the visit to Viktor Nikolayevich having taken several hours.

I wasn't exactly in the mood for merrymaking. Again and again, I replayed the situation in my mind, recalling my mistakes. I hoped there hadn't been any serious ones. In any case, things should calm down for a while. Still, they had achieved their goals. We had lost; it would be impossible to continue to work. The main link in the chain, the typing, had snapped.

And what about Finogenova? I had the protection of my name, but what were they doing to her? I worried about this a great deal. Nor did I have an answer to the main question: What to do next?

I couldn't ask anyone for advice. Father was hospitalized and it was out of the question to talk to him about it. I had to decide alone. The issue was whether to give the signal to prepare the book for publication or not. It wasn't a simple step. Publication of the book would generate a huge furor, and the long-established notion that publishing abroad was immoral still had a hold on me.

To be sure, Father and I had discussed all this two years earlier. But was this indeed the critical moment?

On the other hand, publication would show everyone that the memoirs existed and would survive. Of course, this would throw my

18. *Editor's note:* Lieutenant Colonel Yuri Ivanovich Nosenko defected in the aftermath of the Kennedy assassination. His statements reportedly influenced the Warren Commission's conclusion that there was no foreign involvement in the assassination. Later, however, questions were raised about the legitimacy of Nosenko's motives, and he was reported to have undergone harsh interrogation from 1964 to 1967 by the Central Intelligence Agency.

new "friends" for six loops. The poor guys were so sure they had won a great victory, and then all of a sudden . . .

That night I decided that, yes, what had just happened could be considered the critical moment. We had to publish; there was no reason to wait. The situation would not change for the better.

Of course, it was difficult to make the decision alone, but Father wouldn't be out of the hospital until late in the summer, perhaps not till the fall. Too much time would have slipped away. Who knew what Popov and Rasskazov would think up in the meantime?[19]

The next day was an incredibly full one. I was still being followed but decided not to pay any attention. The prearranged signal was sent to the Western publisher.

I soon found out that the first volume would be out at the end of the year or the beginning of the next.[20] The second book required a lot more work and would take several years. At the moment, I wasn't concerned about the second volume.

Plans were made to announce the book in October and begin serial publication in November. It looked as if everything would go smoothly and I'd have time to warn Father.

I had no doubt what his reaction would be; we had discussed publication many times, and I had followed a plan worked out in advance. But how would he react to my handing over all the material? I must admit I was worried sick about that. From the point of view of logic, I had done the right thing. But ethically, my action didn't look very good. After all, Father had refused to give his memoirs to Kirilenko. Yet, if I hadn't given them up, who knows what would have happened? I still couldn't shake my doubts. They torment me to this day, twenty years after the fact.

The following thoughts also occurred to me at the time: Father had

19. *Editor's note:* Why didn't Sergei wait? What need was there for haste? As long as the manuscript was in the West, couldn't the signal have gone out at a later date? Did Sergei ever think of bargaining with the KGB? Did he and his father ever think through the alternatives open to them? "Of course, there were various possibilities," Sergei replied. "But we had decided not to enter into a conflict with the authorities, but rather to concentrate on preserving the manuscript. And for that to happen, it had to be published. Our first choice was to publish it in our country; only in extremis would we agree to publication abroad. We didn't consider any alternatives other than those mentioned in this book."

20. Obviously, preparations for publication had already been under way for some time. The timetable for publication was cleared with us in Moscow.

lived through the revolution, the civil war, and World War II, through the Leninist, Stalinist, and post-Stalinist periods of our nation's development. Whatever mistakes he made had no meaning now. He had devoted his whole active life to the common cause. Now that he was retired, he was using his memoirs to resurrect history, to make sense of the years he had lived, to prevent those who had replaced him from making avoidable mistakes. This would be of great benefit to society, for without a knowledge of the past, it is impossible to have a clear vision of the future.

But here was the paradox: Not only were the authorities not interested in history, they were hounding us for working on the memoirs, treating us like criminals, and treating the memoirs like illegal literature published abroad.

Yet Father's memoirs were unquestionably one of the Soviet Union's most important party documents. Why then suppress them? At the time, I had no good answer. Even today, to be honest, they're not hurrying to publish Khrushchev's memoirs. Many people still have no need for history, at least for truthful history.

I can't help thinking of George Orwell's wise words: "He who controls the past controls the future, and he who controls the present controls the past."

Hasn't the time come to stop rewriting the past, to leave it as it happened, and to begin to use it to build the future?

THE following day, I managed to find Lora. They had treated her a lot less politely than they had treated me. She had been under surveillance for several weeks. Certain suspicious types had been poking around her building, asking the neighbors questions. My visit to her at the hospital was the clincher.

According to her neighbors, the mysterious visitors were particularly interested in her tape recorder. Where had she gotten it? What was she typing? They tried to strike up an acquaintance with Lora herself but were unsuccessful. Once, when she was away, they tried to get into her apartment. They had to give up, though, because Lora's mother, who was ill, never went out.

Another time, they decided to use an old trick. Lora was summoned to the personnel department (this was just before she began working at our institute) and given an enormous form to fill out. They hinted that her impeccable record qualified her for an interesting although secret job. The time required to fill out the form guaranteed that Lora would be away from her apartment for several hours. Meanwhile, her ill mother was called to the hospital for some kind of urgent, and lengthy, examination.

The path was clear. Without any search warrant, "strangers" broke into her apartment. They had plenty of time but didn't need to look very far. There was a stack of typed pages of the memoir manuscripts inside the closet, along with tapes of my father's voice. The operation was a clean sweep; the "conspirators" had been uncovered.

That day they took only two pieces of carbon paper, trying not to leave any trace of their visit. But the observant Lora noticed that someone had been in her apartment, and that the pack of carbon paper was two sheets thinner.

On July 11, 1970, Lora was returning home. They were waiting for her outside her building. Three men approached her, showing their identification. "We need to clear some things up," one of them said. "Please come with us."

Quickly, they got into a waiting Volga. Two of the men sat in the back on either side of Lora, and the third got into the front with the driver.

They took her to Lubyanka, where she was questioned only briefly, just to get acquainted. Lora hid nothing: "Yes, I was typing Khrushchev's memoirs. Is that really forbidden? What's illegal about that?"

Then they all went back to her apartment, where they conducted a thorough search, without a warrant or any official witnesses. It was then that they seized the tapes and typewritten pages. They didn't stop to prepare the usual protocol on the search, but headed back to KGB headquarters to see Popov and Rasskazov, who apparently felt no need to exercise restraint as he questioned Lora.

"Don't you realize you're a coconspirator against the Soviet government? You're not going to get off easy, you know. You should have come to us at once and reported that you had been approached to type anti-Soviet material! You've been drawn into anti-Soviet activity!!!"

These were but a few of the accusations hurled at the poor woman. A full fifteen years after the Twentieth Party Congress, they were accusing her of anti-Soviet activity for simply typing the memoirs of the first secretary of the CPSU Central Committee.

The same people took a different tack with me. Only two hours later, they told me they were the right hand of the Central Committee and were only acting on orders from the party and in the party's interests. Yet, in spite of that, none of them ever have to answer for their violation of the constitution and of party morality. They'll receive pensions sufficient to live out their lives in comfort, just like their predecessors, who tortured and destroyed our country's best sons. Will it ever be thus?

Lora was in a state of near shock, and I was unable to calm her. It took a long time before she was back to normal, and the interrogations she went through affect her to this day.

They didn't leave either of us in peace for a long while. At first they continued to follow us openly, and to call us in for questioning. Then they seemed to back off, perhaps out of fear that we would resume work on the memoirs, or that I wouldn't keep quiet about their actions.

The final character in this story, Vadim Trunin, returned to Moscow a few days later. Someone from the KGB informed me of his arrival. I called him in the morning, getting him out of bed. I didn't tell him what had been happening, just arranged to go over to see him. He lived in the Volkhonka-ZIL area of Moscow, in the empty apartment of the film director Andrei Smirnov.

When I got there, I told Trunin what had happened over the last several days; I said I was going to take the folders from him, since I had promised to give them to the KGB for safekeeping. I repeated Viktor Nikolayevich's assurance that it was a temporary measure until Father recovered, at which point the materials would be returned and we'd resume work.

I didn't really believe my own words, and Vadim's only response was to grunt, as if to say, "Don't hold your breath until they give it back."

"The material belongs to you, go ahead and take it," he said, neither arguing nor trying to talk me out of it.

I took the folders and delivered them to Rasskazov. He accepted them without giving me any kind of receipt, saying they were covered in the receipts I had been given before.

I didn't press the point — the pages I had just given him were copies anyway. I only wanted to be finished with this nightmare as soon as possible. Yet the question of my own tape remained.

Yevgeny Mikhailovich apologized. "We've been very busy and haven't managed to listen to everything yet. Just wait a bit, and we'll give it back soon."

I got angry. "Why are you taking so long? Make a copy and listen to it as much as you like. It's not difficult to copy a tape."

The notion of copying obviously interested Rasskazov. "Tell me, Sergei Nikitich, how easy is it to copy tapes?"

I understood that he wasn't just curious. "It's very simple," I replied. "All you need is two tape recorders and some time. After all, copying takes the same amount of time as the original recording."

In other words, I would have needed over two hundred hours to copy Father's dictated tapes. However, faced with the time pressure to edit such a mass of material and with constant surveillance, I would have been unable to do this unnoticed. I was counting on Rasskazov's reaching precisely this conclusion.

"Couldn't one of the family have made a copy?" he asked, further indulging his curiosity.

"Out of the question," I replied.

"How about Nikita Sergeyevich himself? Could he have made one?"

"I don't know. That's his business. I never asked him."

The next day Vadim told me that as soon as the door had shut behind me at his apartment, a stranger burst in, flashed some identification, and carted him off to Lubyanka.

They really let him have it: "Who saw and read the memoirs? Where were they being kept?" And so on for hour after hour.

"Thanks to you, I'll go down in history," grumbled Trunin good-naturedly. "Just remember, they're not going to give anything back to you."

Popov and Rasskazov swept many people up in their net. The questioning went on for weeks. They interrogated Andrei Smirnov, mainly about Trunin. They asked Petrov's widow, Yulia, about Lyova, about me, and about Father. My friend Baraboshkin was questioned about me and the tape recorders. The operation involved others whom I knew of and, evidently, still more people I didn't know.

They didn't touch Rada or Adzhubei. Their loyalty was never suspect. In his memoirs, Aleksei Ivanovich touches in passing on the writing and publishing of my father's memoirs. He notes he wasn't involved in the work, says he has no idea how the memoirs came to be published, and hopes that time will provide an answer to the mystery.

I have tried as best I could to answer the question.

LYING in the hospital, Father knew nothing of the events swirling outside. I continued to visit him regularly, trying to appear unchanged on the surface, although I no longer talked in detail about work on the memoirs. I didn't want to lie; after all, I'd have to tell him the whole truth soon enough. He never asked me questions about the manuscript. Meanwhile, his condition began to improve.

Periodically I called Rasskazov about my tape. Finally, during the second half of August, Yevgeny Mikhailovich said, "Come on in, we're ready to return the tape to you. Viktor Nikolayevich would like to speak with you."

At this point, Father's discharge from the hospital was imminent — one and a half to two weeks away. He had refused to enter the Herzen sanatorium for rehabilitation treatments, saying that he would feel better at his dacha.

I still hadn't told him what had happened. I had decided to tell all after he returned to Petrovo-Dalneye. But deep down, I wanted to put off the difficult and unpleasant conversation as long as possible.

Once again I arrived at the old building that was now so familiar. Rasskazov took me up to Popov's office. Victor Nikolayevich greeted me politely and took the gray plastic case containing my tape out of his safe, but he didn't hurry to give it to me.

"We listened to your tape," he began, "and found it very interesting and vivid. You obviously dictated it right after the fact."

I nodded.

"It comes across. I understand that your emotions caused you to make some very sharp and not altogether correct judgments. Now that some time has passed, I assume you're able to evaluate these events more objectively."

I didn't reply, just shrugged.

"We'll return your tape," Viktor Nikolayevich smiled, "but first we'd like to erase it right here, with you present."

What good would it do to object? I could re-create it word for word. I agreed.[21]

As if reading my thoughts, Viktor Nikolayevich continued, "Of

---

21. *Editor's note:* Was Sergei never tempted to tell them to "go to hell" and storm out of the room? "Not only might developments have taken a different turn," he replied, "but I would have had a different character. There is no way of knowing whether we would have achieved our aim, whereas in fact I did achieve it. In our country the sad fact is that direct resistance is ineffective in such cases. Of course, not everyone agrees with me on that."

course, you can re-create the tape, but we will count on your better judgment."

Vladimir Vasilievich entered the room carrying a large, gray, cumbersome piece of equipment, obviously homemade. It began to hum when he plugged it in. Vladimir Vasilievich passed something over the reel and handed it to me. The surgical operation was done: memory was destroyed, the events had never taken place. It occurred to me it was a good thing they had never learned to do that with people.

I was very sorry to have lost the recording. It was as if a part of me had disappeared. After I redid it, it would be the same, and yet different.

"Well, there we go." Viktor Nikolayevich was smiling again. "Take your tape. We always fulfill our promises to the letter." He was clearly pleased with the show and wanted to ring down the curtain. But this time I wasn't so quick to leave the office.

"Thank you for the tape," I began, "but you seem to have forgotten one of your promises."

Viktor Nikolayevich looked at me quizzically.

"You promised me that when Nikita Sergeyevich leaves the hospital all the material you took from me will be returned to him. It is recorded in the receipt. He'll be discharged in a few days and will be returning to the dacha. I would like for the tapes and transcripts to be back where they belong before he arrives. As for the secretary and typist you offered, you'll have to speak to him directly."

Viktor Nikolayevich grinned broadly at me. "Sergei Nikitich, I don't have any memoirs."

I had expected him to refuse to release them. I was ready to argue, but this — I was caught by surprise.

"But you yourself, and Yevgeny Mikhailovich, said several times that they were being kept in your office in your personal safe. You said you wouldn't give them to anyone because you feared for their safety even inside this building." I motioned toward the safe standing in the corner. "So where are they?" I asked helplessly.

"We turned them over to the Central Committee."

"But it was on behalf of the Central Committee that you promised to return them!"

"That's right, I said that and I wasn't deceiving you. But we were ordered to turn them over to the Central Committee, and we followed orders. We're all subordinate to the Central Committee."

He was clearly amused by my confusion.

"What should I do now? Isn't there any way I could meet with Comrade Andropov?" It had suddenly occurred to me that this might be a way out of the blind alley.

"That's not possible. Andropov is at a meeting with voters." Again? Clearly there was a shortage of imagination around here. "From there he's going south for a vacation. He won't be returning to Moscow for quite a while."

There was nothing more to be said. I left. I was in an extremely unenviable position. Father was getting out of the hospital, and all his memoir materials had vanished. Were they really at the Central Committee? Or had they simply been destroyed? I hadn't the slightest idea whom in the Central Committee to approach.

It was a good thing I had given the go-ahead for publication in the West. At least something would be saved. Apparently Father had been right when he said that all our efforts were in vain, that they would seize everything.

I still didn't want to believe that. I was ready to fight and mulled over possible ways to find the memoirs in the depths of the Central Committee. As it turned out, I didn't need to go looking. They found me.

The day after my conversation with Popov, I received a phone call at work from someone at the Party Control Commission. He gave me his name, but I don't recall it. He suggested I pay a visit to the PCC the next day and told me the room number. "A pass will be waiting for you, remember to bring your party card," he reminded me sternly.

He didn't mention the reason for the invitation, and I didn't ask. It was clear enough without my asking. My insistence on my rights in Viktor Nikolayevich's office had shown that I still wasn't sufficiently "reconciled" and that it wouldn't hurt to pressure me a bit further.

The man who had called the day before met me; he seemed a decent enough type. He said he was familiar with the story of the memoirs and asked me to write down in detail everything that had taken place. I wrote for a long time, trying not to leave anything out. I began with Harvey, then Rasskazov's phone call and the seizure of the memoirs, and finished the account with Popov's disheartening answer to my request two days before.

He carefully read the pages I had crammed with writing and went out of the room. I was alone, but not for long.

In a few minutes, he returned and invited me to see the deputy chairman of the PCC, a Comrade Melnikov. A tall, angular man with rough-hewn features, Melnikov was sitting in a dark office at a standard desk. Before coming to the PCC, he had been the first secretary of the Tashkent city party committee.

Melnikov began to question me about the work on the memoirs. I could tell that, apart from anything else, he was just plain curious and wanted to be let in on some secrets about Father's life. I told him everything I had already told Popov, but added a detailed account of how I had been followed. I emphasized how Popov had taken the memoirs in the name of the Central Committee, promised to give them back, and now announced that he didn't have them and didn't know where they were.

Despite everything I had been through, I still cherished the naive hope that the abuse of power would anger Melnikov and that an investigation would be launched, culminating in victory for justice. Instead, he replied as follows:

"We in the Central Committee never made any promises. The material is indeed here at Central Committee, but I have no control over it. There can be no discussion of its being returned at this point. The Central Committee will make the appropriate decision and you will be notified in due time."

At the end of August, Father got out of the hospital and returned to Petrovo-Dalneye. He was pale and weak; he took few walks, preferring to sit on the terrace or doze in a chair in his room. Slowly he began to regain some strength. He began to go down to his favorite place at the edge of the woods to look at the vegetable garden and admire the view of the river.

We hadn't yet talked about the memoirs. Father was silent more often than before, thinking his own thoughts. Perhaps he had an inkling that something had happened, since I was taking such great care to avoid the subject. Whenever we were together, I tried to distract him with tidbits of Moscow news.

The refusal of the Central Committee to return the material, although not completely unexpected, sent me into a deep depression. I felt it was all my fault; after all, I had no right to give them up in the first place.

There came a point at which I could no longer hide the sad story from Father. He might find something out from someone else, or simply ask me straight out, "How are things going with the memoirs?" On the other hand, he was still quite weak. If I told him, he would surely get agitated, at a time when his heart had not yet regained its strength. Yet sooner or later I would have to tell him.

One day, when Father seemed nearly back to his old self, and we were strolling slowly toward the edge of the woods, I got up the courage to tell him everything — about the KGB, the PCC, and the imminent appearance of the memoirs in the West.

He approved of my decision to go ahead with publication. The unforgivable way he had been treated liberated him to authorize such a decision, if only in retrospect. "You can't hide the truth," he said. "Let someone else publish the book for now. It's unfortunate that it has to be done abroad, but there's nothing to be done about it. Someday it will make its way back to us," he complained bitterly.

However, I really caught it for having turned the memoirs over to Popov. Until his death, Father never forgave me.

"You had no right, none at all, to give them up. Never mind about saving the text; it's a matter of principle. They are violating the constitution. You had gall to make decisions about something you had no right to decide in the first place. Contact the man immediately and express the strongest possible protest in my name. Demand that everything be returned! There's no point in going to the Central Committee, they'll just yelp and yap and it'll all be lies. After all, they say they never promised anything. Demand the materials back from the one who gave you the receipt. Tell him that if they don't do what you ask, I, not you, will cause a scandal."

Father was extremely upset. He took out his pill container and swallowed a validol. He never went anywhere without them these days. I was afraid his heart would act up, but, this time, nothing happened.

"It's a good thing we can reconstruct everything. All our work hasn't been wasted," he said, calming down a bit.[22] "But I can't accept the way we were treated. We can't let them get away with it." He was beginning to get agitated again.

"Let's change the subject," he said suddenly. We walked for a while longer but didn't return to the memoirs.

In accordance with Father's wishes, I tried to locate Popov. Of course, he knew about my conversation at the PCC and understood

22. *Editor's note:* This comment by Khrushchev implies that he had hidden another set of tapes and transcripts somewhere in the USSR. Sergei Khrushchev returns to this question at the end of this chapter.

why I wanted to contact him. Now that the memoirs were in their hands, Popov was impossible to get hold of.

"Viktor Nikolayevich is out." "Viktor Nikolayevich will call you back." "Viktor Nikolayevich is away on business."

And so it went, on and on, with me stubbornly calling several times a day. I, too, knew how to play the game. Finally, a miracle: Viktor Nikolayevich was in! We agreed on a meeting. He knew I wouldn't give up and was afraid that if he avoided me any longer I might suddenly decide to do something unpredictable.

When we met I delivered a formal protest; I told him exactly what Father had said. Unfortunately, Viktor Nikolayevich lived up to my worst expectations by repeating his old story: "Sergei Nikitich, I haven't got anything. The KGB gets its orders from the Central Committee. They demanded the material be turned over to them. It is out of the KGB's hands. It's unfortunate that we haven't carried out our part of the bargain. I personally regret that, and I extend my apologies, but we no longer have anything to do with the matter. You need to address your concerns to the Central Committee."

When I told Father about the conversation, he spit in a fit of temper. "To hell with them! There's nothing more we can do. We won't get a thing out of them!!! Don't ever go back there."

As it happened, our acquaintance with Rasskazov and his team stretched for many years. Their interest in me would seem to die out completely and then suddenly flare up with new force.[23]

In early October, I had one more meeting with Yevgeny Mikhailovich and Vladimir Vasilievich. It had been announced in the West that Little, Brown would be publishing *Khrushchev Remembers*. (We had agreed to the title; it was modest, quiet, and unpretentious.) The publisher was said to possess both typewritten transcripts and the tapes themselves with Father's voice on them.

This time Rasskazov looked dispirited, and understandably so. His brilliant July operation had been followed by an October fiasco. We met in the familiar room at the Moskva Hotel. Our conversation wasn't lengthy; only one thing interested them — how the memoirs got to the United States.

---

23. What did they want from me all these years? It's hard to say. I suppose the fact that they had the "Khrushchev docket" meant that they had to keep an eye on me all this time. It was their job to keep track of what I was up to.

My reply was simple. "As long as we had the material, we never talked of publication. So the question should be asked of you, not me." As far as I was concerned, I had told the truth.

In parting, I again demanded that the material be returned to its rightful owner. What was the point of keeping it now that publication was imminent?

"Under the current circumstances," Rasskazov answered spitefully, "I wouldn't advise you to bring up the subject."

Our trials were not yet over. Father was to have yet another meeting with his old comrades in arms. The book had not even come out, no one had seen, much less read, it; yet Father, who hadn't fully recovered, was rudely summoned to the Central Committee.

No one had the slightest interest in what the book was about. Nor, as far as I know, were they interested in the contents of the material they had seized from me.[24] Nevertheless, on November 11, right after the October Revolution holidays, Father received a phone call, not from Arvid Y. Pelshe, chairman of the PCC, but Pelshe's secretariat, ordering him to appear immediately at the Party Control Commission.

It was a time when Brezhnev was gaining in strength, puffing himself up to full size, feeling virtually omnipotent. It wasn't yet the end of the seventies, but neither was it the liberal sixties. Back then, no one would have dared to act so flagrantly.

Father answered that he couldn't come immediately because he had no means of transportation, no car. "A car has already been sent for you," was the answer.

Pelshe and Melnikov were already waiting for Father at the PCC, along with the secretary who had dealt with me two months before.[25]

The scenario they had prepared was destroyed, smashed to smithereens the moment Father walked in the door. He had been infuriated by the way they treated him, by the seizure of his memoirs, by the crude deception, and by Popov's boorish behavior. He could scarcely control his anger. Being summoned by Pelshe was the last straw.

Father's health was not conducive to a heated argument, but he hadn't initiated the confrontation. Bezzubik's advice was not to get up-

---

24. I recently learned that *no one* ever read through the transcripts that were held at the Central Committee. That shows that it wasn't their contents that interested the authorities.

25. *Editor's note:* Did Khrushchev have no choice but to go? "Alas, not," replies the author. "When the Central Committee or the Party Control Commission summons you, party discipline demands that you go."

set, to stay calm and not to take things too hard. But it didn't apply that day; Father went into battle, as always, without looking back.

The "educational" discussion they had intended never came off, and I wouldn't have wanted to be in the shoes of those "educators." They gave Father a prepared text stating that he, Khrushchev, had never written any memoirs or given such memoirs to anyone, and that the book just published was a complete fake. Father shoved it aside.

"I refuse to sign any such document," he said. "It's a lie and to lie is a sin, especially at my age. It's time to think of the next world. It wouldn't hurt you to think about that either," he said suddenly to Pelshe, and continued without waiting for a response. "I wrote my memoirs. Every man has that right. My memoirs were for the party, for our people. I hope they'll help people to understand the time when I lived and worked. I can assure you that I will continue to work on them in the future.

"I'm prepared to sign a document stating that work on my memoirs is not yet finished, that they are not yet in a form suitable for publishing."

With regard to the book's appearance abroad, Father agreed to state that he himself had never given any material to anyone for publication abroad. The compromise satisfied Pelshe. Having agreed on the wording, they had the text typed, and Father signed. The statement was published immediately. I don't have a copy and can't quote it; I don't consider it important anyway.[26]

The main part of the discussion was still to come. Father turned to Pelshe, who thought the subject was closed, and reminded him of the missing memoir material. Pelshe was unprepared to answer and said that he knew nothing about it. When Melnikov didn't come to his chief's aid, Father moved on to an even more painful subject.

"It's been six years since I was in office," he began, "six years since you blamed me for everything. You said that once you were rid of Khrushchev everything would go smoothly. I warned that we needed to

---

26. *Editor's note:* The full text of Nikita Khrushchev's statement was as follows: "It is reported in the press in the United States and in certain other capitalist countries that the so-called memoirs or reminiscences of N. S. Khrushchev are now being prepared for publication. This is a fabrication and I am indignant about it. I have never passed on memoirs or materials of this nature either to *Time* or other foreign publishing houses. I did not turn over such material to Soviet publishing houses either. Therefore I declare that this is a fabrication. The venal bourgeois press has many times been exposed in this way. N. Khrushchev, November 11, 1970."

restructure things, to find a new way to manage the economy, or nothing would work out. But you resurrected the ministries and destroyed whatever had been accomplished.

"Our agriculture is foundering. We raised prices on butter and meat to stimulate their production, but output hasn't risen because you haven't followed through. The stores are empty; that's what they tell me.

"We bought grain from America in 1963 as an exception, but now it's become the rule. Shame on you!! The Soviet Union buying grain!!

"That shows I wasn't the problem; the problem was a faulty agricultural system. You've become resigned to the situation and don't want to do anything about it. You just sit calmly in your swamp when what you need to do is to act, to find new solutions.

"Or take international relations. You said I caused the quarrel with China. Six years have passed, and relations have only worsened. Now everyone can see the causes are deeper and much more complicated. Time will pass and relations will normalize, but it will take new people both here and in China who are able to look at the problem in a new way and throw off old, encrusted views."

Father told me later that Pelshe was about to break in at this point, but Father didn't let him; he hadn't yet spoken his piece.

"You missed your chance [Father used a more colorful expression that rhymes with "missed"] in Egypt. How much money, how much energy, did we invest? Then you let our ally with a modern, well-equipped army lose the war when it was ready to fight."

He went on to other domestic and foreign policy topics, until the tirade had taken almost every ounce of his strength. Finally, he fell silent.

Pelshe attempted a defense, but Father was no longer listening. Instead, he said woodenly, "I've done what you asked; I signed. Now I want to go home. My chest hurts."

That was Father's last meeting with the party leadership, his parting words to his successors. He had told them what had been festering inside him for the past six years, the results of his agonizing reflection in solitude.

I didn't know what had happened until Mama called later that day and said that he had been questioned at the PCC about the memoirs. I dropped everything and rushed to the dacha. Father was sitting at the edge of the woods, staring into the meadow. I sat down next to him and we remained silent like that for some time. Then he began to describe what had happened, becoming more and more incensed as he spoke.

When he had told me everything, he stopped for a moment and then suddenly, as if answering a question in his own mind, said, "Now I am positive that your decision to publish the book was the right one. They'll destroy the material they took. They're afraid of the truth. You did the right thing."

We fell silent again, each thinking his own thoughts.

In the evening, I left since I had to be at work the next morning. When I got home, I wrote down Father's story while it was still fresh in my mind.

Father's meeting had cost him. Pelshe had gotten results — Father had to go back into the hospital. Bezzubik said he had suffered a mild heart attack. "It's not nearly as serious as the one this summer, there's no comparison. It's barely as bad as a cat scratch." The comparison was quite apt; and besides, the cat was a wicked one.

Father was a wise man, and he had anticipated much of what had happened. Back when we were just starting work on the memoirs, he had told me that if he should ever be forced to leave the house and go into the hospital, I was to take everything relating to the dictation and put it somewhere secure for safekeeping. Just to be on the safe side. How right he was!

I began daily visits to the hospital again. Father would grumble at me as usual, while the endless green line on the monitor registered all the ups and downs of his ailing heart.

By now he had aged tremendously, and not only on the outside. All the blows that had recently rained down on him had affected him deeply. He told everybody, doctors, nurses, and visitors, about the confrontation at the Party Control Commission. It wasn't that he wanted their sympathy; he simply had to get the story out of his system.

Before the New Year, 1971, his last new year, arrived, Father was discharged from the hospital. He celebrated New Year's Eve at the dacha.

Life seemed to return to normal: the same walks, more chats with visitors and vacationers at Petrovo-Dalneye, the same old questions and familiar answers. Now, however, there were new questions; many visitors asked him about the memoirs, which they had heard about in Russian-language broadcasts on the Voice of America, BBC, and other foreign radio stations.

Father replied that it was not his business how the memoirs ended up abroad. He had dictated them and felt that there was no reason to hide them. They contained no secrets, nothing at all to prevent their being published.

This time, his recovery went very slowly. His mental and physical powers had suffered greatly. He tired quickly and could no longer walk all the way to the meadow without stopping to rest. Along the way, he would sit down on the folding stool that he always took with him. Arbat was gone. He had died at an advanced age, and there was no one else to carry the stool. Father got a new dog, a mutt. He named her Belka (Squirrel) for her reddish coat and lively character. She ran everywhere after him, gazing into his eyes loyally and licking his hands, but she clearly lacked Arbat's tact and refined manner. We suggested he should get a purebred of some sort, but he refused.

"The mutt is smarter, more loyal, and less capricious. What do I need a blockhead with a pedigree for?"

The talk at the Central Committee had taken its toll, but he had not been broken. As early as February I got a phone call. "We're going to start dictating again," he said. "Get everything ready."

It was slow going this time. He forced himself back into a working frame of mind, but it was different. He no longer lived for his work, but just carried out duties he had given himself. By working, he proved to himself and to those who had offended him that he hadn't given up and wasn't about to.

In the months remaining to him, he filled nearly two reels with recollections about his meetings with cultural figures. He tried to make sense of and to explain his actions, and to understand their motives and behavior.

But he was dissatisfied with these tapes. He told me he was going to do them over again from the beginning, but he never managed to do so. For this reason, I feel that these pages of his memoirs must be approached with a certain amount of care.

In January I received the long-awaited book from America, a black volume with the title in red and gold lettering, and a smiling photograph of my father on the dustcover. I rushed straight to Petrovo-Dalneye to show it to him. He leafed through it, looked at the pictures, and returned it to me. He didn't read English, so the book seemed alien to him. Now, if it had only been our book, that would have been something else entirely. "Why don't you keep it," he said.

The KGB had called me in again in January. Yevgeny Mikhailovich asked me to examine a retranslation into Russian of the English-language version and tell them how closely it corresponded to the original.

I was amazed. "But I don't have the original. You do. The simplest thing would be to compare the two texts. Any differences would be obvious."

"Viktor Nikolayevich already told you we don't have the memoirs. We turned them over to the Central Committee, so we have nothing to compare the English version with. That's why we are asking you — as the person most familiar with the memoirs."

It was hard to believe that they couldn't get hold of the text. I had no idea what they were trying to accomplish by asking me for my opinion. Nevertheless, I eagerly agreed. I read English quite well, and their professional retranslation into Russian would make it easier to see exactly how authentic the English-language text was.

They gave me a room in which to work and assigned Vladimir Vasilievich to help with anything I needed; I plunged into reading the typewritten retranslation.

Edward Crankshaw's short introductions to each chapter grated on me. It's been a long time since I read the book, but I clearly remember the disagreeable reaction I had at the time. But apart from that introductory material, the rest was fine. The text didn't differ in substance from the dictations, nor from the stories my father would tell over and over again.

In my report, I noted that the material had been shortened considerably, that almost everything that had to do with the war, except for certain episodes, had been deleted. Absent also were several other passages pertaining to various periods of Soviet history.[27]

I gave my conclusions to Vladimir Vasilievich, who thanked me, and departed. Neither Viktor Nikolayevich nor Yevgeny Mikhailovich showed the slightest interest in speaking with me further. Apparently, my report was just a formality to fill out the file they had on me. Meanwhile, people stopped asking Father questions about his memoirs. As we had anticipated, the book's publication had calmed the waters.

Nineteen seventy-one also saw the publication by Progress Publishers of the reverse translation from English back into Russian. Of course, it was for a limited circle of readers, and bore the stamp "for official

27. I refer here to cuts made by the American editor, who deleted what he thought wouldn't interest American readers. I should add that I hold no grievance on this account.

use only." In this sense, the second edition of the book was in Russian after all, although in a translation from the English.[28]

By now, Khrushchev's memoirs have been published in fifteen more languages and read in practically all the countries of the world, except in the one for which it was intended, and for which Father had undergone the trials that became his lot.

He could have chosen not to write his memoirs, as had others. He had several other pastimes that he enjoyed: gardening, taking walks, and photography. If not for the memoirs, his behavior would have pleased those in power just fine and undoubtedly would have added several years to his life. He chose a different path because he was convinced that the Soviet people needed to hear what he had to say, and that no matter what happened, his words would someday reach them. The world reaction to the publication of his memoirs only emphasized how right he was.

On my shelf at home I have English, German, French, Italian, Japanese, and even Turkish editions. Only a Russian edition is missing, but I hope one will soon appear. Meanwhile, Father's memoirs have taken on a life of their own, independent of the author.

NEW editions kept appearing in the east, west, north, and south, but it seemed Yevgeny Mikhailovich and company had forgotten about me. Only rarely, during visits by important foreign dignitaries, for example when the UN secretary general came to Moscow, would I catch a glimpse of the familiar Volga in my rearview mirror. Eventually they began using different models of cars, but I had grown too old to be interested in what the latest KGB cars looked like. The game was over for me.

Once in a while I would hear about preparations for a second volume, but nothing was asked of me and nothing depended on my participation.

Finally, in 1974, the second volume of memoirs came out, entitled *Khrushchev Remembers: The Last Testament*. On the white dustcover the title appeared in dark, mournful-looking lettering together with a photograph of Father in retirement. He was sitting, on a winter's day,

---

28. *Editor's note:* As far as I know, this is the first time we have had confirmation that a Russian edition was published for a limited readership in the USSR.

on his favorite bench at the edge of the woods, leaning on his home-made walking stick.

At this point, the KGB remembered me again. I met Yevgeny Mikhailovich and his constant companion Vladimir Vasilievich in the same room at the Moskva Hotel. We talked about the same old thing — the memoirs and how they had gotten into the hands of the publisher, Little, Brown.

They showed me a letter they had prepared for me to send to an American journalist, Norman Cousins, editor of the *Saturday Review*. The letter was quite lengthy. Unfortunately, I can't find it among my papers — either I've lost it or I never had a copy in the first place. The gist of it was that I considered the book's publication to be a provocation directed against the Soviet Union and against our family. The letter proclaimed the book a fake.

I was aware at the time that of the many memoirs of various national leaders published in the West, not all turned out to be authentic. My letter was designed to create a scandal and discredit the memoirs. The plan was simple. As a competitor of Time Inc. (which owned Little, Brown), Cousins would presumably be only too pleased to take advantage of the opportunity.

The proposal being out of the ordinary, I said I couldn't decide on my own and needed to consult with my mother. We agreed to meet again in a few days.

I told Mama that same day. She asked if I had read the book. "No," I answered.

"Then how can you write that the book is a fake if you haven't even examined the text?" she objected logically. "You shouldn't make a statement like that about a book none of us has ever laid eyes on. You could always say, as your father did, that we just don't know how the material got to the West."[29]

With this in mind, I went to my next meeting. I knew they wouldn't like what I was going to tell them and armed myself with an immovable

---

29. *Editor's note:* Contrary to what Nina Petrovna said, the formulation her husband used was slightly different. Khrushchev himself had declared not that he didn't know how the manuscript had gotten abroad but that he himself had not sent it. "True enough," replies Sergei. "Mama did *not* in fact know how the materials had reached the West, although of course she could guess. But she had been careful not to ask Father or me. Our task at this point was to deny the authorities any possibility of declaring the book a fake."

argument — my mother had forbidden me to sign the letter. It was true, and they would never approach Nina Petrovna. It had been apparent at our earlier meeting that the matter was not as critical as four years ago.

I read the prepared text once more and asked to rewrite it in line with Mama's position.

There was a small argument, but I insisted. "Give me the book. Both my mother and I read English, slowly, to be sure, so it will take at least a couple of weeks to look over the text. If it doesn't correspond to the memoirs, then I'll proclaim it a fake on every street corner. I'll write letters to whomever you wish. But without reading it first, I just can't."

Yevgeny Mikhailovich shot back: "How can we give you a copy of the book? We haven't got a single copy; we haven't even seen it ourselves."

I seized on his words. "How can I make a statement about a book that neither I nor anyone else has ever seen?"

Rasskazov understood that his admission that they hadn't seen the book clinched it: I would never sign the letter as written. Instead, we went through the text of their letter word by word, arguing at each turn. Finally, we managed to agree on a version that followed the pattern of Father's statement four years before.

As before, they asked me to copy and address the letter in my own handwriting. When I had finished, the letter was mailed off to Mr. Cousins, Washington, D.C., United States of America.

That was the last time I saw Yevgeny Mikhailovich and his trusty friend Vladimir Vasilievich. But more than once I've noticed or otherwise felt traces of their interest directed either at me or at Lora Finogenova. Such instances have always been nebulous and insubstantial. A strange hissing on the telephone line, an oddly familiar car behind us, the inordinate attention of a passerby on the street, or a nagging suspicion that things on a table have been moved slightly by an unknown hand.

In general, life has taught us to keep our eyes open and to sniff if something smells a little funny. Occasionally I've looked around if a situation seemed odd, only to think I've seen Yevgeny Mikhailovich peering from around a corner.

When I regularly rewrite my address book to delete names I no longer need, I always stop at the letter *Ye*. I can never quite bring myself to cross him out of my life, so I write him in again: Yevgeny Mikhailovich, no last name, extension number 224.

I'm sure that by now there's another person in his old office, someone who's busy with other matters and doesn't even know I exist or that I have his phone number in my little book.

Or perhaps he has inherited me, and he knows my every move, what I do, what I eat, with whom I drink, even that I haven't thrown out his phone number, and that I'm writing about him at this moment.

If so, he's sitting and biding his time. *Perestroika* and *glasnost* are in the air, so his time is not now. Will it come again? That depends on us all.

MY letter reached Mr. Cousins and attracted his attention as a way to trip up the competition. He sent a correspondent (I don't remember his name and have no one from whom to find out) to Moscow with instructions to meet me and to offer to publish a series of exposé articles, if I wanted to.

At the time, I was devoting all my efforts to putting up a headstone at my father's grave and had become friends with the artist and sculptor Ernst Neizvestny. Neizvestny was always surrounded by foreign correspondents. It was easy for Cousins's emissary to contact Neizvestny and convey a request for a meeting. Ernst knew nothing about the story of the memoirs and took the request as a novice's desire to interview me. He warned him that I didn't give interviews and that under the circumstances nothing good would come out of attempts to contact me.

The correspondent answered that he did not want an interview, but that he had something of great importance to discuss with me, and that I already knew what it was.

Neizvestny recounted to me his conversation with the man and offered to let a meeting take place in his studio. My mission was not one of the most pleasant, but I actually was glad that events had taken this turn. The letter still worried me and now I had the opportunity to regain some control over the situation. I knew what I would do.

I had been to Neizvestny's studio so many times that my visits had long ceased to attract any attention at the "Big House." This time, however, Ernst Iosifovich warned me that a car with special antennas was parked nearby, and that they would be listening to our every word.

"It always shows up for foreigners they're interested in," Neizvestny said offhandedly.

We had just sat down in a small room when there was a knock at the door. It was the correspondent. He didn't know Neizvestny well and was quite businesslike. We greeted him warmly and invited him in to share our meager repast. A bottle of vodka already stood on the table, next to a modest selection of snacks. Our guest spoke Russian fairly well, which facilitated communication.

We each drank a glass, and ate. "How are things in America?" we asked. We talked about art and religion, and drank some more. We discussed the latest international events, talked about the dissidents, and had a third round. After the conversation turned to Neizvestny's artistic style, we opened a second bottle and then inspected the sculpture in the studio.

Our guest couldn't figure us out. He repeatedly tried to bring up what he had come to discuss, but we always eased the conversation in another direction. Finally, he had had enough. The confusion on his face said it all: "Where am I? Who are these people? What's going on here?"

He stood up and thanked us for the chance to meet us. When we responded with a warm good-bye, his confusion only mounted. I walked him out to his car.

I didn't know if they were listening to us on the street. "Our" car was parked thirty feet from his Volvo. I didn't want to upset Yevgeny Mikhailovich and preferred he not know what I told the correspondent. However, it was impossible to delay any longer.

The man had opened the door to his car when I prolonged our final handshake. "I apologize. We were being listened to inside," I began. He broke into a broad smile; finally it began to dawn on him.

"Please give my apologies to Mr. Cousins," I told him. "A number of circumstances compelled me to deceive him. Strange things happen in life. The memoirs are authentic. There is nothing to expose." After that, we said good-bye.

That was the authorities' last attempt to meddle with Western editions of my father's memoirs. Since then, they have lived the respectable life of the memoirs of a retired prime minister of a great nation. They are quoted and referred to and have become a part of world history.

Meanwhile, in the Soviet Union itself, the authorities continued to spread the word that the memoirs were a fake. Even today, when talk turns to Father's memoirs, someone never fails to say: "It will be good when the authentic memoirs are published, instead of those fakes." Nonetheless, despite the Brezhnev-era ban on Father's name, certain other occurrences offered hope of a change in his posthumous fate and that of his book.

Once, at the end of the seventies, Aleksei Vladimirovich Snegov called to say that the historian Roy Medvedev was writing Khrushchev's biography. Aleksei Vladimirovich had told him everything he knew and now, at Medvedev's request, was urging me to meet with Medvedev. I had heard a lot about him, and had read his book on Stalin, *Let History Judge*. At the time, its publication in the West was an extraordinarily brave step, one that could not help but evoke admiration and respect. Neizvestny had good things to say about him, too, and had intended to introduce us, but never managed to.

One mustn't forget the circumstances of the time. Today there are plenty of things about my father in print. Back then, however, simply mentioning his name was taken by my family as a gift, a gift that could easily get its author in trouble.

Medvedev and I agreed on a meeting, and before long an intelligent-looking gray-haired man was sitting across my kitchen table from me. We talked about his project and about the necessity of maintaining objectivity when writing history. We seemed to understand each other, and our meetings continued. I told him about my father, and he used my stories in many chapters of his book.

Roy Aleksandrovich brought me the final draft of his book to look at. He said the book was already being typeset in London. This was just about the time when Brezhnev died.

I didn't like what I read. Several sections were full of hostility for Khrushchev's reforms. Only indisputably correct steps, like the Twentieth Congress and disarmament, escaped the author's wrath. As I remember, Medvedev particularly attacked Father's "mistakes" in agriculture that led to reduced production of agricultural vehicles, tractors, and combines. Yet today, our world leadership in the output of tractors and combines has turned out, after sober analysis, to be wholly unnecessary. Father had the same thoughts twenty years before.

A large portion of Medvedev's book was devoted to a critical discussion of educational reform, which was a low priority issue for Father but was very close to Medvedev's heart.

I tried not to succumb to a son's subjectivism, tried to look historical facts in the face. But nothing came of my attempt. I openly told Roy Aleksandrovich all of this. I suggested that he use the new atmosphere under Andropov to redo the book so as to take into account the positive aspects of Khrushchev's career, as well as his mistakes.

We parted coolly. Medvedev said that each historian has his own view of past events, and added that the book was already in the process of being published. I couldn't argue with that. For my part, I'm using these pages to express my personal view of past events.

A few days later, Snegov called me. He was even more categorical in his evaluation. Eighteen years of Stalinist prison had given him the right to his views.

Some time later, I picked up the phone to hear Roy Aleksandrovich's voice on the other end. We met again, and neither of us brought up our last conversation. Medvedev gave me a blue-covered book, *Khrushchev: A Political Biography,* in Russian. It is the one that is so widely quoted today. It differed substantially from the previous version, although, in my opinion, it still contained quite a few inaccuracies. Roy Aleksandrovich told me he was in the midst of writing a book on Brezhnev, and asked me for help. I agreed.

Whatever my opinion of his books, Medvedev was the only historian working on Khrushchev when Father's name was in dark disfavor; for that I am deeply grateful to him.

The changes that began after Brezhnev's death in November 1982 prompted me to attempt to have Father's memoirs published in our country, so as to restore his good name.

I began to formulate a letter to Yuri Andropov, the new general secretary, but didn't write it in time. Andropov passed away early in 1984, to be succeeded briefly by Konstantin Chernenko. Dark clouds again began to gather over the country, and it was not only senseless, but even dangerous, to approach Chernenko with my request.

Happily, the retreat was short-lived, and after long reflection and some hesitation, I decided to write to General Secretary Mikhail Sergeyevich Gorbachev. His speeches, his words, and his deeds inspired optimism and instilled faith in change for the better. His style of action, his dynamism, his sociability, and his dedication to the new and innovative, all reminded me of my father.

It was the beginning of 1986. I agonized over what my letter should say. So much depended on it. Finally I came up with this:

To the General Secretary of the CC CPSU,
Comrade Gorbachev, Mikhail Sergeyevich.

Most respected Mikhail Sergeyevich!

I am Sergei Nikitich Khrushchev, son of former Secretary of the CC CPSU, N. S. Khrushchev.

Please forgive me for intruding on your other concerns, but I have been induced to write to you by the changes now occurring in our public life and by personal problems that, unfortunately, only you can resolve.

I sincerely support your initiatives aimed at pulling our country out of stagnation, and I hope they succeed. The most important thing is that those who want to work, and they are a majority, now know that their labor is needed, and so the wall of indifference is coming down. I could write more about this, but your time is valuable.

Your style of work, your quick reactions, your urge to see life with your own eyes and to become personally involved and make decisions independently, all remind me a great deal of my father, Nikita Sergeyevich. I am his ardent supporter not just as his son, but also as a Communist. It would be a great shame if you encountered failures along this path, especially since you are so sincere in your desire to lead our nation forward.

Sometimes my own ideas seem trivial to me, and other times important. It's quite possible that you already know all you need to know. Nor can I relate everything I want to in this letter — it would be quite difficult to do so, and anyway, I fear I might be unconvincing. I fully understand the small possibility of realizing my hope, but I would very much like to speak with you. Perhaps it would help our common cause. But since this may not be possible, I will try to set out my ideas in writing, although I fear they won't come out right.

You no doubt know that N. S. Khrushchev dictated his memoirs during his retirement. His efforts were halted before he could finish, first by the seizure of his tapes, and soon after that by his death. The tapes are being held at the Central Committee. Partial excerpts of them were published abroad and here in the Soviet Union in a limited edition for official use only. The published version doesn't fully reflect what he dictated, especially his thoughts on internal matters, although no one has ever checked the published texts against the tapes. I was his only assistant in editing the very "raw" transcripts into readable form. It was beyond my powers to do this at a sufficiently high literary level, but I was familiar enough with the events described to make sure their meaning was not distorted.

N. S. Khrushchev is a part of our history, and, in my opinion, far from the worst part. His memoirs might be of some use today, if only in making sense of that period.

I'd like to ask your permission to complete the work on my father's memoirs. Without me, they will be lost, for the dictation is often simply a collection of words that need to be properly arranged, without altering my father's meaning.

I am past fifty years of age and it would be imprudent to put the matter off. Moreover, I feel that I owe the completion of the work to the memory of my father. He sometimes said the memoirs were senseless because publication would never be permitted. I am hardly insisting on immediate publication; the work will take several years, and in the meantime what should be done will become clear. However, the memoirs should be preserved for history.

In conclusion, I would like to wish you success in your difficult cause. May good fortune be your companion!

> With deep respect,
> S. N. Khrushchev

It was relatively easy to reach Gorbachev's aide Anatoly Sergeyevich Chernyaev on the phone. He received me the very next day. I was nervous as I entered the familiar Central Committee headquarters building on Staraya Ploshchad. How long it was since I'd been there!

Anatoly Sergeyevich questioned me in detail about everything. "I won't be able to reach Mikhail Sergeyevich tomorrow," he said, "because he's very busy. I'll try the day after, but definitely by the end of the week."

I had counted on waiting at least a few weeks, if not months. Obviously, a new age had begun in earnest. Sure enough, three or four days later, when I called Chernyaev, the matter had been resolved. "You mean no one called you yet?" Anatoly Sergeyevich was surprised. "I

reported it all to Mikhail Sergeyevich. He consulted with other Politburo members, and they decided that in keeping with the spirit of our
policy to fill in the blank spots in Soviet history, work on Nikita Sergeyevich's memoirs is important.

"You'll be given everything you need to do your work. Comrade
Aleksandr Nikolayevich Yakovlev will be in charge of implementing this
decision. Let me give you a telephone number," he said, and dictated
to me the number of Valery Alekseyevich Kuznetsov, one of Yakovlev's
assistants. "If you have any problems, please call. I think everything
will be fine. Good luck."

I was in seventh heaven. Here I had been assuming a long struggle
with red tape. So that's what the "new thinking" was all about.

But I rejoiced too soon. I couldn't help recalling how during my
father's last years in office the indestructible apparat had slowly but
surely sabotaged all the decisions that did not suit them. The apparat
was using the same methods now at the dawn of *perestroika*.

Yakovlev's aide turned me over to the head of the Central Committee Propaganda Department, Yuri Aleksandrovich Sklyarov. He returned my phone call promptly, and our conversation was extremely
courteous. Sklyarov assured me that he would sort everything out in
the next few days and get back in touch with me.

A good beginning, it seemed. It was the first spring after the
Twenty-seventh Congress of the CPSU. It was sunny and I had a song
in my heart.

A month passed. Silence. I called again. It turned out that not only
had no one been working on the memoirs all these years, no one even
knew where they were. A search had to be conducted in the archives.
Yuri Aleksandrovich again assured me he would call as soon as he had
news.

The calls continued back and forth in this way for nearly two years,
and in August 1987 we resolved to appeal to Mikhail Sergeyevich once
again. I was away and Rada Nikitichna took the initiative. More orders
were given, confirming the previous ones.

With renewed hope, I took to calling Yuri Aleksandrovich again.
At first the archives were under repair. Then they were being moved to
a new building. Finally, in August 1988, they found something. I rushed
to the Central Committee. Rada Nikitichna was already there in Yuri
Aleksandrovich's office. Another man, Vasily Yakovlevich Morgunov
was also seated at the table. He had been assigned to help us in our
work on the memoirs.

Yuri Aleksandrovich opened a high-quality cardboard folder, actually more of a box. "They brought me four hundred pages. You can begin working on them," he said politely.

"Why four hundred? Where are the rest? And where are the tapes?" I asked, becoming agitated. I looked through the text from the box and could see that it was neither my edited version nor the familiar reverse translation from English that the KGB had shown to me. Apparently, someone else had started the job over again at one point.

Working with the material I saw in front of me would be impossible. I would need the original text to organize the sections and the tapes to verify the contents. Only then could I be sure that nothing was missing and that the original text had not been distorted.

Before coming in, I had reread Popov's itemized list of the seized materials and tapes, and copied it down. I showed Sklyarov my copy of the list, suggesting that it would make the search for all the material easier. He was astonished that there existed such a list. He promised to look into the matter further. Our conversation over, we agreed to get in touch again in September.

MEANWHILE, there had been promising developments on another front. One day, when I was living on Starokonyushenny Lane, a neighbor in the building, Jane Tempest, called me on the phone. Her father was a British Communist who had worked in the Soviet Union for many years. Jane had been born here and was a real Muscovite. Our families often got together. Now she teaches in the United States, at one of the universities in Boston.

"A new acquaintance of mine wants to meet you. He's done a lot of work on Nikita Sergeyevich's memoirs," she said. I invited them to come over the next day.

Thus did I make the acquaintance of Strobe Talbott, a *Time* correspondent, the translator and editor of *Khrushchev Remembers,* and a likable young man who spoke excellent Russian.

He had devoted a significant part of his life to my father's memoirs and had made his mark with them in journalism. He understood perfectly every nuance of our life. Through his work on the memoirs, he came to feel a bond with my father and to understand him. He described to me how he had worked on the memoirs, what he had edited out and why. A lot of material on the war had been taken out, as well as sections on housing construction and, especially, on agriculture.

"Your father talked a lot about corn, trying to convince the reader of its virtues. The American reader doesn't understand why; there's no need to convince American farmers about corn," explained Strobe.

Until meeting Strobe, I had little idea of who had worked on the memoirs and how. It was a very pleasant surprise to see how much attention, and even respect, the publisher had lavished on my father's dictations.

We didn't talk about how Time obtained the memoirs. Our meeting occurred at the end of the period of stagnation, and it wouldn't have been prudent to discuss such matters.

I didn't think we'd ever see each other again. But fate directed otherwise. In 1988, Time's Moscow correspondent asked Rada Nikitichna for a meeting to discuss an important proposal. In mid-June we met with representatives of the magazine in Yulia Leonidovna's apartment. Over the years she, too, had become involved indirectly in the saga of the memoirs. Strobe Talbott was there, along with Ann Blackman and Felix Rosenthal from Time's Moscow bureau.

We had no idea what they could want from us. Everybody sat down for tea around a large round table. "The main reason we are here," Strobe said, "is that we can't consider our mission accomplished and the matter closed until the Russian edition of Khrushchev's memoirs is published and turned over to the people for whom it was originally written. We are prepared to make every effort, to give you as much help as we can, to see that this happens.

"Time Inc. is extremely proud that it had the honor to first publish the memoirs of this great man.

"When I first read the interview that Sergei Nikitich gave to the Yugoslav press, I called my boss and said it was time to act and that we needed to go to Moscow. They approved my idea, and here we are."

In the spring of 1988, I had been asked for an interview by a correspondent for the Croatian paper Vestnik. Since the winds of change had begun to blow, I agreed to talk to him. In answer to a question about Khrushchev's memoirs, I said that they were in the hands of the Central Committee, and that, given glasnost and perestroika, I thought they might be published in the Soviet Union. Unexpectedly for me, the interview was reported very widely, with all the major press agencies picking it up.

On behalf of my family, I thanked the Time representatives for their kind words and intentions, and said that the Russian text of the memoirs, transcribed from the tapes, would help us more than anything else.

Talbott answered that Time had given all the tapes over to the Harriman Institute at Columbia University, where oral histories of many notable world leaders were held. "The tapes are available to any researcher. It won't be difficult for us to get them for you," he said, raising my hopes.

We agreed on our next meeting. Less than a month later, in early July, we welcomed *Time* executives Henry Muller and John Stacks to my apartment, along with Talbott, Blackman, and Rosenthal.

Muller and Stacks had not taken part in publishing the memoirs, but they spoke with great respect about Nikita Sergeyevich and his period. They gave us several copies of Khrushchev's memoirs in English. I already had one, but Rada and Yulia now received them for the first time.

They assured us once again that *Time* felt it was a matter of honor to see the publication of Khrushchev's memoirs through to the end and said that we would have the transcripts of the tapes in the near future.

It wasn't long before a beaming Rosenthal appeared at my apartment followed by his driver carrying a large cardboard box.

"It was too heavy for me to carry," he explained. "Everything we agreed on is there. My bosses in New York send their best to you and wish you success."

Rosenthal left. After such a long journey and so many years of separation, the memoirs had finally returned home. Here they were before me, without any seals or stamps, to look through as I wished.

I opened the first folder and read through the familiar text. It was definitely my father's own words in my own unprofessional but diligently edited version:

"My comrades have long been asking me, and not just asking but urging me, to write down my memoirs, because I, indeed my entire generation, lived through a very interesting time. . . ."

THE transcripts I received from Time included everything except the material omitted when the memoirs were sent abroad. They were very helpful to me in two ways. They directly facilitated my work on editing Father's memoirs. And they afforded me some leverage (which I must admit didn't work very well) with the authorities. I gave them to understand that I now had a copy of the text. But to this very day [February 1990 — ed.] they have yet to turn over to me what I now understand are nearly six thousand pages of text in the Central Committee archives. The reason I want that material is that its release would turn my unofficial work on Father's memoirs into an officially sanctioned project. In that case, I would no longer have to worry about possible bans and prohibitions and KGB interference.

I must admit something else that I haven't felt I could reveal until now. I had access to one other complete set of tapes and transcripts (including the sections removed from the materials sent abroad for safekeeping and eventual publication), which had been hidden inside the Soviet Union. The hiding place turned out to be a safe one. The tapes and transcripts lay there quietly all these years.

One might well ask why I didn't retrieve this set of materials much earlier. Why did I engage in lengthy and fruitless negotiations if all I had to do was reach out my hand? I can't say I wasn't tempted; I often considered doing so. What stopped me was my overly optimistic hope of gaining Central Committee cooperation, along with an innate sense of caution built up over the years. As the saying goes: God protects him who protects himself. I kept expecting to get the Central Committee's copy at any time. In addition, I hadn't forgotten that years ago I had assured the KGB and the Party Control Commission that I had handed over all existing copies to them. I couldn't get out of my mind the thought that I could still be called to account if events took a turn for the worse.

Yet another concern was to preserve the last set of copies themselves — just in case, because who knew what tomorrow would bring. What if the last set were to be seized? Then the results of all our labors might perish forever. On the other hand, to sit at home with folded hands would be criminal. So eventually I decided to act. That's how I came by the full set of tapes and transcripts that I am using today to prepare the Russian edition of my father's memoirs.

LEAVE-TAKING

BY New Year's 1971, Father had aged a great deal. Confrontations with his former colleagues had wounded his heart and left a mark on his soul. What troubled him most was not the way the boors unceremoniously confiscated his memoirs. In his last conversation with Pelshe, Father said he had given his whole life to the country, to the people, and that was the truth. And yet today it was as though he had never existed. Even in official editions of correspondence between governments, letters from their side were signed by real leaders, but ours only by the faceless "Chairman of the Council of Ministers of the USSR." In the rare instances where the name Khrushchev appeared in the press, some ritual reference to "voluntarism" inevitably accompanied it. More often they didn't mention the name at all, preferring to refer only to "voluntarism."[1]

In my opinion, the accusation of voluntarism amounts to accusing someone of making decisions. The succeeding epoch was inclined to avoid making any decisions at all.

In Father's soul, bitter resentment at his former friends' betrayal blended with disturbing economic news. Khrushchevian innovations

---

1. *Editor's note:* As with other former high Soviet officials who later became "unpersons," Khrushchev's name was replaced by the label officially used to identify his transgression. "Voluntarism" conveyed the new leadership's charge that his activist policies had been arbitrary and unilateral.

had been scrapped, the old ways had returned, and the situation had worsened. The stores were emptied of goods before one's very eyes. Goals were not achieved. All efforts came to naught.

"First and foremost, we've got to feed, clothe, and provide shoes for the people," he always said. He remembered the famine and devastation of the civil war [during which Khrushchev's first wife, whom he married in 1914, died — ed.], and then the postwar famine in the Ukraine, when corpses lay in the streets and there were cases of cannibalism. All his overflowing energy had been aimed at ensuring that none of this would ever happen again. He was determined that our country take its rightful place among the world's most powerful and wealthiest states.

In his time, of course, things hadn't always gone as he had wanted. Many undertakings had ended badly. Now even the little that remained of his legacy was falling apart, not merely through the authorities' toleration, but with their connivance. This was what he found most terrible; it seemed his entire life had been in vain. Everything achieved through years of stubborn toil lay rotting. That was how the transition from the tempestuous sixties to the stagnant seventies was ending.

Father's physical strength was also on the wane; his seventy-seventh birthday was approaching. Nikita Sergeyevich weakened seriously that winter. It was obvious even to the untrained eye that the physiological moment had come when the vital organs all begin to give way at once. Gloomy thoughts overcame him even more frequently.

"No one needs me anymore," he would say bitterly. "I'm just wandering around aimlessly. I could go hang myself and no one would even notice."

We always objected in chorus and as vigorously as we knew how, but to no avail. His dark mood was obviously not a reaction to any concrete event but rather a manifestation of something taking place deep inside him.

On the surface, life went on as before, and the daily routine continued. As I have already mentioned, little by little Father began to dictate again. This was his way of demonstrating his strength to those who had wronged him: they had not broken him, and he would not give up.

Spring came, and with it Father's birthday. As usual, everyone who could came to Petrovo-Dalneye on April 17. He didn't encourage any celebration and indeed grumbled about it, but of course he liked the attention. It was our custom to take a walk through the meadow and gather on Grass Snake Hill. The earth was warming up, and the first flowers had appeared.

We walked around the garden, which had fallen on hard times during his illness. It lacked the master's caring hand. Father strolled between the rows, picked up a handful of dirt, sniffed it, and announced, "The doctor forbids me to work, so this year we won't be tending the garden."

It saddened him to have to say that. We all protested, even the laziest among us, and so the garden got tended after all, although not with the same intensity as before. All of us pitched in. When the ground thawed, my friends came out, and together we dug and hoed and planted. This pleased Father, who made sure we did everything by the book, scolded us for our "clumsiness," and showed us how to level the earth and shape it into beds.

The spring sun and reawakening nature seemed to dispel his depression. He seemed his old self again — active, smiling, energetic. But he could no longer work with shovel and hoe. Two or three swipes and his face would turn ashen, he would begin to breathe heavily, and he had to return to his faithful folding chair.

After resting a bit, he would joke sadly, "Now I'm a good-for-nothing. Can't do anything but give orders."

We worked in the garden on weekends throughout the summer. We carried out all his agrotechnical orders, and as a result the beds didn't look bad at all.

Father himself still couldn't work, and he eagerly anticipated our arrival. In advance he would lay out a plan of action for his "work force." There was a lot to do. We had to accomplish in two days what he used to do in a week. At last the children would arrive. That normally meant me, Lena's husband Vitya, and less often Yulia Leonidovna and her brother, Yura, the test pilot. Rada and Aleksei Ivanovich usually spent the weekend at their own dacha.

Father led the "brigade," as he called us, to the field, assigned tasks, and kept an eye on our progress. Gradually becoming engrossed in the work, he began to give instructions and to get angry — once again we weren't doing it right. Unable to hold back, he would jump in and show us how to hold a hoe or weed dandelions.

Summer arrived and I decided to celebrate my birthday at the dacha. A noisy company gathered at Petrovo-Dalneye. They all knew and respected Father, and he enjoyed seeing the familiar faces and meeting new people. Sometimes he seemed bored with us, his relatives.

As always, the first thing Father did was to take everyone out to the garden. He listened to well-deserved compliments and lamented his assistants' lack of qualifications.

Then everyone went back to the house, where he provided a musical treat. The guests crowded into his bedroom, where he kept his favorite record player. Those who couldn't squeeze in found a place on the terrace next to the open door.

Eagerly, anticipating the enjoyment he would both provide and receive, Father began picking records out of piles that stood on an end table next to his armchair and on the windowsill. We all knew the program, but no one disturbed the ritual.

Rummaging through the records, Father said with a smile: "We'll begin with some of my favorite Ukrainian songs."

Amiable approval from everyone. Then the sounds of "I'd Take Up the Bandura," "The Wide Dnieper Roars and Moans," and finally, his favorites, "I Wonder at the Sky" and "Black Lashes, Brown Eyes" — both performed by Ivan Semyonovich Kozlovsky, the well-known Russian tenor of the 1940s and 1950s.

Father sat in the armchair, his eyes half closed, his lips moving, singing to himself. Then came Russian folk songs, operatic arias, and in conclusion Lidia Ruslanova's voice, her ardent song reminding Father of his youth.

Finally the concert ended, and everyone scattered into the woods. The main treat, shashlik, would require a fire, and the guests went looking for firewood.

Father disappeared briefly and then returned with his favorite camera, a Hasselblad. The ritual picture taking began. Everything around the dacha having been photographed many times, Father now took up his camera only when someone new appeared.

First, a general photo around the bonfire. Then the guests asked to be photographed with Father. As usual, there was no picture of Father and me together because I was the photographer.

After a while, the party broke up. It was the last gathering at Petrovo-Dalneye.

At the end of July, I was to go on vacation, planning as usual to travel by car and sleep in a tent. But I wasn't sure I should go: I thought perhaps I should stay, so I asked Father.

"There's nothing for you to do here. You'll just get in my way. . . . Go!" He sent me packing.

Father couldn't stand the thought that his condition demanded any extra attention or obliged his loved ones to give up their plans for his sake. More than anything else, he hated the idea of becoming a burden.

There was no reason to be especially concerned, so I left. While on the road I called often; everything was all right at home. I came back a month later, at the end of August, intending to spend the last few days of vacation at home.

Father looked about the same, no better, no worse.

Mama said he had begun talking about his uselessness again, about the pointlessness of life. Several times he began to talk of suicide. Vladimir Grigorievich Bezzubik took this very seriously. He thought it was connected with the developing arteriosclerosis. After a long talk with Father, he advised us not to leave him alone for any length of time. I myself think it wasn't just the sclerosis. I was sure that Father couldn't forgive the insults inflicted on him. But the attacks of melancholy passed, and once again Father joked and told stories and went for walks.

At the end of August, granddaughter Yulia brought the poet Yevgeny Yevtushenko as a guest. Zhenya had long been asking to meet with Khrushchev. Father was happy to see him. The two spent several hours in a lively conversation, with Father recounting the story of Stalin's death and the arrest of Beria.

I should mention that after Father's dismissal, I took endless pictures and movies of him. Earlier, professionals had done this. There were more than enough people who jotted down his every word, and snapped his every movement. Mountains of albums piled up in our house.

Now I had no competitors, but I firmly believed that the time would come when history would need these pictures. I was convinced that this would happen in my lifetime; youth is optimistic. But later I wasn't so sure. More and more, I wondered to whom I should give these treasures. The very name Khrushchev seemed forgotten, except by those whose job it was to fashion an image of a fool, the undereducated, eccentric "man who loved corn" featured in innumerable jokes. Happily, life turned out differently.

That year I managed to obtain a movie camera with a synchronized tape recorder. In the last few weeks, I had tested it out thoroughly during Father's encounters with guests from the lodge next door. Now it was Yevtushenko's turn. Concentrating on my filmmaking, I listened to the conversation with only one ear.

I remember that they talked about the sixties, about their memories of the many sharp and unfair words that created a split between Khrushchev and the young and not-so-young writers, artists, and moviemakers who were a product of his times and who had sincerely supported his cause.

Father often recalled these meetings. By now he had reflected on those heated confrontations and took a different view of what he had said. He told Yevtushenko that he felt guilty for the sharp words he had directed at the young artists and others.

We returned to the house. Father was chilled, and asked for some tea. Yevtushenko began recounting his recent travels around the country. What particularly astonished him was that young people had no idea what had happened in Stalin's time, no notion of the extent of the repressions.

"I was recently on Lake Baikal, where I met some workers and some intellectuals. I steered the discussion around to the Stalinist repressions. They claimed to know about them, and when I asked how many people they thought had perished they said, 'A couple of thousand.' Someone interrupted, 'More — around twenty thousand.' People haven't the faintest idea what happened back then." Then Zhenya mentioned having seen an album of Chagall paintings with an inscription from the artist to Khrushchev; it was at Mikhalkov's dacha.[2]

"They stole it, the bastards," Khrushchev swore quietly.

They continued their conversation over tea. When it was time to part, Father accompanied his guest to the porch. The sun was setting; the autumn air seemed transparent.

Zhenya thanked Father, and Father invited him to come another time. Unhappily, there would be no "other time," but no one knew that then.

Autumn came and my vacation ended. Once again I could come to Petrovo-Dalneye only on weekends.

On Sunday, September 5, Father and Mother were planning to visit Rada at her dacha. It was a long way away, sixty kilometers; these trips had a way of turning into expeditions, but they brought variety to Father's life. He met new people and came home recharged with new impressions.

Alas, the excursion didn't work out well. Father felt ill; his heart

2. *Editor's note:* Sergei Vladimirovich Mikhalkov, well-known writer, poet, and dramatist, coauthor of the words of the Soviet national anthem, and a secretary of the USSR Writers Union.

bothered him. Mama gave him a pill, and he sat for a while on the little folding chair that accompanied him even to the Adzhubeis.

They returned home earlier than usual. He took some more medicine, and although it didn't help, he didn't feel any worse. There was no point in disturbing the doctor on Sunday.

Night didn't bring any relief. The thick darkness pressed down on his chest; he began to have difficulty breathing. He called Mama, who had not closed the door to her room — just in case.

"Sit with me, I'm in pain. Obviously, I'm not going to live out the autumn," Father said in a frightened voice, almost like a child.

Bezzubik came in the morning. He examined Father, listened to his heart, found nothing threatening, but advised going into the hospital. Father didn't want to do that, and Vladimir Grigorievich didn't insist.

That afternoon there was another attack. Now Bezzubik couldn't be dissuaded, and Father really didn't put up any resistance. He just pleaded: "Let's go in my Volga. I just don't like your ambulances — they make you feel like you're already dead."

Vladimir Grigorievich agreed. They waited for the car.

Mama called me at work to say they were taking Father to the hospital. I dropped everything and dashed to the dacha. Mama was there alone, confused and pitiful.

She tried to reassure herself. After all, it hadn't been a heart attack. That was a good sign, but Father had felt very bad.

"Maybe it will pass," Mama said without conviction.

I began my regular routine; I took the tape of Father's last dictation out of the machine, put it in my briefcase, inserted a fresh tape, and put everything back in place. I sat for a while in Father's armchair with a big lump in my throat.

At last the telephone rang, and Vladimir Grigorievich informed us that they had arrived safely. Father's condition was satisfactory. They were admitting him and would do a cardiogram. We could visit him in the evening.

Ah, yes, once again that word "satisfactory." I had heard it a year earlier in response to my question, "How's he doing?"

This time I didn't hold back and pressed Bezzubik.

"Explain to me just what this word means."

Vladimir Grigorievich remained silent for a moment; I imagined him looking at the ceiling. Then he spoke in the quiet, soft voice I associate with that extinct breed, the personal physician who makes house calls.

"You know Nikita Sergeyevich is at an age when you have to be prepared for anything. We say 'bad' when there isn't much hope. Everything else is 'satisfactory.' "

I had no further questions.

That evening I went to the hospital. The door of his ward opened onto a staircase, the window onto a courtyard where the last autumn flowers bloomed. He didn't look bad. He was sitting on the bed watching television. The pain had lessened.

He didn't let me stay long. As he sent me packing, he said jokingly: "No sense wasting time. Don't you have anything to do? Go home and give my best to Galya and Nikita [my wife and son]. Don't bother me, can't you see I'm busy: it's time to swallow some pills, and have my temperature taken. They don't let you get bored here! When you come tomorrow, bring me something to read."

The tone, and the words, were so familiar that they gave me hope. It was all right. Everything would turn out okay.

But it didn't. The books I brought the next day weren't needed: during the night he had suffered a massive heart attack. The doctors were even wary of trying to transfer him to the intensive care unit, fearing he couldn't stand the move.

I tiptoed into the ward to confront a sad sight. There was an intravenous apparatus next to the bed. Father's face was gray, his breathing laborious. He couldn't do without oxygen, but he hadn't lost his spirit. Two transparent tubes to his nostrils supplied him with oxygen; they had taped them to his face. Father still found the strength to joke with the nurse who stood on duty next to his bed.

"My whiskers are all messed up — do something, please."

He was hooked up to various monitors, and a little green snakelike line was running across the screen.

Vladimir Grigorievich didn't set me at ease.

"His condition is very, very grave. You can expect a sad ending at any moment. We'll keep hoping — maybe he'll pull through. Nikita Sergeyevich has a healthy constitution for a man his age."

I too hoped for the best, wanting to believe any optimistic prognosis. The day passed, then Wednesday came. His condition did not improve.

Each day Mama, my sisters, and I took turns visiting Father. I sat quietly in a chair, staring at the medical apparatus, listening to the heavy breathing. The oxygen hissed softly, the intravenous device measured out one drop after another.

We hardly spoke; Father found it difficult even to listen. Nevertheless, he still had strength to smile, even joke. He didn't want to give up and wouldn't tolerate pity.

Thursday morning I called the nurse on duty to get a report. She answered, "He's still breathing," and hung up.

Alarmed, I tore off to the hospital. The doctor explained: "He had a terrible night. He lapsed into a Cheyne-Stokes breathing syndrome, but we managed to control it. Now he's doing a little better."

I knew about Cheyne-Stokes from the medical bulletins at the time of Stalin's fatal illness. The words smelled of death, inevitable death.

Carefully opening the door a little, I looked into Father's room. He lay gravely weakened on a high bed with a sparkling, nickel-plated back and side rails. Catching sight of me, he tried to smile, but no smile materialized. I sat for a while, tried to say something, then fell silent. Father closed his eyes either in sleep or because it was simply too difficult to keep them open. After a while, he opened them again.

"Go away," he muttered. Then the familiar joke. "You see I'm busy. Don't waste time."

I sat a little longer, then left. Mama, Rada, and Lena took my place.

All of us — and Father too — were torn. We didn't want to leave him alone, we wanted to help, to distract him, but at the same time we didn't want to tire him, to force him to react in one way or another. Thus we came and went.

On Friday, Father was a little better. But what did "better" mean? The medical team assembled and stated that, compared to yesterday, the patient's condition was not "extremely grave," but just "very grave." Even *this* inspired some illusory hope.

On Saturday morning, Father seemed to feel a bit better. Mama went to the hospital first. When I called, she said: "Rada and I are both here. Don't come now, or he'll get angry and chase us out. We'll sit a while longer and then leave. You come later."

I allowed myself to leave the telephone. I went down to the courtyard and worked on my car. For some reason, I went back up to the apartment half an hour later. As I approached the door, I heard the telephone ringing; I ran in and with a terrible premonition grabbed the receiver. Those days, every call generated anxiety.

It was Mama again.

"Father's doing very badly. Come immediately."

It isn't even five minutes from Stanislavsky Street to Granovsky Street. Nevertheless, I was too late.

They didn't permit me to enter the ward.

Mama sat on a wooden bench in the corridor.

"I went out for a minute, and when I returned . . . the doctors are doing something to him. . . . Resuscitation. . . . They asked me to leave. I heard them say, 'Nikita Sergeyevich, breathe, breathe!' "

I sat down next to her. Nurses and physicians dashed past, paying no attention to us. Spotting a nurse I knew, one who had been with Father these last days, I rushed up to her.

"Well?"

"Very, very bad."

"No hope?"

"So it seems. None."

I went over to Mama and told her that it looked grim. She sat there with a stony expression.

Yevgenia Mikhailovna, the physician on duty, emerged from the ward. We had known her for years; she'd been working in this hospital a long time. She sat down on the bench next to Mama but didn't say anything.

Confused, Mama asked, "Is he in terrible pain?"

Yevgenia Mikhailovna took a deep breath; she couldn't bring herself to tell the truth. "No, not so much pain now."

Her words gave hope to Mama, who began asking more questions. Yevgenia Mikhailovna remained silent a while longer, then made her decision. Putting her arms around Mama's shoulders, she said simply, "He's dead."

Mama burst into tears. Yevgenia Mikhailovna cried along with her.

I called home. Half an hour later, the other members of the family appeared. Rada had been at the hospital the whole time.

They took us into the next ward, which was empty, and asked us to wait. For the time being we couldn't visit "in there."

Mama wept.

After a while, Yevgenia Mikhailovna called to me, "You can go in."

On the landing, outside the door to the ward, three robust young men who had worked at resuscitating Father were now smoking with great relish. They looked at me sympathetically as I entered alone.

Father had changed markedly. His face was quite different, unfamiliar: the nose seemed much sharper, aquiline; the lower jaw was bandaged; a sheet covered him up to the throat. Drops of blood streaked the wall, a sign of the resuscitators' efforts.

My throat tightened, but I knew I couldn't falter; strength would be needed. I stood there a few moments, then touched his face: it had already grown cold. I kissed his forehead, then left.

My legs were cotton, my mind a fog.

I entered the ward where they all were sitting. I thought how agonizing it was going to be for Mama and, not really realizing what I was saying, said, "Maybe you shouldn't go in just now."

"What do you mean? Of course we must."

They all went in and took seats around the bed. I stood in back, near the window. Time passed, I don't know how much.

Yevgenia Mikhailovna, anxious about Mama, whispered in my ear, "It's time to leave. Tell Nina Petrovna."

We left the room. A cart from the morgue was already waiting at the door. They took Father away. We accompanied him as far as the elevator. The doors closed. It was over.

We made our way to the exit.

On the way, Yevgenia Mikhailovna asked softly, so that the others couldn't hear: "Did Nikita Sergeyevich have any gold teeth?"

"Yes," I answered, not understanding.

"How many?"

I shrugged my shoulders.

She wasn't about to explain that the people in the morgue would extract even a former premier's gold teeth so as to make a little money on the side. Everyone was equal in their eyes. As for me, I knew nothing about that side of life.

When we got to the ground floor Father's car was waiting for Mama at the entrance. I had left my own by the service entrance; there was a stairway there that led directly to Father's ward. How long ago that was! It seemed an eternity.

That's how it all ended.

Mama and my sisters got into the car, but I held back.

"Sergei Nikitich . . . stay a moment," Yevgenia Mikhailovna said. "What about the death certificate, and the funeral arrangements?"

It finally dawned on me that my work had just begun. I had never had to deal with a funeral.

During all those years, everything that concerned Father's contacts with the outside world had been handled by the chief of security. All problems, all requests had been directed to him. Expressionless, he would merely nod, and then within a few hours, days, or — rarely —

weeks, deliver an impersonal answer: This will be possible, but that will not.

I rushed around the hospital trying to locate Kondrashov or Lodygin, who had recently headed the security detail. No luck. The object of their supervision dead, their function had come to an end.

I was completely at a loss. Seeing that, Yevgenia Mikhailovna took the matter into her own hands. We entered the hospital administrator's office.

A battery of telephones stood on a large desk. Through the window you could see the huge, gray Lenin Library building. The glass reverberated with noise from the traffic below.

Yevgenia Mikhailovna sat down confidently behind the desk and grabbed the nearest phone. But it was not going to be easy. Whoever was on the other end couldn't give any answers; they had never encountered such a situation and couldn't make up their minds what to do. The decision had to come from somewhere else. The very conversation was potentially dangerous for them and they hastened to put an end to it.

At last Yevgenia Mikhailovna reached some boss of hers who agreed to talk. However, he couldn't answer even simple questions: "Can you give me the death certificate? Will it be a state funeral or private?"

It was Saturday, and we needed answers as soon as possible. But it was explained to her that the death certificate could be issued only after an autopsy. All we could do now was wait.

Obviously, all these questions had to be decided at a high level. Until then, no one would show any initiative.

But I was in shock and scarcely realized what was happening. Yet, aware that everything rested on my shoulders, I wanted action.

Yevgenia Mikhailovna reassured me: "In a couple of hours everything will be settled and I'll call to tell you about it."

I finally realized that there wasn't anything I could do and went home. No one was there; they had all gone to Petrovo-Dalneye. I wandered aimlessly through the apartment. Various scenes came back to me, but I just couldn't summon up an image of Father, and for some reason this seemed very important. I felt a lump in my throat, and I burst into tears. After a few moments, I pulled myself together. I had to get control of myself.

It occurred to me that soon "they" would be discussing matters and deciding what to do. Even in death, Father's fate would be decided by strangers, outsiders, people hostile to him. They'd try to bury his name in some official communiqué. They wouldn't want to let people know of our misfortune.

The decision soon came to me: we had to act on our own. At least this much was up to us. Let people learn of our sorrow as quickly as possible. After all, it wasn't just my father who had died but an important statesman who had done so much good in his life. Let "them" keep quiet, or even put out dirt about him; still there would be people who would sympathize with us, and bow their head before Father's ashes. I knew what had to be done, how to notify the world; deep down I had foreseen the possibility of such a situation.

I picked up the phone and dialed the number of an English journalist whom I knew quite well. Through him, the world would learn.

He answered promptly, as though he had been waiting for my call. He expressed his sympathy; you could tell from his voice that the words came from the heart.

I asked how he thought events would unfold and in my confused state requested his advice. How should I behave?

"Don't get into a tizzy. Go and support your mother. You'll get nowhere on your own, so just wait. Those in a position to make the decision about the funeral will make it, and the only thing for you to do is accept it. Let's get in touch this evening."

I decided to take his sensible advice and go to Petrovo-Dalneye. Before leaving, I dialed the dacha. Lena picked up the phone.

"It's terrible what's going on here — we found the house locked and a guard at the door. He didn't want to let us in without permission from his superiors. Mama wanted to leave — we barely persuaded her to stay."

Fortunately, those in charge of security returned, obviously having contacted the high command. They opened the house but refused to let anyone into Father's room: the door had been sealed and in front of it stood a guard.

Lena had always been the most uncompromising of all of us. Now she was boiling over with indignation.

Our lives had shaped themselves around Father, he was the axis around which we lived, acted, and thought. We automatically measured every step: How would Father look at this? Would he approve, keep silent, or say simply, "You shouldn't do that."

That was all it took.

And so his death did not merely remove someone near and dear to us; it shattered our normal existence. The locked, sealed door somehow served as a symbol of the collapse.

I hurried to the dacha. The situation Lena had described didn't surprise me. Sergo had told me about similar cases. In recent years it had become standard practice to ensure that not a single document of any kind went astray. I don't think they were worried about state secrets; but what if there were some notes evaluating our thriving present-day leaders? They had special people who conducted these searches. No one cared about the feelings of people who had lost a loved one, let alone about the constitutionally guaranteed inviolability of one's dwelling.

I knew every rut in the road, having traveled it for years, and within half an hour I was signaling at the green gate. The situation hadn't changed in the meantime. The guard at the door to Father's bedroom shifted his weight from one foot to the other; you could see from his look of dismay that he was ashamed, ashamed of himself for disrupting people's grief, ashamed of those who had sent him, and of those who had issued the orders to them. But no one could help him, or us. We simply tried not to notice him.

I went to Kondrashov to find out what was going to happen, and what we could do. He said: "Some comrades are coming from the Central Committee. They'll examine Khrushchev's personal effects and decide what to do with them."

That meant a search was imminent.

Evening came. It was damp outside. The little asphalt square in front of the house was slippery with yellowed, wrinkled leaves. The weather matched our mood. The evening, the dampness, and the darkening tips of the pines against the low-hanging clouds — all this deepened our agitation and uncertainty.

After a while I was unable to restrain myself, and returned to the guardroom. It turned out there was some news. Kondrashov himself didn't consider it necessary to keep us informed, but in response to my question said that a commission on Nikita Sergeyevich's archives had been formed under the chief of the Central Committee's General Department, Comrade Klavdy M. Bogolyubov. Comrades Stepan P. Avetisyan and Mikhail I. Kuvshinov were on their way to the dacha.

I knew Kuvshinov, the assistant business manager of the Central

Committee, having encountered him in connection with household matters. I had a good impression of him. This was the first I'd heard of Avetisyan.

I wanted to alert Mama so that these new visitors wouldn't arrive like a bolt from the blue. But before I could finish my conversation with Kondrashov, a car drove up. Two men in dark overcoats and hats emerged. They stamped their feet at the entrance but didn't enter the house.

The taller one was Kuvshinov. I figured the shorter man with thin gold-framed spectacles was Avetisyan.

Kondrashov and I hurried out to meet them. We greeted each other and introduced ourselves; Kuvshinov shook my hand heartily as if to cheer me up. I invited them in. Kondrashov followed us.

They expressed their sympathy to Mama and asked her to forgive the intrusion. What could you do? It was the way things were, and they weren't responsible. They were just doing their duty.

Dismissing the guard, they broke the seal and opened the door; they had a key. They asked for the key to the safe that stood in the room.

The first things they looked for were papers and tapes. Recalling how the KGB had seized materials for the memoirs from me the previous year, I realized it would be useless to interfere.

Having cleaned out the safe, they moved on. They dumped all the magnetic tapes into a briefcase without sorting them out and without paying any attention to our objections that some had music, others calisthenics instructions, and a few had not been used at all. For some reason Mama really didn't want to give up the calisthenics tape, on which the physical education instructor, reading a text, began with the words, "Good morning, Nikita Sergeyevich! How did you sleep?"

Our weak protests didn't help; the visitors were implacable. They promised that everything that had no historical value or was not a state secret would be returned after it had been examined. After repeated reminders, they actually returned the calisthenics tape a few months later. The others, including the blank ones intended for dictation, remained "there."

The examination of Father's papers went quickly; essentially, he had none. All official papers were kept at the Central Committee, they had seized his memoirs the previous year, and his correspondence did not interest our "guests."

What they were interested in gradually became clear; meanwhile, they methodically examined the room. For some reason, the record player attracted special attention. They peered into every drawer, every box, and into the closet. They leafed through the books that lay in heaps on the table next to the armchair and on the windowsill. When a piece of paper caught their attention, they studied it carefully, showed it to Mama, and then Avetisyan put it away in his capacious briefcase.

Lena and I looked on in dismay. Understanding that it was hopeless to intervene, I kept quiet. Lena, however, was seething. She kept making caustic comments. She exploded when Avetisyan found a typewritten copy of Mandelshtam's verses about Stalin[3] among the books on the windowsill, read it, and started to stuff it into the briefcase.

Not long before, the nuclear physicist and academician Lev Andreyevich Artsimovich and his wife, Nelly, had come to congratulate Father on his birthday and had brought the verses as a gift. Lev Andreyevich had written a very meaningful dedication to Father in one corner. I don't remember the exact words, but it had to do with the repressions and the cleansing wind of the Twentieth Congress. Nothing seditious. But it was the dedication that caught Avetisyan's attention. He wanted to know who had written the verses. Upon being told it was Mandelshtam, he grunted and asked who had written the inscription.

He didn't comment on our answer.

At this point, Lena was unable to contain herself and burst out that he didn't have any right to confiscate a gift from the academician to our father, that it was now a family remembrance.

Both men listened impassively. When Lena stopped for breath, Avetisyan politely explained in a calm, colorless voice that Mandelshtam's verses and the inscription from Artsimovich to Khrushchev were a great historical treasure that had to be preserved in the Central Committee archives.

The indignant Lena practically shot out of the room.

What else did they take? One thing I remember is the original copy, signed by all members, of the Presidium's greeting to Father on his seventieth birthday. As I mentioned in chapter one, it said they were all happy to work with, and under the leadership of, Nikita Sergeyevich,

3. *Editor's note:* Osip Mandelshtam, one of the great Russian poets of the twentieth century, perished in a Stalin prison camp. His caustic poem about Stalin was one of the things that led to his first arrest in 1934.

and they wished him a long life of productive labor. At the time, the text had been published in all the newspapers.

I understood: nowadays the words didn't correspond to the spirit of the time. Why they also took some award certificates signed by former President Mikhail Kalinin we had no idea. Nothing else seemed to interest them.

Comrade Avetisyan asked us to inform him if we found anything interesting. All documents connected with Khrushchev's life, he emphasized, had great historical importance.

I already knew the value of such words, but Mama naively suggested: "I've got a recording of Nikita Sergeyevich's speech at the Sixteenth Congress of the Ukrainian Communist party, also some gramophone records with his voice and materials for other party congresses."

Comrade Avetisyan said we could keep these in the family.

The courtyard was absolutely dark; night had fallen. I glanced at my watch: a little after eight.

All this time, one question had been throbbing in my head like a nail: how and when would the news of Father's death be made public, and what kind of funeral would there be? I waited in vain for them to get around to this topic.

The commission completed its work and was about to leave. Only then did I ask whether the matter of the funeral had been decided. Apparently it had. But they themselves didn't remember how, since they were absorbed by other concerns.

This was what had been decided: There would be a private, family funeral in Novodevichy Cemetery. Nikita Sergeyevich's death would be announced Monday morning, at ten o'clock, the very same hour when the wake was scheduled at Kuntsevo Hospital. The funeral would follow at noon. The Central Committee would pay for the funeral.

It had been worked out very efficiently; there would be no delay. Kuvshinov gave me his office and home telephone numbers.

"If you have questions about the funeral, contact me directly."

Mama said she had called Kiev. Yulia Nikitichna and her husband, her niece Nina Ivanovna, and other relatives were coming.

I realized immediately that word of Father's death would reach people simultaneously with the funeral ceremony, even in the best circumstances, and most likely even later. Nor, of course, was this accidental; everything had been thought out beforehand. I decided to call and inform as many people as possible. I was in a rage, and for a time could think of nothing except how to thwart this shabby, disgusting provocation.

But I quickly had second thoughts. "History will judge them for this," I thought to myself. "It's our job to bury Father with dignity."

I recalled that my English friend and I had agreed to get in touch by phone that evening. He said that all the major press agencies in the world had already reported Khrushchev's death: they were publishing extensive commentaries and obituaries. The general tone was positive, not hostile. The reports praised Nikita Sergeyevich's role in making a reality of peaceful coexistence and took note of his other good deeds.

"Listen to the radio. The whole world's talking about your father," my friend said.

The conversation ended, and I felt a little better. After all the tense hours, I really needed a kind word.

I told Yulia and Lena about the call, then sat down again at the telephone.

I called all my friends and acquaintances to inform them about the funeral. I listened to their condolences, and asked them to tell everyone they could.

I thought especially about Mikoyan. I wanted very much to invite him; he was Father's old friend and the only one who had supported him in those difficult days of October 1964. But I knew Mikoyan's own position was complicated. Like Father, he wasn't in favor these days, and his appearance at the funeral might be taken as an act of defiance, a challenge. I wavered, then dialed Sergo's apartment. He was at home but hadn't heard anything yet.

He commiserated with me and promised to come by to pay his respects. He was going to his father's dacha that very evening and would tell him what had happened.

While I was on the phone, it suddenly occurred to me that people would have to get up at the crack of dawn to attend a wake scheduled for 10:00 A.M. This was a funeral, after all; fuss and haste were inappropriate. Yet they had arranged the wake in a suburban hospital, in Kuntsevo. How were people going to get there? In those days, that was much more complicated than it is now.

On the advice of Mama and my sisters, I decided to call Kuvshinov and ask him to postpone the start of the ritual to a later hour. I reached him at home; it was already late evening. He was extremely kind but unyielding; it was obvious that he had strict instructions.

"The decision has been made. It would be impossible to find

another place for the wake, and we can't change the time. There are others who have died, too — there's a queue. Other people are also grieving. No, there's no way to change the time of the funeral."

Obviously finding it unpleasant to say this, he found a way to help on something within his sphere of competence.

"Tomorrow they'll prepare a grave at the cemetery. Look at the spot, and if you don't like it, the comrades will try to accommodate you. I'll call the cemetery and issue orders."

This turned out to be a great kindness indeed. The organizers of the funeral hadn't managed to think of everything; we succeeded in finding a gravesite that would be easier to visit.

I have to admit that I kept waiting to see whether any member of the Politburo would call. After all, Nikita Sergeyevich had worked for decades not only with Brezhnev but also with several of the others. The majority of them had developed under his leadership, had been his friends, had visited his home and he theirs. They knew Mama and our entire family well. Death equalizes everyone; what do personal quarrels and political conflicts mean in the face of death?

Unfortunately, a certain degree of culture and intellect is required to understand this. Not one of them called.

Late in the evening, we turned on the radio. For some reason, we were still afraid to be overheard listening to Western broadcasts, so we went out on the porch. It was a damp, cold night, but we sat there on the bench in darkness. Foreign radio stations resounded hollowly through atmospheric interference and jamming. All the stations, except for Moscow, reported extensively on Khrushchev's death, complete with commentaries and recollections.

The first official condolences to the Soviet government came over the air; they came from the foreign minister of the Malagasy Republic, Didier Ratsiraka. Out there on Madagascar they evidently hadn't analyzed all the nuances of our internal politics, but they knew their international protocol.

These condolences created a unique problem for the functionaries of the Council of Ministers and the Ministry of Foreign Affairs. No one knew what to do with them. Every situation, however, has an out, and they found one. For a long time, an apologetic postman kept bringing dirty, carelessly torn packages of messages from heads of state, presidents, leaders of Communist parties, public figures, and — most treasured by us — ordinary people who remembered and respected Khrushchev. There were many of them.

I kept the condolences in a suitcase. I'm looking through the stacks of cables and letters now; I'll pick out a few at random. My hand alights on those from Josip Broz Tito and János Kádár, Italian leader Amintore Fanfani and Urkho Kekkonen, Jacqueline Kennedy and Ambassador Thompson's family, the families of the Iowa farmer Roswell Garst and the Russian painter living in India Syatoslav Rerikh. (Father had particularly warm feelings toward the Garsts and Rerikhs). There's no enumerating them all.

The letters came to our home address, to my sister Rada at the journal *Nauka i zhizn,* and simply to "Khrushchev's widow, Moscow." Many never reached us, including the one from Madagascar; we learned about them through the newspapers.

For the rest of that year and into the beginning of the next, Mama wrote thank-you notes. If the note was to be sent abroad, it had to be translated. She did the English translations herself, and asked friends to do the others. I'm sure that by no means all of them reached the addressees; instead, they were buried somewhere in the archives of the "responsible agencies" [i.e., KGB — ed.]. But that's probably not what's important.

In front of me are copies of some of Mama's replies. One of them has a special history.

Academician Andrei Dmitrievich Sakharov had written some particularly warm lines. He was already in great disfavor, and his disagreements with the government had begun when Khrushchev was in power. By the end of the fifties, he was a legend to me — the youngest academician and the father of the hydrogen bomb. I was a young engineer and didn't have even a nodding acquaintance with him, but Father often talked about him and regarded him with — I can't find another word — a certain reverence.

This feeling survived their sharp divergence of opinion concerning our resumption of nuclear tests after the moratorium. They couldn't agree on the moral merits of the decision to explode a nuclear device of monstrous megatonnage on Novaya Zemlya. They spoke different languages, and they didn't understand each other. Neither changed his mind. Khrushchev won; might was on his side, and he made the decision. The series of tests concluded with an explosion that shook the entire world.

As usual, the awarding of medals crowned successful labors, and this time there was a special abundance of them. Nikita Sergeyevich ordinarily did not pay much attention to these affairs; the appropriate departments prepared the lists and the Central Committee Presidium signed off on them. I happened to be present at the dacha when they informed Father that the lists were ready, and that it remained only to obtain the go-ahead to register the decree with the Presidium of the USSR Supreme Soviet.

Father had only one question: "Is Sakharov on the list to be designated Hero of Socialist Labor?"

At that time, Andrei Dmitrievich had already won this medal twice.

It turned out that Sakharov's name was missing. It was said that he hadn't taken an active role and moreover had come out against conducting the tests.

Father was indignant.

"This is outrageous. Sakharov's contribution to our defense is enormous. Let there be differences of opinion, but everyone does his own work — we as leaders of the state, he as a scientist. It's a good thing that we can disagree, express different opinions and debate the issues. That decreases the chance of error. We didn't agree with Sakharov, we didn't go along with his recommendations — so awarding him a medal will testify all the more to the government's respect for his point of view. You have to talk with people like Sakharov, persuade them. There's a lot they don't understand; they live in their own world, far from the ups and downs of politics and interstate relations — where there's more dirt than there should be. Sakharov's views are naive, but they're interesting. They come from the heart, from his wish for everyone's happiness. We have to listen to him."

Thus Andrei Dmitrievich Sakharov became a Hero of Socialist Labor for the third time.

Each man followed his own difficult path. In his retirement, Father still counted himself a member of the anti-Sakharov camp, but that was out of inertia, and he watched with dismay the developing rift between the academician and the Soviet leadership.

"What are they doing? You have to talk with a man like that, not call him on the carpet. You have to hear him out, debate with him. That's the only way to reach a constructive decision, to get back to common principles. They're making him their enemy, and that's an unforgivable mistake."

During our strolls along the paths of Petrovo-Dalneye, he came back to the subject of Sakharov more than once. It seems odd, but by that time Khrushchev and Sakharov were both dissidents. Each in his own way, to be sure, but that didn't change the main thing: no one had any use for their views of how to make the world a better, more just place. If only Sakharov and Khrushchev had never existed — things would have been more peaceful for the powers that were. They could also do (and did) without many others of intelligence and conscience for whom there was no place in the Motherland.

Sometime in November, Mama wrote a response to Sakharov's condolences; the question of how to get it to him arose. We knew his address but had no doubt that the post office would never deliver the letter. I decided to take it myself. I won't conceal the fact that I wanted very much to meet the academician.

The weather was nasty, a cold wind blew, and the last soggy leaves drooped listlessly from the trees. My headlights were reflected in the puddles. I had a long way to go. He lived in an unfamiliar part of the city.

At the time, the KGB had again begun following me, and I wasn't surprised to see two well-known Volgas as I approached the fork in the Volokolamsk Highway.

Dirt from the road covered my windshield. The cleaning fluid had run out, and the wipers just streaked the windshield, through which I could barely make out the road.

What are they doing? I thought to myself in annoyance. If they'd just pick me up and take me there, it would save all of us a lot of trouble.

The gloomy weather evoked gloomy thoughts: Who knows what instructions they have? Maybe they'll seize me and take away the letter.

I went around and around the Shchukino district without finding the right street. After asking a couple of the rare pedestrians I encountered, I found the building. You couldn't get to it by car; the road didn't reach it. I had to take the path around it. My "escorts" remained behind, or perhaps they were waiting for me at the door. I was nervous, but I found the right entrance and entered without incident. Climbing the stairs, I heard steps below. I rang the bell and the door promptly opened; I identified myself.

Disappointment awaited me. Andrei Dmitrievich wasn't at home, and the meeting didn't take place. There was nothing to do but hand over the envelope and retreat.

At the entrance, two tall men in autumn coats were conversing. We paid no attention to each other, pretending to attend to business, to care nothing about a chance passerby.

Having delivered the letter, I felt at ease. I didn't even feel like picking out my companions in the rearview mirror, even though it was clear they were there. I simply drove home, thinking about the twists of fate with which the Most High liked to amuse Himself. Here I was, threading my way around dark back streets in order to deliver a thank-you note to our outstanding scientist for his expression of sympathy on the death of a man who, albeit long retired, had been the head of our government.

MORE melancholy trouble lay ahead for us.

On Sunday, we — I think Vitya was with me — drove to Novo-devichy Cemetery. I had been there only once or twice in my life; I had a lot to learn about this new world where I was to be a constant visitor. The director was waiting for us. He was a man with the astonishing name of Arakcheyev.[4] In those days, every coincidence seemed sinister. Arakcheyev and I didn't actually become friends, but we treated each other with respect. He turned out to be an extremely decent, principled man. Later on, when they closed the cemetery to visitors [in large part to discourage paying respects to Khrushchev — ed.], he antagonized the higher-ups by proposing to organize tours and issue a catalogue. After a heated party meeting, a new director appeared at the cemetery.

Some people — evidently his bosses — had crowded into Arak-cheyev's office. They escorted us to the far wall of the cemetery. Very near the extreme right-hand corner was a freshly dug grave that would be at the head of a new row. I didn't like the site. I had already thought about erecting a monument. But this plot wasn't easily approachable, nor was there room to move around. It was separated from the path by thick, impassable bushes.

I asked whether we couldn't switch the burial to a site beside the broad avenue that cut across the cemetery. Back then, there were many unoccupied plots; nowadays the graves of academician Mikhail Yangel, the former finance minister Zverev, the son of Brezhnev's aide Georgy Emanuilovich Tsukanov, and others are located there.

My companions consulted with each other and refused; it could not be done. I understood: it was too public and prestigious a place.

"How about the row you suggested, but nearer the path?" I asked.

---

4. *Editor's note:* Count Aleksei Arakcheyev, adviser to Tsars Alexander I and Nicholas I, was instrumental in founding and maintaining the brutal military colonies of the early nineteenth century.

This time there were no objections. The workers came and began to dig the new grave. I stood nearby until they finished.

The first gravesite they had proposed didn't stay empty long. A little time passed, and in December they lowered the poet and citizen Aleksandr Trifonovich Tvardovsky into it.[5]

Having finished our business at the cemetery, we returned home. Everyone was busy with the sad bustle of getting ready for the next day: we collected Father's medals, hunted for a dark suit, prepared the dishes for the funeral banquet.

Vitya and I tried to find a suitable photograph of Father. We found one from ten years earlier and had it laminated in polyethylene to protect it against the autumn rains.

In the evening, we listened to the radio again. In every country there were commentaries about Khrushchev's death, but Moscow maintained silence.

Out-of-town relatives were gathering. Some remained in the city and spent the night at the apartment, others came to Petrovo-Dalneye. The house was full.

New arrivals had to be put up for the night. There wasn't enough space; they occupied all the sofas and we got out folding cots. Only Father's room remained empty.

Mama suggested that I sleep in his bed. I hesitated, I felt extremely uncomfortable: only a week ago he had slept there . . . But I didn't say anything, and lay down. All night I thought about Father, stared at the ceiling, and replayed in my mind the recent, already irrevocable past. Father had loved me more than his other children, perhaps because I was his only son, or because he saw in me the fulfillment of his own dream of becoming an engineer. I had been absolutely devoted to him. I remembered our frequent walks together, sometimes in silence, sometimes with him telling me about his new ideas. For me, these walks had been a gift; I recalled listening impatiently for the sound of the car door slamming shut, for that meant he was home from work. As we walked, I would tell him about my affairs, about new projects at our design bureau, and he would listen with great interest. Beginning when I was a child, he had taken me hunting — ducks in the winter and rabbits in

---

5. Tvardovsky was the poet who became editor of the liberal journal *Novyi mir*. It was he who sent Aleksandr Solzhenitsyn's *One Day in the Life of Ivan Denisovich* to Khrushchev, and who, with Khrushchev's help, managed to publish the work in his journal.

summer. Our work on his memoirs, just he and I, had brought us even closer. But now he was gone. It just wouldn't sink in.

We arose early on the day of the funeral, Monday, September 13, so as to get to Kuntsevo by ten o'clock. I dashed out for the newspapers. *Pravda* did not have an obituary; instead, at the bottom of page one, in small type, was this notice:

> The Central Committee of the CPSU and the Council of Ministers of the USSR regretfully announce the death on September 11, 1971, after a protracted, painful illness, of the former First Secretary of the Central Committee of the CPSU and Chairman of the Council of Ministers of the USSR, personal pensioner Nikita Sergeyevich Khrushchev, age 78.

I immediately fixed on the omission of the customary "with deep regret." In this case, the Central Committee and the Council of Ministers weren't grieving deeply. I was told later that they at first wanted to limit themselves to a black-bordered announcement on the back page, but the chief editor categorically rejected that idea and threatened to resign — he'd have to answer for that to the rest of the world.

Until the day Khrushchev died, obituaries of ranking political figures had always been published on either the second page or the last, depending on the rank of the deceased. This time, they obviously didn't know what to write, so they took the easy way out and kept silent.

No one thought about the consequences, about the fact that they were establishing a precedent: former ministers who were now retired would get an obituary, while retired former members of the Central Committee Presidium might not, because "such is the custom."

This is what happened when Andrei Andreyevich Andreyev died right after Nikita Sergeyevich. A tradition was born. Nikolai Bulganin, Aleksei Kirichenko, Mikhail Pervukhin, and many others were buried this way.[6]

Mama made everyone eat breakfast; a difficult day lay ahead. The food stuck in our throats, but we ate. Finally, we left for the morgue.

---

6. *Editor's note:* Andreyev was one of the top leaders around Stalin in the late thirties and forties. He dropped out of the leadership in 1952. Kirichenko, a protégé of Khrushchev's, was second secretary of the Central Committee until his sudden fall from power in 1960. Pervukhin, a top-level industrial administrator, was a member of the post-Stalin Presidium until he joined with Molotov, Malenkov, Kaganovich, and others in the 1957 attempt to oust Khrushchev. He was dropped from the Presidium in 1961.

On the road to Kuntsevo I thought, We will put up a monument. We've got to find something out of the ordinary, something striking, worthy of Father's memory.

But how? Where to begin? I didn't know any sculptors; their world was distant from mine. And anyway, who would agree to do it? Some would be afraid, and Father had cursed others at the Manezh — it was unlikely that *they* would agree. Fortunately, as it turned out, I was wrong.

We arrived at the hall for the wake. It was a small, red-brick building with a cramped little auditorium reserved for relatives of the deceased. A crowd made up mostly of foreign newsmen had gathered out in front. But they were quiet and obliging and moved out of our way without trying to ask us questions.

Kuvshinov and Avetisyan had already warned us that the burial would be a strictly family affair. The state would play no role. Around the coffin were wreaths from relatives and friends — plus a modest one "To Comrade N. S. Khrushchev from the CC CPSU and the Council of Ministers of the USSR."

However, the state was present after all. Not only was the place full of KGB agents; in the woods behind the fence were armored personnel carriers loaded with soldiers in full field gear. Their commanders could be seen walking back and forth and talking into field radios. All looked battle-ready.

At last we were all there. There weren't many of us, but it wasn't easy to get to the hall that day. It wasn't only that the hospital was out of town; in addition, the police checked the identification papers of all those approaching the hall; in order to enter, you had to prove you were a family member or a close friend. They didn't allow anyone else in.

We entered the hall. Chairs for relatives surrounded the coffin, and more chairs lined the walls. No one, however, sat down. Funeral music could be heard over the loudspeakers. The family and a group of old Communists, many of whom had worked with Nikita Sergeyevich in the Donbas in the old days, stood in a half circle around the coffin. Family friends, friends from work, and neighbors were also there. So were other people I didn't know. Journalists remained just outside the door.

Officials stood in a separate group that included Comrade Georgy S. Pavlov, business manager of the Central Committee, and someone I didn't know, evidently from the KGB.

Father lay stiffly in the coffin. He didn't look at all like himself; the face was entirely different.

Standing by the coffin, Mama pulled at my hand. I bent down and she asked in a whisper, "Do you know who'll speak at the funeral?"

I shook my head.

"Go find out," she whispered.

You could see the suffering in her face, but she didn't cry. The question of the funeral had evidently been bothering her for some time. The way she saw it, a public man simply could not be buried without some ceremony.

Above all, the authorities did not want any speeches, which was why they had decided on a private, family funeral. The last thing I wanted at that moment was to argue with them, to cross them; I simply didn't have the strength, and beyond that I didn't attach much significance to graveside speeches. I was wrong about that, as events would soon show. But the main thing was to be guided by Mama's wishes, which were more important to me than anything. Later she would recall everything down to the most minute details, and any false step would echo painfully.

I approached Comrade Pavlov with the question. He replied that since the ceremony was unofficial, no assembly was planned. I couldn't take that answer back to Mama.

"You won't object if I and maybe one or two of our friends say a few words?"

It was obvious that he was in an embarrassing position. He disliked his mission and decided to limit himself to his formal instructions. He shrugged his shoulders. "Go ahead."

I knew I had to speak. I had already been thinking about what I might say, looking for the right words. Another speaker had to be found as well; it wouldn't do for me to be the only one. I approached the group of old Communists, and asked if one of them would speak. They whispered among themselves, then one of the women replied, "Gavryusha Pilipenko can speak. Talk to him."

But Pilipenko refused, citing his ailing heart. Or was it that he was simply afraid to speak on his own without sanction from on high?

Standing next to him was a small, gray-haired woman, Nadezhda Dimenshtein, who also knew Father from their days in the Ukraine. She interrupted brusquely: "If he can't do it, I will."

I immediately agreed. I wanted to find still another, younger speaker. My thought was to pick one of the old comrades and someone from the younger generation, but I couldn't think of any candidates.

My eyes lit on Yevtushenko and Trunin, who were standing together. I had alerted Trunin about the funeral, and Zhenya had obviously learned of it from Yulia. I recalled Yevtushenko's recent visit, and his conversation with Father; surely he wouldn't be afraid.

"Zhenya, would you be willing to say a few words over the grave?"

He was taken aback, but quickly recovered. "I think that would be superfluous. Silence would be more meaningful."

That was the last I saw of him that day. Apparently he had gotten frightened after all.

I turned to Trunin with the same request. It was easier with him; we had known each other a long time. But he didn't want to speak either. I understood why. Such a thing would be duly noted, and no one could foresee the consequences.

"If it's necessary I will," he said, "but I really don't know what to say. You decide — whatever you want, I'll do."

But I had already changed my mind. Vadim barely knew Father; he had met him for the first and last time on July 3 that year. Vadim later reproached me. He had rehearsed what he would say all the way from the hospital to the cemetery but I didn't call on him.

I noticed Vadim Vasiliev, my old friend from the institute. His father had perished in Stalin's camps, and you could depend on Vadim; he wouldn't be afraid.

"Yes, of course I'll say something," he answered without even thinking.

While I was selecting the speakers, the time for the farewell passed; now we had to depart for the cemetery. I went up to Mama and whispered in her ear that I had arranged everything; naturally I didn't say how. The Central Committee's position was very important to her, and the fact that its representative had approved reassured her.

I can still see the scene in the hall just before we left — the two sobbing Yulias, older and younger, Rada stone-faced, and Mama in a state of near collapse. And cutting through all the weeping Aleksei Ivanovich's hissed whisper: "The dog is alone at home. She needs to be walked."

The others left the auditorium, and we remained there alone. These were the most difficult moments. Mama summoned all her strength and managed to hold herself together. Rada stood next to her. We kissed

Father. It was horrible — just yesterday he had been alive, an active, cheerful man, and now his lips were cold and unknown.

I have a photograph showing the pallbearers: Anton Grigoriev (a singer at the Bolshoi Theater), Valery Samoilov and Semyon Alperovich (my friends and colleagues at the design bureau), Misha Zhukovsky, professor and physician.

We got on a bus; the coffin stood in the aisle. The bus set off. A police car led the way, an innovation, I think.

Behind us came a car with a nurse from the polyclinic — just in case. Then came several more automobiles, and a cavalcade of journalists brought up the rear.

No sooner had we pulled away than soldiers began spilling out of the woods around the auditorium, many more, it seemed, than we had noticed when we arrived.

We drove along Rublevsk Highway and quickly reached Kutuzovsky Prospekt. Without stopping, we sped right through the intersections, indecently fast, in my view, for a funeral procession.

Why are we in such a hurry? I wondered. What are we going to be late for?

Next, the Borodinsky Bridge. There's no left turn allowed here, but on this occasion a special traffic policeman stood just beyond the bridge. A sharp motion of his baton halted oncoming traffic, and we made an unhindered, and for me unexpected, left turn onto the embankment. That meant we wouldn't drive along the Garden Ring. They didn't want us on streets crowded with people.

We approached the Novodevichy Cemetery ringed by soldiers; behind them stood groups of people. We turned in through the gates. The grounds were normally open to visitors; I was struck by a sign that read, "Cemetery Closed Today for Cleaning."

While we drove inside, the other vehicles remained near the entrance. We passed the central square, where a wooden speakers' platform and a pedestal for a coffin usually stood. Today there was nothing; they'd been farsighted enough to remove them. *This* funeral would proceed without any speeches.

At the time, Vitaly Petrovich Kurilchik was deputy chief of the Moscow City Executive Committee's Administration of Communal Services; cemeteries came under his jurisdiction. He remembers what happened.

The day before the funeral, Sunday, the authorities became concerned about the possibility of people gathering at the cemetery. Someone from the Central Committee tracked down Vitaly Petrovich at home and asked whether there was a speakers' platform at the cemetery. Learning that one stood on the traditional spot for such rituals, the man ordered him to remove it — just in case a spontaneous meeting materialized.

Vitaly Petrovich objected quite reasonably that neither the presence nor the absence of the platform could "determine the weather," and proposed instead that he simply close the cemetery for cleaning. But, in the end, he removed the platform, too.

Kurilchik also recalls the crude violation of the generally accepted rule for funerals — that no vehicles enter the cemetery grounds. On that day, the organizers had no time for such niceties. Today it's difficult to imagine what they were afraid of. I won't speculate; but they were *very* frightened.

We came to a dead end and stopped. Ahead was a narrow path. My friends Yura Dedov, Yura Gavrilov, Volodya Modestov, Petya Krimerman, and others carried the coffin on their shoulders the last few meters.

They put the coffin on a metal pedestal next to the grave. I hurried to the gates — we had to let everyone in. Several times I ran there to escort family and friends and anyone else who managed to get through the thick cordon of soldiers.

The authorities had been thorough. Passengers were not permitted to leave the trains at the nearest Metro stations, and bus and trolley lines that passed near the cemetery didn't operate that day. KGB agents and policemen carefully examined identification papers; it took more than a little persistence and resourcefulness to get through.

Some teacher had led a squad of Young Pioneers with a banner to the cemetery. It was too late to send them home, so they were shoved behind a police bus. As for Petya Yakir, son of my father's old friend Iona Emanuilovich Yakir, he never made it to the cemetery because they sent him to a police station.

We later learned that other regrettable incidents took place. Plainclothes agents, present in abundance, openly photographed everyone inside the cemetery and at the gates.

Sitting beside the coffin all the way to the cemetery, I had been anxiously wondering what I would say. I had no prepared speech, only scraps of nighttime thoughts. I didn't want to talk about Father's contributions. First of all, evaluations like that are inevitably controversial, and that day it might have sounded like a challenge. I didn't want to pick a quarrel with the authorities. This was a funeral. Ahead was eternity; for my father, vanity remained behind.

I didn't come up with anything concrete as we drove along, but a general idea took shape in my mind. The words would have to come by themselves.

Another problem arose at the cemetery: in the absence of a speakers' platform, I would be neither seen nor heard. A rather large crowd had gathered around the grave. It was now clear why Pavlov had raised no objection to my proposal; he had counted on the physical impossibility of conducting an assembly.

As I glanced around in confusion, the mound of earth from the grave caught my eye. Next to it stood the pedestal with the coffin that contained Father's body. At the head of the coffin stood Mama, Lena, Rada, the two Yulias, Yura, and others.

A scene from an old movie flashed through my mind — someone standing on some hill, delivering an oration. Maybe I dreamed the whole thing, but it gave me an idea, and I climbed up on the mound of earth; from the top I could see everything clearly. No one paid much attention; not many knew me. They were all waiting silently for something to happen.

I looked around the cemetery. Close by, berries on a rowan tree; on the left, birches and maples were changing color, turning gold. I didn't know how to begin; the words wouldn't come. I opened my mouth . . . but said nothing. The crowd began to press in around the grave.

I made up my mind. "Comrades, today we say farewell to our father, Nikita Sergeyevich Khrushchev . . ."

Clouds covered the sun. Raindrops began to fall.

"The heavens are weeping with us."

The words suddenly came of their own volition, and after that they formed their own chain, one after the other. I said roughly the following:

"We are not conducting an official funeral assembly, and we have no designated speakers. Nevertheless, I want to say a few words about the man whose body we lower into the grave today.

"I don't want to speak of Nikita Sergeyevich's role as a statesman. As his son and contemporary, I can't be objective in my views. History will render its own judgment, put everything in its proper place, evaluate each according to his merits.

"The one thing of which there can be no doubt is that Nikita Sergeyevich sincerely tried to do everything he could to build a new world, a better world for everyone. Of course, he made mistakes along the way; the only way to avoid mistakes is to do nothing. And Nikita Sergeyevich did a great deal.

"Khrushchev's personality certainly won't be forgotten. He left no one indifferent, nor does he today: he has his friends, and his enemies. The arguments about him and his work will long continue; that, too, testifies that he did not live in vain.

"I want to speak about him as a father, my father, the father of our entire family. I cannot pronounce the word 'was' . . . it's so painful.

"We knew another side of his life, at home. He was a good father, husband, friend. He lives on in our hearts. Let him remain in the hearts of his loved ones, in the hearts of his many friends. There are no words to express our feelings.

"And one more thing. We have lost a man who had every right to be called a Man. There aren't many people worthy of being ranked alongside him."

What else I said, I don't remember. I closed with the traditional farewell: "May he find the earth soft as down!"

From the mound of earth I could see the journalists' microphones pointed at me, and I tried to speak loudly. I wanted my words to be remembered, wanted them to remind people once again of the man who had devoted his entire life to them.

I saw something else, too. Next to each journalist stood people — all dressed alike — who were talking loudly, noisily trying to interfere with the recording of the proceedings.

I was later told that confusion had erupted among these plainclothesmen when I began to speak: this couldn't be happening, it wasn't permitted! But no one dared stop me; they hadn't been ordered to do so.

I introduced Nadya Dimenshtein and moved to the side.

Despite her small stature, she easily scrambled up the slippery clay. Looking down on the crowd, she began to speak, her voice ringing out clearly.

She talked of Nikita Sergeyevich's time in the Ukraine, where they had worked closely together, and about how he had successfully resolved the problems that arose. Then she turned to the bloody subject of Stalinist repressions, and to Khrushchev's role in rehabilitating innocent victims.

She ended with these words: "Our Nikita Sergeyevich was always an honest, just man, a real Leninist. Farewell, dear comrade."

After her, Vadim Vasiliev spoke. He spoke first about his own pain. About his father who died too young, about his father's rehabilitation, and about other victims of that era.

"I bow deeply to you, dear Nikita Sergeyevich. The Russian people will forever remember you," he concluded.

The speeches ended. It was time for a last good-bye. The people in back began pressing forward, hoping to say a final farewell.

My friends and I linked arms, made a chain, and cleared a path. People came through our tunnel to lay flowers and bid Father good-bye. After about fifteen minutes, security men blocked the way; again pressure built up and again we intervened. The police didn't argue with me. Finally, everyone got through. The last to struggle by one after the other were foreign journalists. There were no Soviet journalists present. Like so many others, this sad event has left no documentary trace in the archives.

The time had come for our family to say adieu. Mama was barely holding up. Then it was all over. The coffin was lowered into the grave. We tossed in handfuls of earth. The gravediggers' shovels went to work; the small mound of earth was covered with a few wreaths of live flowers.

Mama couldn't hold back any longer. She covered her face with a kerchief. Anton Grigoriev carefully supported her with two hands.

At that moment, I noticed a man running along the path from the gate, a wreath in his arms. A stranger. With the satisfaction that comes from honorably doing one's duty, he managed, panting and puffing, to lay the wreath carefully on the grave. On the ribbon was this inscription: "To Nikita Sergeyevich Khrushchev from Anastas Ivanovich Mikoyan."

It turned out Sergo hadn't immediately told his father what had happened. When he arrived late Saturday night at the dacha, Anastas Ivanovich was finishing his tea and looked tired. They talked about this and that. Sergo wasn't sure he should mention Khrushchev's death with night coming on. His father would be upset and wouldn't sleep.

Sergo decided to put it off until morning. He had to leave early for the city, and so he asked the secretary assistant who lived at the Mikoyan dacha to convey the sad news.

She strongly supported Sergo's decision to put the matter off until the next day and assured him she would inform Anastas Ivanovich first thing in the morning. But, of course, she said not a word. Her controllers didn't exactly need to have Mikoyan show up at Khrushchev's funeral. Anastas Ivanovich learned of Khrushchev's death from Monday morning's *Pravda*.

Thus we buried Nikita Sergeyevich. The crowd began to disperse. I noticed a journalist, evidently a Japanese, pick up a trampled flower and place it carefully on the grave.

Mama had invited friends, relatives, and just acquaintances to Petrovo-Dalneye. As we drove there, the clouds parted and the sun appeared.

We gathered around the big table; we had pulled it apart and added extra leaves. It was tight, but there was room for all. Misha Zhukovsky perched on the same chair with Mama. Everyone spoke — some very well, some not so well, all warmly. I especially want to single out Pyotr Mikhailovich Krimerman and Mikhail Aleksandrovich Zhukovsky, who didn't know Nikita Sergeyevich before 1964. During the bad times, when old "friends" scattered, they became his companions and admirers. Today, too, they had come to share our grief, and their comments about Father rang with special sincerity.[7]

A few other episodes from that difficult day come to mind. I recall a young man, a student of journalism, who couldn't get inside the cemetery grounds, but somehow learned our address and came to the dacha to express his condolences. Afterward, he called me off and on for several years, came by once in a while, and then disappeared.

Several hours passed, and as it got pretty noisy around the table some of the guests broke up into little groups and went out to stroll around the grounds. It was then that an insignificant but memorable encounter took place. I was standing on the porch when Misha Zhukovsky ran up looking absolutely beside himself.

There was a line at the toilet, and he had been looking for a secluded spot. "I went around the corner," he said, pointing to the guardhouse, "and I hear a voice. I listened, and it was *us*, one of *us* holding forth!" He was less frightened than fascinated.

I had long since ceased to worry about such things, and I reassured him: "It's just the regular eavesdropping system."

The story about what Lev Andreyevich Artsimovich did on the day

7. Professor Zhukovsky, the reader will recall, was the doctor who treated grandson Vanya Adzhubei at the Petrovo-Dalneye dacha. Krimerman was the director of a series of photo supply stores in Moscow who helped Father a lot with his photography hobby. Both men loved to talk with Father and did so at great length.

of the funeral warmed our hearts. He couldn't attend because he was heading a delegation at a scientific congress in Switzerland. On the day of the funeral, he asked those present at the session to honor Khrushchev's memory. I don't think anyone else would have dared.

The day after the funeral, the mayor of San Francisco, George Christopher, called to express his condolences. He had arrived in Moscow the day before, on what business I don't remember. Hoping to see Father, he had brought some souvenirs. When he learned from the newspapers of the grief that had overtaken us, he ferreted out my telephone number through some mysterious means.

I shrank a bit at the prospect of seeing him: every contact with foreigners added a black mark to my official image, which already had plenty. But we agreed to meet the next day in his room in the National Hotel. I decided not to invite him to my home.

Father had met Mr. Christopher during his trip to the United States in 1959. He was the first head of the Soviet government, as well as the first secretary of the Central Committee, to set foot on American soil. Father was proud of the invitation, and saw it as recognition of the growing might of our country, of its authority in international affairs.

Preparations for the trip had taken place at the government dacha at Pitsunda. Father, Gromyko, and their aides discussed strategy on the beach, under a tent that protected them against the heat. They tried to anticipate possible surprises, and agreed on the final text of speeches. Father was excited, and he kept making the same point.

"Who would have guessed, twenty years ago, that the most powerful capitalist country would invite a Communist to visit? This is incredible. Today they *have* to take us into account. It's our strength that led to this — they have to recognize our existence and our power. Who would have thought the capitalists would invite me, a worker? Look what we've achieved in these years."

He kept ramming this into his listeners. He arrived in the United States in this mood. The visit was successful, but each side gingerly tested the other's strength.

The farther west we went on the trip around the country, the more often we encountered signs that didn't exactly welcome the Soviet guest. I remember one small place where a young man waved a placard that had "Welcome Khrushchev" on one side and "Freedom for Kazakhstan" on the other. His face radiated love of peace and genuine curiosity, and I had no doubt he had a very vague personal notion of Kazakhstan.

More and more often, local leaders' speeches contained what Fa-

ther considered interference in our internal affairs. At first, he acted as
though he didn't notice, but he was getting very irritated. He took every
word as a lack of respect for our country, and *that* Father was not about
to tolerate.

The eruption occurred in Los Angeles, at an evening reception honoring our delegation. The mayor, Norris Paulson, started talking about
the lack of personal freedom in the USSR. His barbs were the sharpest
so far. Our hosts obviously wanted to find out where Khrushchev's limit lay.

They had reached it. Father exploded. He said he represented a
great power and would not tolerate such treatment. The United States
might be accustomed to dealing with its vassals this way, but from *us*
it could expect only a well-deserved rebuff.

He spoke heatedly, loudly, and at length. The mayor kept shifting
from one foot to the other, nervously fiddling with a carafe of wine in
his hands. The audience looked on in silence, wondering how the spectacle would end.

Finally, Father began to calm down. He turned to Aleksei Andreyevich Tupolev with a question, "Is our plane ready? We can fly out of
here for home immediately. It's not so far to Vladivostok."

Rising to his feet, Aleksei Andreyevich responded: "The aircraft is
ready. We can be in Vladivostok in a few hours."

"If this continues, we're flying home," Father repeated. "We've
lived a long time without you, and we'll live some more. We insist on
being treated as an equal."

He concluded his impromptu remarks and turned to the final toast
protocol required.

The hall was buzzing at the Soviet premier's fiery performance. The
mayor took his seat looking relieved.

It appeared that the whole show was spontaneous — the explosion
of a very emotional man. But it just looked that way on the surface.
Deeper down, it was quite another matter: there, calm calculation pre-
vailed.

Following the reception, the entire delegation, including the aides
and others who accompanied Khrushchev, returned to the huge presidential suite in the hotel. Everyone except Father was confused and
depressed by what had happened. He took off his suit jacket and sat
down on a banquette. The rest of us settled ourselves in sofas and armchairs.

Father's face was stern, but there was a twinkle in his hazel eyes.

There was a long, bewildering pause. Why were we gathered here? "We represent a great power," Father began, "and we don't allow anyone to treat us like a colony."

For the next half hour, he expressed his opinion of the way our delegation had been received. He didn't stint on colorful phrases. At times his voice rose to a scream; his fury seemed to have no limits. Only his eyes, which sparkled with mischief, gave him away. Now and again Father raised a finger and pointed to the ceiling as if to say, "This isn't for you; it's for those who are listening in."

The monologue finally ended.

A minute or two passed; we all were still confused but kept still. Father wiped the sweat from his bald head — the role had demanded a fair amount of intensity — and turned to Gromyko.

"Comrade Gromyko, go at once and tell Lodge everything I just said." Henry Cabot Lodge, the former U.S. representative to the United Nations, accompanied Khrushchev around the country as the president's representative.

Andrei Andreyevich stood up, cleared his throat, and headed for the door, a gloomy resoluteness on his habitually unsmiling face. His hand was already on the doorknob when his wife, Lidia Dmitrievna, couldn't contain herself any longer.

"Andryusha, be more polite with him," she implored.

Andrei Andreyevich showed no reaction. The door closed silently behind him. I glanced at Father. There was rejoicing in his face: Lidia Dmitrievna's words proved that his speech had been convincing.

The next day, we arrived in San Francisco. It was as if they had changed hosts: all around were friendly faces, not a word was said that could possibly offend the guests.

Mayor Christopher's instincts matched the State Department's preference: guests should be received politely. From then until the end of the trip, the high-ranking Soviet guest was treated respectfully.

This memorable encounter in San Francisco sparked the mutual regard between Khrushchev and Christopher. They later exchanged souvenirs and greetings on holidays; and Christopher's attitude toward Father didn't change after his ouster.

When we met in the National Hotel, Mr. Christopher expressed deep regret that he had been unable to attend the funeral. He spoke warmly of Father and extended his sympathy to our family. He talked on and on about Khrushchev.

Finally we said good-bye. To this very day, I have warm memories of the mayor of San Francisco. I keep the pen he wasn't able to give Father as a sign of the friendship between these two men, between our two countries.

Soon after Father's death, they moved Mama to Zhukovka, a dacha community reserved for Council of Ministers personnel. It wasn't far from Petrovo-Dalneye. There, among other pensioners, she lived out the rest of her days.

In the latter part of the 1970s, I began urging her to write her memoirs. She resisted for a long time, began to write, stopped, and began again. Her memory was no longer what it had been, and many events got confused. She gave part of her manuscript to me, and after her death, in 1984, part went to my sister Rada, whence it found its way into Adzhubei's memoirs.

Mama's facts are accurate, in my view, but chronology is blurry, and the result is a real muddle. For example, she writes that Nikita Sergeyevich had a heart attack after the conversation about his memoirs with Kirilenko, but the conversation took place in April 1968, while the heart attack occurred on May 29, 1970. There are other inaccuracies.

Mama is buried next to Father in Novodevichy Cemetery. In the last years, when her legs just wouldn't obey her, she rarely visited his grave — maybe two or three times a year was all.

"Bury me here," she requested, pointing to a spot under the birches I had planted.

I didn't think I'd be able to grant her this wish. For about that time, the question of burial in Novodevichy Cemetery became extremely complicated; special permission was necessary. The most I could hope for was to be allowed to place an urn with her ashes in Father's grave.

Fate intervened to help. At the moment of her death in August 1984, Chernenko was on vacation, and Mikhail Sergeyevich Gorbachev was at the helm in Moscow. I appealed to the Central Committee business manager, asking that I be permitted to bury my mother next to my father. I received a positive reply in an hour and a half.

THE life and death of Khrushchev are inextricably bound up with the fate of our country. Totally forgotten in retirement, he has suddenly and unexpectedly sprung back into existence in connection with recent and not-so-recent developments. There is a lot of talk about Khrushchev today, to which I shall return in my conclusion. But before that, I cannot omit an account of how we barely managed to erect a monument to him in Novodevichy Cemetery.

CHAPTER SIX

THE MEMORIAL

I 'VE already mentioned that the first time I gave any real thought to a memorial headstone was on the way to the wake. I couldn't get the idea out of my head.

After the funeral, Vadim Trunin and I ended up in the same car. On the way to Petrovo-Dalneye, I asked his opinion. Hesitating only a second, he answered, "The only sculptor worth asking is Ernst Neizvestny."

At the time I knew practically nothing about Neizvestny. My world had been one of missiles and satellites, of successful and unsuccessful launches. I was firmly convinced that this was the real world. All I had heard were echoes of the scene at the Manezh Exhibition Hall, where Father had smashed the "abstractionists" and other "ideological diversionists infiltrating from the West" in modern art.

Under Stalin, all artistic schools except Socialist Realism were prohibited as "imperialist ideological sabotage." After Stalin's death, when art began to revive, hidebound party ideologues set out to make short shrift of artists they didn't like by turning Khrushchev against them. Everyone knew that Father wasn't well informed about art, that he preferred simple, easily understandable compositions, and they decided to take advantage of this. An exhibit celebrating the thirtieth anniversary of the founding of the Moscow Artists Union was being held at the Manezh Exhibition Hall across from Red Square, and Khrushchev was scheduled to pay it a visit in December 1962. On the eve of his

361

visit, champions of the long-dominant Socialist Realism arranged to have the work of certain avant-garde artists displayed at the Manezh. Meanwhile, they prepared Father in advance, explaining that the innovative works were really "anti-artistic" and ideologically hostile. Naturally, they added that real artists couldn't conceal their indignation at the modernist works. Just as they expected, Father didn't like what he saw and told off in no uncertain terms the painters and sculptors, including Ernst Neizvestny, who had been gathered there. A real argument broke out. As a result, the bureaucrats of official art obtained powerful backing in the person of Khrushchev himself.

Although I wasn't very interested in these noisy squabbles, I tried to understand where the truth lay. My usual answer, "Father is right," didn't sit right; his words rang with the usual force and conviction, but somehow they didn't convince. As it turned out (and this often happens with strong-minded people), Father sensed the weakness of his own position, and this caused him to be more harsh and uncompromising.

I was present at a conversation he once had about the film *The Ilyich Gate*.[1] The whole style and aggressiveness of his critique distressed me greatly. I remember it to this day. Gradually, I became convinced that Father was making a tragic mistake, and thereby eroding his authority. I felt I had to try to do something, but it was far from easy.

I had to choose the moment, to express my feelings to him carefully, to try to persuade him that such categorical judgments were harmful. I had to make him understand that he was fighting against his own political allies, against those who supported his cause. After all, it was Father who had personally authorized publication of Yevtushenko's *Heirs of Stalin*, Tvardovsky's *Terkin in the Other World*, and Emanuil Kazakevich's *Blue Notebook*.[2]

I remember him squabbling with Mikhail Suslov, who thought the reference to Zinoviev's first name in Kazakevich's book was unacceptable.[3] Father disagreed, laughing good-naturedly: "But that's the way

1. Marlen Khutsiev's film provoked bitter attacks for its alleged lack of progressive ideological content. The film raised ethical questions having to do with relations between the wartime and postwar generations.

2. All these works, which were banned for various reasons, were released only after their authors appealed personally to Khrushchev.

3. *Editor's note:* Grigory Zinoviev was a colleague of Lenin's who lost out to Stalin in the succession struggle of the 1920s and was later executed after a show trial in 1936. Until his name was rehabilitated under Gorbachev, Zinoviev was unmentionable except as a traitor and a spy.

it happened. What do you want, that Ilyich not call Zinoviev by his first name in Razliv? How should he address him? You can't just change history like that."

This was where their primary difference lay: should you or shouldn't you rewrite history based on contemporary interests and opinions? However, although they differed fundamentally, from time to time they would use the same ideological phraseology.

Father was considerably weaker in the labyrinth of isms, and relied more on his intuition. Toward the end of his time in office, both Suslov and Leonid Ilyichev gained in strength, to the point that it might even be said that they dominated him to a degree. He joined them in fighting against "foreign ideological influences" in literature and film, against formalism in music and sculpture, and against other such things.

My attempts to turn the conversation in this direction met with the same irritation provoked by the incident involving Lysenko: "Mind your own business! You don't understand the first thing about it. Someone said something to you, and you go around repeating it like a parrot." Our conversation was over before it had begun.

Father could discuss issues relating to agriculture, construction, and defense for hours; here he was in his element. The problem of "bourgeois ideological infiltration" was utterly foreign to him, but the thirties and forties had ingrained in him a hard-line algorithm dictating that such things must be mercilessly resisted. And he threw himself into the fight.

Sculpture and the fine arts in general constituted a "theater of military action," and the confrontation at the Manezh exhibit was one episode in the ideological battle. The plan was to use Father himself to crush the upstart intellectuals. Unfortunately, the plan was a success.

I remembered the Manezh confrontation when Vadim mentioned Neizvestny's name. I knew very little of him as an artist. But I was convinced of one thing — my father's headstone must be done by a master. It should be done in such a way that Father's image would leave no one indifferent.

Vadim's words became fixed in my mind, but I doubted he was being realistic. "Do you think he would take it on?" I asked Vadim later. "My father gave him and his friends a good tongue-lashing at the Manezh. He closed all doors to them. Neizvestny will probably just kick me out. What I'd essentially be asking him is to make a memorial for his adversary."

Trunin disagreed. "You're wrong. Neizvestny is a highly cultured man. He sees Khrushchev's personality objectively and values the role he played in our history. Of course, he hasn't forgotten what happened between them, but those events are no longer of primary significance and he sees them in a different light now."

I didn't reply right away. I wanted to agree with him, but Vadim hadn't convinced me entirely. Still, I had little choice since I wanted only the best sculptor to do my father's headstone.

"If you want, I can call him," suggested Trunin. "If he tells me to go to hell, you'll have nothing at all to do with him. If he agrees, you can go see him. I'm sure you'll be able to reach an agreement."

That brief conversation in the car on the day of the funeral was the start of a new stage in the fight for Khrushchev, and the first step toward a man whom I now think of with great affection and whom I would like to believe I can call my friend.

At the wake, I asked Yulia Leonidovna what she thought about the idea. She was considered our family's expert on culture. Without thinking about it very long, she repeated practically word for word what Trunin had said. "The only one worth considering is Neizvestny. Many feel he's the top sculptor in the country. Unfortunately, I don't know him and can't help you contact him."

Two unrelated people had told me the same thing. I decided to turn to Neizvestny and waited for some signal from Trunin, who as bad luck would have it, had disappeared somewhere. It was then that another candidate for the job turned up: Zurab Konstantinovich Tsereteli. At the time, his name was on everyone's lips. A rising star, he had collaborated in the creation of the new Lenin memorial complex in Ulyanovsk. We had become acquainted only a short while ago, but had seemed to hit it off. We met soon after Father's funeral at the home of mutual friends, where we ended up sitting next to each other at the table.

I hadn't yet spoken to Neizvestny, and the uncertainty of the situation was troubling me. My doubts were beginning to gain the upper hand. Naturally, I asked his advice: "Zurab, there should be a monument to Nikita Sergeyevich, but I don't know where to begin."

He became suddenly animated. "You don't need to look for anyone. I'll do it myself. Let's go to the cemetery tomorrow and look the place over, and I'll get to work."

I was unprepared for such a vigorous response. To tell the truth, I didn't know what to say, so I mumbled something about my plan to contact Neizvestny.

"An excellent idea! I would be glad to work with him on the project."

The next morning we went to Novodevichy. Zurab walked around the gravesite, examining everything very carefully. He paced off distances to the path and the wall, and seemed satisfied. "We're lucky there are no other graves nearby; we can put up a real monument. We'll need an area of about five by six meters. I am going home to Tbilisi today and will put together a first draft. I'll be back in a couple of days, and we can discuss it. Your job is to take care of arranging for the space."

With that we parted, feeling very pleased with each other, hardly realizing that we'd never see each other again.

Meanwhile, I launched a frontal attack to obtain a five-by-six-meter plot. That matter was much more complicated than I imagined it would be. Either no one could change the standard size for the plot, or no one wanted to. The days passed quickly as I went to office after office. It never occurred to me, as I went knocking on doors, that new characters were making their entrance onto the stage.

I had still had no news from Trunin and hadn't managed to contact Neizvestny, but those who needed to know what I was up to had managed to find out everything. My uncertain steps were analyzed, conclusions reached, decisions taken, and appropriate actions carried out.

Less than two days after the visit with Tsereteli to the cemetery, a good friend passed on a warning: "I want to give you some friendly advice," she began. "*They* aren't very happy with you. You didn't make the best impression on them with those memoirs of your father's published in the U.S. They think you deceived them. You pretended to be a simpleton but turned out to be a trickster."

"I have no idea why they think of me that way," I objected. "I always gave them straight answers to their questions."

"Okay." She shrugged. "But look what you're doing now. You've decided to put up a memorial to your father; that's only natural. But we're talking about Khrushchev! On one hand you want to ask Neizvestny, an artist whom your father abused, and on the other hand you've asked a Georgian, Tsereteli. They think that combination isn't a coincidence."[4]

---

4. *Editor's note:* Taking part in a project to honor Khrushchev was a veritable political demonstration in those years. The fact that Stalin, whom Khrushchev had unmasked, was undergoing a political semirehabilitation made the participation of his fellow Georgian, Tsereteli, seem symbolic as well.

I was amazed. I hadn't thought of the situation that way at all.

"You shouldn't talk to Neizvestny," she said, obviously transmitting their advice. "It would be best to go to the artists union and let them recommend a good sculptor. Who knows whether or not Neizvestny can manage such a complicated project; meanwhile, the political effect wouldn't be very good. He's the kind of guy who enjoys a good scandal, and a scandal is just what you don't need. Do you really want trouble with the authorities? You could ask the artists union about Neizvestny; maybe they'd even recommend him."

I wasn't exactly delighted with her advice. Although no threats had been made, it was a warning and couldn't be dismissed casually. After the affair with the memoirs, I didn't feel like annoying the authorities.

I decided to consult with Sergo. It turned out he knew Neizvestny and was ready to call him right away. Sergo had very definite ideas about the "friendly" advice I had received.

"Spit on it! You have no idea where it will lead. You and they have opposite goals: you want a good monument for your father, their main concern is to make sure the memorial doesn't stand out. Think about it. You go to the union and they'll recommend a sculptor you don't like. You'll be forced into a conflict, into arguing with them, and you'll be at a disadvantage.

"Much better to go straight to Neizvestny; just go as a man who wants to commission a memorial for his father. If you propose him to the union, they'll object, and your situation will be entirely different. If you decide to go ahead against their recommendation, it will mean a conflict."

I had to agree with him. I decided to contact Neizvestny without delay.

Sergo dialed the number. He was about to describe my problems to Neizvestny, but the sculptor cut him off. "I already know what's going on. Trunin called me, and I told him I'd be glad to meet with Sergei Nikitich. I'm inclined to accept his offer."

The next day, Sergo and I set off for the workshop. It was located near the present-day sports complex on Olympic Prospekt, in a small, one-story building that has since been torn down. After tramping up and down the cluttered courtyard, we found the right door. We knocked, entered, and found ourselves in a small entryway. On the floor stood a sculpture entitled *Orpheus Playing the Strings of His Heart*. To tell the truth, I didn't like it at the time. I had been raised to respect Socialist Realism, and my primary yardstick for evaluating a work of art was the degree of likeness. This looked nothing like its subject, not to mention the fact that the chest was torn open. Not very realistic, I thought.

It took months and years of being around Ernst Iosifovich to lead me out of the thicket of ignorance. But for the time being, I fortunately decided not to broadcast my opinions.

Neizvestny came out of a small room. He was a solidly built man of medium height, about fifty years old. He gave the impression of a kind of thickset sturdiness. I noticed his small, piercing eyes and the thin strip of mustache across his upper lip.

He greeted us politely, but it was obvious that he was sizing us up, watching our every move to figure out what sort of people we really were.

The place was small. The workshop itself was about thirty-five or forty square meters. There were also two smaller, auxiliary rooms of about eight to ten square meters each. In the one into which Neizvestny led us there stood a couch covered with an army blanket, two bookcases, a table, and a couple of chairs. That was it for furniture. On the walls hung pictures by Neizvestny.

In another room, more like a hallway, there was a workbench surrounded on the floor by various tools. Some I knew were for casting and welding, while others were unfamiliar. This was the first time I had ever been in a sculptor's workshop and I was finding it very interesting.

After a few words of introduction, Ernst Neizvestny showed us some of his work. There was so much of it that it was impossible to absorb or to make sense of it all. In the middle of the room stood a scale model of a most improbable building. At its center was the head of a man, deep in thought, while a wing strained away from him with reliefs of symbols and human faces on its surface.

"That's a study for the Palace of Thought, the central building in Akademgorodok, in Siberia," explained Ernst Iosifovich. "While your father was in power, they stopped me from working for a very long time, then they finally allowed me to continue. The design was approved in 1964, then it was shoved deep in the drawer again."

Hanging from the ceiling, all around the perimeter of the room, were drawings. Together they comprised a single colored composition, with particularly bright spots of color leaping out at you. Having finished our quick tour, we got down to the reason we had come.

"I would like to make something clear," began Neizvestny. "I went through some difficult times as a result of my arguments with Nikita

Sergeyevich, but all that's in the past. I respect him greatly, and although it may seem strange, I remember him fondly. He was a man who knew what he wanted, and one can't help being sympathetic to his aspirations, especially now when a lot of things are clearer. So let's not talk about personal grudges, but rather about a memorial for a statesman. I'm ready to take on the job."

Well, it looks like we've made a good start, I thought to myself.

Right then and there, Neizvestny began to draw a sketch on a pad: a vertical stone, one half white, the other shaded to look black, and at the bottom a large slab.

I couldn't understand what he was up to. "Why white and black? What does that mean?" I asked.

"Nothing concrete as yet. I'm trying to embody a philosophical idea. Life, and the development of humanity, progress through a constant struggle between life-asserting and death-asserting principles. Our age is an example, with its conflict between man's intellect and the machines created by his intellect that are killing him. Take the atom bomb, for instance. In the ancient world, the centaur exemplified this idea.

"In our tombstone, black and white can be interpreted in various ways: life and death, night and day, good and evil. It all depends on us, on our views, on the way we perceive the world. The coupling of black and white is the best way to symbolize unity and the struggle of life against death. These two principles are closely interwoven in every individual; therefore the two stones should be irregular, and merge to create one whole.

"The entire thing will sit on a bronze plate. I don't think it looks bad at all," he said, looking to me for a reaction.

I had decided in advance not to meddle and not to interject my opinions. You can't expect a worthwhile result if you try to second-guess the artist. One must either put one's faith in talent or be satisfied with hackwork. There's no middle ground.

"I leave the matter entirely up to you. Will there be a portrait?" I asked.

"I don't think there should be any portrait at all. We are providing a kind of symbol. A portrait is for a man whom no one knows, when what you want to do is preserve his outward appearance for posterity." Neizvestny shrugged his shoulders. "Nikita Sergeyevich's face is well known to all, so there's no need for a portrait."

He hadn't convinced me, but I kept my feelings to myself for the time being. There would be plenty of time to discuss things, and besides, I was a bit timid in the face of Neizvestny's fame.

With some trepidation, I told Neizvestny about Tsereteli and how he wanted to take part in the project. "I'll work with him, if you like," said Neizvestny simply.

"Also," I continued, "we should somehow formalize our arrangement. There should probably be a contract."

I had been made wary by the warning from Lubyanka, and I wanted to take out some sort of insurance, to legalize our relationship as much as possible. With that we parted.

My fear that further pressure would be brought against us was not unfounded. Tsereteli and Neizvestny were each invited to have a "conversation," but with opposite results. Tsereteli apparently received his warning or, if you will, his advice, the same time I received mine. He didn't bring the promised study from Tbilisi nor did he call me. For my part, I decided not to call him. I didn't see how a joint effort by him and Neizvestny could work out very well. I would be caught between two fires. Some time later, I ran into Tsereteli in the entryway to my building. He averted his eyes and slipped past.

Several years later, after the monument had been put up and everything was over and done with, Ernst Iosifovich told me his side of the story. His "conversation" had occurred in a certain well-known building shortly after Sergo and I had been to see him. He was strongly urged to decline the project. At first they tried telling him lies about me and about our family, but that primitive tactic had no effect. Next, they tried more weighty arguments. Neizvestny had been working at the time on reliefs for a new building under construction at one of the institutes in Zelenograd. It was a prestigious assignment, and his work stood a good chance of winning him a state prize. Neizvestny's "advisers" showed great concern: What if his work on Khrushchev's memorial hindered his being nominated for the prize? Wouldn't that hurt his career in general? His "well-wishers" were deeply mistaken. They hadn't mastered the psychology of their subject.

"It was their threats that made up my mind once and for all. Before that I might have hesitated because we didn't know each other well; but after talking to them, I decided to remain firm to the end."

Two such different reactions from two people, both sculptors. Which one was right? Who won? There are no answers to these questions. All I know is that Neizvestny didn't win the state prize, while Tsereteli walked away with a Lenin Prize and a state prize.

After our first meeting, the project really began to roll. The very next day we drew up our contract in the notary's office and went to the cemetery. Ernst Iosifovich promised the first sketch would be ready for inspection several days later.

I went to the cemetery. The gravesite needed to be cleaned, since autumn and the passage of time had done their work. The wreaths had wilted and the photograph of Father had been soaked. Despite all our efforts, water had seeped under the plastic.

Friends lent a hand. Back at my former design office, they made a good-quality, temporary stanchion for a new photograph enclosed in Plexiglas. Official likenesses of Father seemed inappropriate for his grave, and I wanted one that was a little more human. Let people see not a former premier, but a human being, as we had seen him only a short while ago. On the grave I put a picture from July 3, the last photograph taken while he was alive. He was dressed casually in the picture, without a necktie, and was looking at the camera with a tired smile.

Mama didn't like the picture and asked me to replace it. I resisted for a while, but she wasn't alone in her sentiment; others of my father's admirers didn't like it either. I gave in eventually, substituting a picture taken shortly before his seventieth birthday, a smiling, happy Khrushchev, with all his medals and awards on his chest. Now I see that I was wrong. Neizvestny was right: Khrushchev was a symbol and shouldn't be seen by the people with his collar open.

I kept ringing all the bells, trying to increase the size of the plot for the memorial. Neizvestny agreed with Tsereteli that the plot should be bigger, although he characterized the latter's notion as "typically Georgian in sweep."

Decisive steps had to be taken, so I appealed to the Central Committee business manager. Pavlov didn't undertake to resolve the matter himself. "I'll call Comrade Promyslov, he'll help you. Call him tomorrow."

I knew Vladimir F. Promyslov well. He and I lived in the same building and always said hello to each other. He had been appointed mayor of Moscow under my father. I was absolutely certain of a quick and favorable response. I had no notion of the kind of person my amiable neighbor had become. As it turned out, he wouldn't even speak to me. His office told me to address all my requests to his deputy, Valentin Vasilievich Bykov.

Bykov received me courteously enough but said he was in the dark as to what had been going on. He ran straightaway to Promyslov and came back dejected. "He says no one ever called him. He just snapped at me, 'Give him another thirty centimeters on each side.' I don't know what to do."

It seemed Promyslov had decided to have some fun at my expense. Bykov, on the other hand, really wanted to help and was ready to do anything he could. We agreed that by virtue of his own authority he would allocate additional space measuring two and a half by two and a half meters. Bykov signed the necessary papers then and there.

Things were moving. I thought the job would take a year, a year and a half at the outside. I couldn't have imagined it would stretch out over four long years.

When I told Mama about my visit to Neizvestny, she wasn't overjoyed. But she didn't object, either. She left the black-white motif up to the sculptor, but she categorically rejected the idea of a memorial without a portrait.

"A headstone is a deeply personal work," Neizvestny responded. "It is a memorial to someone who was close to you. Nina Petrovna's opinion should be decisive. I'll find a way to incorporate a portrait of Nikita Sergeyevich."

The work progressed. Once or twice a week I visited the studio in the evening. Ernst Iosifovich worked day and night, and sometimes we would sit up late in his small room, talking about everything: the memorial, politics, his work, my work, Neizvestny's meetings with my father, God, life in general.

As a youth of seventeen, Neizvestny had gone to fight at the front. He graduated from the military academy at Kushka and fought as a paratrooper. He had been given more than one decoration and had been seriously wounded. His spine had been broken, which put him into the category of the most seriously injured invalids. "In need of constant care," stated the conclusion in his medical records. But he refused to accept that; his character wouldn't tolerate it. The life of an invalid wasn't for him. He overcame his injury and went on to higher education in art and philosophy.

Whenever he moved heavy pieces of sculpture around, he would always say, grinning, "In need of constant care."

He had an unusually large and diverse circle of interesting friends. People were drawn to him. Evenings spent in his company often turned into noisy disputes. Sometimes, when he was in an especially good mood, Ernst Iosifovich would amuse us by telling stories — serious

stories about India, a humorous story about the half-length portrait he
did of Marshal Choibolsan, one of the leaders of the Mongolian People's Republic, or sad stories about things that had happened to him
right here in Moscow.

Each time I met him I, ignoramus that I was, understood more
about his art. Many of his pieces that had confused me before, or that
I had disliked, I now began to admire. I already mentioned the zinc
Orpheus that stood in his entryway. The more I looked at it, the more
it intrigued me. I began to see the profound philosophical statement the
work made, and I began to feel that it expressed the essence of my
father's spirit. Like Orpheus, he had given his last ounce of strength to
others. I would stand and look at the sculpture, trying to see inside it.
I had become a regular in the studio and my presence ceased to be a
distraction.

Once I even suggested to Neizvestny that we use the sculpture of
Orpheus as the memorial for my father. He was quite surprised.

"I always like to see my work displayed," he said, "but that
wouldn't do at all. We need something much more austere, more mon-
umental. Orpheus is much too frivolous; he would be more appropriate
for a memorial to a poet rather than a statesman. What I've thought
up for your father is much better, much more fitting for Khrushchev's
grave."

In getting to know Neizvestny, I tried to understand his philosophy
and views on art. Gradually I learned a bit about these things.

I was uneasy during our first several meetings. Of course Neizvestny was a great artist, but he was known as an "abstractionist," a
word that for me was not very respectable, if not downright abusive.
How would he express his artistic approach in my father's memorial?
The main thing that concerned me was that the portrait be a good
likeness. I was afraid of seeing little cubes, triangles, and distorted facial
characteristics.

One day I expressed all my fears to Ernst Iosifovich. He laughed
heartily. "Art is much simpler and more complex than that. For example, I don't consider myself a member of any artistic movement. I'm
not an abstractionist, which your father accused me of being, nor am I
a realist. Any such affiliation limits and impoverishes an artist. Every
style is good in its place. Take our memorial: Nina Petrovna would like
there to be a portrait of Nikita Sergeyevich. It should be *his* portrait,
not my vision of his philosophy expressed as a portrait. In this case,
everything must be as realistic as possible: realism bordering on natu-

ralism. That's the way it should be. And that's how I'm going to sculpt it, because it's a memorial. When you and your family come to the grave, you'll want to see your father, not my representation of him.

"Let's look at the concept of the memorial as a whole, its idea. It embodies the eternal conflict, the struggle between the bright and progressive and the reactionary. How could that be expressed in real, photographic images? Such images would distract the viewer, lead him off into the mundane. What is needed is an abstract idea reflecting the trajectory of the artist's thoughts — in our case, light and dark locked in combat."

My education continued. I had previously accepted our ideologists' argument without question: "Anyone can draw an abstract picture, but try to produce a true likeness — that takes some real sweat." I now saw that abstraction demands far more talent.

The conclusion that followed from this was a bitter one: Father had fought with the wrong people for the wrong reasons. Unfortunately, he only realized it when it was too late.

Only later did Neizvestny recount the ill-fated confrontation at the Manezh. "Why don't I, or any of my friends hold any grudge against Khrushchev? He was a contradictory person, but he pursued an honest and progressive policy. His attack on us at the Manezh was a setup. The exhibition was arranged deliberately, and they invited all of us artists to participate at the last minute. None of us could understand what the hurry was. They needed to crush us in order to survive themselves.[5]

"The artistic conflict between styles wasn't of primary importance. The main thing for them was money. At the time, I had collected a lot of evidence of corruption and bribe-taking among the bosses of the Moscow art world.

"They even invited me to join the mafia. When I refused, they decided to give battle and destroy me.

5. Here is what Gennady I. Voronov, then a member of the Central Committee Presidium, remembers (in the journal *Druzhba narodov*, January 1989): "I won't categorically confirm, but I will suggest, that the exhibition, and Khrushchev's visit to it, were specially arranged. Both the level of his artistic insight and the nature of his aesthetic views were well known to those who arranged the exhibition. If that is so, then the result of his visit could have been foretold as well." As to the identity of those who set up my father in this way, I'll limit myself to saying that they included the Moscow Artists Union mafia, in league with ideologues at the Ministry of Culture and the Central Committee.

"This all started long ago, when I was still a student at the institute. They announced a closed competition for the design of a monument commemorating the three hundredth anniversary of the union between the Ukraine and Russia. They had chosen a site on the square at the Kiev railway station and had laid the foundation.

"This was the first and last truly closed competition. I was a third-year student, but I won it. The model of my *Bandura Player* is over there on the shelf.[6] Your father saw a photograph of it; he liked it, at least he never said anything against it. Everyone else praised me, and the newspapers wrote about how a former frontline soldier who was now a student had won. But they didn't erect the monument, and they never will.

"The pretexts were quite plausible: they hadn't allocated the resources, there wasn't any concrete, the stone wasn't available, the excavator had broken down. But the truth lay elsewhere.

"At the time, I wanted to join the Moscow section of the artists union. Everyone was 'in favor,' and they accepted me. Right away they took me aside and began explaining the facts of life: 'Sculptors get big honoraria — you can live well. Of course, there's a certain, shall we say, unofficial procedure. We take turns: today you won the competition, tomorrow it'll be someone else. We all play by these rules — and you'd be well advised to do likewise.'

"I was young and hotheaded in those days, so I said, 'Fuck off! If it's a competition, it's got to be honest. Anyway, I'll beat you all with sheer talent!'

" 'We'll see about that,' they jeered.[7] 'Without us, you'll have no future.'

"Unfortunately, they knew what they were talking about. They didn't exhibit a single one of my works in Moscow: not the *Bandura Player* at the Kiev station, not the wings on the square in front of the Zhukovsky Academy,[8] not the *Builder of the Kremlin*. Yet these were all commissioned by government decree, and had powerful high-level supporters. Shepilov took a personal interest in the *Builder of the Kremlin*. But again, either there was no cement, or no stone, or no workers.

---

6. The bandura is a Ukrainian stringed folk instrument. The bandura player sits holding the bandura on his knees.

7. I am deliberately omitting the names Neizvestny revealed to me.

8. Neizvestny referred to the Professor Nikolai Yegorovich Zhukovsky Higher Engineering Academy of the Soviet Air Force.

Time went by, and you just had to write it off. Everybody forgot about what had been decided earlier.

"I got angry and put together a whole dossier on the bribe-taking of our maîtres and the top people at the ministry. There was one department head to whom everybody gave a 'backrub.' For some reason, that's what they called payoffs.

"I decided to get this out into the open, to expose the mess. I'd go to Khrushchev. I called Vladimir Semyonovich Lebedev, who set a day and time for a meeting.

"In my youthful naïveté, I blabbed the secret to someone. The evening before the meeting, I dropped by the National Hotel for dinner. Some guys I didn't know sat down next to me. One thing led to another, and a fight started. You know me — it's not easy to get the better of me. When I was a commando they taught me not how to hit, but how to kill. But this time I wasn't dealing with errand boys — those guys were experts. They beat me up quite professionally.

"Next day I had to go to the Central Committee. Someone had already reported 'the drunken debauch engaged in by the sculptor Neizvestny.' I couldn't go to Lebedev and open his eyes with bruises under my own.

"I called and begged off, claiming illness. He grunted sympathetically and postponed our meeting, but it never took place.

"They decided to finish me off at the Manezh and teach others a good lesson at the same time. We all stood around by our pieces on exhibit, waiting to see whether your papa would show up. He had never seen us before; he didn't know us or anything about our work. Of course, they had already explained everything to him; they had primed him and were bringing him now just to confirm our 'bourgeois idealism' and 'abstractionism.'

"That was where our stormy conversation took place. You know, I felt that the fact that I wouldn't give in actually pleased your father, the fact that I jabbed back at him the way he did at me. He always respected strong people. When he announced at the end that I didn't even know my own profession — and his whole entourage happily nodded agreement — I said to him: 'Why don't you appoint a commission to find out?'

"He stopped short, stared at me intently, and in very different, much calmer voice said: 'We'll do just that.'

"On the spot, he barked out an order: 'Appoint an authoritative commission — let *it* determine what he's really capable of.'

"Then he left.

"To be sure, there were some who understood everything. After it was all over, Lebedev whispered to me, 'If it gets real bad, call me. We'll pick the right moment and report to Nikita Sergeyevich.'

"It all began after the Manezh. They thought they could act with impunity, so they came at me like tigers at live meat. First they accused me of stealing bronze, a strategic raw material. Again they denounced me to Khrushchev.

"They started an investigation. I turned out to be clean. I proved that I had collected old stuff for my casting — faucets, mortar, scrap. So they failed.

"Then they dredged up the accusation of lack of professional fitness: I didn't know *how* to do realist sculpture, and that's why my works were abstract. Professionals said this, academicians!

"I reminded them that Khrushchev had ordered the appointment of a commission. They got the commission together. In their presence, over the course of a few days, I made a two-and-a-half-meter sculpture of a steelworker pouring steel — all exactly according to the canon of Socialist Realism. Here's a photograph. They circulated it around the union. I received the kind of fee I had never even dreamed of. But it wasn't art, just an odd job. No thought involved at all.

"Again they had misfired. So they decided to call a meeting. They accused us of lack of patriotism.

"We, the accused, had served at the front, been wounded, decorated — while our accusers managed to spend the war safely defending the Motherland in the rear. So we decided to have a little joke: we arrived in soldiers' blouses with battle decorations on the chest and stripes indicating wounds. But the people on the tribune still droned on about patriotism.

"I didn't get to see Khrushchev. I called Lebedev, who kept putting it off; either he was busy or he simply thought the time wasn't right.

"Later he helped me. Evidently, he had reported to Khrushchev: in 'sixty-four they suddenly commissioned my design for the Palace of Thought in Akademgorodok. But if your luck's bad, it's bad. I had just started to get into the thing when they dumped your father. Once again it came to nothing.

"Now they were the winners, and they[9] gave me a warning.

9. Neizvestny was referring to sculptors whom he considered members of the Moscow Artists Union mafia. Once again, I deliberately omit specific names.

" 'Sit still. Don't make a move. No matter who decides what or where — not one of your works will ever be put up in Moscow.'

"It seems they were right. So you see, my misadventures involve your father very slightly indeed. He himself turned out to be the victim of a well-thought-out provocation, and when all's said and done, he suffered more than I did. They settled accounts with us and deprived him of allies, all with one blow at the Manezh."

NEIZVESTNY continued working on the tombstone. The job of doing a portrait turned out to be anything but simple. Variation after variation was discarded. At first he put a bust on a stele in front of the stone, but that destroyed the composition's harmony. Then he removed the stele, leaving a bust that simply emerged from the stone and hung, as it were, without any support. Ernst Iosifovich made plaster models of all these variations.

Finally, he found a solution: a bronze head the color of old gold would stand in a niche on white marble, against a background of black granite.

We had many arguments about the color of the head. I tried to persuade Neizvestny to give it a darker tone, but he didn't agree. Finally we decided to do it in old gold, the more so since the bronze would inevitably darken with time.

Half a year was devoted to these efforts. Summer 1972 came. The idea for the tombstone had taken final shape; it remained to carry it out. We decided to give formal family approval to the project. Mama and Rada came to the studio; Yulia wasn't in town, and Lena was already mortally ill.

Ernst Iosifovich related his ideas in detail. The tinted mock-up stood on a revolving base in a large room. We talked, asked questions, listened to the answers, and approved the general design.

There was still a lot to do before beginning to erect the monument. First, the details of the monument itself had to be worked out; but the main problem was to get it approved by the artistic council of the Russian Republic Art Fund. Without its official seal on the drawings, the factory wouldn't undertake to do the work, nor could it be erected in Novodevichy Cemetery.

Ernst Iosifovich didn't hide his fear of the council; his experience with it was too rich and sad. But to our astonishment, everything went smoothly. After a half-hour discussion, the members of the art fund council congratulated Neizvestny on his great artistic success. Our joy knew no bounds.

By the way, a curious thing happened at the council. While Ernst Iosifovich was preparing his presentation, I bustled about, moving the mock-up from one place to another, answering questions, asking the secretary if he had a draft of the council's decision.

When it was all over, the council secretary turned to Neizvestny: "What's your collaborator's name?"

At first Ernst Iosifovich didn't understand. He was startled and he answered defensively: "I work alone."

But then he smiled and said, "This man is a client, not a collaborator. Let me introduce you to Sergei Nikitich Khrushchev."

We had a good laugh about that.

Certain practical problems surfaced. We had to decide where to get the materials for the tombstone. Bronze was considered a strategic metal, so to obtain it you had to get special permission from the USSR Council of Ministers. The business manager of the council, Mikhail Sergeyevich Smirtyukov, helped us on this. He responded to my request without hesitation, and the next day some bronze was allocated. Simultaneously, the Moscow City Council's Construction Materials Office was charged with helping us obtain the stone. The office wanted to be of assistance, as its director had begun his career under my father in the early fifties and recalled him with great warmth. But they didn't have a stone of the required size — almost two and a half meters high — nor would they be able to get one. It wasn't a standard size.

Ernst Iosifovich insisted on a special order. They didn't turn us down, but they warned that such stones are produced by blasting, which produces insidious microcracks that can show up only at the last moment, during the final polishing of the finished work. Standard-size stones, cut by special machines, don't have cracks.

It was tempting. If we went ahead with the special order, who would pay for the waste that might result? And how many months or years might the work take? Ultimately, it was up to the artist. The problem was whether the design could be altered without destroying the concept.

The to-ing and fro-ing went on for several days, then finally Neizvestny made up his mind. In the new version, the black half and the white half each consisted of three standard-dimension stones.

"It's even better," he said in a satisfied voice. "The sculpture has become more dynamic."

Now came the final step, finding someone to execute the work. The Construction Materials Office recommended a factory in Vodniki. Armed with a letter from the Council of Ministers Business Office, we went there, only to be disappointed.

It was 1972, a time when the name Khrushchev was mentioned only in connection with "voluntarism" and "subjectivism," or sometimes even in the context of the "historic decisions" of the October 1964 plenum.

We appeared at the factory in the summer. The director being away on vacation, we were received by the chief engineer, a pompous, self-satisfied fellow. I don't remember his name. Giving us a casual nod, he said: "Have a seat. What do you want?" He seemed to bulge with a sense of his own importance.

Neizvestny began to explain, and I produced the letter from the Business Office. All this had no effect whatsoever. Our host remained ice-cold.

"We can't take on this work," he declared importantly. "We're swamped with important assignments. The Ninth Directorate of the KGB" — he pronounced the words with relish — "has commissioned us to repair the Lenin Mausoleum. We can't risk disrupting the schedule for you."

Puffing himself up even more, he went on: "I don't think you want stone anyway. Khrushchev himself was all for reinforced concrete — he even wanted to shut our plant. So you ought to do his monument in reinforced concrete. Just concoct something fancy. I was abroad recently," he couldn't refrain from boasting. "They've got a lot of stuff like that there."

We obviously weren't going to get anywhere with him. Neizvestny's face turned red and his nerves were tight as a drum. His mustache twitched at such boorish behavior, his eyes bored into the offender's, he seemed ready to handle this jerk commando-style. Ernst Iosifovich didn't tolerate insults from anyone, and it was only with great difficulty that I restrained him.

"Let's not stir up trouble and compromise what we want to achieve," I told him. That argument alone saved the chief engineer's face from undergoing unplanned restructuring.

We left in a hurry, never to return.

The art fund had its own plant in Mytishchi. Knowing there was always a considerable waiting period, we hadn't gone there at first; now we had no alternative.

Pavel Ivanovich Novoselov, the director, received us courteously, but his response to our inquiry was rather discouraging. Before any project could be launched, it had also to be approved by the Chief Architectural Planning Administration (GlavAPU) of the Moscow City Council.

Neizvestny feared this outfit even more than the art fund council. At first he wanted to try to outfox them by simply presenting the finished tombstone.

While we were occupied with all this busywork, autumn crept in unnoticed. And we hadn't even had time to approach GlavAPU yet.

Meanwhile, rumors about the proposed tombstone had already circulated rather widely, and many people took a lively interest. My friends, and people who had always wished Father well, wanted to know what kind of memorial would be placed on his grave. How were things going? When would the monument be installed? Endless questions.

I decided to show the plans to the people closest to me. Neither Mama nor Neizvestny objected. One September day, a couple of friends went with me to the studio, where my niece Yulia was waiting for us. Nothing indicated any impending misfortune. When we entered the studio, she was already there, engaged in animated conversation with Neizvestny. Standing next to Yulia, buried in his beard, was a friend of hers, the film scenarist Igor Itskov. She hadn't warned us he'd be there; and his presence greatly troubled me. We all knew very well where he worked. I had my doubts but didn't say anything. I couldn't exactly kick him out.

The events of recent months, and the courteous assistance of the Council of Ministers Business Office, had dulled our vigilance. The "preventive" discussions with me and with Ernst Iosifovich, the disappearance of Tsereteli, the warnings and hints — all that had somehow faded into the background.

Neizvestny displayed his models and talked about his work, including versions of the memorial he had rejected. Everyone was pleased.

Itskov asked about the idea embodied in the tombstone.

"In a philosophical sense, life itself is based on antagonism between two principles," Neizvestny declared in his usual way. "One is bright, progressive, dynamic; the other is dark, reactionary, static. One strains to move forward, the other pulls back. This basic idea fits Nikita Sergeyevich's image quite well. He began to lead our country out of the darkness, and he exposed Stalin's crimes. The dawn broke for all of us, heralding the imminent rise of the sun. The light began to dispel the darkness.

"This approach helps us to understand the basic ideas reflected in the tombstone. The main component is white marble, its dynamic form bearing down on black granite. The darkness resists, struggles, refuses to yield — as with man himself. It's no accident that the head is on a white pedestal, or that the background remains dark. In the upper corner of the white is a symbolic representation of the sun. Rays extend down from it, dispelling the darkness. The head, the color of old gold on white, not only pleases the eye, it's also a symbol: the Romans immortalized their heroes this way. It all rests on the sturdy foundation of a bronze slab. It can't be budged. There's no reversing the process that's begun.

"On the left of the slab, seen from the stele, there's a heart-shaped aperture. Red flowers ought to grow there, to symbolize enthusiasm and self-sacrifice.

"Then there are the letters: on one side KHRUSHCHEV NIKITA SERGEYEVICH, and on the other the dates of birth and death. Nothing else, no explanation of any kind. It all has to be laconic, majestic.

"Remember the inscription on Suvorov's grave? 'Here Lies Suvorov.' That's it. Nothing about rank, decorations, medals."

It was the first time Ernst Iosifovich had explained his concept in such detail to strangers. Usually he limited himself to a few general comments about good and evil, life and death.

Later, when we ran into trouble, he justified himself by saying, "You brought your friends, and I thought I could speak freely."

Soon after this meeting, we had to suspend our activity for a while. Neizvestny had long planned to go to Poland on private business, but he had been obliged to postpone the trip. Today it's difficult to imagine the difficulties he had arranging it, but permission finally came through, and at the end of the year he was able to leave.

The Polish friends who had invited him had scheduled an extensive program; he wouldn't return until the New Year. This forced interruption didn't occasion any special concern, because for all practical purposes the work was finished. It was even a good thing: in the meantime, everything would be settled, and one could look at the project with a fresh eye. Next we would get final permission, and then off to the factory.

With a light heart, I saw my friend off on his journey. He was elated: it wasn't a long journey, but at least it was abroad.

Ernst Iosifovich wanted to arrange a small exhibition of his works in Poland. At the time, there was no way he could get official permission, so he decided to take only a few engravings with him. They would attract less attention and wouldn't take up much space.

Because the sheets were quite large, the problem of transporting them without damage arose. Rummaging around in my dacha attic, I came across a huge suitcase. At one time, it had contained Father's uniforms; Mama had neatly packed them up after the war. Now it was empty.

I gave the suitcase to Neizvestny. The engravings fit nicely on the bottom without being crumpled. Neizvestny liked the sturdy old leather-belted canvas suitcase, besides which he got a kick out of setting off on a journey with Khrushchev's luggage.

After Ernst Iosifovich left, our work came to a standstill, and only rarely did I call the studio to check up on the news from Poland.

Neizvestny returned toward the end of January or the beginning of February. He was full of impressions. He had been warmly received, the exhibition of his engravings had been a success, and he had promised them to the organizers.

But there was an amusing episode at the border on the way to Poland: the odd-looking, outsize suitcase caught the eye of the Soviet customs official. Neizvestny didn't have any contraband, but when they got down to the engravings he became a bit concerned. He wasn't an officially approved artist, and he hadn't obtained special permission to export his work. Not without reason, we had feared there'd be red tape, consultations, and in the end, a refusal. Now they could hold up the engravings.

The customs official listlessly picked through the suitcase until he reached the engravings. A palpably bewildered expression appeared on his face. He obviously hadn't encountered art of that style. He looked at one, two, three — ten sheets in all. His perplexity was growing; he didn't know what to do.

"What's this? Whose drawings are these?" he finally asked.

"They're mine," Neizvestny answered casually. "Drew them myself."

"I see," the customs man said with relief, slamming the suitcase shut. "You can go."

A lot had changed during Neizvestny's absence. I don't know who reported Ernst Iosifovich's candid remarks, but one thing was certain: the authorities reacted very badly, a fact that was brought to the attention of everyone involved in the construction of the Khrushchev monument.

We alone remained ignorant of this, and so we counted on finishing the work in 1973.

It was time to get GlavAPU's approval. We started at the bottom, in the section where they usually stamp "Approved" on a project. Ernst Iosifovich knew all the angles there. A lady he knew leafed through our papers, heaved a sigh, expressed her sympathy — and said there was no way to avoid having the work examined at a session of the artistic council. She put us on the waiting list.

We arrived early on the appointed day so as to have a look around and set up the model just the way we wanted it. The circumstances were much more pompous and imposing than at the art fund: a huge hall, a huge table, a small multitude of people.

The model attracted a lot of attention; unquestionably, many had come especially for "Neizvestny and Khrushchev." When the council members entered the hall, they gave the works on display a cursory inspection, then suddenly their gaze fell upon the familiar image of Khrushchev. With this, they came alive; some looked around intently with conspiratorial expressions on their faces.

It wasn't accidental, I think, that the chief architect of Moscow, Mikhail Vasilievich Posokhin, wasn't present. His deputy, Comrade Burdin, had been appointed to chair the meeting.

The session began. The first item of business involved discussing designs for memorial plaques on buildings. As usually happens during such meetings, everyone yawned and stared into space.

At last our turn came.

Burdin briefly presented the work, then Neizvestny took the floor. Everything went normally, in businesslike fashion. We didn't know that the necessary job had already been done on the council members: the scenario called for them to turn us down, but only after a "democratic, creative discussion."

Having made his presentation, Ernst Iosifovich answered numerous questions, and then the discussion began. It was my first time at such an assemblage. It would have been fascinating if it hadn't involved something on which we'd expended our blood. I was extremely worried.

It all came down to this: the project was very interesting, but the black-white symbolism wasn't clear.

"Such a contrast," the sculptor Tsigal observed, "breaks up the composition, and indicates the artist's lack of taste. Wouldn't it be better to keep the form but substitute gray granite? And perhaps smooth out the sharp corners?"

Neizvestny sat silently, staring at the floor and breathing noisily through his nose. He and Tsigal had studied together, but their creative paths had led them into different camps. The flood of words left me at a loss. I was about to say something, but Ernst Iosifovich hissed: "Keep quiet. It will get worse."

The next speaker took the floor. The proposed monument seemed much too tall to him; it would oppress the viewer. He recommended reducing the height from two meters thirty centimeters to two meters ten centimeters. I didn't understand a thing; it was as if he were talking about the height of the entryways in apartment houses.

The spectacle continued. A new member of the council had the floor; he too was bothered by the black and white. Another alternative was proposed: red porphyry, symbol of the revolution, of Khrushchev's revolutionary past. The gathering liked this idea. Other speakers supported it, with this addition — that it would be good to make the memorial fifty times larger. In that case the tombstone, or more precisely not a tombstone but a cyclopean structure, would be seen to best advantage on a large city square. The author of the proposal didn't specify which square.

Along with all the other views came a proposal to place a bust on a stele — like the ones at the Kremlin wall. I don't remember who suggested this, and at the time I didn't pay much attention. It soon became clear that the idea hadn't arisen accidentally, but was the product of a lot of mind-numbing discussion in various offices. The bureaucrats liked the ordinariness, the lack of thought, the adherence to established standards.

Following a "detailed and comprehensive discussion," the project was not approved. My presentation — in which I cited Nina Petrovna and the family — didn't help.

The decision rang out: "Project to be returned to the artist for revision taking into account comments expressed, then resubmitted."

We put the mock-up in a case and, downcast, went back to the studio. Friends were waiting, but we didn't bring anything to make them happy.

Ernst Iosifovich did a terrifically funny imitation of the speeches at the session, but he didn't know what to do next. Somebody suggested writing to Brezhnev. When I recalled my own unsuccessful attempt to contact him in 1968, they dropped the proposal.

Everyone was perplexed. Why the sharp change in the official attitude toward the project? Only a few months earlier, the doors had been wide open. Somebody recalled that comments on the monument had appeared in the Western press. Apparently, it had been reported that the black-white combination reflected the contradictions in our society and in the role of Khrushchev himself in the process of democratization. And so on. Where and how they got this information is hard to say. Many people had seen the project, and there was a lot of interest in it. Exactly what caused the reversal in official attitude remains unclear. Perhaps the Western press comments played a role; during these years especially, our functionaries had an allergic reaction to almost any such publicity, whether in the West or the USSR. What is clear is that someone who had seen the project must have denounced it to authorities.

We parted without having come up with any ideas. The next day, I began trying to call highly placed people, but things had changed there, too. It hadn't been easy to get through to the Council of Ministers Business Office earlier, but it had been possible. Now Smirtyukov became elusive. Either he was with Kosygin, or he was discussing the five-year plan, or he was somewhere else.

It was the same at GlavAPU, where they informed me that Posokhin either had "just left" or "hasn't come in yet." He sent Burdin, who cheerlessly tried to convince me of the necessity of revising the project. I wouldn't agree, knowing from past experience that as soon as I gave in, there would be nothing at all left of the monument.

It was the combination of black and white that disturbed my interlocutors most. They kept trying to figure out what it concealed, each of them coming up with his own interpretation, one more terrible than the other.

Full of emotion, I said to Burdin: "You think the black personifies Brezhnev? What stupidity! The monument will stand forever. If we accept your interpretation, then what shall I do with it when Brezhnev dies?"

Burdin kept silent. He was powerless; the decision had been made elsewhere.

Neizvestny's spirits fell, but somehow, slowly, he kept working on the project. At the time of our unsuccessful council debut, the stone and the slab had been worked over thoroughly. He hadn't even started on the head, and he didn't want to expend his efforts in vain. Nevertheless, I managed to convince him to begin work on the portrait.

Difficulties arose immediately. In those first hours after Father's death, I had been too upset to think of a death mask. Now the mold would have to be based on photographs.

At first it seemed Ernst Iosifovich had found a way out. He thought he remembered that the president of the Academy of Art, Nikolai Vasilievich Tomsky, had a bust for which Khrushchev had posed.

"I don't like Tomsky's work at all," Neizvestny said, "but you can't deny he's an excellent portraitist. If your father sat for it, then we can use the bust instead of the original."

I tried to dissuade him. I didn't recall that Father had ever posed for a sculpture. Nevertheless, I called Tomsky. He wasn't about to talk to me either. Instead, an assistant responded dryly: "Yes, we've got a portrait, but it's the property of the Ministry of Culture. It can't be lent to anyone without their approval."

Listening to my account, Neizvestny muttered, "We'll get along without them, we'll work from photographs."

This fruitless struggle with various agencies took up all of 1973, and now it was 1974. Mama was upset, even though each time I tried to calm her by saying, "Just one more little step, one last call . . ." But each call wasn't the last, and beyond each little step waited another. My mood deteriorated a little more each day. The deputy chief architect, Burdin, the city council, and the Council of Ministers all recommended doing a bust on a stele. This variant suited everyone except our family. The tombstone would be featureless, expressing nothing, just what they wanted.

I came up with a new argument: so long as the family, not the state, was footing the bill, then we had the final say. We would never approve a bust on a stele.

We had reached a stalemate. Each side looked for a way out of the situation. Rumor reached us that the Moscow City Council wanted to assume the costs. That meant *they* would have the final say.

I stubbornly insisted on a second review by the GlavAPU artistic council. Burdin broke down and promised to approve the project.

Once again we were sitting in the same hall, with the same mock-up. Burdin kept his word. The tone of the discussion had changed. Those who spoke acknowledged that they could approve the revised project[10] — with some critical comments. Up until the session itself, there had been no mention of any such comments; they appeared at the last minute and transformed the approval into a worthless piece of paper.

The final text of the decision ran as follows:

> Taking into consideration the urgent request of Nikita Serge-yevich Khrushchev's family, the artistic council of the Main Architectural Planning Administration of the Moscow Execu-tive Committee approves artist E. I. Neizvestny's project for N. · S. Khrushchev's tombstone. However, the artistic council rec-ommends that lowering the height of the wall and changing the material to gray granite be considered. Further, the artistic council deems it advisable to substitute a tombstone in the form of a bust on a stele for the proposed project.

I thought we had won since we had the word "approves." Neiz-vestny was skeptical, and he turned out to be right. While he and I were arguing, the art fund council annulled its positive decision. We now had good cause to give up.

I tried to catch Posokhin, but he was keeping out of sight. Finally, I went to his apartment. That was the last straw for him. "It doesn't make any difference whether I like the project or not," he declared categorically. "Until they give the command from on high, I'm not going to approve anything. I won't sign a single piece of paper."

The circle was closed. On top of everything else, more misfortune knocked at our door. A new man, a retired colonel who had com-manded one of the Gulag camps in the north, became director of the main administration in charge of cemeteries. I don't remember his name. In one stroke, he reversed the earlier decision authorizing en-largement of the plot for the monument.

I waited half a day in his reception room until he finally deigned to receive me — and rudely refused my request that he reconsider.

I called Bykov, the deputy mayor. He was astonished at the arro-gation of power and immediately summoned the new director. I came along, too. Five minutes sufficed for the restoration of justice; the issue of reducing the space for the monument no longer existed.

---

10. Actually, there had been no revision in the design. "Approve the revised proj-ect" was simply a ritualized bureaucratic phrase.

Valentin Vasilievich Bykov was unique in his decency. He was the only man who didn't change his opinions, the only one who kept his word.[11]

It had become abundantly clear that no decision would be forthcoming from the lower echelons of power. One had to get to the very top.

I suggested we begin with Viktor Grishin. He was secretary of the Moscow party committee, had worked side by side with my father for many years, and had often been in our home. Neizvestny got the telephone number, and to my astonishment I quickly reached Grishin's aide, a man named Izyumov. He promised to report to Grishin. A week later the answer came: "These questions are not within our competence. It's a matter for the Moscow City Council and GlavAPU on the one hand, and the Council of Ministers Business Office on the other. Talk to them. We can't help."

A rumor reached Neizvestny that was obviously designed for our ears. In a conversation with his aide, Grishin allegedly lamented his inability to help in the matter: "If the situation were different, naturally I'd give permission. But it's developed in such a way that I can't do anything."

The refusal thoroughly discouraged us. Except for Brezhnev himself, there was no one else to call.

With great reluctance, I took on the task. There was no other way.

Since I had last tried to reach the general secretary's office in 1968, all the telephone numbers had been changed. Trying to find the new ones took up the better part of a month. Having at last reached the Secretariat, I stated my business. They advised me to consult Georgy Emanuilovich Tsukanov, an aide to Leonid Ilyich, and gave me his number.

Once again I made innumerable unsuccessful attempts to get through. I don't remember how many calls it took, but finally I heard a lordly voice: "Yes, I'm listening."

"Hello, Comrade Tsukanov," I said agitatedly. "This is Sergei Nikitich Khrushchev. I'm calling about erecting a monument to my father.

---

11. *Editor's note:* Had the various officials who put obstacles in the way of the Khrushchev monument actually been ordered to say no, or had they simply not been told to say yes? "The problem," Sergei Khrushchev answered, "was that in the absence of any instructions, they feared to say yes. They would not risk much by cooperating with me, but it was easier not to help us. Bykov really ran no risk at all; he was just more honest and more decent than the others."

The whole thing's come to a halt. We've been beating our heads against a wall for a year and can't get anything done. Our only hope is that Leonid Ilyich will help."

"I don't understand why you've called *me*. The Council of Ministers Business Office handles such matters — call there." He sounded extremely displeased.

"I've tried for a year to settle the problem with them, but I can't get any sense out of them. That's the only reason I've turned to you."

I began to speak faster, knowing that my cause had just about had it.

"You think we don't have anything more important to do? We're not involved in this business, and we're not going to *get* involved."

"But who can help me?" I pleaded, almost in despair.

The dial tone indicated Tsukanov had hung up on me. Now what could we do? There was no way of knowing. Go higher? Only the Lord God was higher. March 1974 came to an end.

I wanted very much to avoid involving Mama in all this. In her old age she didn't need to suffer the behavior of boors. But there was no way around it. I explained the situation to her briefly; to my surprise, she listened calmly.

"I told you long ago that it was time for me to get involved. All right, I'll call Kosygin."

I didn't think it would work. Such tactics had brought too many disappointments. It didn't take long to reach Kosygin. Upon learning who was calling, a secretary said that Aleksei Nikolayevich was busy, asked for Mama's number, and promised to get back in touch at the first opportunity.

An hour and a half later, the telephone rang. "Nina Petrovna? This is Kosygin's secretary. I'm going to connect you with Aleksei Nikolayevich."

Kosygin was cordial and attentive. He asked about Mama's health and lamented the passing years. Then, turning to business, he said, "All right, I'm listening, Nina Petrovna. What's happened?"

Mama told him in a few words about our misfortunes. Kosygin listened without interrupting. "And you yourself, do you like this design for the monument?" That was his only question.

"Yes, of course I like it — otherwise I wouldn't be calling."

"All right. I'll have someone look into it. We have your telephone number. Someone will call you."

He said a kindly good-bye.[12]

Mama called me at work and told me about the conversation. Encouraged, I decided to go to Neizvestny's studio immediately with the joyful news. I had just replaced the receiver when my phone rang again. The deputy director of the Council of Ministers Supply Department (in charge of construction, supplies, and related matters), Vladimir Alekseyevich Leontiev, wanted me to provide a drawing for the monument as quickly as possible so that a report could be made to Kosygin.

The machine was in motion. A day later, the colored drawing lay on Leontiev's desk. He looked at it a long time, turned it this way and that, then said, "Comrade Posokhin has given us his version of the tombstone — a bust on a stele, like the monuments near the Kremlin wall. What do you think — shall we report both proposals?"

He showed me a small sheet of notebook paper with a slapdash india ink sketch of a bust on a stele.

I objected, citing all my arguments. They didn't work.

"Well, we'll see," said Leontiev. "We'll send both of them forward and inform you of the decision."

The suspenseful wait began. A week passed. Silence. Unable to restrain myself, I called the Supply Department. "Aleksei Nikolayevich still hasn't looked at anything," they told me. "As soon as we report to him, we'll inform you."

More waiting. Another week passed.

The call finally came on a sunny April day as I and my co-workers at the office were getting ready to go to Leninsky Prospekt, to our regular assigned lamppost, the one marked number 88. Along with groups of people from other offices, we were supposed to greet some visiting dignitary, I don't recall whom, on his way into town from the airport.

They caught me going out the door. It was the chief of the Supply Department office that was handling my case.

---

12. *Editor's note:* Was Kosygin, too, more decent than the others? Or was he simply so powerful that he didn't have to be "indecent"? Or was it that Brezhnev himself really didn't care anymore by this time? Sergei Khrushchev: "As far as I know, there had never been any high-level ban on our project. If there had been, Kosygin wouldn't have given his approval. Of the functionaries who opposed us, some feared to make a mistake by helping us, while others had hated Khrushchev and were now getting their revenge. As chairman of the Council of Ministers, Kosygin was sufficiently independent to act. Moreover, he had preserved a certain amount of human decency, witness his having allowed Svetlana Alliluyeva to travel to India, as mentioned in chapter three."

"Aleksei Nikolayevich has examined the drafts. We would like you to come in."

"What's the decision?" I couldn't hold back.

"I can't tell you anything on the phone. You'll have to come down."

I dashed to my car. It wasn't easy to get to Razin Street that day. In preparation for the ceremonial procession, they had already begun closing Leninsky Prospekt. I had to thread my way through the back streets. At last I arrived and rushed up the stairs to the office.

Leontiev's colleague greeted me warmly: "Congratulations. Let's go see Comrade Leontiev. He's waiting for us."

Leontiev recounted the meeting with Kosygin.

"Aleksei Nikolayevich looked over the drafts and gave the order to erect the monument. He thinks that if the family has approved it, there's no reason for the Business Office or anyone else to interfere. We've already called Comrade Posokhin. Get in touch with him — he'll give the necessary orders. If there's a hitch, or if you need assistance, don't be shy — call us. We'll help you."

"The Russian Republic Ministry of Culture has to allocate the bronze," I recalled. "They'll need a letter."

"We'll do it immediately. Just tell us how the letter has to be worded."

"And an order has to be given to the plant." In my mind I was feverishly sorting through all our problems.

"We'll issue it today."

Leontiev was obviously pleased with the way things had worked out. The source of our troubles wasn't his office, but rather another one [Central Committee headquarters — ed.] located nearby.

Returning to work, I dialed Posokhin's number first thing. The secretary, who in recent months had almost run out of pretexts to get rid of me, now sounded as though I were her close relative.

"How wonderful that you've called, Sergei Nikitich. Mikhail Vasilievich has been trying to find you — every five minutes he asks if I've been able to get hold of you. We just couldn't locate you anywhere. I'll put you through. And just in case, may I please have your telephone number?"

Posokhin was the very personification of goodwill: "Hello, Sergei Nikitich! I already know everything. My congratulations! They called me from the Council of Ministers. We'll approve your project immediately!"

"When does the artistic council meet?"

"What are you talking about? No council is necessary! We'll stamp it today. When can you come by?"

"Immediately. I have the blueprints with me."

"But can't we stamp the drawing that Aleksei Nikolayevich had?" Posokhin stammered.

I was on the point of erupting in laughter.

"Impossible," I replied sternly. "We've got to have several copies — for you, the art fund, the plant, for me. Nothing else will do. Especially since the drawing doesn't have the dimensions and the blueprints do. Otherwise, there'll just be new misunderstandings about the height — two hundred thirty centimeters or two hundred ten centimeters."

Posokhin was silent for a moment, weighing his response. "Come on over. I'll be waiting."

Posokhin's reception room was crowded; his associates rushed to congratulate me. Many of them had been on my side earlier; they liked the monument. Today they all were delighted.

I went up to the door of Posokhin's office, but his secretary politely but firmly restrained me. "Sergei Nikitich, you have to go to the chief of section," she said, giving the man's name. "He'll sign everything."

"But why not Mikhail Vasilievich?" I was genuinely astonished. "I just spoke to him."

"No no — he's already given all the orders," she said, backing me away from the door.

Posokhin had obviously thought it over while I was on my way and had decided not to affix *his* signature. Just in case. In any event, we had done it. I now had the blueprints with the long-awaited seal of GlavAPU, the stamp "Approved," and a signature.

I called Neizvestny. "Come over immediately," he demanded happily. "Tell me all the details."

When I finished telling the story, I had a happy, holiday-like feeling in my soul. Ernst Iosifovich smiled contentedly.

"The main thing now," he said, "is not to lose momentum. We've got to hurry, hurry, hurry. We've got to build the monument before something else changes."

Life had taught him many bitter lessons. He knew whereof he spoke. That same day, we went to my place and selected the necessary photographs of my father. Within a couple of days, the assistants had made the mold for the head.

When I came to the studio to see how the work was going, I received quite a jolt: before me stood Lenin's head.

Ernst Iosifovich laughed.

"In the beginning any form will do — you just need ears, nose, eyes, mouth, and so on. I'll do the rest, I'll do Khrushchev's head. The technicians are so skilled at doing Lenin that for them his head is the easiest of all to sculpt."

The work went beautifully. More and more, the head came to resemble Father, but Neizvestny wasn't satisfied.

"It has to be a very, very close likeness. For other headstones I've introduced a certain stylization," he said, repeating words I'd already heard, "but for this one — he has to be realistic, I'd even say naturalistic."

For a long time, he couldn't get the shape of the eyes right, or the lower part of the face. Finally, the clay head was ready. The last hypercritical inspection. Both he and I were by now accustomed to the head; a fresh eye was needed.

We gathered our domestic "commission" of Mama, Rada, and Yulia. We put a large photo of father next to the sculpture and compared the two again and again. Everyone approved without reservation.

The work was finished. It was time to turn it over to the plant.

We went to Mytishchi, where the plant was located. The director was pleasant but unyielding: "Where's the art fund council's approval?"

I tried to pass off the former approval, but the trick didn't succeed. We returned to Moscow empty-handed. I called the art fund. The director was away; his deputy came to the telephone.

"You're asking about the manufacture of Khrushchev's headstone? Do you have approval to erect it?"

"We've got a positive decision from GlavAPU," I said proudly.

"Well, if that's the case," the man said, relieved, "we'll put the question to the next meeting of the council."

This time the council wasn't as well disposed as before. They didn't start carping, but you could sense they were all rather afraid.[13] Suddenly they were discussing the cost: the project would exceed the three

13. *Editor's note:* What happened in the meantime to explain this change? Had they not gotten wind of Kosygin's support? Sergei Khrushchev: "I have no clear explanation. Before considering the project for the first time, they had also received positive phone calls from the Council of Ministers. But then everything turned around; it was just that the chairman of the council was taking out some extra insurance."

thousand rubles allocated by the state. The fears of the council members were palpable: if the authorities set aside three thousand, then they must know what they were doing. Here's something substantially more expensive. Could it be a trap? How could something that wasn't right be approved?

The chairman also had some doubts. He wanted to see the clay model — you never knew what this notorious Neizvestny might get it into his head to do.

The council's decision was as follows: "Approved conditionally, pending a visit to the studio to see the model."

Two weeks later, the council members came to the studio. The head, done in the best realist tradition, pleased them.

You could read on their faces what they were thinking: "Well, he can do it right when he wants to."

Ernst Iosifovich received congratulations.

At last, all imaginable councils were in the past. It was time to start constructing the monument. The necessary letter was sent off to the factory, after a telephone call from the Council of Ministers. The plant gave our project top priority.

On July 2, 1975, my fortieth birthday, they laid the foundation for the monument at the cemetery, and they did it conscientiously. They dug a pit at the edge of the grave and poured in concrete, having reinforced it with a steel frame.

The same work brigade undertook the job of erecting the monument. The Council of Ministers Supply Department provided the necessary equipment. Everything proceeded as if in a fairy tale, and gradually we began to forget our recent trials and tribulations.

On a sunny but already cool day in August 1975, the final stage of our four-year labor was at hand: the installation of the headstone. Early in the morning, Neizvestny and I set out to the plant in Mytishchi so as to be there when the truck arrived at ten. The hour came; no truck. Eleven — still no truck. We were beginning to worry. We assumed the delay was purely technical; nevertheless, forgotten fears sprang back to life. Could it be that it was starting all over again?

The truck finally appeared. It had blown a tire, and they had to replace it. Now the stones were loaded. They'd get the slabs on the next trip. We carefully put the head in my Zhiguli.

In little more than an hour, we arrived at Novodevichy Cemetery. The crane was already in place, waiting. A comrade from the Council of Ministers walked up and down, supervising the unloading. We decided not to assemble it the first day. We put the stones and the bronze next to the foundation and took the head to the studio.

The day for assembling the monument arrived. The weather didn't let us down: again sunny, as if we had ordered it that way. The crane carefully picked up the first bronze slab. Foreign correspondents bustled around, photographing every step. As at the funeral, there were no representatives of the Soviet press.

Neizvestny appealed to the journalists not to publish anything until the work was completed. We wanted to insure ourselves against every contingency.

In those days, the cemetery was open to the public, and an impressive crowd gathered at the grave. Someone produced a rope and they cordoned off the work site. They constantly had to chase the too-curious away.

Finally, the last step: installation of the head. The late afternoon sun shone brightly on the monument. Neizvestny took the head and went up to the stones. The niche was too high for a man of his height to reach. We found a box. He climbed up on it, and, in a brief, triumphal moment, the head was in place. The work was finished!

Photographs of Neizvestny standing on the box appeared in newspapers around the world.

The finishing touches remained: they covered the little square around the monument with sand, an entire truckload. A week later, there wasn't a trace of it left; visitors had tracked it away on their shoes.

We thanked the man from the Council of Ministers warmly for his assistance. It was obvious that he was pleased, too. He had done his best.

As we bade each other good-bye he asked, "Can I report that you have no criticisms to make?"

"That," I replied, "together with our enormous gratitude." By this time, the area around the gravesite was full of people — some of them my friends, others friends of Neizvestny, acquaintances, strangers. Everyone was excited, they were all laughing and congratulating Ernst Iosifovich and me. A holiday!

No officials were present, and only one member of the artistic council, Tsigal, came. He walked around the monument and congratulated Neizvestny, but couldn't resist saying: "You didn't take into consideration our recommendation that the height be reduced."

"It's payday!" I said happily, turning to Neizvestny. Our agreement provided for an honorarium to be paid on completion of the work.

When we first met and began our discussions, Neizvestny refused to take any money. But on reflection he agreed that unpaid work might be taken as a kind of political demonstration. We then agreed on the honorarium.

"Well, what of it?" he said, hiding the envelope containing the money in his back pocket. "It was a big job and I've earned my pay. Now let me invite you to commemorate the happy occasion."

We set off for the National Hotel, where an improvised banquet capped that joyous day.

The next morning, we were again at the cemetery. A crowd stood around the monument. The entire slab was covered in autumn flowers. People were talking, arguing, and taking pictures. Such disputes about the monument continue even today: some, the majority, like it, while others don't at all. No one is indifferent. We achieved our aim — an exceptional monument to an exceptional man. Many people go around to the side, looking for the artist's signature. Far from everyone has heard his name. There is bewilderment.

"Artist Unknown [*Neizvestny* in Russian — ed.]. Why did he want to keep his name secret?"

"That *is* his name — Neizvestny. He's known the world over."

The black-white combination generates the most questions. When they ask me, I generally don't explain the artist's conception.

"Every real work of art lives its own life, and you see yourself in it, it expresses your thoughts," I say, like a real expert. "Look, and think."

People explain the contrast in various ways — good and evil, life and death, and, more rarely, Khrushchev's successes and failures. One woman explained it this way: "The white, that's the good he did, and the black, the bad."

What can you say? Everyone is right in his own way.

The head has spurred a lot of discussion. The majority don't understand the artist's concept: "It's like the head was cut off" goes a typical reaction.

The old gold color likewise didn't please the early visitors, but that's already a thing of the past. Time has dealt with the color of both the head and the slab. Today the head is almost black, the slab grayish.

It seems to me that Neizvestny's efforts, and mine, and those of all the people who helped us, were not in vain, and that the monument to Khrushchev is worthy of his name and his complicated life.

Although we had tried to complete the monument by the anniversary of Father's death, we didn't intend an official ceremonial unveiling. We didn't want to irritate the authorities: speeches of any kind would inevitably have reverberations and attract unwanted attention to the monument. Having learned from bitter experience, we couldn't foretell where that might lead. To an order to dismantle the monument? Our experience suggested this wasn't such an absurd possibility. More likely, there would be trouble for everyone who had assisted us, not excluding Aleksei Nikolayevich Kosygin himself.

I remembered Yevtushenko's words, "Silence would be more meaningful," and I decided to follow his recommendation. But it didn't work out that way.

On the anniversary of Father's death, Mama intended to go to the cemetery late in the day, after the closing, when all the visitors had left. That way she could stand silently at the grave.

September 11, 1975, was a cold, cloudy day with an occasional shower. As we drove up to the cemetery gates, we glimpsed a large group of people. In addition to people we knew who came each year on this day to honor my father's memory, there were some unknown admirers of his, and foreign correspondents.

A lanky figure ran up to the car: Zhenya Yevtushenko. He opened the door and helped Nina Petrovna out, carefully supporting her by the elbow. He opened a large umbrella over her head.

Standing next to her the whole time, at the center of attention, he asked me quietly, "Who's going to speak?"

Evidently his refusal to say anything four years ago had given him no peace, and he wanted to rectify his error.

But you can't turn back time. We didn't want an assembly, or speeches. Nevertheless, he said a few warm words about Father at the monument. Thanks be unto him. We stood by silently.

Flashbulbs popped as the foreign press took pictures, but they didn't ask any questions. It was no time for interviews. After half an hour, we left. Behind us in the dark, covered over with flowers, was the monument.

When Neizvestny and I met a few days later, he told me that a delegation of former prisoners of Stalin's camps had paid him a visit. They tried to give him some money they had collected as a way of thanking him for the monument.

"We've arranged a watch at the monument," they told him. "We'll change the flowers every day."

Some Armenian sculptor put a marble likeness of Father at the base of the monument, along with a touching note.

Every day a huge crowd gathered at the monument. Sometimes they spread out, sometimes they huddled together.

Naturally, all this didn't escape the attention of those whose duty it is to know everything. Their gloomy predictions had come true: the monument had stirred up interest in Khrushchev and raised it to the surface. Khrushchev and Neizvestny: the fame of one supported and illuminated the fame of the other. Their names were linked, and rumor had it that they had in fact been friends. Memories of the stormy fifties and early sixties that had been extinguished were reborn.

This couldn't be tolerated very long. Novodevichy Cemetery was closed to the public "for renovation." It remained that way for ten years. Only now, under *perestroika,* do flocks of tourists appear there once again.[14]

14. I can't end this chapter without mentioning that not all that long after the monument was completed, Ernst Neizvestny was forced to leave the country and emigrate to the West. The conflict between him and the official Moscow artists had escalated to all-out war, and in this unequal struggle, he was doomed. They denied him appropriate honors on his fiftieth birthday; they refused to arrange an exhibition in a suitable hall; when his studio was torn down to make way for an Olympic sports complex, they denied him an acceptable substitute, even though he had the formal backing of the first deputy chairman of the Council of Ministers, Kiril Trofimovich Mazurov; they put every possible obstacle in the way of his completing a major commissioned work in Ashkabad, lest the authorities turn out to like it; and finally, when he decided to leave, they turned down his request to keep his Soviet passport, so that he would be unable to return easily. Only in 1989 did Neizvestny return to his homeland for a visit.

CONCLUSION

T HE story of my father's final years might well end right here — his memorial in place, the final chapter written. He and his generation have long since been replaced by other world leaders, and the events I have described are now part of history.

However, it's not quite as simple as that. Reading today's newspapers, I keep coming across familiar problems, problems Father agonized over for many years, and I find that his thoughts on these issues have a contemporary ring. It's almost as if those decades of oblivion didn't exist. But they did.

Back in October 1964, it seemed as if the censors slammed shut the forbidden book and put it away in the *spetskhran*.[1] Father's name disappeared from the newspapers. It was as if he not only didn't exist, but had never existed. The ominous expression given currency by Orwell in *1984* seemed to apply to Father: Khrushchev had become a "nonperson."

The new regime didn't publicly analyze or criticize the decade just past, or even my father's indisputable errors. He simply vanished —

---

1. *Spetskhrany* are special depositories in Soviet libraries where books inaccessible to the general reader have been kept. These have included books by "enemies of the people," works by Western Sovietologists, and works by dissidents. My father's memoirs were grouped with these banned works. In order to gain access to material in the *spetskhran* one must have special clearance granted by the authorities. These closed archives are presently being gradually eliminated and their holdings made accessible to readers.

along with all his victories and defeats, all his virtues and shortcomings, all the love of his friends and the hatred of his enemies.

Instead, newspapers kept repeating variations of the two officially sanctioned charges, "voluntarism" and "subjectivism," to which they counterposed the meticulously trimmed lawn of the unified "collective leadership." I had never perceived my father's "voluntarism" and "subjectivism" as negative traits. In my view, these are two natural aspects of any personality that separate it from the herd.

Any man who agonizes over decisions through long, sleepless nights will try to bring them to fruition, if he really is a man, by insisting, persuading, even forcing. Who among us would agree to abandon an idea or project to which he is deeply committed without a long, fierce struggle against his opponents? Alas, there are many people who can't be convinced by any arguments.

The notion of "subjectivism" is hardly worth mentioning. We are partial to a particular country, or city, or woman, or melody; we prefer a fir tree wrapped in a snowy mantle, or a sun-baked palm. Personality only exists so long as individuality and subjective perceptions remain intact.

When the bureaucrats were thinking up words to use against my father, they apparently didn't give much thought to their meanings. Or perhaps the very existence of personality was itself intolerable. One way or the other, the previous period's "voluntarism" and "subjectivism" became buzzwords. They explained all our failures and mistakes. Father was never mentioned by name in any of it; it was as if they feared him, as if some sort of mystic or shamanistic aura stopped people from uttering the forbidden name. No one knew (nor did I) what might follow. Brezhnev decided not to tempt fate.

I have tried, wherever it was relevant in this book, to describe how the "house" Father began to build was demolished. The regional economic councils he added on were torn down. The pillars of self-sufficiency were uprooted and hastily replaced by the high though somewhat rundown walls of the ministries and agencies that divide our economy into princely domains.

Sadly, it didn't take much time to accomplish all this. Father's innovations never had time to put down deep roots, and some of them just didn't take at all.

Father was criticized for various things. Many denounced him because it was their job to do so; it's been that way with us for a long time. Others had simply grown tired of his long speeches. But the resurrected ministers, those whom Father had sent out to manage the regions and who had now returned to the capital, hated him with all their might. The bureaucratic system was taking revenge on its deposed enemy.

Time does its inevitable work. In the years immediately following Father's removal, the mere mention of his name provoked a quick reaction, whether negative or positive. Gradually reactions became more muffled, and people started to forget. This was only true in the USSR, however, and from time to time I managed to acquire books published in the West that discussed Khrushchev in detail. I had to agree with some of the conclusions they reached; other, less pleasant ones made me want to leap up and protest. But the main thing was he continued to live. The fact that he was still talked about in the West offered hope he had not vanished forever.

Meanwhile, a new generation that knew nothing of the past was growing up in our country. For them Khrushchev was only a name in political jokes, some about corn, others about that shoe that had made such an indelible impression when it was banged on a table at the United Nations.

His reforms in industry and agriculture, his reductions in the army, the window he had opened to the world, none of this, it seemed, had ever happened. Even I had begun to adopt an apologetic tone in conversations about my father. It was as if I were asking for sympathy, for reassurance that he had done some good, hadn't he? This pitiful half question presupposed that his mistakes had predominated.

At the same time, another process began. Gradually the authorities began to clean up Stalin's image. It is not my task to examine this phenomenon. I'll mention one aspect, though, not because of its significance, but in connection with the psychological peculiarities of Father's successor as first secretary. Brezhnev very quickly became known as the general secretary, the same title held by Stalin in the 1930s.

Father appointed the young Brezhnev to his first party post in Dnepropetrovsk during the years of terror. In those days, Stalin seemed an untouchable deity; even in his wildest dreams, Brezhnev couldn't imagine himself close to the Leader. But now he had replaced not just Khrushchev, but Stalin himself.

Brezhnev's memoirs are larded liberally with passages describing his telephone conversations with Stalin. Whether they ever happened isn't important; their mere mention conferred grandeur on Brezhnev. The higher he rose, the more taken with himself he became, the more captivated by the fate that had lifted him unexpectedly into his Kremlin office.

It was hardly an appropriate time to bring up the arrests, interrogations, and camps. References to these violations of socialist legality became less distinct and more infrequent, while books and films began to depict Stalin as the wise leader, pipe in hand, strolling through his oak-paneled office, expounding immutable truths. It's true that our leaders lacked the courage to take the final step. Virtually all of Moscow expected Volgograd to get back its old name, Stalingrad; even the date was supposedly known. But it never happened. As with his condemnation of Khrushchev, Brezhnev didn't see the resurrection of his idol through to the end.

Meanwhile, what was occurring in the economy? The mechanisms put in place during the fifties continued to work, but without careful attention, they began to run down. The economic self-sufficiency that was just beginning to take hold in enterprises and regions gave way to a harsh centralized diktat. The modest artistic freedom that was developing, punctuated to be sure by my father's abusive criticism, was replaced by criminal trials and exile. Disarmament and the reduction of armed forces gave way to an unrestrained buildup of missiles, tanks, and aircraft of use only to the generals. The notable reduction in international tension was followed by adventurism, culminating in the invasion of Afghanistan.

The nation was sliding toward a crisis, and unfortunately, it wasn't our wisdom and resolve that changed the situation but rather the senile, medal-bedecked general secretary's natural death. Things changed imperceptibly at first, then faster. New hope appeared.

But Father's name was still strictly forbidden. All that happened was that talk of the subjectivist and voluntarist period grew less frequent, while a new phrase was born: the "years of stagnation."

I have already mentioned my appeal to General Secretary Gorbachev regarding the fate of my father's memoirs. During one of my conversations with members of his immediate circle, someone had said these encouraging words: "Wait a little longer. We're proposing a report for the anniversary of the revolution. It will tell all, everyone will get his due. Khrushchev won't be forgotten."

Sure enough, there it was in Mikhail Gorbachev's solemn speech in the Kremlin Palace of Congresses on November 6, 1987. Father's name was mentioned along with those of other prominent state and party figures who had seemingly been erased from our history. They got but a few lines, and extremely cautious ones at that. Gorbachev stated that despite his mistakes, Khrushchev was responsible for much good accomplished in those distant years.

I reread those two short paragraphs many times. I would have liked more, but consoled myself that it was impossible to fit everything in one speech. We had to await developments.

Silence, however, soon reigned once again. It wasn't that there were no references at all to Khrushchev. Newspapers and journal articles occasionally paid tribute to the Twentieth Congress and to the famous "secret speech" — without, of course, quoting from the speech itself, which remained secret in the USSR even though it had been published in the West as early as 1956. These pieces condescendingly patted the former leader on the back. Yet, at the same time, they complained about his alleged lack of culture, and recalled how rudely he conducted himself in meetings with writers and artists.

The press had begun to paint a picture of a dim-witted hooligan cast upon the throne by fate. Such a Khrushchev suited a bureaucracy that hadn't forgiven him for reorganizing the administrative structure, for taking away its privileges, or for setting limits on the amount of time they could spend in office.

However, the logic of societal development is governed by its own objective laws. Once under way, *perestroika* meant breaking with the old and seeking out new and progressive solutions. One can't help remembering a similar period thirty years ago, when a restless leader roamed the country, peering into every crevice and shaking up apathetic bureaucrats.

On the other hand, though, no further signals were given from above, so that when functionaries talked with me about my father, they lowered their voices and instinctively glanced around to make sure no one else could hear. Stalin had taught us that our own shadow might be an informant. Therefore, all such conversations ended with a nod to the "well-known mistakes" of those years.

The first to violate this "proper" tone was Fyodor Burlatsky, who published a long article in the middle of 1988. His Khrushchev was both a statesman and a human being with virtues and failings.

I liked Burlatsky's article, but my sisters did not. Understandably, both they and I would have liked more, but I was content with what there was and felt it was a good beginning.

Burlatsky couldn't illuminate all aspects of my father's work in one article. Moreover, he had hardly known Father. He used information from third parties and supplemented it with what he remembered from Khrushchev's meetings with Central Committee functionaries. In those years, Burlatsky was a young man working in the Central Committee department for relations with other socialist countries. The head of this department was Yuri Andropov, who together with other activists from the younger generation was often invited by Khrushchev to participate in developing new ideas.

It was from Andropov that Burlatsky learned much about Khrushchev. When Andropov was included in the group that accompanied Khrushchev to Yugoslavia in 1961, he took along his smart young assistant. Tito had invited Father to rest for a few days on the island of Brioni. It was in that relaxed atmosphere that Burlatsky heard Khrushchev tell the stories that he recounted in the *Literaturnaya gazeta* in 1988.

The issue is not whether or how often Burlatsky met my father. The main thing is that he was a man after Khrushchev's model, a man who had grown to maturity in that period of reform and bold experimentation. It was this quality of Burlatsky's, rather than the facts he cited (some correct, some not), that won his article national recognition.

Perestroika continued to evolve and gain momentum. Gorbachev soon needed new people to help in his cause, people on whom he could rely in his struggle against conservatives. Not surprisingly, it was Khrushchev's fledglings, the men of the sixties, who answered the call. Excluded from active political involvement for a quarter of a century, they seemed to have disappeared from the political arena completely. Twenty-five years is certainly long enough to wither one's ideals, to dry up a thirst for struggle, to grow old and tired. However, they were made of sterner stuff.

It would take some time to list all of their names, but I will mention three: Aleksandr Yakovlev, who returned from his prestigious exile as ambassador to Canada to become one of Gorbachev's most active supporters in the Politburo; Yuri Voronov, the former chief editor of *Komsomolskaya pravda,* and now heading one of the hot spots, the Central Committee's Cultural Department; and the journalist Yegor Yakovlev, who has managed to turn *Moscow News* from a sheet whose primitive lexicon was favored by students studying for their foreign language tests, into a respected newspaper that stands in the forefront of the struggle for *perestroika.*

Despite a growing amount of published material focusing on Father, the authorities maintained their silence. But it was no longer possible to hold back the swelling tide. In October 1988, *Ogonyok* published my account of Father's removal from office in October 1964.

By coincidence, *Ogonyok* came out just when many old-guard leaders were being ushered into retirement as a result of the September 1988 Central Committee plenum. The news of these retirements exploded like a bomb. No one had foreseen this development, including the editor of *Ogonyok*. As a result, many connected my account with ongoing events, seeing it as a warning of some kind.

The telephone in my apartment wouldn't stop ringing. My callers had limitless imagination. Just one example that I particularly remember: A correspondent from the Japanese paper *Asahi* asked me a single question: "Wasn't it Mr. Gorbachev who ordered you to write your account?" Amused, I shot down that notion, but in the days that followed I got the same question from all sorts of people, Soviets as well as foreigners.

The foreigners generally were satisfied with my answers, but my compatriots nodded in a knowing way, as if to say, "All right, we know. After all, we're not children. It's a matter of state; you can't discuss it."

I became a popular man; I was invited to speak before many groups in Moscow and in other cities, and I gave many interviews. I decided to make use of the situation. I had to find a way to talk about Father's memoirs and to get them published. The Central Committee was still saying nothing on the subject. Now there was a new reason — the reorganization of the bureaucracy. This was not the time to recall Khrushchev.

I first mentioned Father's memoirs in an appearance on Moscow radio in October 1988. To tell the truth, I hedged a little. It was difficult to overcome my habit of acting only with official approval. What I had to say was well received by a small number of listeners. After all, it was only a local radio show.

I expected to "hear it" from above, but nothing was forthcoming. Of course, I would have continued my campaign in any case, but this was a good sign: Khrushchev's enemies up there, opponents of *perestroika,* were feeling a bit weak.

I soon made an appearance on the TV show "Vzglyad" ("View"), where I discussed the memoirs on camera with the well-known commentator Genrikh Borovik. I continued to make appearances at large gatherings; I spoke to thousands of people interested in hearing about

Khrushchev. Soon, many items large and small were appearing in all sorts of publications. The articles varied enormously in form and content. Some of them rushed to offer new facts of one sort or another, others aspired to interpret the period, and still others dealt in dirt, trying to dig up a little scandal.

Of all that appeared in print, I must single out Anatoly Strelyany's article entitled "The Last Romantic," published in the popular journal *Druzhba narodov* in November 1988. Strelyany was the first to try to get to the heart of the matter, to understand events as they occurred at the time, to determine the reasons for Khrushchev's successes and failures. He accomplished this with great tact and sympathy for Khrushchev, with the help of Andrei Shevchenko, a former assistant to Father for agriculture, who retained a soft spot for his patron throughout all the difficult years.

Partly as a result of this and other articles, public opinion regarding Father changed dramatically. From the hapless butt of jokes, he changed back into a respected national figure. In May 1988, one of the public opinion surveys that are increasingly being conducted in the Soviet Union showed that fewer than twenty percent saw Khrushchev as a positive figure. By the beginning of 1989, the number had climbed to more than fifty percent.

My own efforts had not been in vain, and I was deluged with questions about my father's memoirs. I decided not to bother the powers that be anymore. I might have to wait years for their approval. I had Gorbachev's oral answer, which could be interpreted as agreement, opening the way for publication.[2]

The first step would be crucial — the first excerpts from the memoirs had to get wide circulation, and I also wanted the magazine that published them to be independent.

Over the past months, I had developed close ties with the staff of *Ogonyok* and without much hesitation I chose them. I felt I could rely on the chief editor, Vitaly Korotich, and his team. Not without a strug-

---

2. *Editor's note:* According to Sergei Khrushchev, he had sent another letter to Gorbachev informing him that even without having received memoir materials from the Central Committee, he was now in possession of a text that was suitable for publication. Gorbachev's answer was transmitted orally by Ivan T. Frolov, then a top aide to the Soviet leader and now chief editor of *Pravda* and a Central Committee secretary. According to Frolov, Gorbachev had discussed the issue with the Politburo and they looked favorably on the idea of publication. Yet in spite of this oral approval, Sergei Khrushchev reports, high-level efforts to prevent publication of his father's memoirs have continued.

gle, he proceeded to publish lengthy excerpts, the millions of copies of *Ogonyok* not only confirming the memoirs' existence, but also driving a battering ram through the conspiracy of silence. After being ignored for a quarter of a century in his own country, Father's memoirs had begun at last to make their way to their readers.

Not everyone is pleased. Even today, many bureaucrats feel that we published too soon. I understand their concerns. They would have preferred their readers to remain unaware of, or indifferent to, Khrushchev's views. Luckily, their preferences were not to be.

I also thought the manuscript might lose some of its relevance after all these years. I feared it would appeal only to those with an interest in history; after all, life does not stand still. It hasn't turned out that way. On many issues we are about where we were twenty-five years ago. Reading Khrushchev's thoughts on the development of the economy, and on reducing the armed forces, we are amazed to discover that he pondered the very issues we are debating now. In this way, Khrushchev has lived on, returning to take an active part in the political process.

This is the main reason there is so much interest in him in the Soviet Union today. Another is that we must understand the preceding period if we are to avoid repeating its mistakes and having to reinvent the wheel.

I am often asked, "Might not Gorbachev suffer the same fate as Khrushchev?"

It's not a simple question. History doesn't repeat itself, nor would the victory of *perestroika* be Gorbachev's alone, but rather our common victory. It depends on us all, on our maturity, on whether we make the right decisions or mistakes. Unfortunately, no one is insured against defeat. However, we must believe in victory. Otherwise, there's no sense in fighting for change.

The main thing people have asked me in various cities around our country is, "How does *perestroika* differ from what went on in the fifties and sixties?" That requires careful thought. First of all, what is *perestroika*? Just a catchword or slogan? I think not. Gorbachev found a very exact way to describe something that has been going on, with interruptions, for many years.

How do I understand *perestroika*? *Perestroika*, restructuring, is the process of changing a situation with which we are no longer satisfied. One can take the term either literally, or more broadly, in which case it applies to the transformation of our entire society.

In this sense, the process is a permanent one. It consists of forward movement and temporary setbacks, of successes and defeats. *Perestroika* did not begin today, or yesterday. It began in 1917, when our people decided to transform their society through revolution. Perhaps the roots of *perestroika* lie somewhere even deeper.

The *perestroika* that Lenin began in the 1920s was brought to a halt by Stalin. He succeeded in exchanging economic progress for a barrackslike existence that we now call the administrative-command system. I'm not about to analyze this period in this book. I will say only that when Stalin died, the country was economically stagnant. In order to survive, it was necessary to change the system for managing the economy. There was no time to hesitate or reflect. There wasn't enough food; long breadlines formed early every morning, even in Moscow.

Our fate depended on the effectiveness and wisdom of the decisions we made. That is one way the *perestroika* of the fifties and sixties resembles the stormy period we are now experiencing. But although the situations then and now have much in common, and Khrushchev's advice on particular issues seems relevant today, there is an essential difference between the two periods.

My father's economic reforms often relied on economic self-interest, from which it was but a short step to self-sufficient economic enterprises, and to the notion of the market as the universal regulator of relations between consumers and producers. In his memoirs, he often came back to the question of a market within a socialist system. But Father never took the final step; the stereotypes laid down in the thirties were just too strong.

No matter how much his reforms incorporated the concept of material incentives, he always carried them out within the framework of the administrative-command system. He kept adjusting the system, constantly moving functionaries from one chair to another, but never altered its basic shape. The time wasn't ripe. One is sadly reminded of the fable of the orchestra whose music sounded terrible: "We're just not sitting in the right places," they explained.

The naive thought at the time was that if wise, competent people could just be chosen and put in the proper places, everything would work well: we would soon amaze the world by beginning to live better than anyone else. The plan of action during those years was simple: first, determine the needs of each member of society, then give every factory and collective farm a concrete task. If the system worked correctly, each person would receive what he or she needed. Nothing more, nothing less! All you had to do was count correctly.

After Father's ouster, I once went to a lecture given by a mathematician, a computer specialist, a talented man who had become interested in economics. He thought that if we could enter several tens or hundreds of millions of equations into a computer, we could create an ideal plan, one that would satisfy the demands not only of society as a whole, but of each of its members as well.

This, in my opinion, was the apotheosis of the development of administrative-command methods. In order to break with this approach, one must force oneself to think differently, to move to a different level. This is as difficult as a shift from our ingrained cause-and-effect understanding of the world around us to a view that accepts the seeming chaos captured by the paradoxes of modern atomic physics. And it is precisely these paradoxes, not our notions of cause and effect, that reflect processes going on in real life.

By the end of his years in power, Father had already begun to understand that the existing system of economic management would never be able to function efficiently. He began to grope for other paths, looking at the experience of Yugoslavia, or at the timid proposals put forth by our own economists. However, the new ideas could only be realized in another time. Father himself wasn't really ready, and in any case, the omnipotent bureaucratic apparatus did not allow him to go very far. Then came October 1964.

The fate of *perestroika* in the fifties and sixties suggested that the economy couldn't function in an administrative-command system. The next twenty-five years only confirmed that fact. Today's *perestroika* began at a different level. Mikhail Gorbachev immediately declared the need for a new economic mechanism. That is a fundamental difference between today's *perestroika* and yesterday's.

I'm not going to discuss which specific decisions are good and which are not. That's not my task. There is a long struggle ahead, for the past never gives up without a fight. There will be victories, but there will be defeats as well, possibly crushing ones. But we believe we will succeed, because progress cannot be halted.

We have taken the next step in the development of our society, and I rejoice that my father's efforts were not in vain. Our successes will be due in no small part to his labors.

The two periods of which we are speaking are closely connected, and one flows naturally out of the other. As I see it, people's attitudes toward my father are a kind of indicator of their attitudes toward *perestroika*. We have begun to move forward, and interest in his work is growing. When the brakes are put on, a voice can be heard from inside some office, "It's not the right time. Let's wait a bit. Who's benefiting from all this, anyway?"

As I write these lines today, interest in Khrushchev is greater than ever before. This pleases me both as his son and as a citizen.

I would like to hope that my book will make its own small contribution to *perestroika*, that it will help us to understand the past and thus ease our progress into an unknown, but greatly desired, future.

Moscow–London, 1964–1989

INDEX